Ōoku

THE INNER CHAMBERS

by Fumi Yoshinaga

VOL. **16**

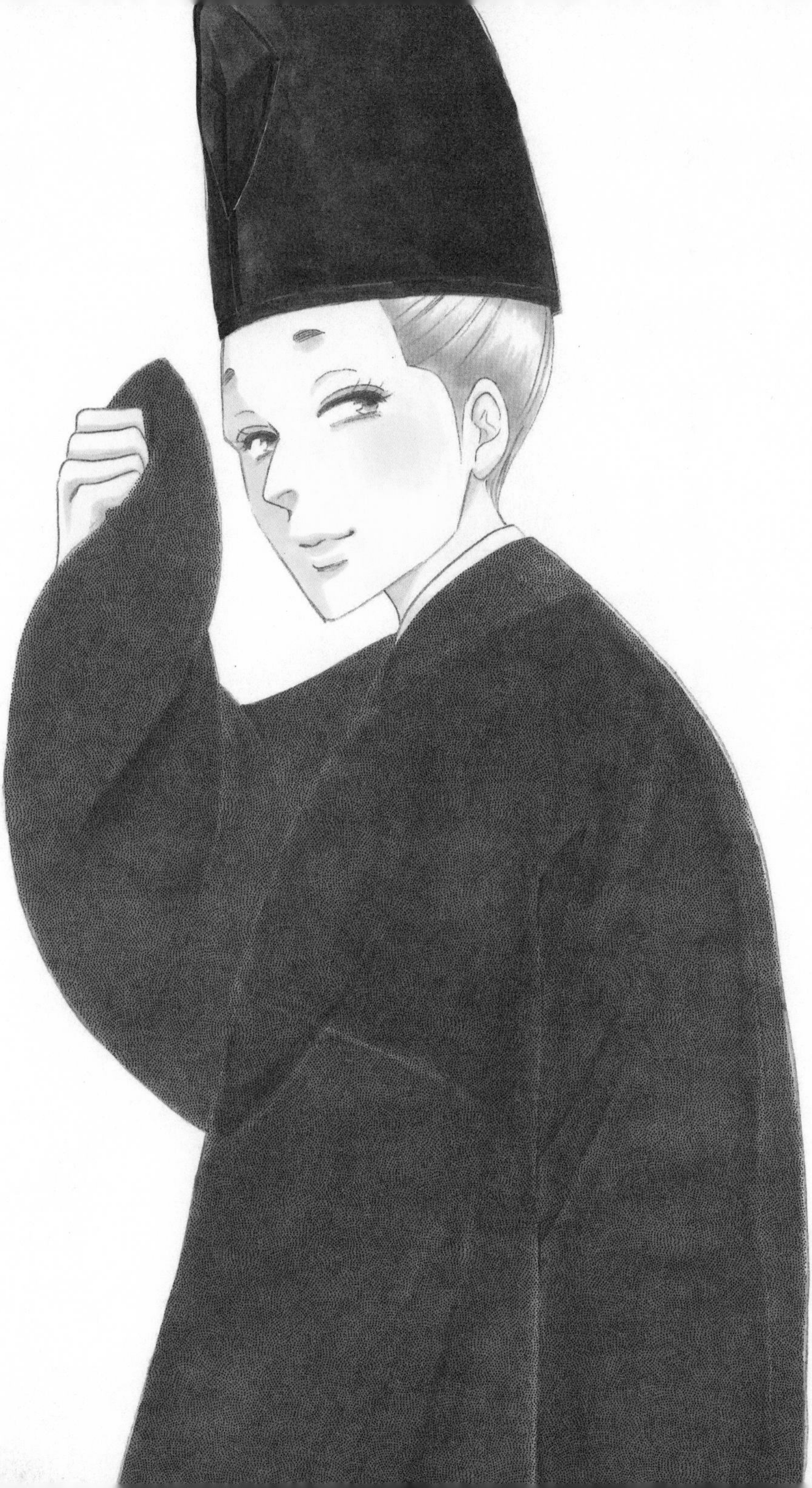

TABLE *of* CONTENTS

Ōoku

THE INNER CHAMBERS

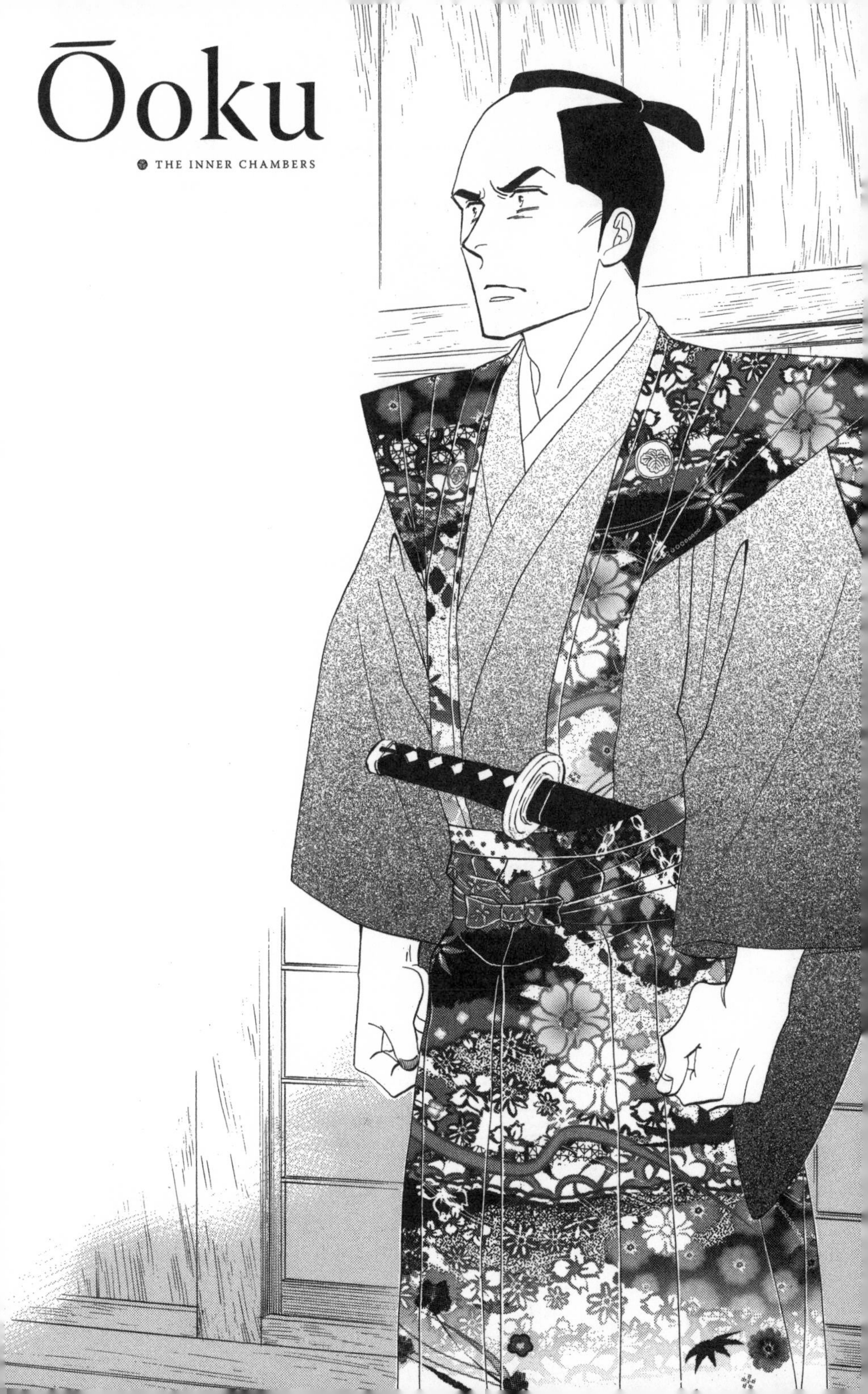

THE INNER CHAMBERS

CAST *of* CHARACTERS

From the birth of the "inverse Inner Chambers" to its zenith, to eradicating the Redface Pox, and now to the end of Tokugawa rule...?

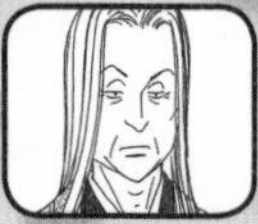

SENIOR CHAMBERLAIN

LADY KASUGA

↓

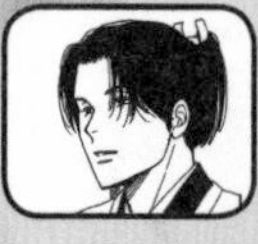

MADE-NOKOJI ARIKOTO (SIR O-MAN)

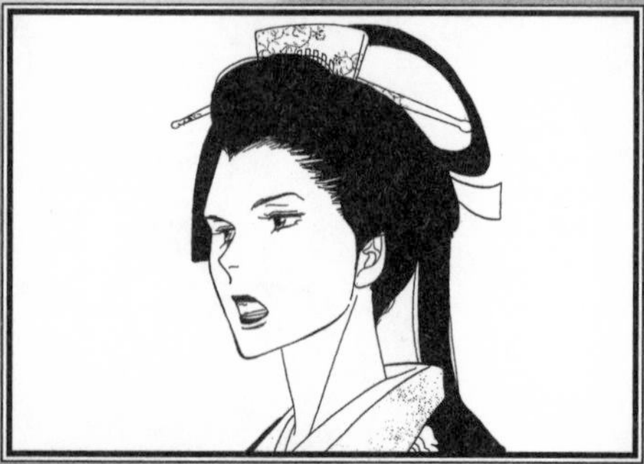

TOKUGAWA IEMITSU (III)

Impersonated her father, Iemitsu, at Lady Kasuga's urging after he died of the Redface Pox. Later became the first female shogun.

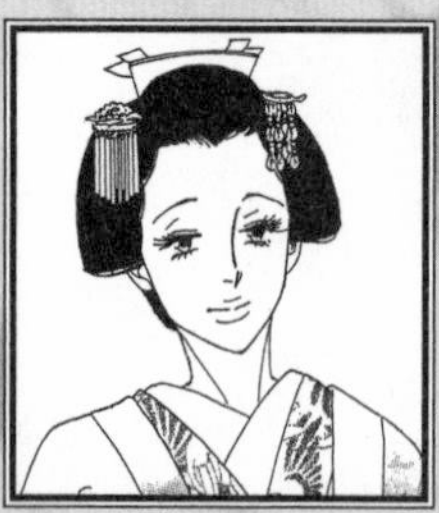

TOKUGAWA TSUNAYOSHI (V)

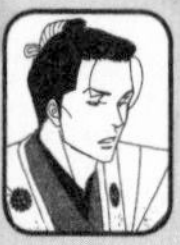

SENIOR CHAMBERLAIN

EMONNOSUKE

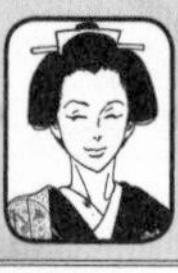

PRIVY COUNCILLOR

YANAGISAWA YOSHIYASU

TOKUGAWA TSUNASHIGE

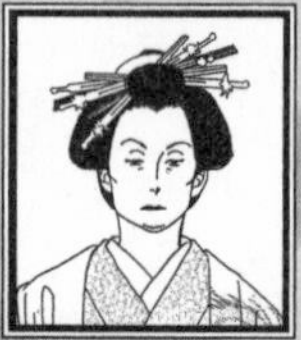

TOKUGAWA IENOBU (VI)

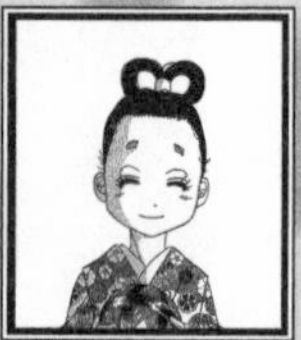

TOKUGAWA IETSUGU (VII)

TOKUGAWA IETSUNA (IV)

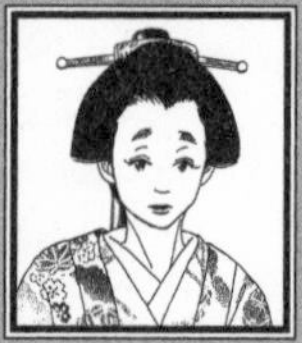

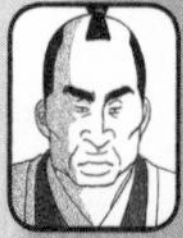

SENIOR CHAMBERLAIN

EJIMA

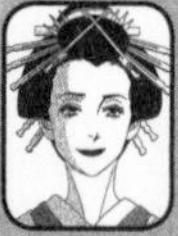

PRIVY COUNCILLOR

MANABE AKIFUSA

PRIVY COUNCILLOR

KANO HISAMICHI

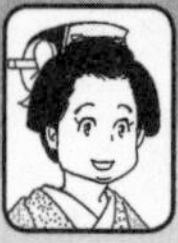

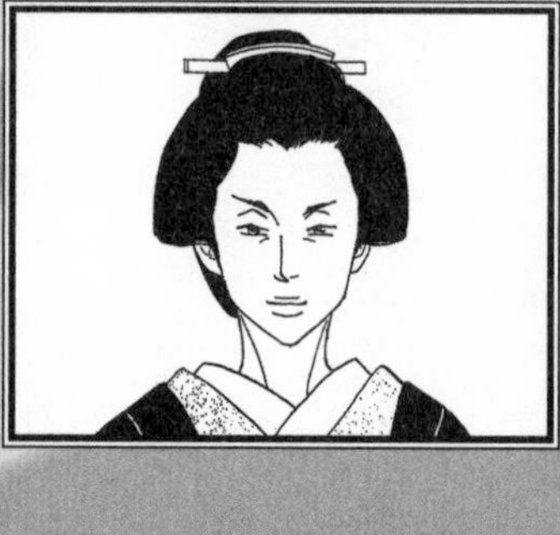

TOKUGAWA YOSHIMUNE (VIII)

Third daughter of Mitsusada, the second head of the Kii branch of the Tokugawa family. Acceded to domain lord and then, upon the death of Ietsugu, to shogun. Imposed and lived by a strict policy of austerity, dismissing large numbers of Inner Chambers courtiers and pursuing policies designed to increase income to the treasury.

TOKUGAWA YOSHIMUNE (VIII)

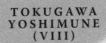

MUNETADA

MUNETAKE

TOKUGAWA IESHIGE (IX)

MATSUDAIRA SADANOBU

TOKUGAWA HARUSADA

TOKUGAWA IEHARU (X)

TOKUGAWA IENARI (XI)

TOKUGAWA IEYOSHI (XII)

SENIOR CHAMBERLAIN

TAKIYAMA
Former Kagema courtesan, discovered by Masahiro and brought to the Inner Chambers.

SENIOR COUNCILLOR

ABE MASAHIRO

SENIOR CHAMBERLAIN

TANUMA OKITSUGU

TOKUGAWA IESADA (XIII)

TANEATSU (TENSHO-IN)

Iesada's consort, renamed Tensho-in after her death.

GREAT ELDER

II NAOSUKE

TOKUGAWA YOSHINOBU

Head of the Hitotsubashi branch, condemned to house arrest and stripped of his title during the Ansei Purge.

PRINCE KAZU

Iemochi's consort, from the imperial court in Kyoto. The purpose of their marriage is to foster closer relations between the court and the shogunate.

TOKUGAWA IEMOCHI (XIV)

Winner of the succes
contest against Toku
Yoshinobu. Young, b
wisdom and compo
beyond her years

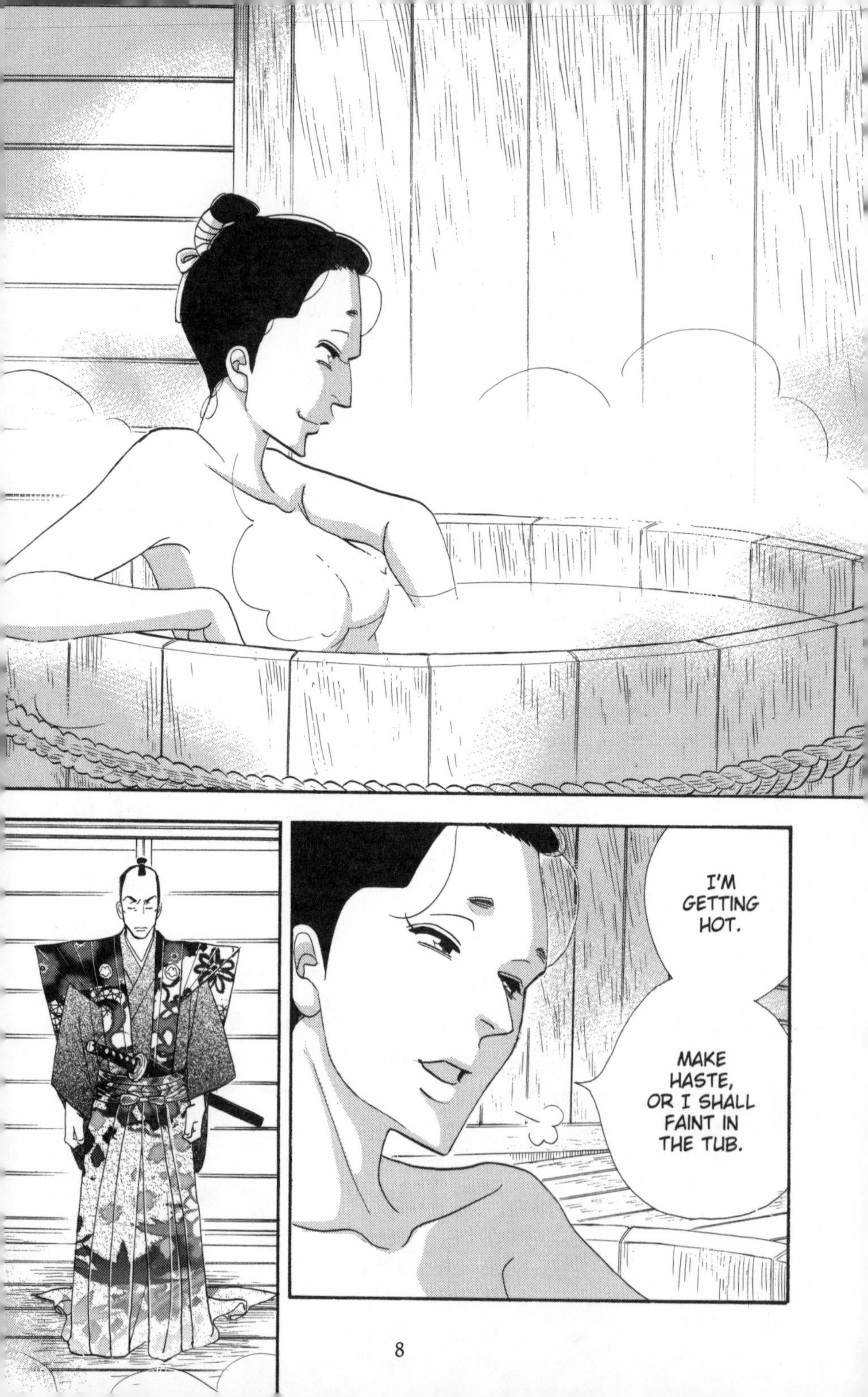
I'M GETTING HOT.
MAKE HASTE, OR I SHALL FAINT IN THE TUB.

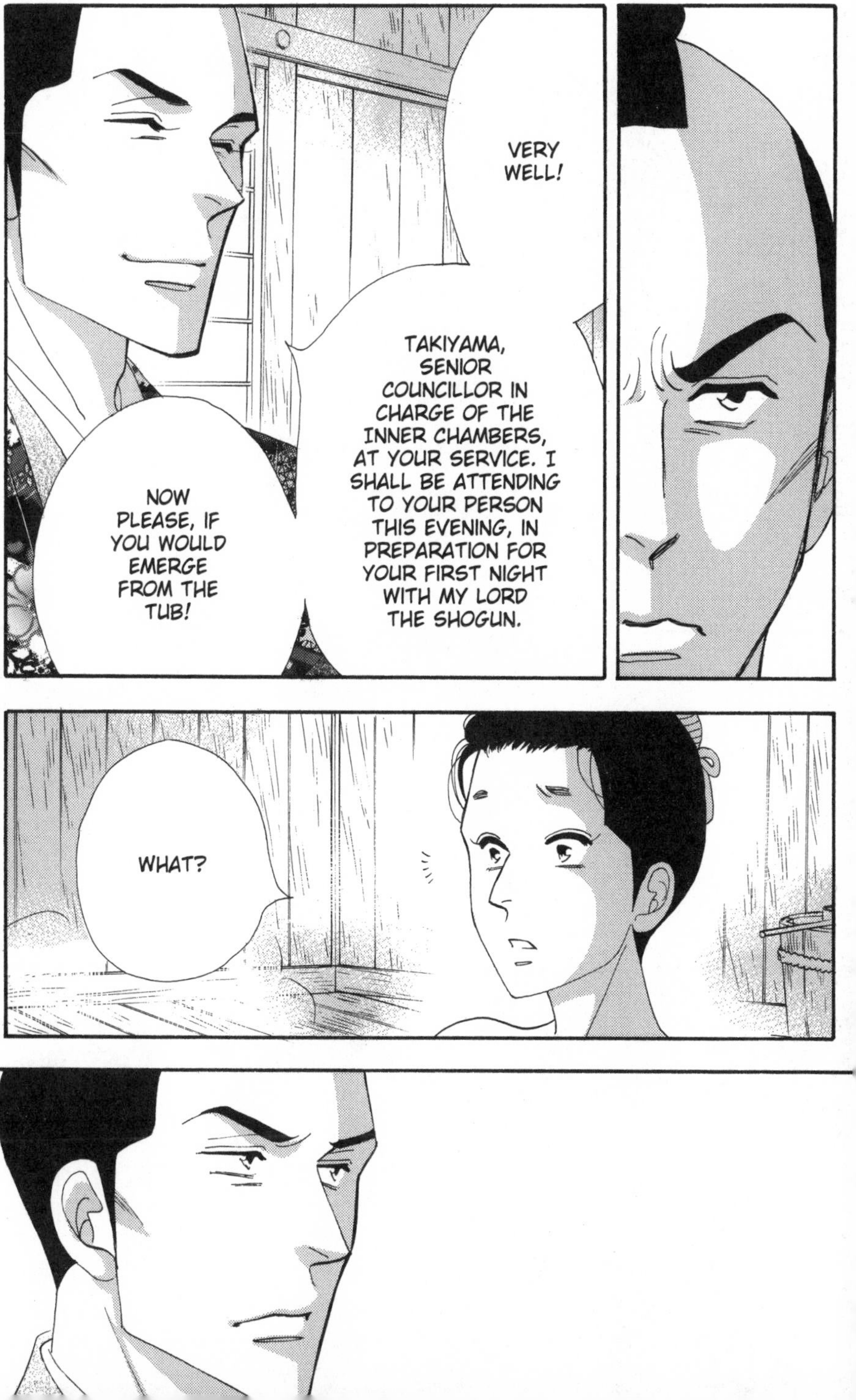
VERY WELL!
TAKIYAMA, SENIOR COUNCILLOR IN CHARGE OF THE INNER CHAMBERS, AT YOUR SERVICE. I SHALL BE ATTENDING TO YOUR PERSON THIS EVENING, IN PREPARATION FOR YOUR FIRST NIGHT WITH MY LORD THE SHOGUN.
NOW PLEASE, IF YOU WOULD EMERGE FROM THE TUB!
WHAT?

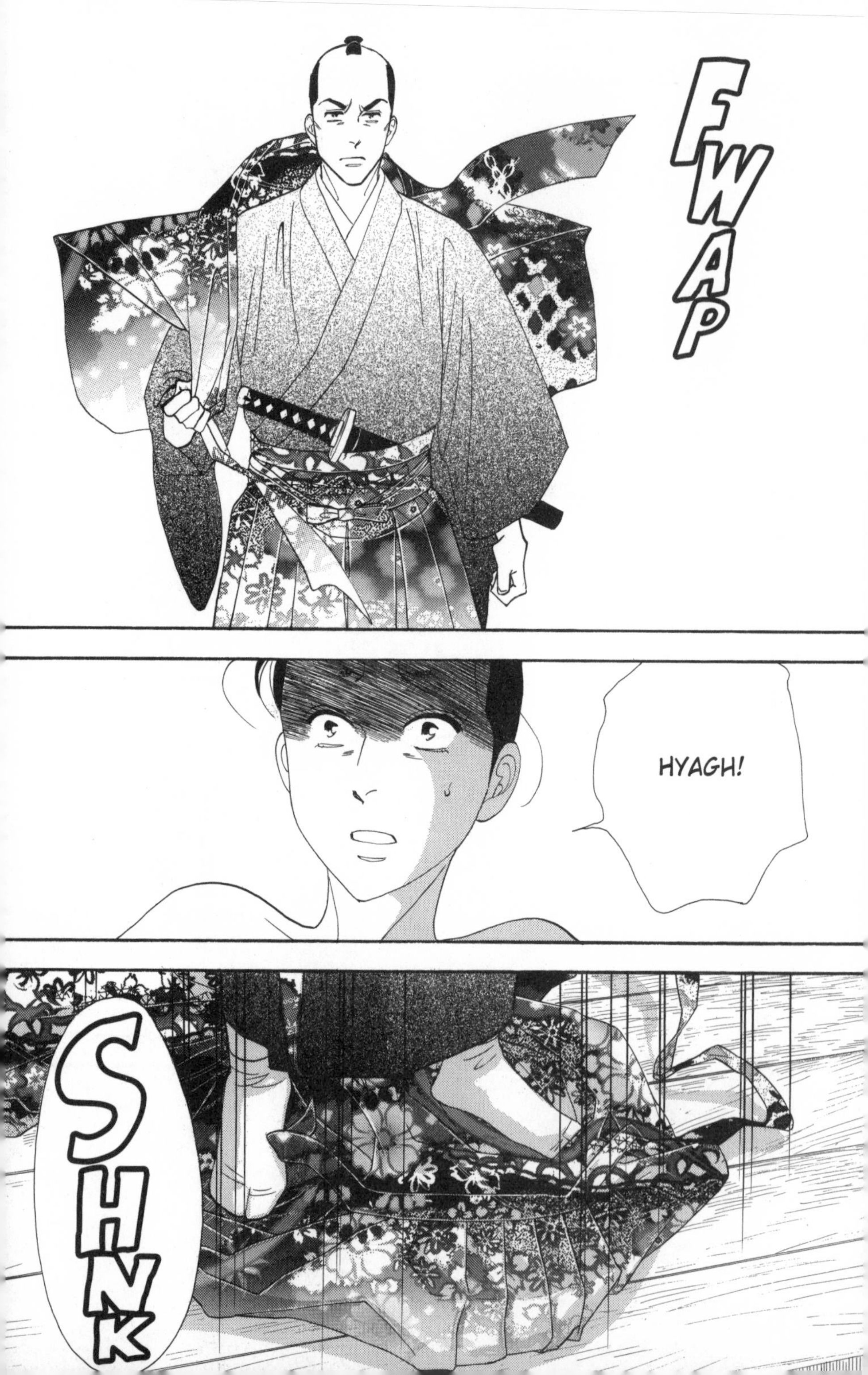
FWAP
HYAGH!
SHNK

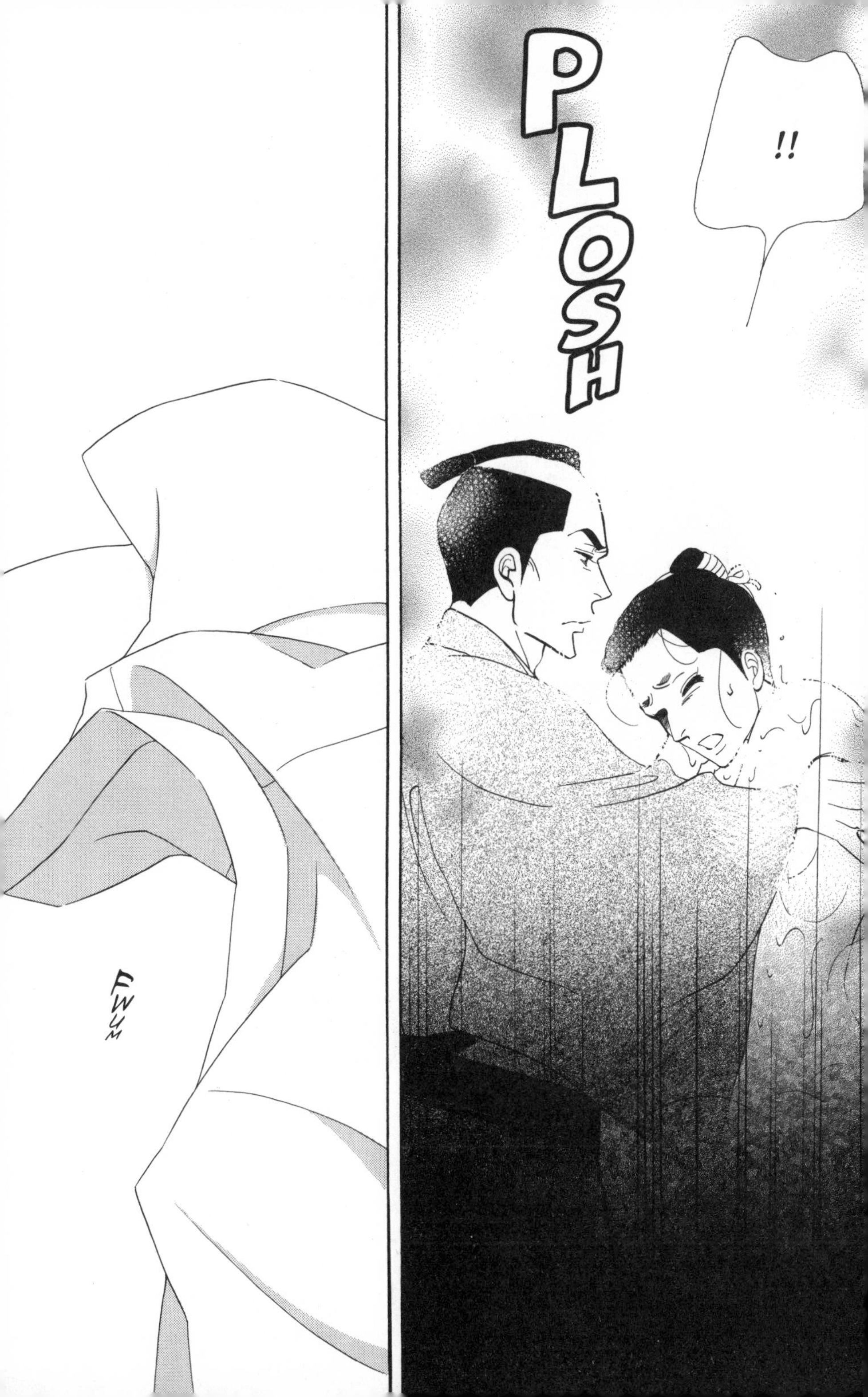
PLOSH
!!
FWUM

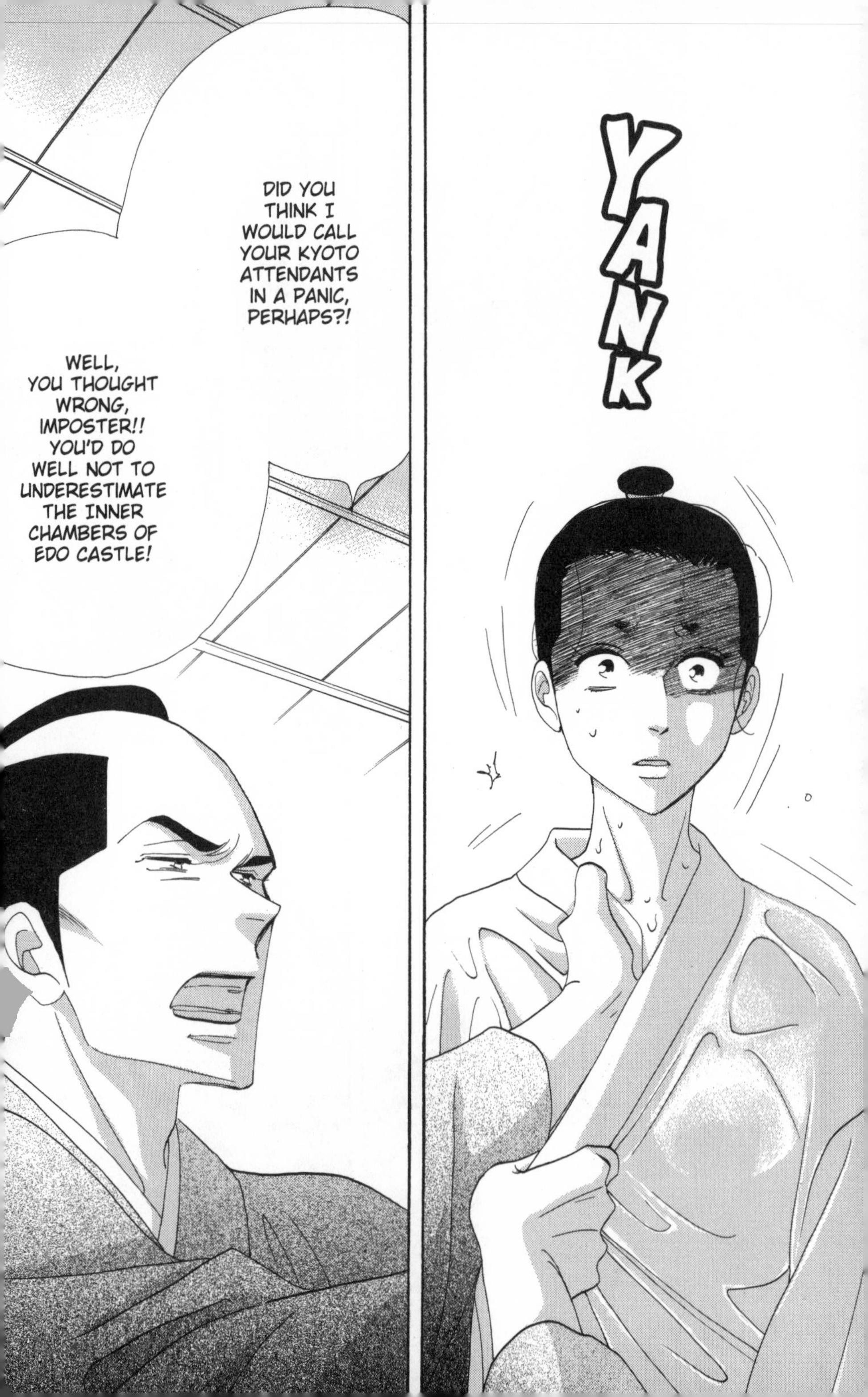
YANK
DID YOU THINK I WOULD CALL YOUR KYOTO ATTENDANTS IN A PANIC, PERHAPS?!
WELL, YOU THOUGHT WRONG, IMPOSTER!! YOU'D DO WELL NOT TO UNDERESTIMATE THE INNER CHAMBERS OF EDO CASTLE!

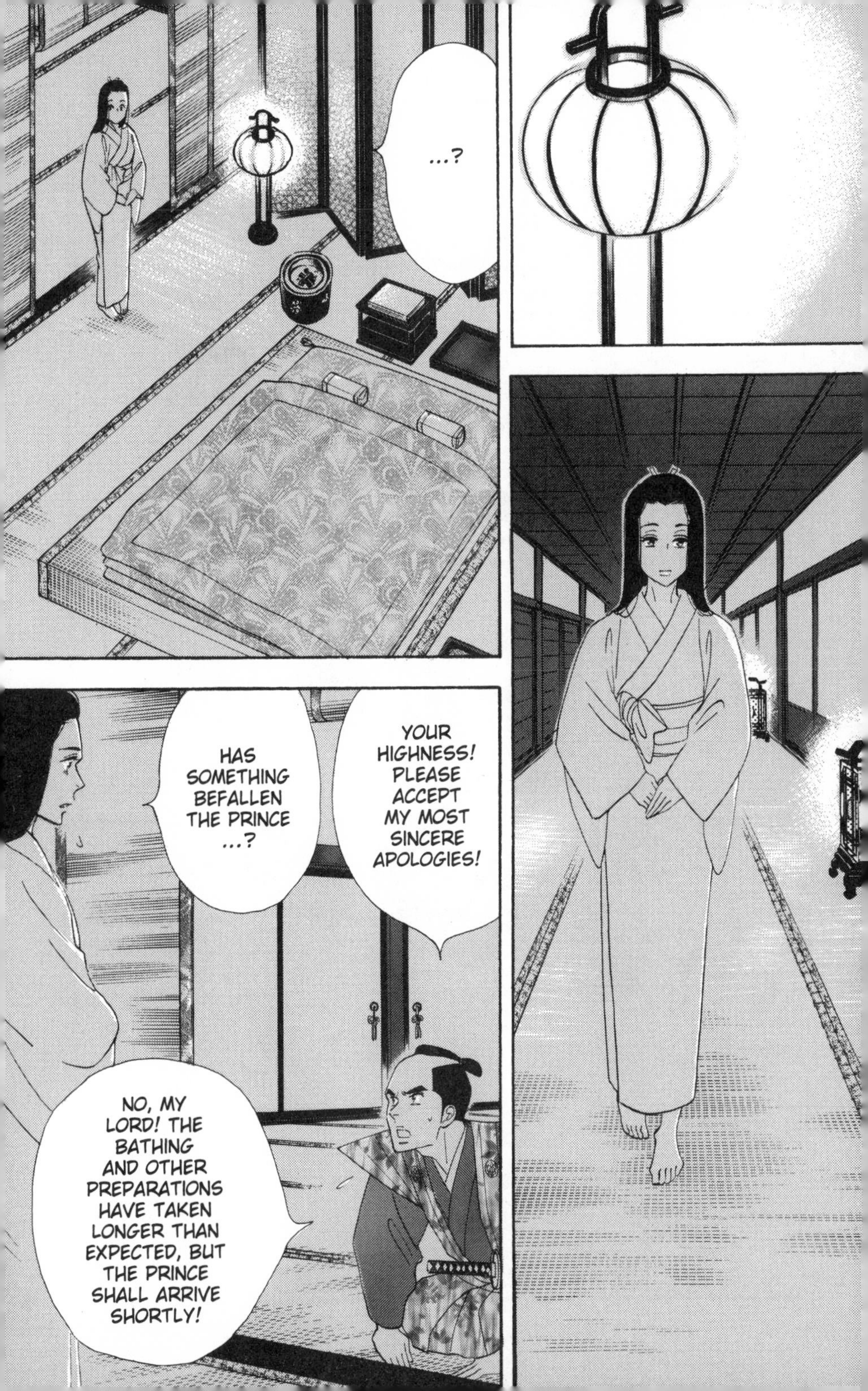
...?
YOUR HIGHNESS! PLEASE ACCEPT MY MOST SINCERE APOLOGIES!
HAS SOMETHING BEFALLEN THE PRINCE ...?
NO, MY LORD! THE BATHING AND OTHER PREPARATIONS HAVE TAKEN LONGER THAN EXPECTED, BUT THE PRINCE SHALL ARRIVE SHORTLY!

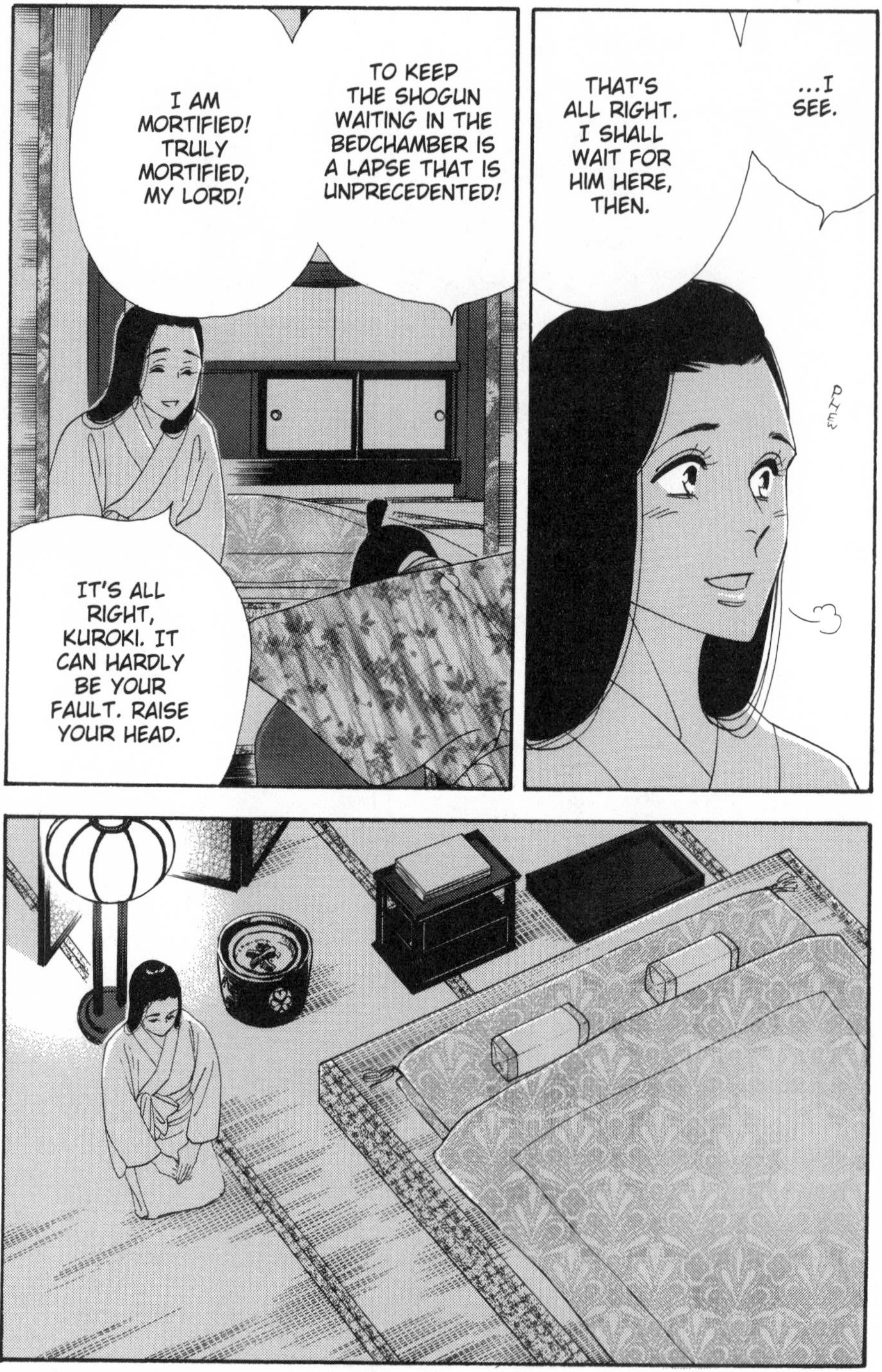
...I SEE.
THAT'S ALL RIGHT. I SHALL WAIT FOR HIM HERE, THEN.
PHEW
TO KEEP THE SHOGUN WAITING IN THE BEDCHAMBER IS A LAPSE THAT IS UNPRECEDENTED!
I AM MORTIFIED! TRULY MORTIFIED, MY LORD!
IT'S ALL RIGHT, KUROKI. IT CAN HARDLY BE YOUR FAULT. RAISE YOUR HEAD.

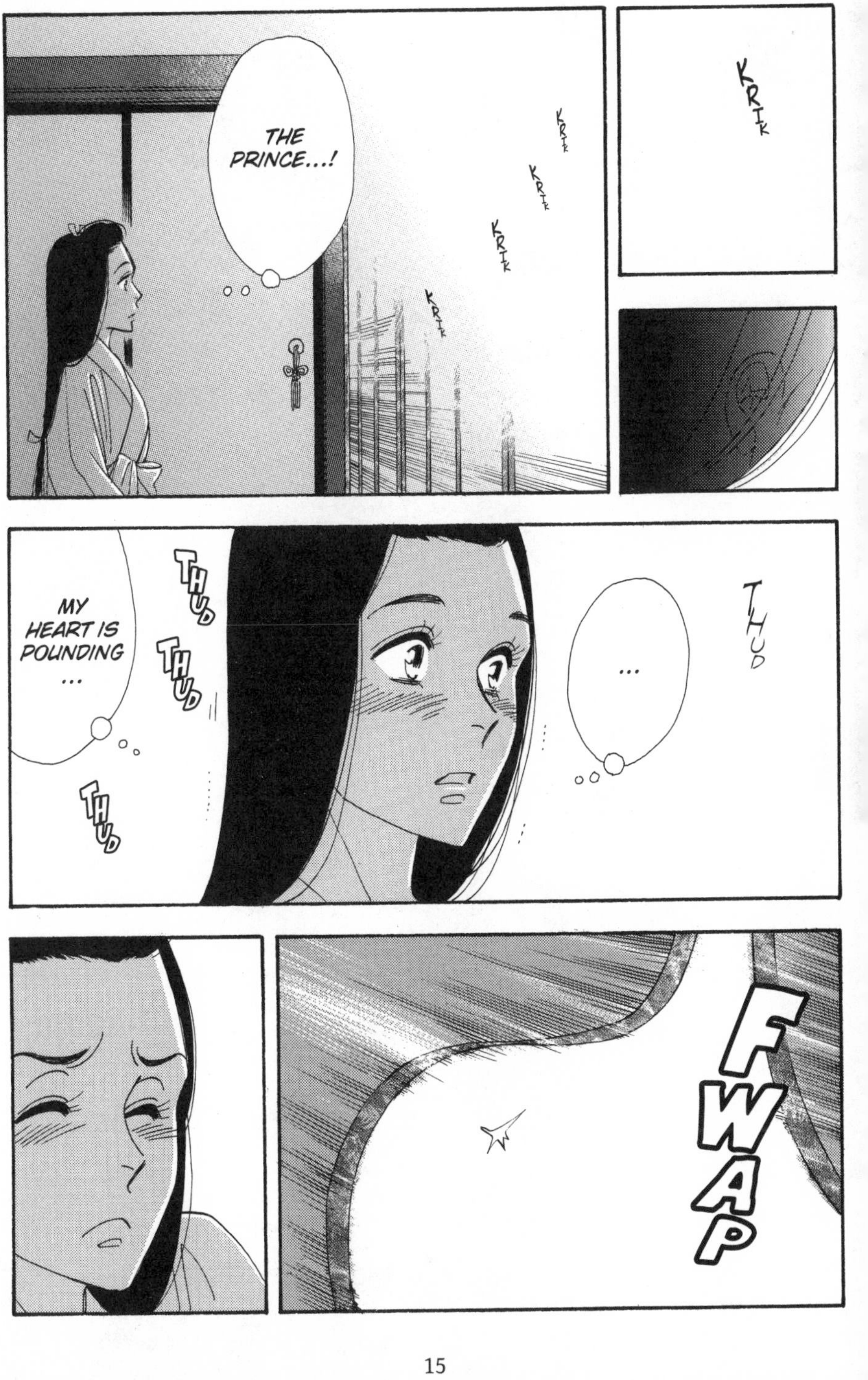
KRIK
KRIK
KRIK
KRIK
KRIK
THE PRINCE...!
THUD
...
THUD
THUD
MY HEART IS POUNDING ...
THUD
FWAP

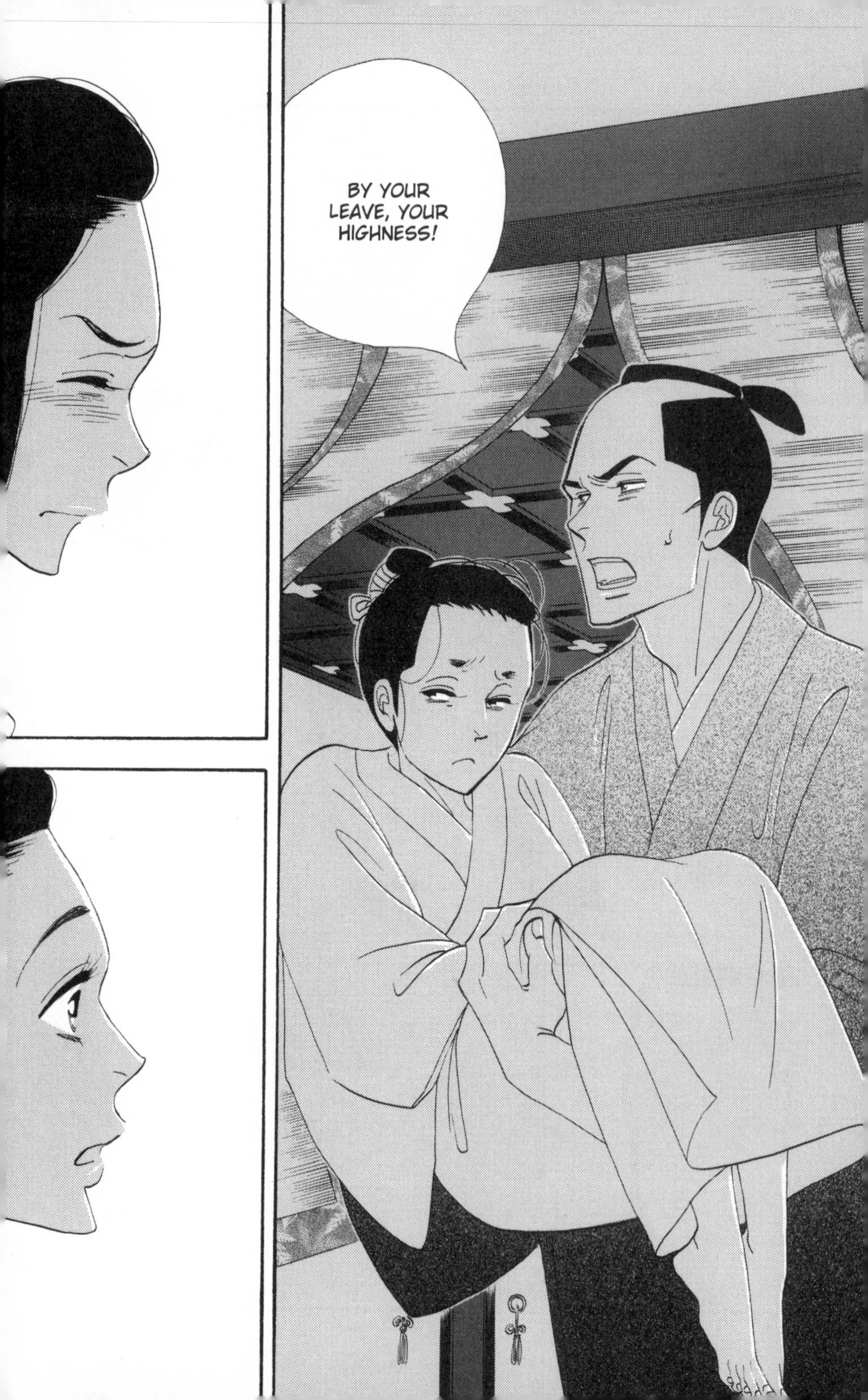
BY YOUR LEAVE, YOUR HIGHNESS!

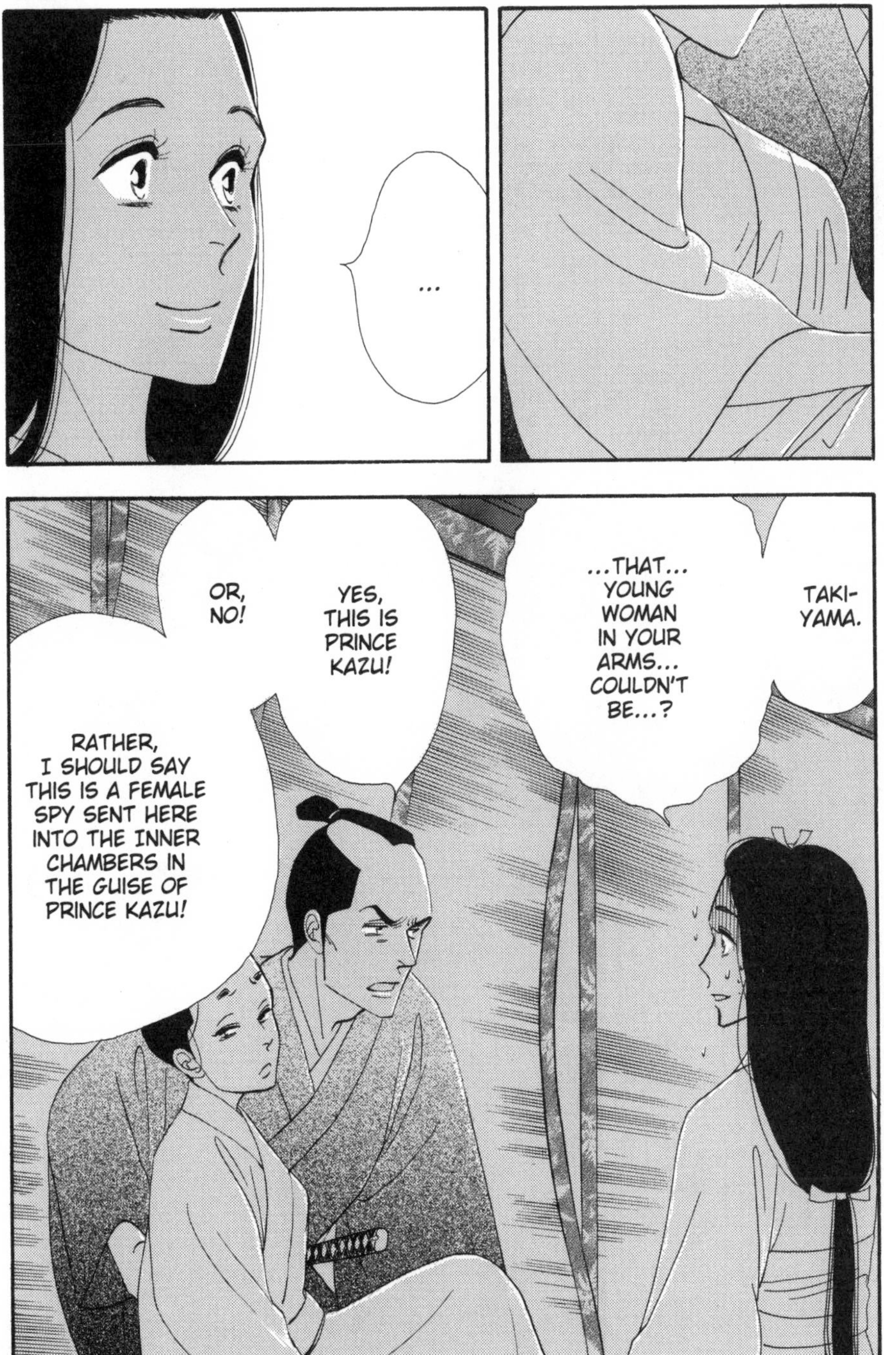
...
TAKI-YAMA.
...THAT... YOUNG WOMAN IN YOUR ARMS... COULDN'T BE...?
YES, THIS IS PRINCE KAZU!
OR, NO!
RATHER, I SHOULD SAY THIS IS A FEMALE SPY SENT HERE INTO THE INNER CHAMBERS IN THE GUISE OF PRINCE KAZU!

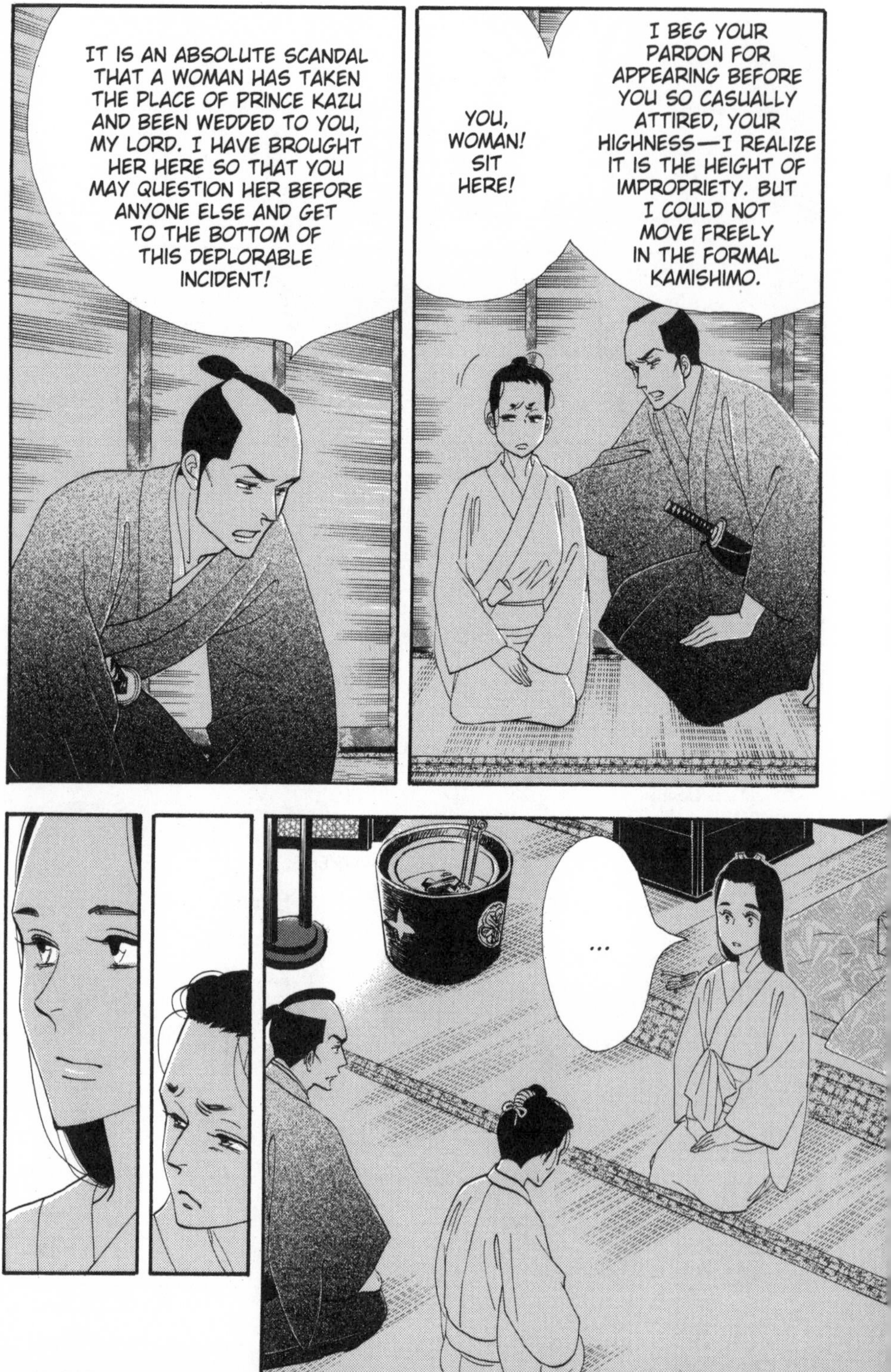
I BEG YOUR PARDON FOR APPEARING BEFORE YOU SO CASUALLY ATTIRED, YOUR HIGHNESS—I REALIZE IT IS THE HEIGHT OF IMPROPRIETY. BUT I COULD NOT MOVE FREELY IN THE FORMAL KAMISHIMO.
YOU, WOMAN! SIT HERE!
IT IS AN ABSOLUTE SCANDAL THAT A WOMAN HAS TAKEN THE PLACE OF PRINCE KAZU AND BEEN WEDDED TO YOU, MY LORD. I HAVE BROUGHT HER HERE SO THAT YOU MAY QUESTION HER BEFORE ANYONE ELSE AND GET TO THE BOTTOM OF THIS DEPLORABLE INCIDENT!
...

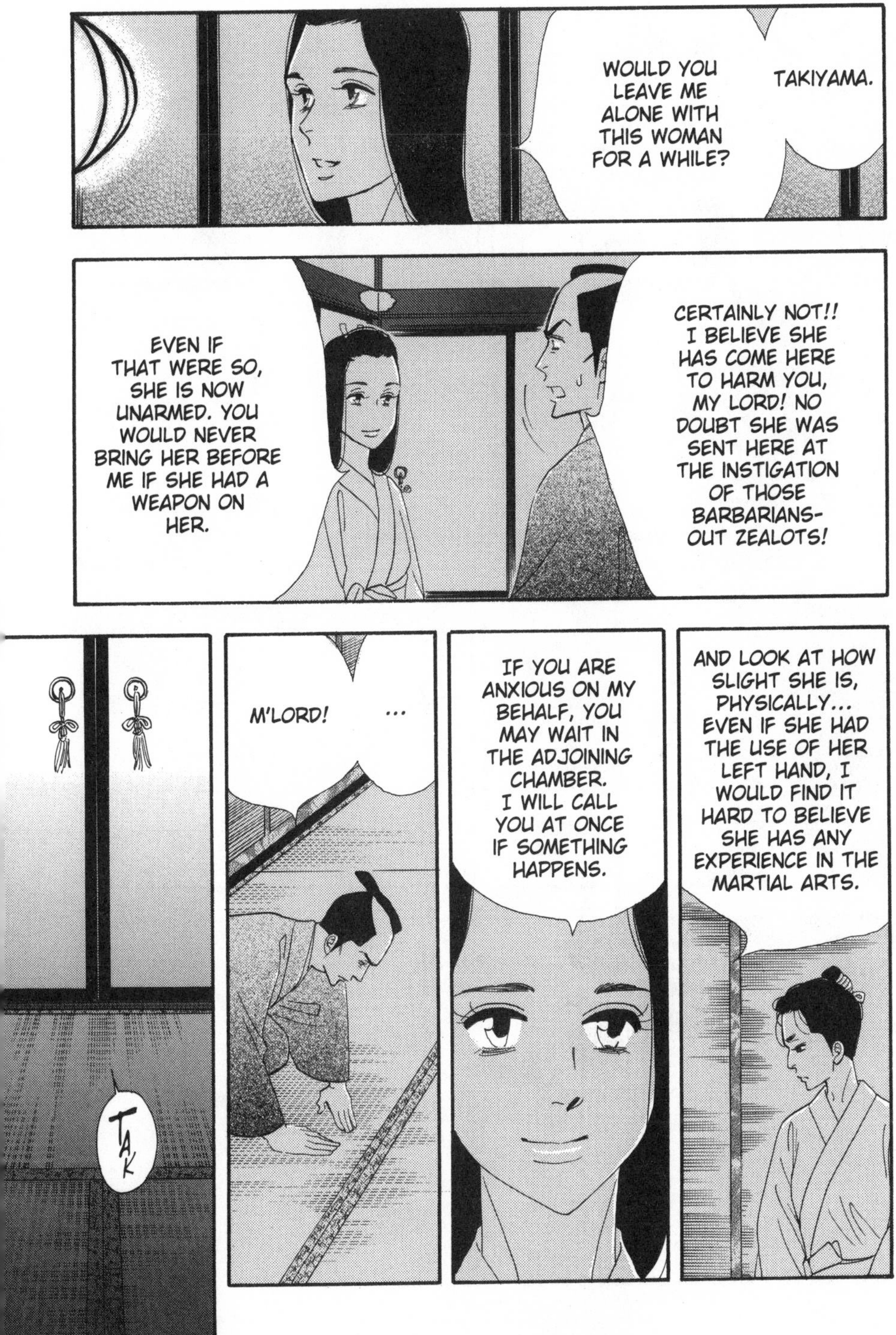
TAKIYAMA.
WOULD YOU LEAVE ME ALONE WITH THIS WOMAN FOR A WHILE?
CERTAINLY NOT!! I BELIEVE SHE HAS COME HERE TO HARM YOU, MY LORD! NO DOUBT SHE WAS SENT HERE AT THE INSTIGATION OF THOSE BARBARIANS-OUT ZEALOTS!
EVEN IF THAT WERE SO, SHE IS NOW UNARMED. YOU WOULD NEVER BRING HER BEFORE ME IF SHE HAD A WEAPON ON HER.
AND LOOK AT HOW SLIGHT SHE IS, PHYSICALLY... EVEN IF SHE HAD THE USE OF HER LEFT HAND, I WOULD FIND IT HARD TO BELIEVE SHE HAS ANY EXPERIENCE IN THE MARTIAL ARTS.
IF YOU ARE ANXIOUS ON MY BEHALF, YOU MAY WAIT IN THE ADJOINING CHAMBER. I WILL CALL YOU AT ONCE IF SOMETHING HAPPENS.
...
M'LORD!
TAK

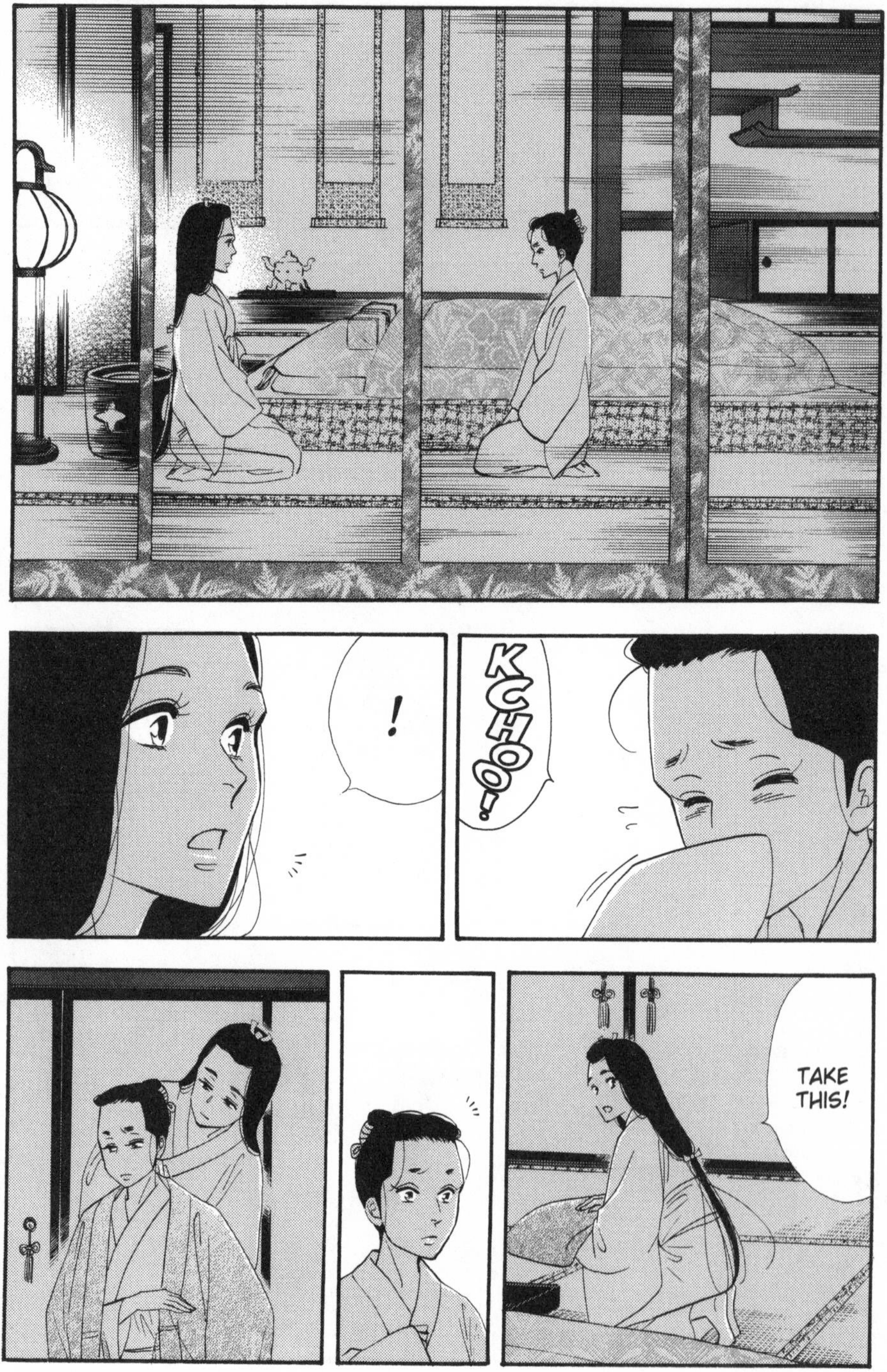
KCHOO!
!
TAKE THIS!

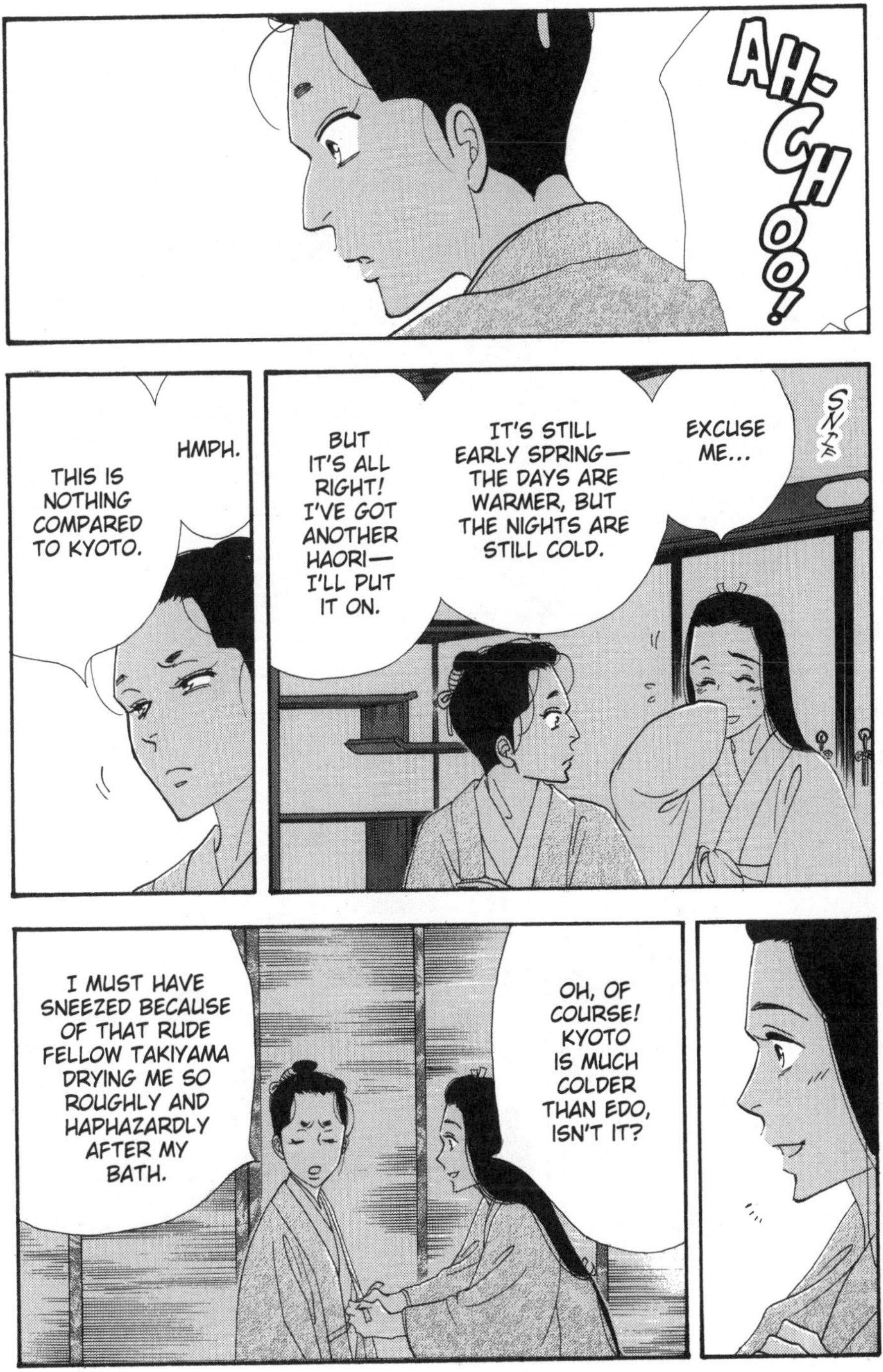
AH-CHOO!
SNIF
EXCUSE ME...
IT'S STILL EARLY SPRING— THE DAYS ARE WARMER, BUT THE NIGHTS ARE STILL COLD.
BUT IT'S ALL RIGHT! I'VE GOT ANOTHER HAORI— I'LL PUT IT ON.
HMPH.
THIS IS NOTHING COMPARED TO KYOTO.
OH, OF COURSE! KYOTO IS MUCH COLDER THAN EDO, ISN'T IT?
I MUST HAVE SNEEZED BECAUSE OF THAT RUDE FELLOW TAKIYAMA DRYING ME SO ROUGHLY AND HAPHAZARDLY AFTER MY BATH.

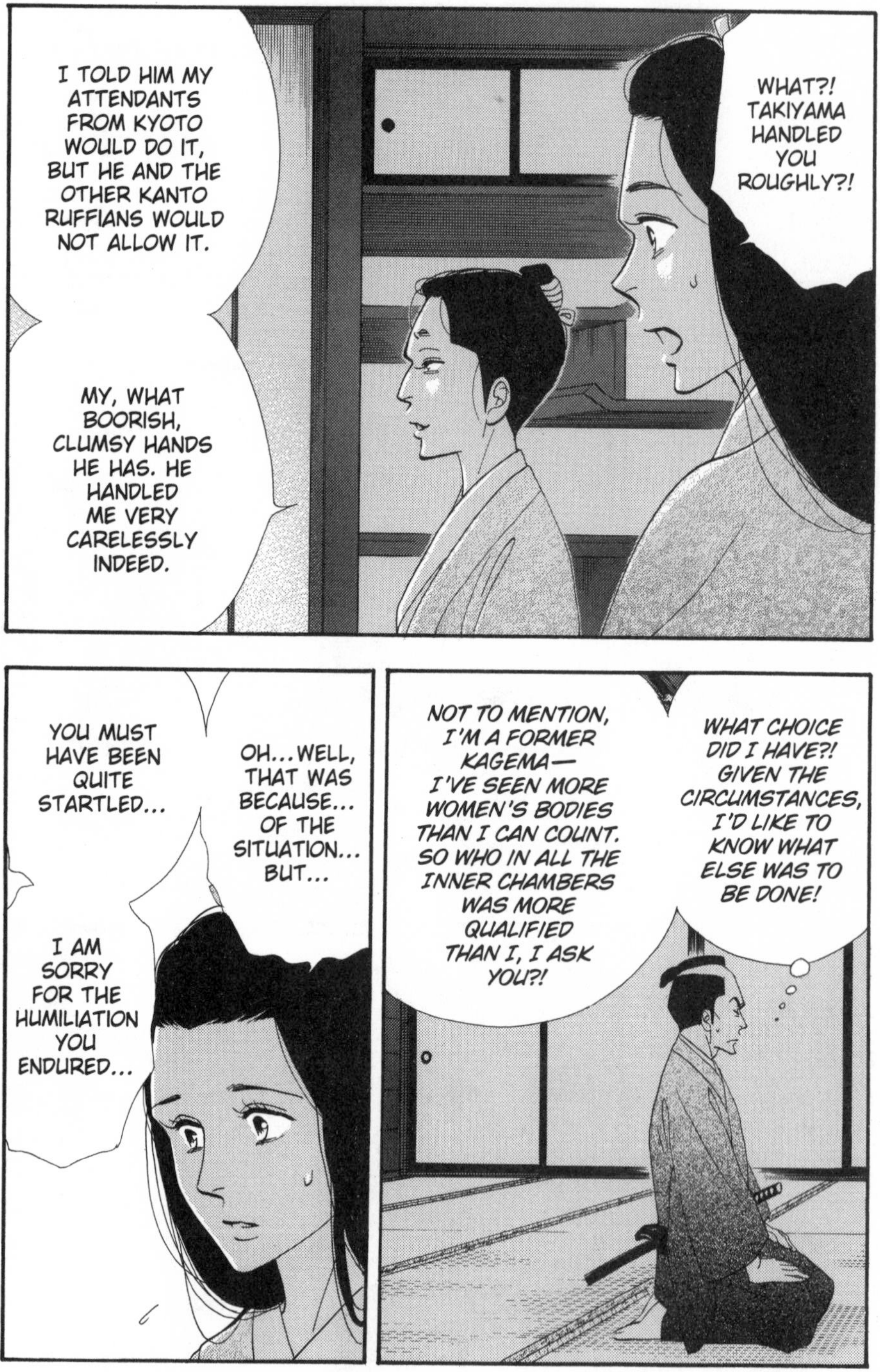
WHAT?! TAKIYAMA HANDLED YOU ROUGHLY?!
I TOLD HIM MY ATTENDANTS FROM KYOTO WOULD DO IT, BUT HE AND THE OTHER KANTO RUFFIANS WOULD NOT ALLOW IT.
MY, WHAT BOORISH, CLUMSY HANDS HE HAS. HE HANDLED ME VERY CARELESSLY INDEED.
WHAT CHOICE DID I HAVE?! GIVEN THE CIRCUMSTANCES, I'D LIKE TO KNOW WHAT ELSE WAS TO BE DONE!
NOT TO MENTION, I'M A FORMER KAGEMA— I'VE SEEN MORE WOMEN'S BODIES THAN I CAN COUNT. SO WHO IN ALL THE INNER CHAMBERS WAS MORE QUALIFIED THAN I, I ASK YOU?!
OH...WELL, THAT WAS BECAUSE... OF THE SITUATION... BUT...
YOU MUST HAVE BEEN QUITE STARTLED...
I AM SORRY FOR THE HUMILIATION YOU ENDURED...

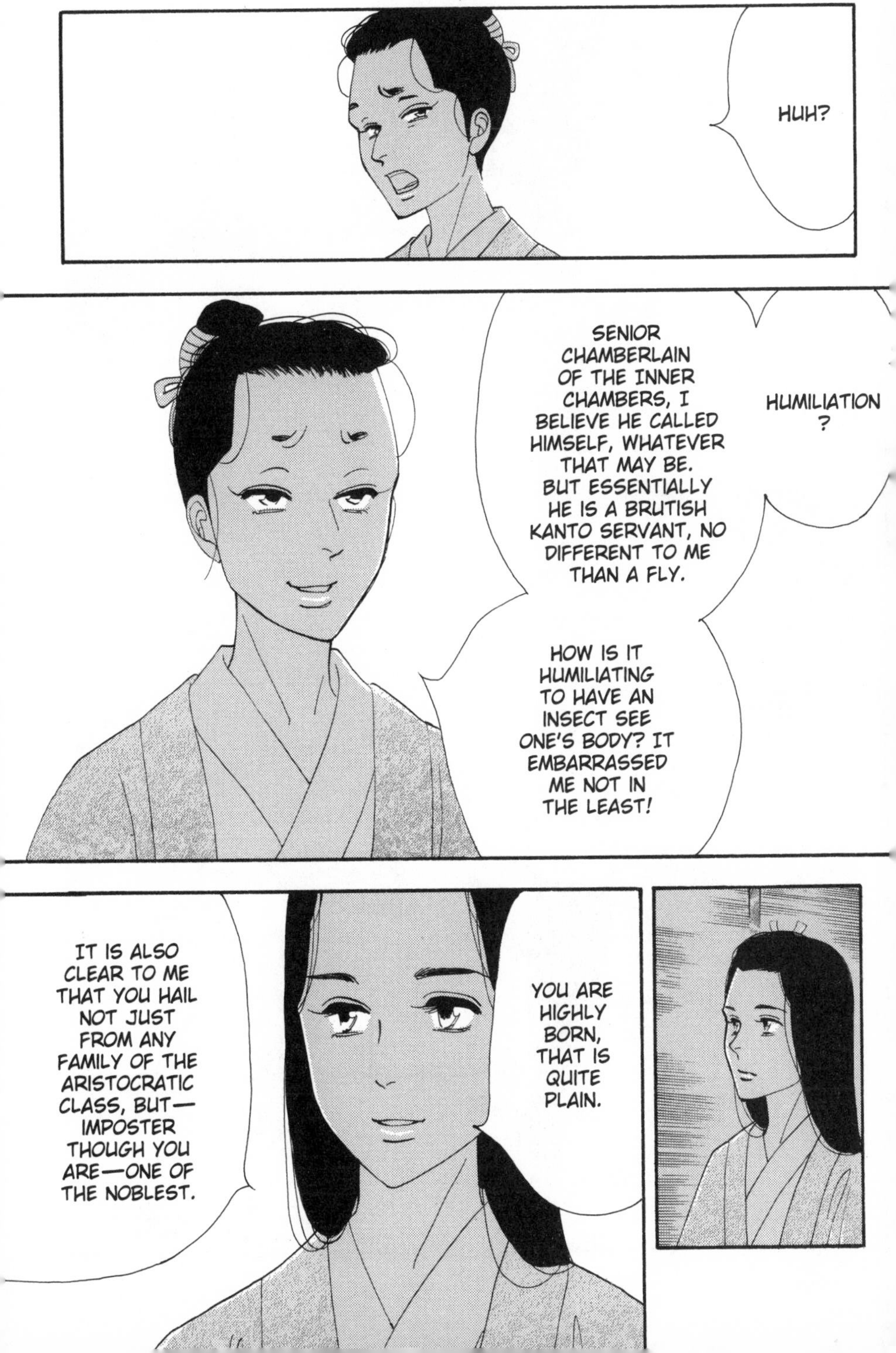
HUH?
HUMILIATION?
SENIOR CHAMBERLAIN OF THE INNER CHAMBERS, I BELIEVE HE CALLED HIMSELF, WHATEVER THAT MAY BE. BUT ESSENTIALLY HE IS A BRUTISH KANTO SERVANT, NO DIFFERENT TO ME THAN A FLY.
HOW IS IT HUMILIATING TO HAVE AN INSECT SEE ONE'S BODY? IT EMBARRASSED ME NOT IN THE LEAST!
YOU ARE HIGHLY BORN, THAT IS QUITE PLAIN.
IT IS ALSO CLEAR TO ME THAT YOU HAIL NOT JUST FROM ANY FAMILY OF THE ARISTOCRATIC CLASS, BUT—IMPOSTER THOUGH YOU ARE—ONE OF THE NOBLEST.

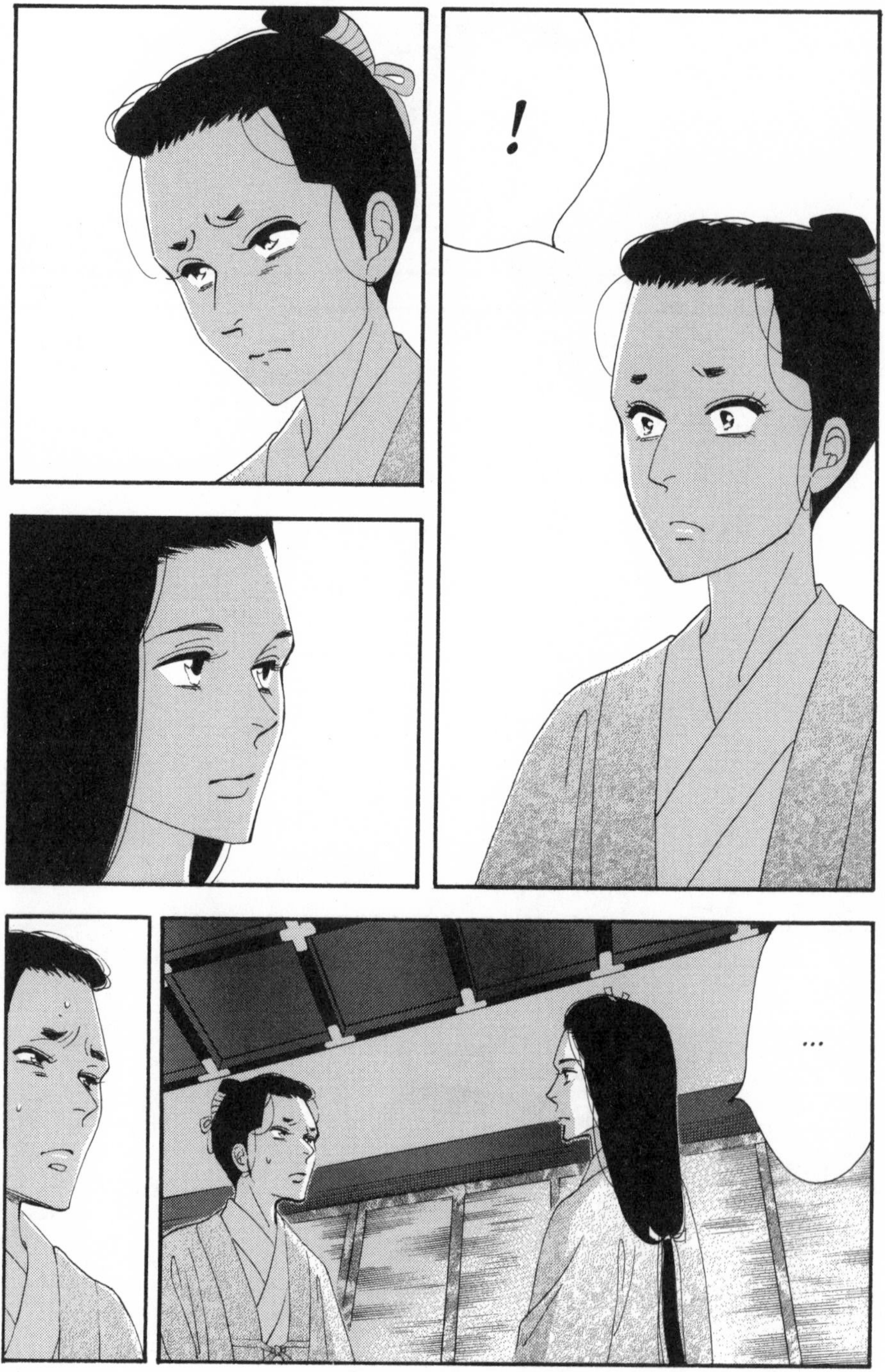
!
...

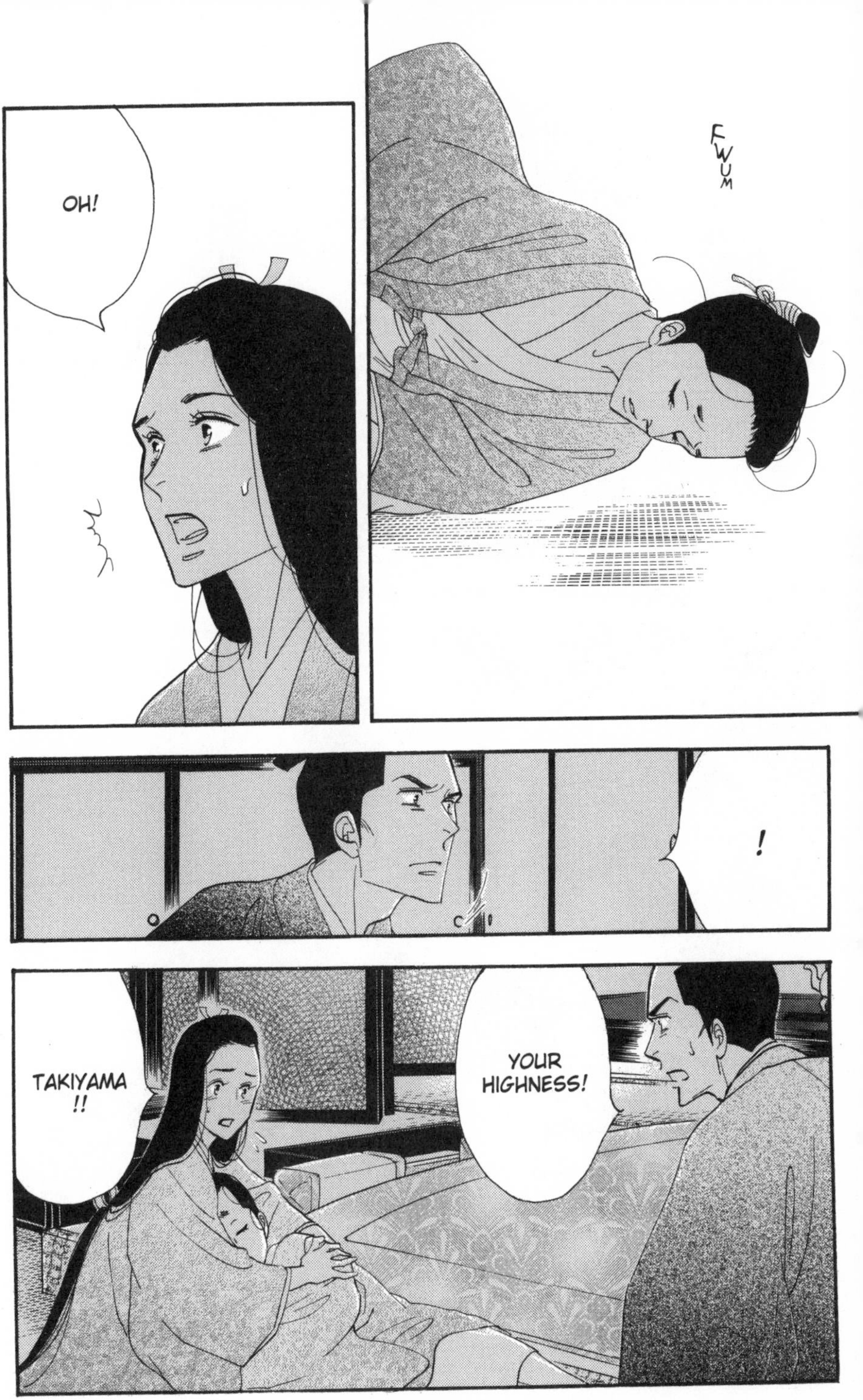
FWUM
OH!
!
YOUR HIGHNESS!
TAKIYAMA !!

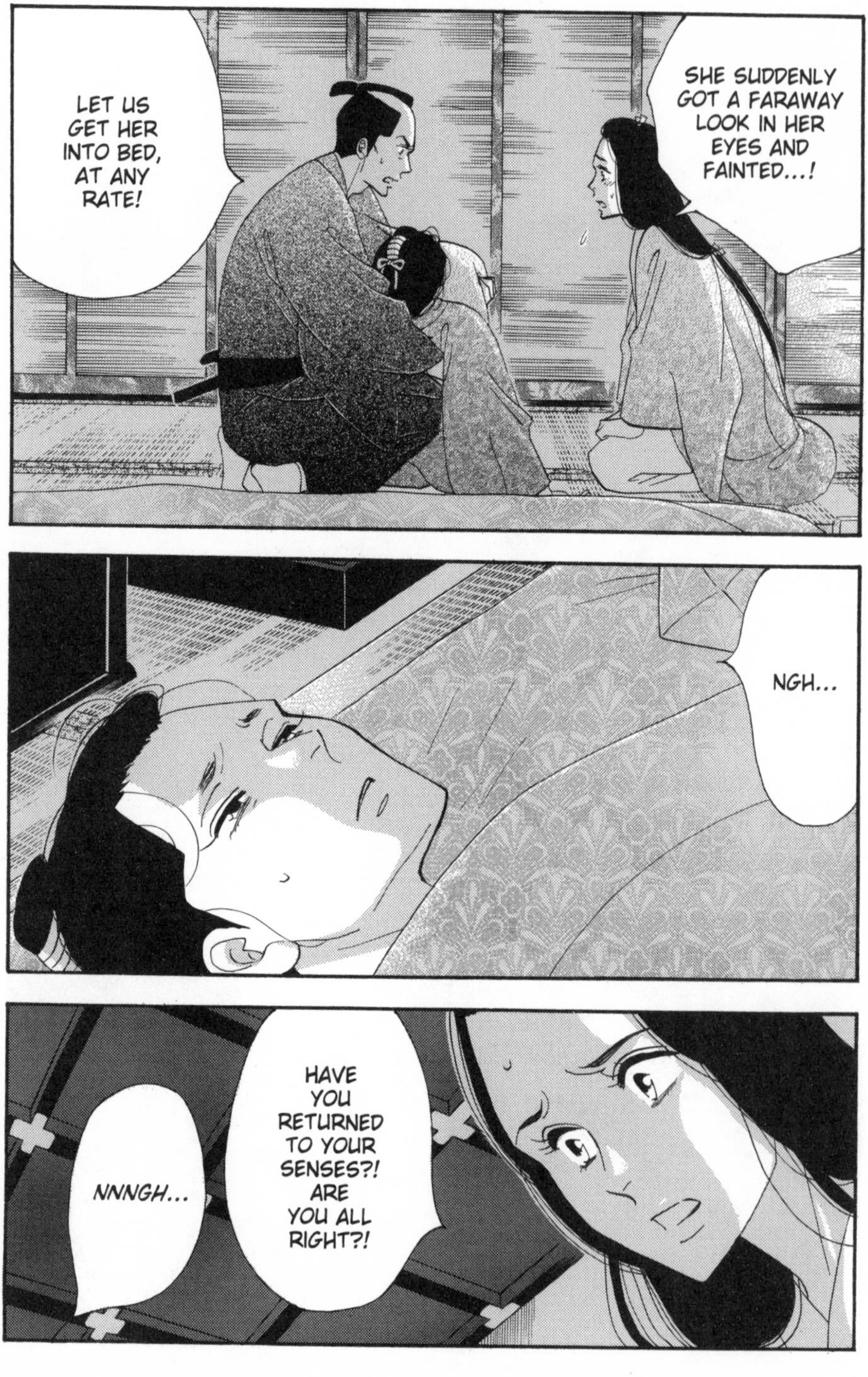
SHE SUDDENLY GOT A FARAWAY LOOK IN HER EYES AND FAINTED...!
LET US GET HER INTO BED, AT ANY RATE!
NGH...
HAVE YOU RETURNED TO YOUR SENSES?! ARE YOU ALL RIGHT?!
NNNGH...

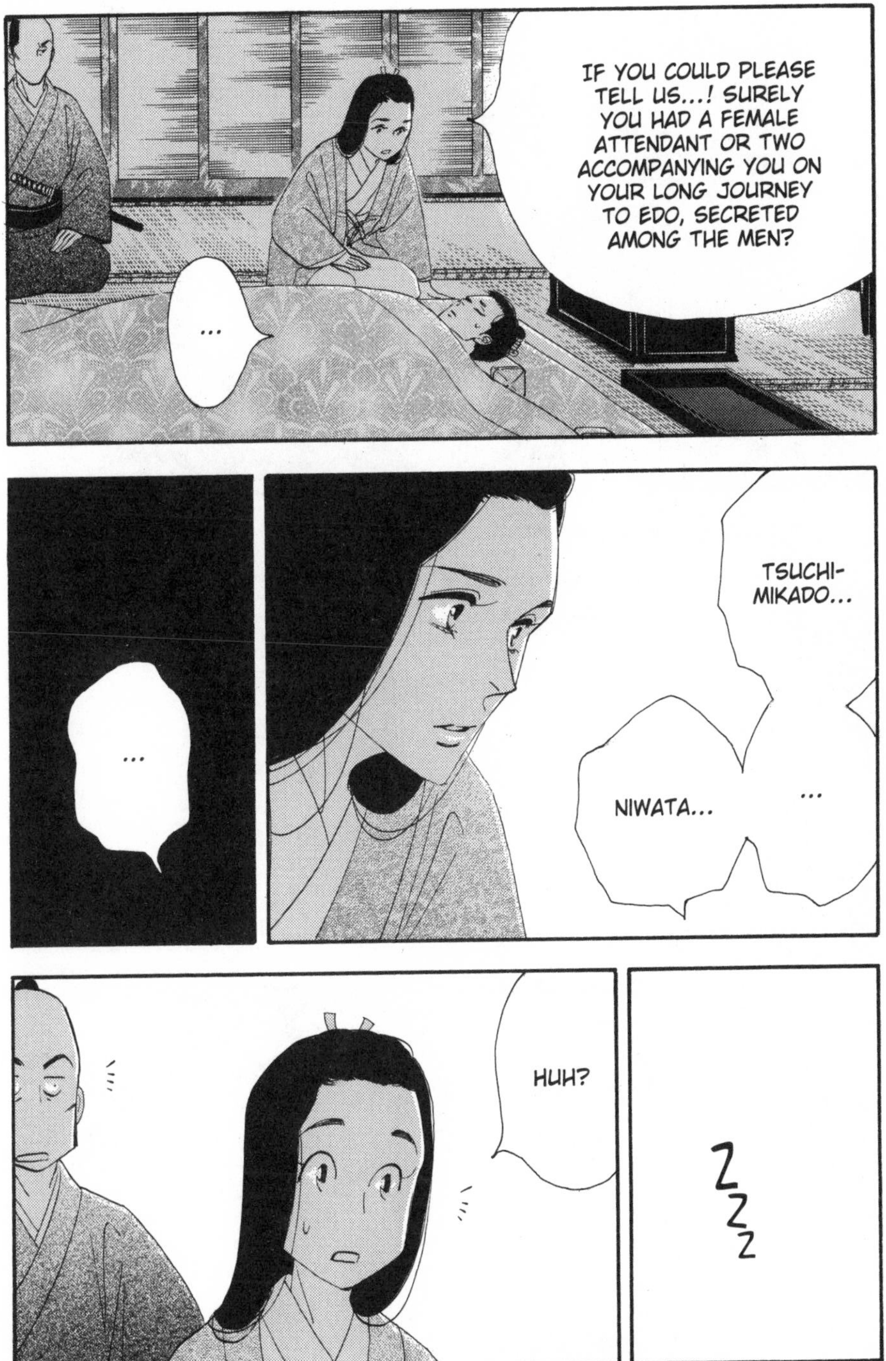
IF YOU COULD PLEASE TELL US...! SURELY YOU HAD A FEMALE ATTENDANT OR TWO ACCOMPANYING YOU ON YOUR LONG JOURNEY TO EDO, SECRETED AMONG THE MEN?
...
TSUCHI-MIKADO...
...
NIWATA...
...
Z Z Z
HUH?

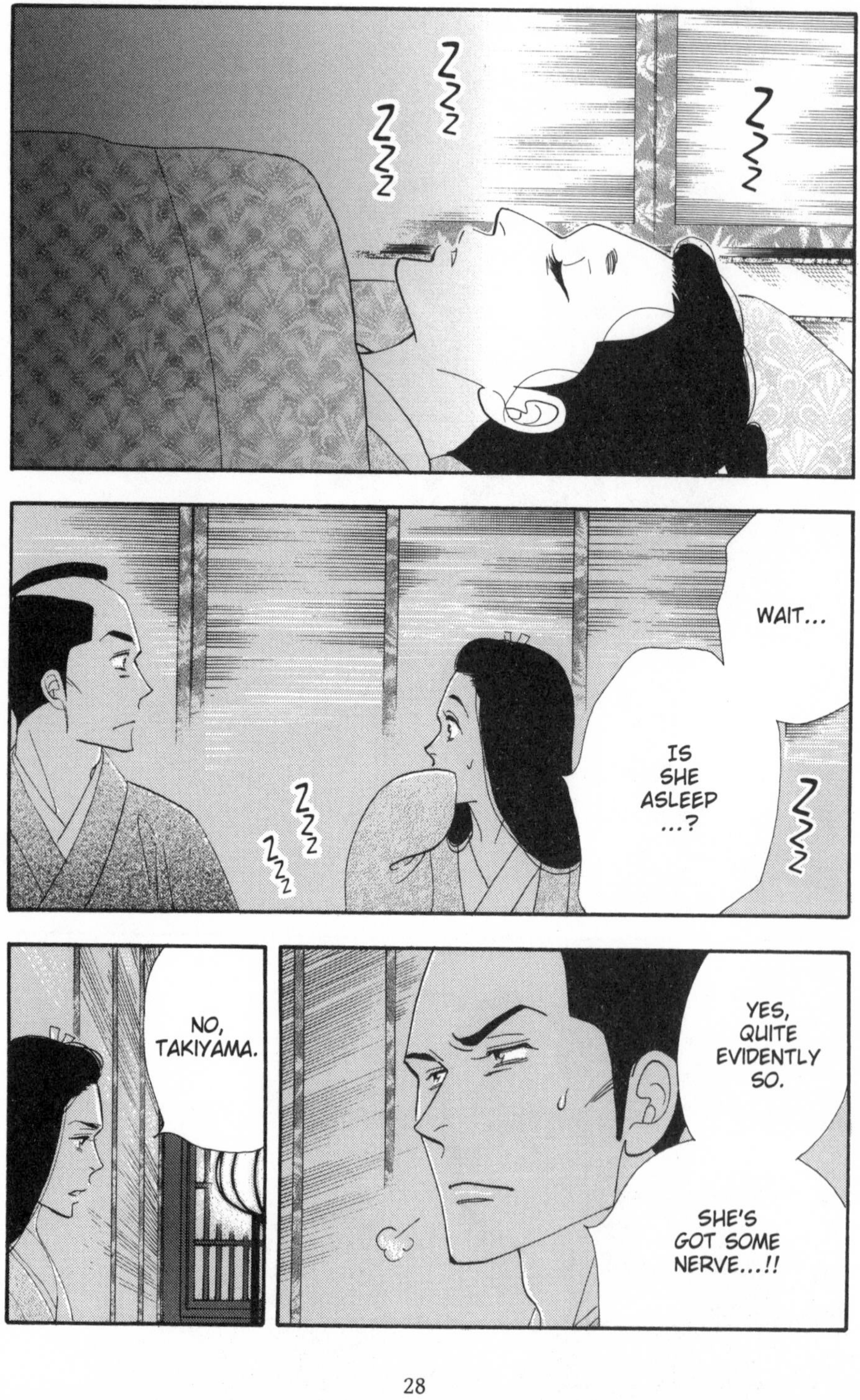
ZZZ
ZZZ
ZZZ
WAIT...
IS SHE ASLEEP...?
ZZZ
ZZZ
ZZZ
YES, QUITE EVIDENTLY SO.
SHE'S GOT SOME NERVE...!!
NO, TAKIYAMA.

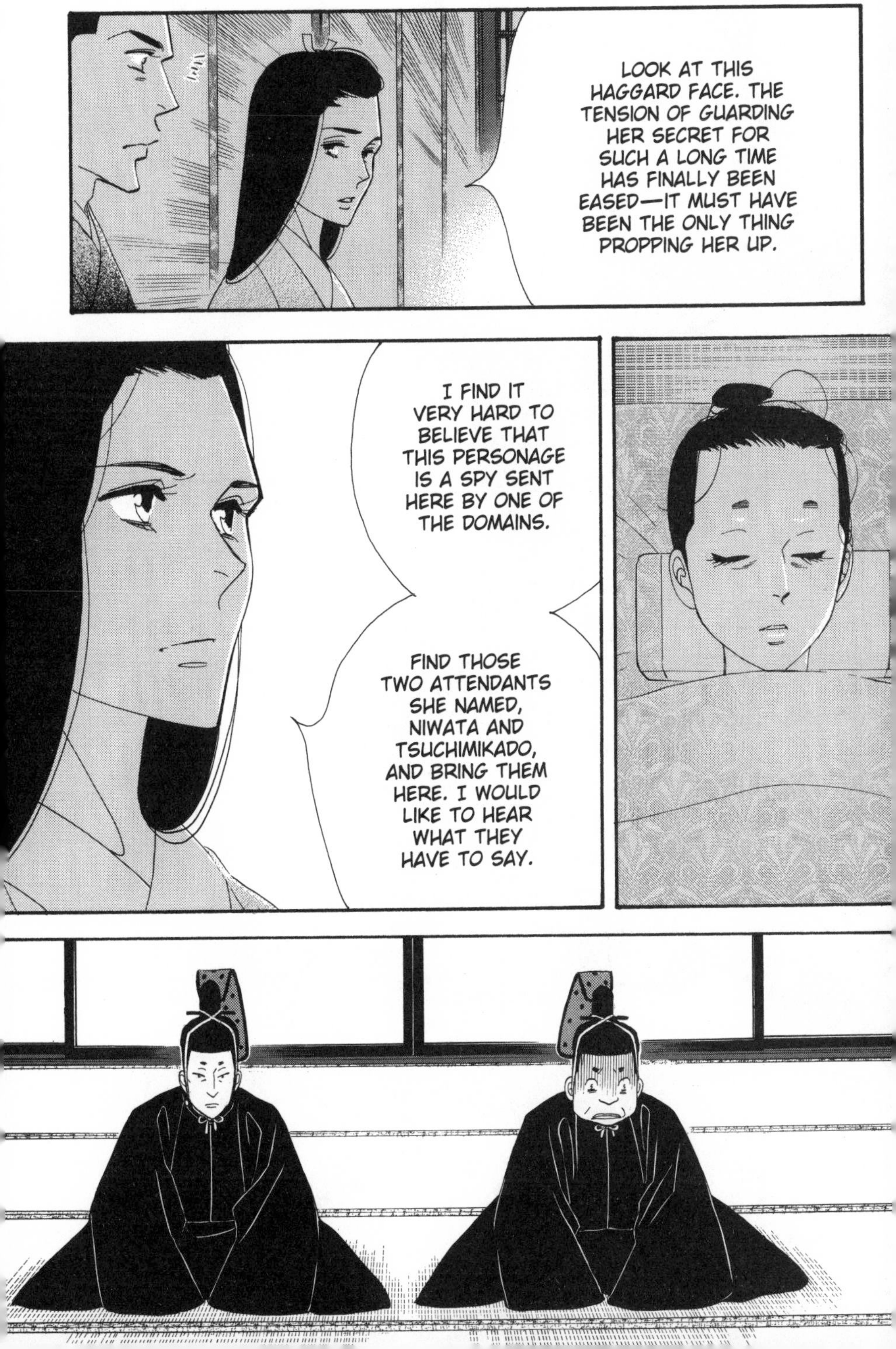
LOOK AT THIS HAGGARD FACE. THE TENSION OF GUARDING HER SECRET FOR SUCH A LONG TIME HAS FINALLY BEEN EASED—IT MUST HAVE BEEN THE ONLY THING PROPPING HER UP.
I FIND IT VERY HARD TO BELIEVE THAT THIS PERSONAGE IS A SPY SENT HERE BY ONE OF THE DOMAINS.
FIND THOSE TWO ATTENDANTS SHE NAMED, NIWATA AND TSUCHIMIKADO, AND BRING THEM HERE. I WOULD LIKE TO HEAR WHAT THEY HAVE TO SAY.

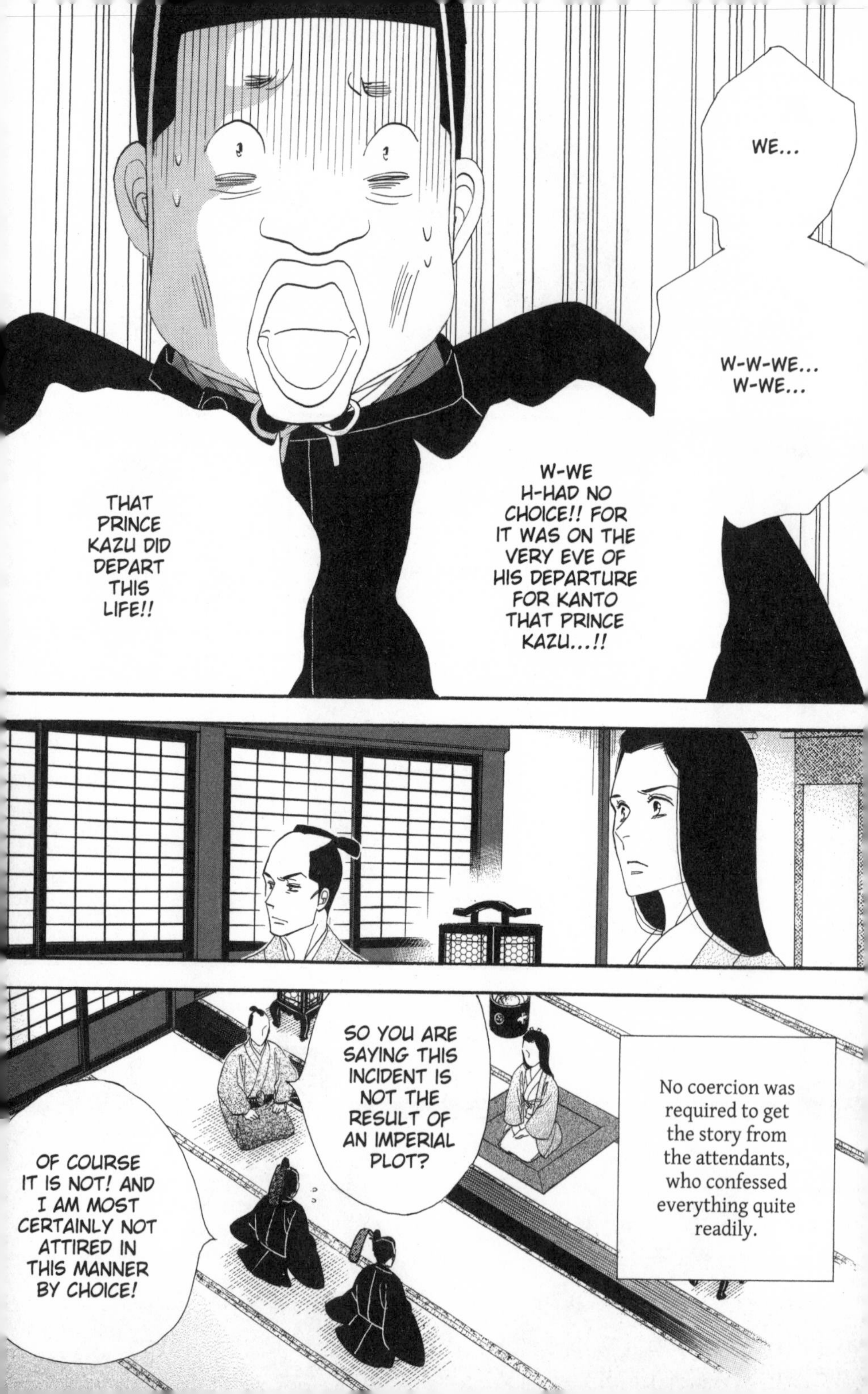
WE...
W-W-WE... W-WE...
W-WE H-HAD NO CHOICE!! FOR IT WAS ON THE VERY EVE OF HIS DEPARTURE FOR KANTO THAT PRINCE KAZU...!!
THAT PRINCE KAZU DID DEPART THIS LIFE!!
No coercion was required to get the story from the attendants, who confessed everything quite readily.
SO YOU ARE SAYING THIS INCIDENT IS NOT THE RESULT OF AN IMPERIAL PLOT?
OF COURSE IT IS NOT! AND I AM MOST CERTAINLY NOT ATTIRED IN THIS MANNER BY CHOICE!

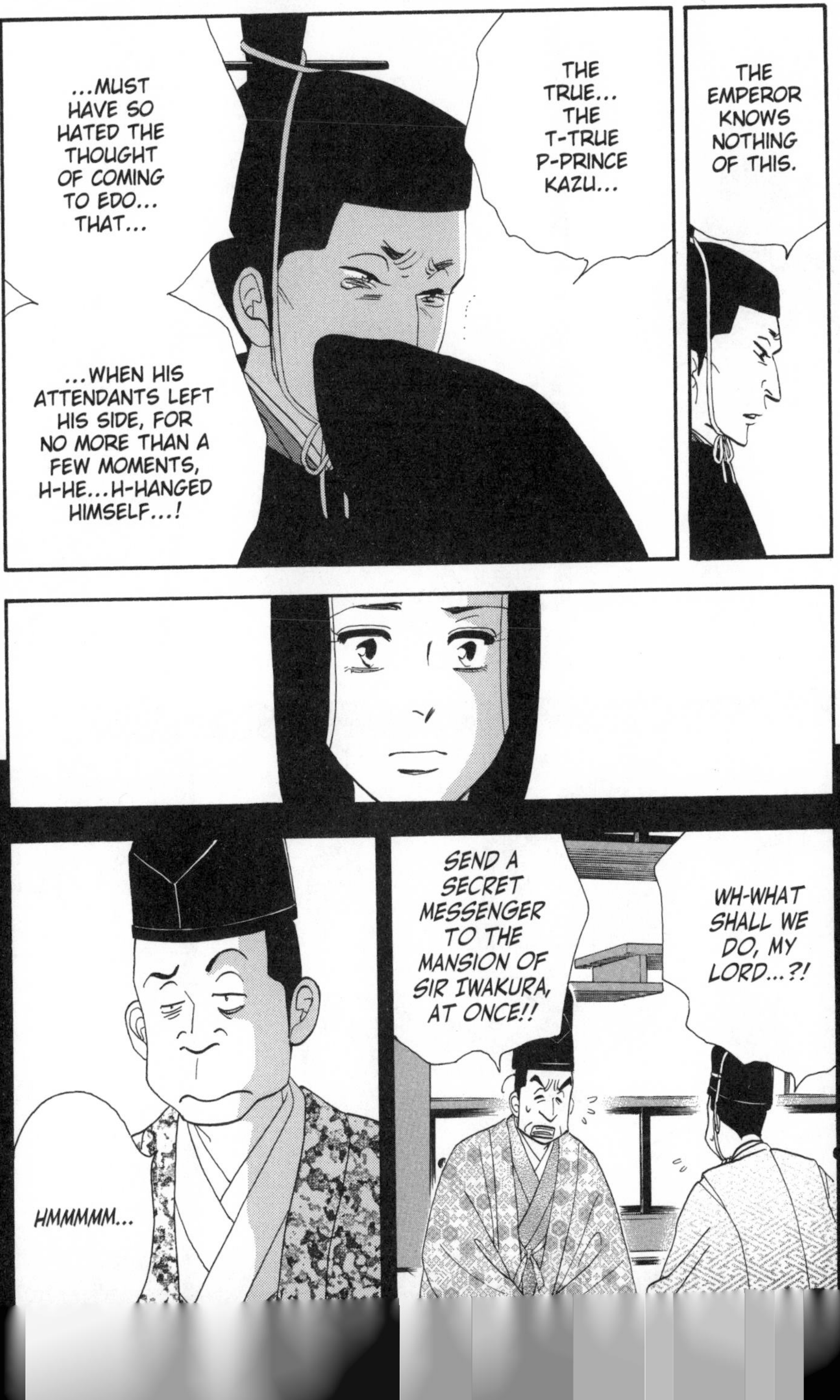
THE EMPEROR KNOWS NOTHING OF THIS.
THE TRUE... THE T-TRUE P-PRINCE KAZU...
...MUST HAVE SO HATED THE THOUGHT OF COMING TO EDO... THAT...
...WHEN HIS ATTENDANTS LEFT HIS SIDE, FOR NO MORE THAN A FEW MOMENTS, H-HE...H-HANGED HIMSELF...!
WH-WHAT SHALL WE DO, MY LORD...?!
SEND A SECRET MESSENGER TO THE MANSION OF SIR IWAKURA, AT ONCE!!
HMMMMM...

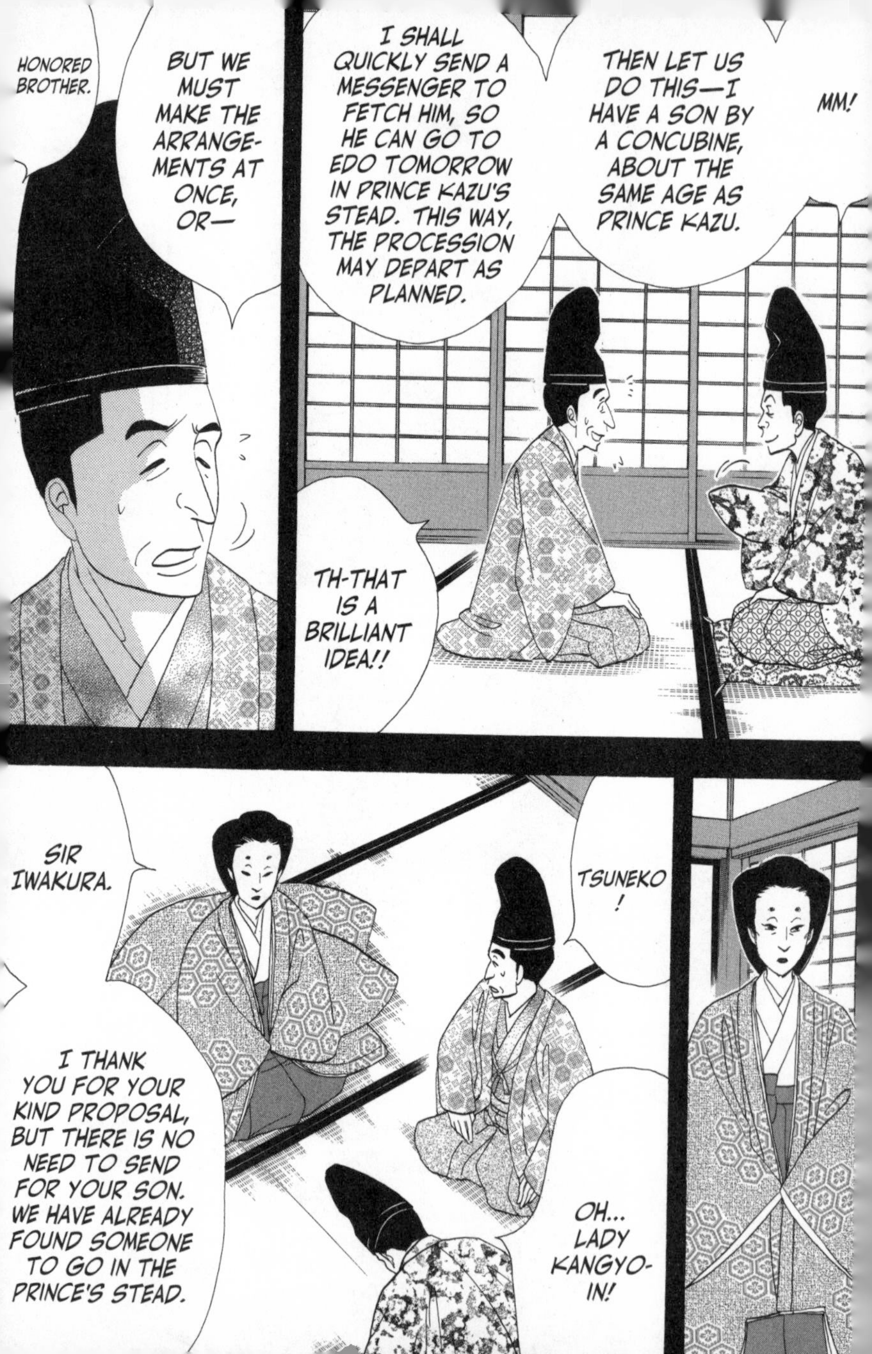
MM!
THEN LET US DO THIS—I HAVE A SON BY A CONCUBINE, ABOUT THE SAME AGE AS PRINCE KAZU.
I SHALL QUICKLY SEND A MESSENGER TO FETCH HIM, SO HE CAN GO TO EDO TOMORROW IN PRINCE KAZU'S STEAD. THIS WAY, THE PROCESSION MAY DEPART AS PLANNED.
TH-THAT IS A BRILLIANT IDEA!!
BUT WE MUST MAKE THE ARRANGE-MENTS AT ONCE, OR—
HONORED BROTHER.
SIR IWAKURA.
TSUNEKO!
OH... LADY KANGYO-IN!
I THANK YOU FOR YOUR KIND PROPOSAL, BUT THERE IS NO NEED TO SEND FOR YOUR SON. WE HAVE ALREADY FOUND SOMEONE TO GO IN THE PRINCE'S STEAD.

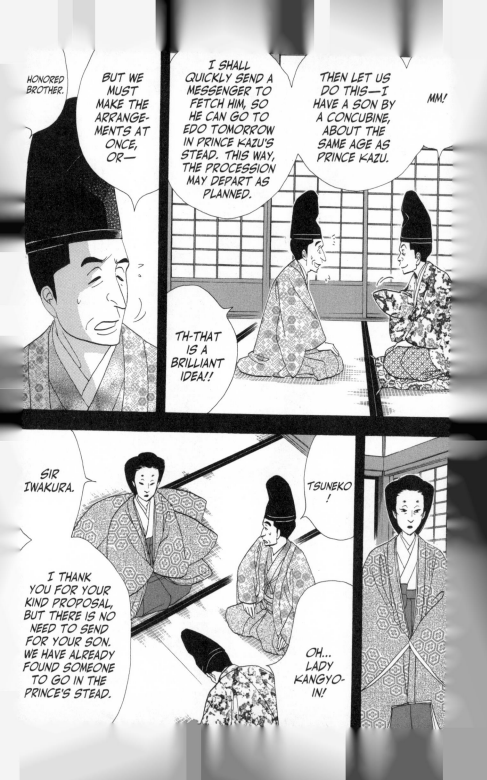

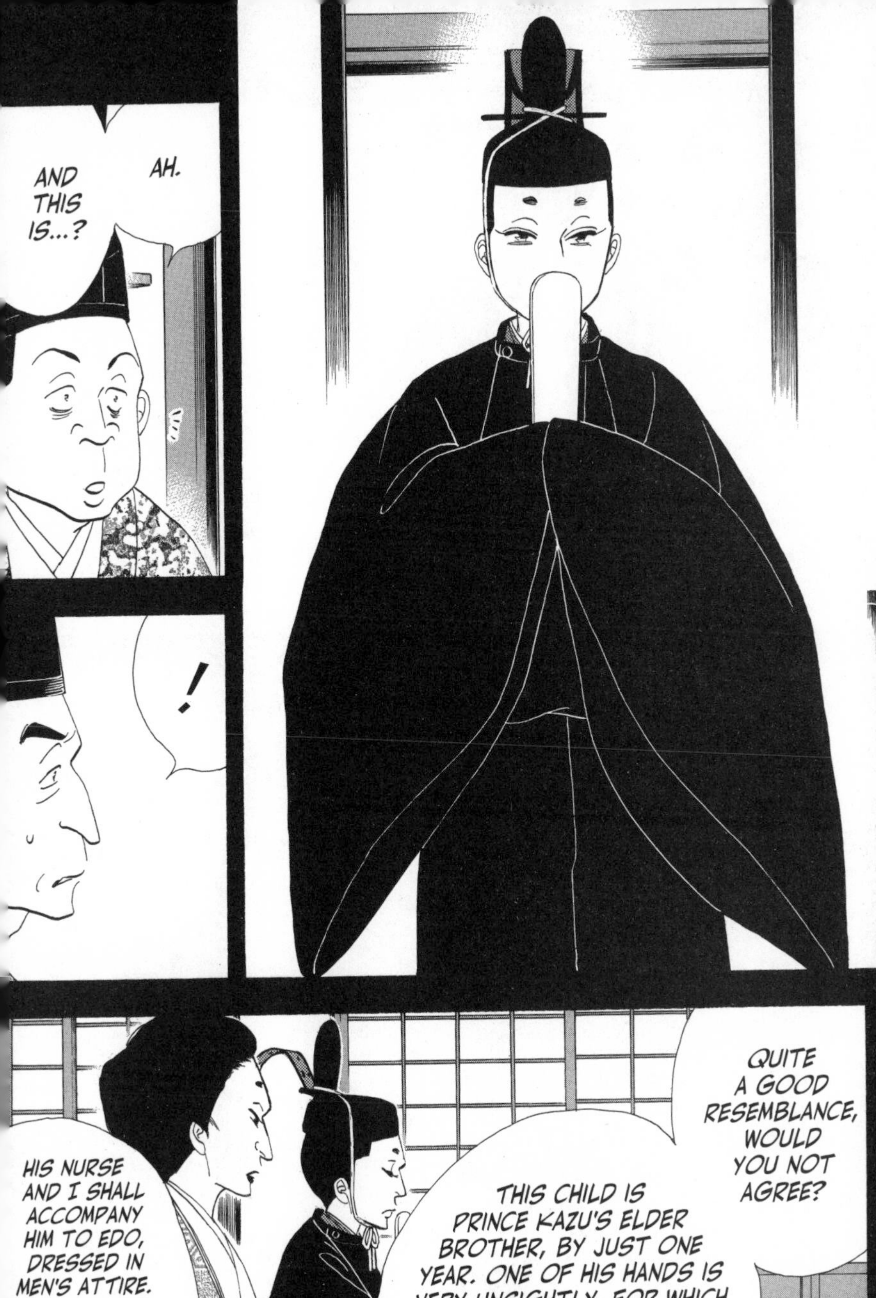

AH.
AND THIS IS...?
!
QUITE A GOOD RESEMBLANCE, WOULD YOU NOT AGREE?
THIS CHILD IS PRINCE KAZU'S ELDER BROTHER, BY JUST ONE YEAR. ONE OF HIS HANDS IS VERY UNSIGHTLY, FOR WHICH REASON WE HAVE RAISED HIM SECRETLY IN THE DEPTHS OF THIS MANSE, OUT OF SIGHT OF THE WORLD.
HIS NURSE AND I SHALL ACCOMPANY HIM TO EDO, DRESSED IN MEN'S ATTIRE. WHAT SAY YOU THAT WE GET THROUGH THIS JUNCTURE THIS WAY, FOR THE TIME BEING?

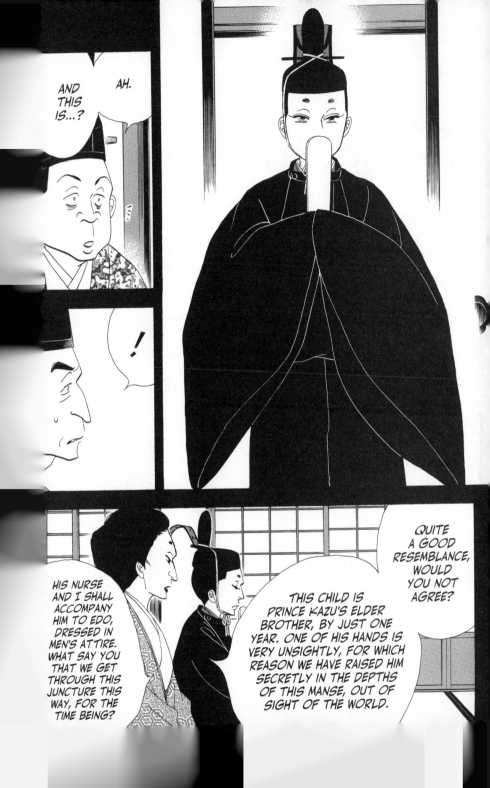

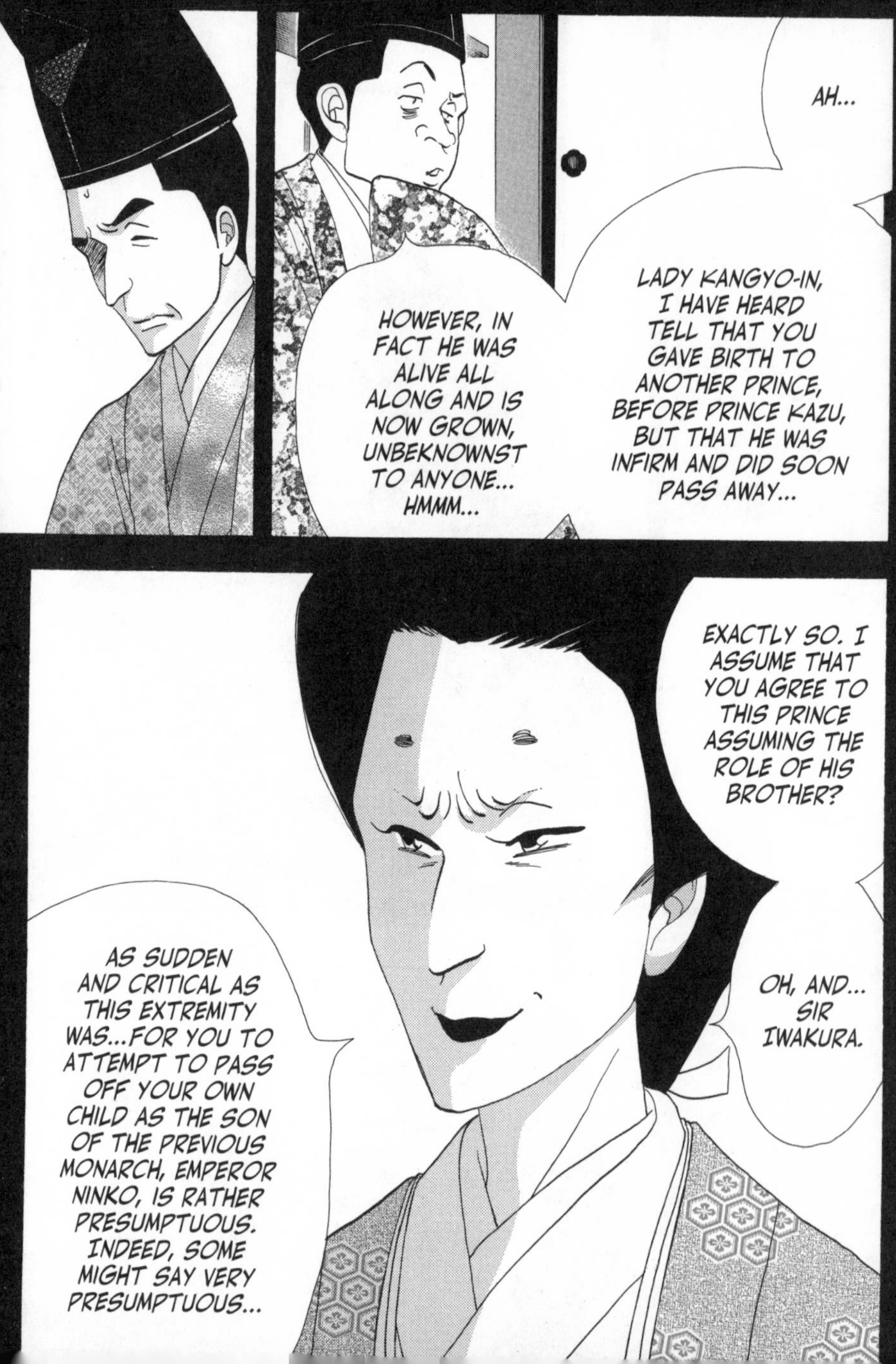
AH...
LADY KANGYO-IN, I HAVE HEARD TELL THAT YOU GAVE BIRTH TO ANOTHER PRINCE, BEFORE PRINCE KAZU, BUT THAT HE WAS INFIRM AND DID SOON PASS AWAY...
HOWEVER, IN FACT HE WAS ALIVE ALL ALONG AND IS NOW GROWN, UNBEKNOWNST TO ANYONE... HMMM...
EXACTLY SO. I ASSUME THAT YOU AGREE TO THIS PRINCE ASSUMING THE ROLE OF HIS BROTHER?
OH, AND... SIR IWAKURA.
AS SUDDEN AND CRITICAL AS THIS EXTREMITY WAS...FOR YOU TO ATTEMPT TO PASS OFF YOUR OWN CHILD AS THE SON OF THE PREVIOUS MONARCH, EMPEROR NINKO, IS RATHER PRESUMPTUOUS. INDEED, SOME MIGHT SAY VERY PRESUMPTUOUS...

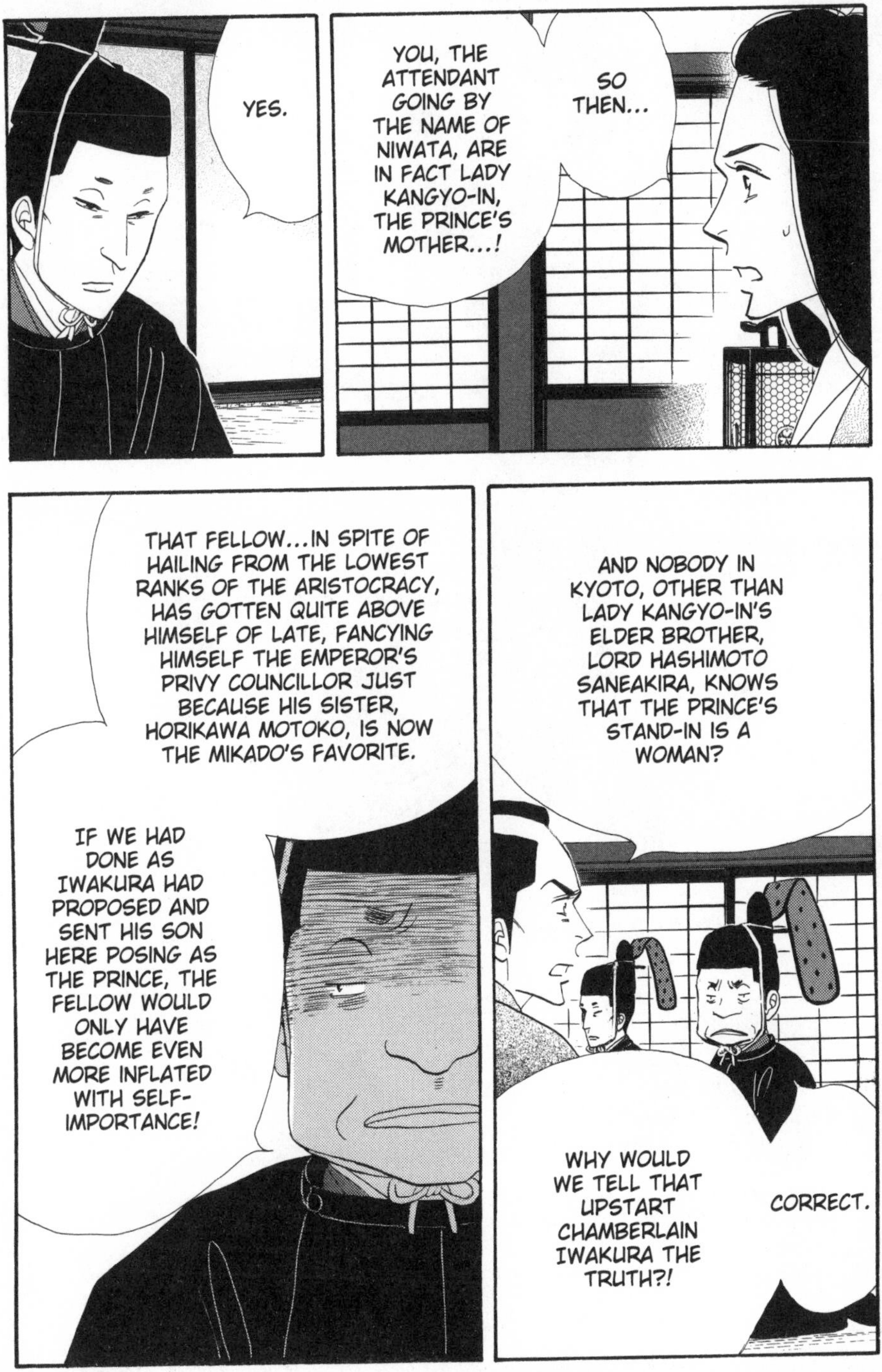
SO THEN...
YOU, THE ATTENDANT GOING BY THE NAME OF NIWATA, ARE IN FACT LADY KANGYO-IN, THE PRINCE'S MOTHER...!
YES.
AND NOBODY IN KYOTO, OTHER THAN LADY KANGYO-IN'S ELDER BROTHER, LORD HASHIMOTO SANEAKIRA, KNOWS THAT THE PRINCE'S STAND-IN IS A WOMAN?
CORRECT.
WHY WOULD WE TELL THAT UPSTART CHAMBERLAIN IWAKURA THE TRUTH?!
THAT FELLOW...IN SPITE OF HAILING FROM THE LOWEST RANKS OF THE ARISTOCRACY, HAS GOTTEN QUITE ABOVE HIMSELF OF LATE, FANCYING HIMSELF THE EMPEROR'S PRIVY COUNCILLOR JUST BECAUSE HIS SISTER, HORIKAWA MOTOKO, IS NOW THE MIKADO'S FAVORITE.
IF WE HAD DONE AS IWAKURA HAD PROPOSED AND SENT HIS SON HERE POSING AS THE PRINCE, THE FELLOW WOULD ONLY HAVE BECOME EVEN MORE INFLATED WITH SELF-IMPORTANCE!

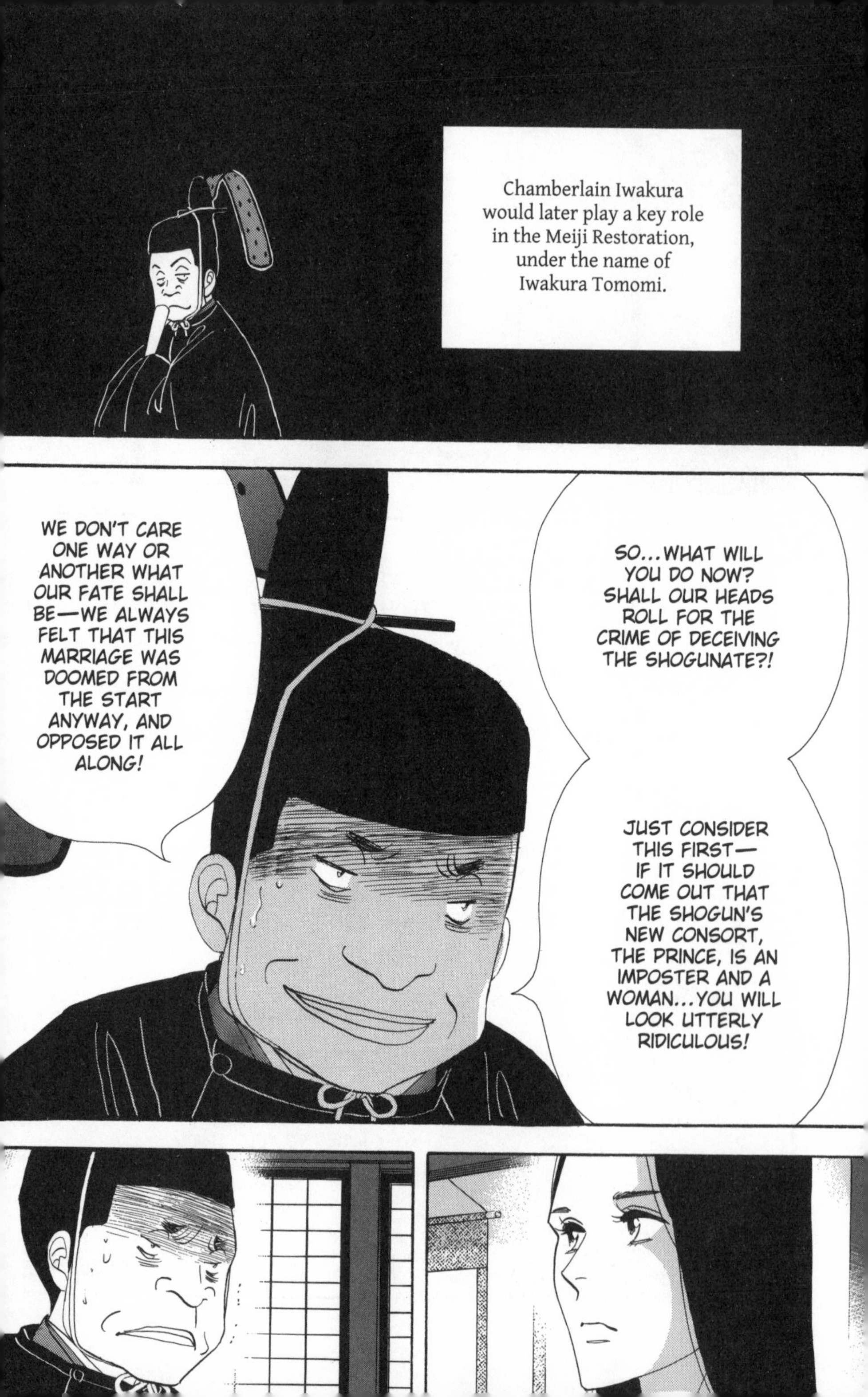
Chamberlain Iwakura would later play a key role in the Meiji Restoration, under the name of Iwakura Tomomi.
SO...WHAT WILL YOU DO NOW? SHALL OUR HEADS ROLL FOR THE CRIME OF DECEIVING THE SHOGUNATE?!
JUST CONSIDER THIS FIRST—IF IT SHOULD COME OUT THAT THE SHOGUN'S NEW CONSORT, THE PRINCE, IS AN IMPOSTER AND A WOMAN...YOU WILL LOOK UTTERLY RIDICULOUS!
WE DON'T CARE ONE WAY OR ANOTHER WHAT OUR FATE SHALL BE—WE ALWAYS FELT THAT THIS MARRIAGE WAS DOOMED FROM THE START ANYWAY, AND OPPOSED IT ALL ALONG!

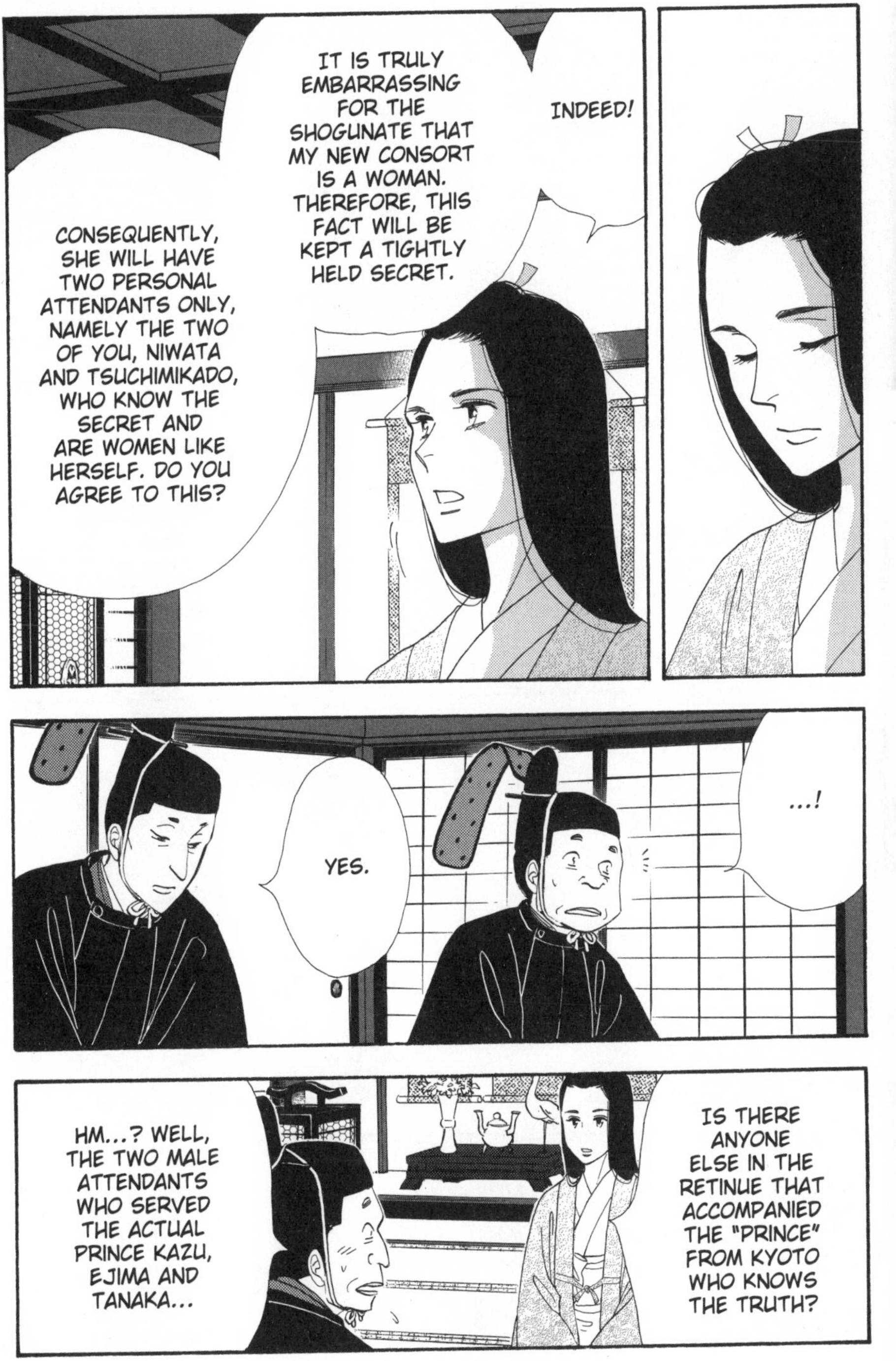
INDEED!
IT IS TRULY EMBARRASSING FOR THE SHOGUNATE THAT MY NEW CONSORT IS A WOMAN. THEREFORE, THIS FACT WILL BE KEPT A TIGHTLY HELD SECRET.
CONSEQUENTLY, SHE WILL HAVE TWO PERSONAL ATTENDANTS ONLY, NAMELY THE TWO OF YOU, NIWATA AND TSUCHIMIKADO, WHO KNOW THE SECRET AND ARE WOMEN LIKE HERSELF. DO YOU AGREE TO THIS?
...!
YES.
IS THERE ANYONE ELSE IN THE RETINUE THAT ACCOMPANIED THE "PRINCE" FROM KYOTO WHO KNOWS THE TRUTH?
HM...? WELL, THE TWO MALE ATTENDANTS WHO SERVED THE ACTUAL PRINCE KAZU, EJIMA AND TANAKA...

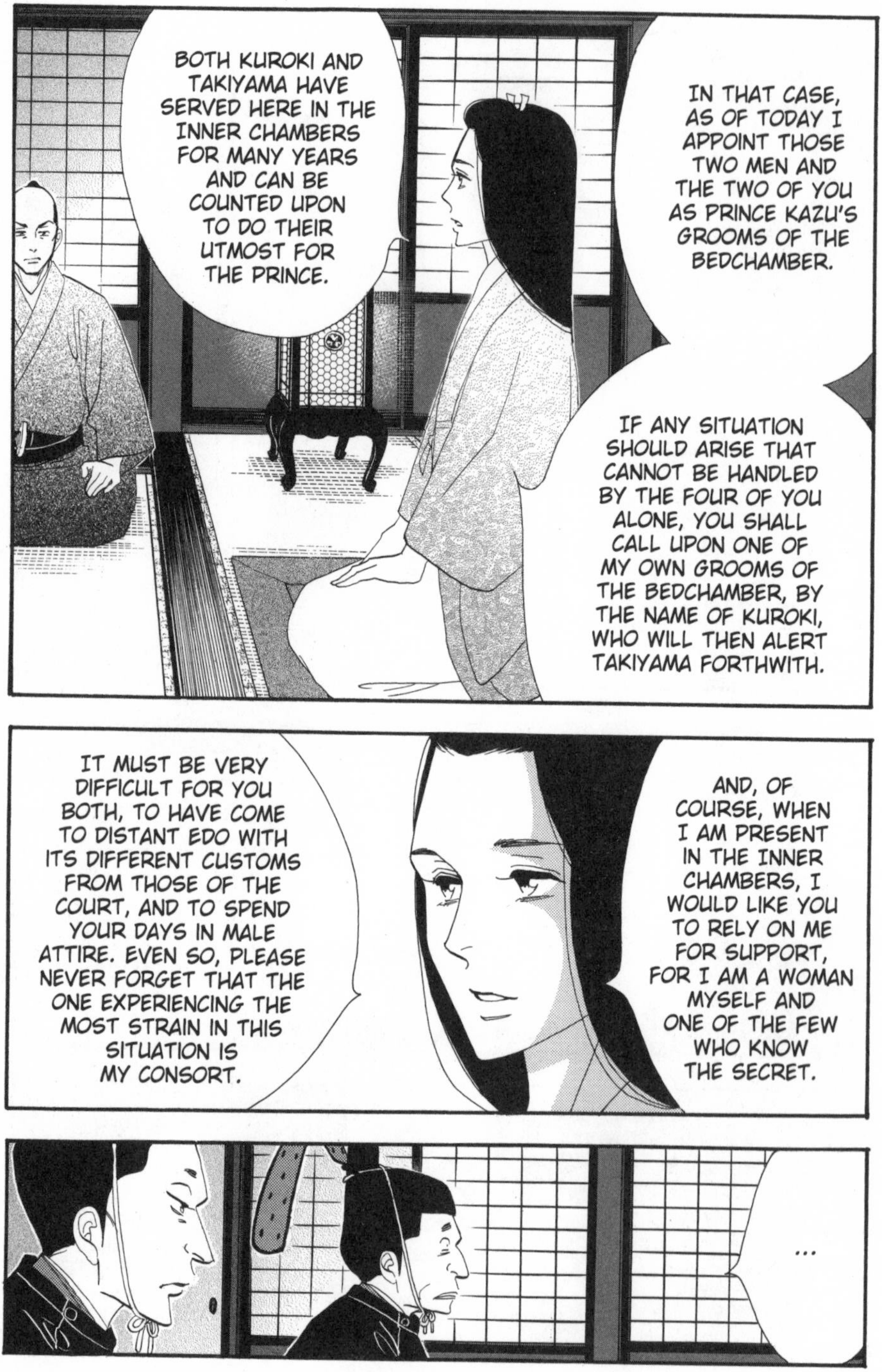
BOTH KUROKI AND TAKIYAMA HAVE SERVED HERE IN THE INNER CHAMBERS FOR MANY YEARS AND CAN BE COUNTED UPON TO DO THEIR UTMOST FOR THE PRINCE.
IN THAT CASE, AS OF TODAY I APPOINT THOSE TWO MEN AND THE TWO OF YOU AS PRINCE KAZU'S GROOMS OF THE BEDCHAMBER.
IF ANY SITUATION SHOULD ARISE THAT CANNOT BE HANDLED BY THE FOUR OF YOU ALONE, YOU SHALL CALL UPON ONE OF MY OWN GROOMS OF THE BEDCHAMBER, BY THE NAME OF KUROKI, WHO WILL THEN ALERT TAKIYAMA FORTHWITH.
AND, OF COURSE, WHEN I AM PRESENT IN THE INNER CHAMBERS, I WOULD LIKE YOU TO RELY ON ME FOR SUPPORT, FOR I AM A WOMAN MYSELF AND ONE OF THE FEW WHO KNOW THE SECRET.
IT MUST BE VERY DIFFICULT FOR YOU BOTH, TO HAVE COME TO DISTANT EDO WITH ITS DIFFERENT CUSTOMS FROM THOSE OF THE COURT, AND TO SPEND YOUR DAYS IN MALE ATTIRE. EVEN SO, PLEASE NEVER FORGET THAT THE ONE EXPERIENCING THE MOST STRAIN IN THIS SITUATION IS MY CONSORT.
...

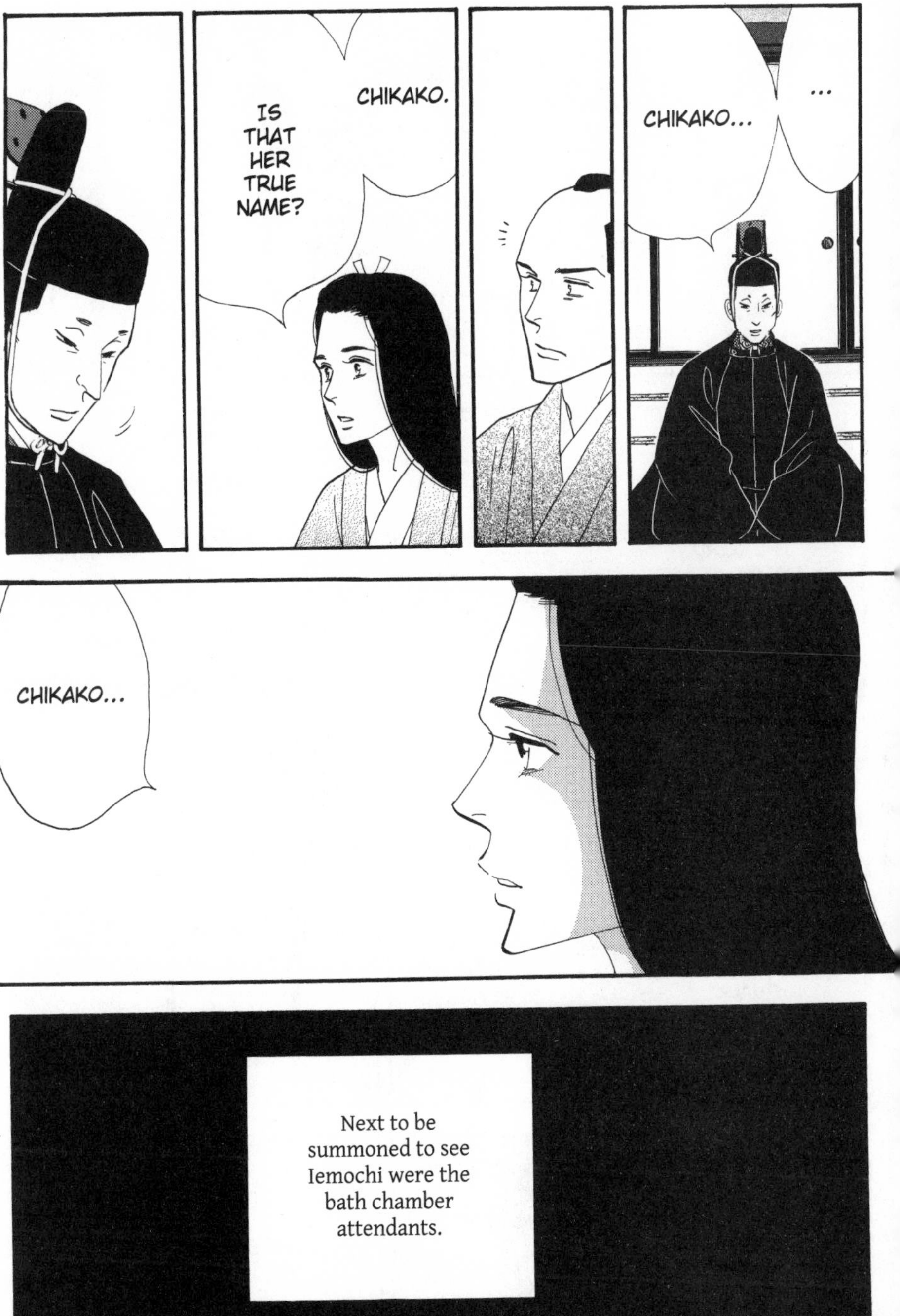
...
CHIKAKO...
CHIKAKO.
IS THAT HER TRUE NAME?
CHIKAKO...
Next to be summoned to see Iemochi were the bath chamber attendants.

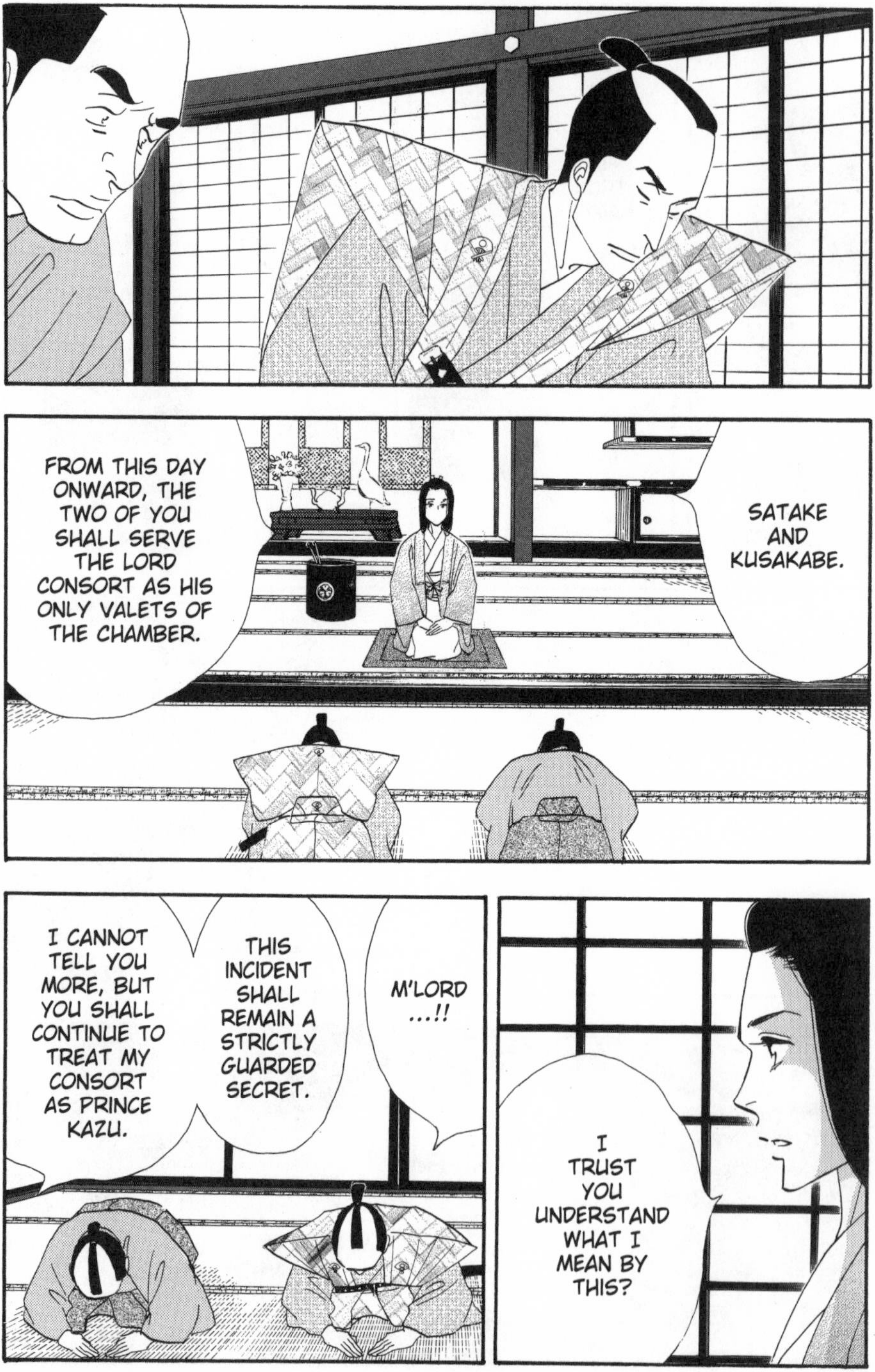
SATAKE AND KUSAKABE.
FROM THIS DAY ONWARD, THE TWO OF YOU SHALL SERVE THE LORD CONSORT AS HIS ONLY VALETS OF THE CHAMBER.
I TRUST YOU UNDERSTAND WHAT I MEAN BY THIS?
M'LORD ...!!
THIS INCIDENT SHALL REMAIN A STRICTLY GUARDED SECRET.
I CANNOT TELL YOU MORE, BUT YOU SHALL CONTINUE TO TREAT MY CONSORT AS PRINCE KAZU.

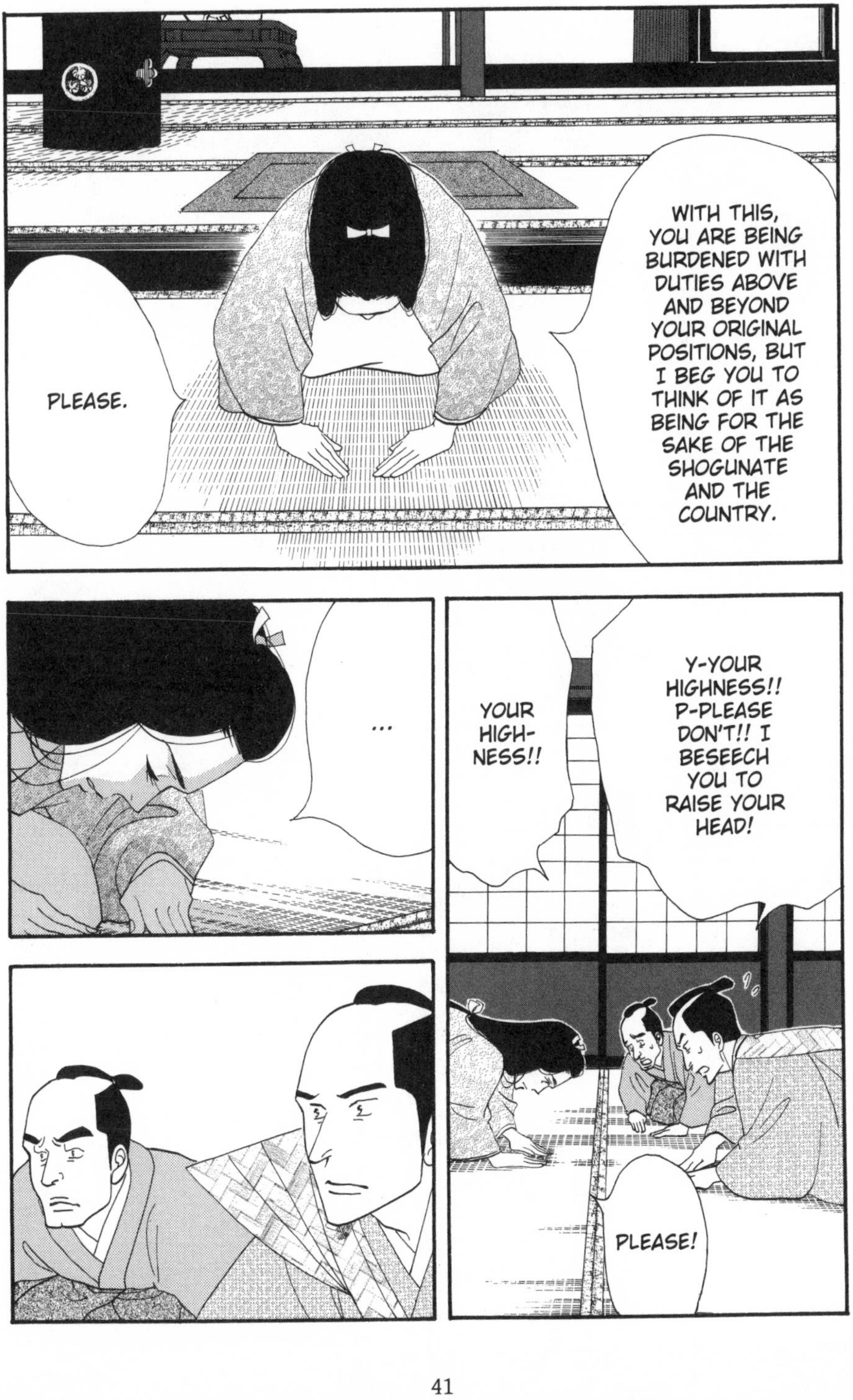
WITH THIS, YOU ARE BEING BURDENED WITH DUTIES ABOVE AND BEYOND YOUR ORIGINAL POSITIONS, BUT I BEG YOU TO THINK OF IT AS BEING FOR THE SAKE OF THE SHOGUNATE AND THE COUNTRY.
PLEASE.
Y-YOUR HIGHNESS!! P-PLEASE DON'T!! I BESEECH YOU TO RAISE YOUR HEAD!
YOUR HIGH-NESS!!
PLEASE!
...

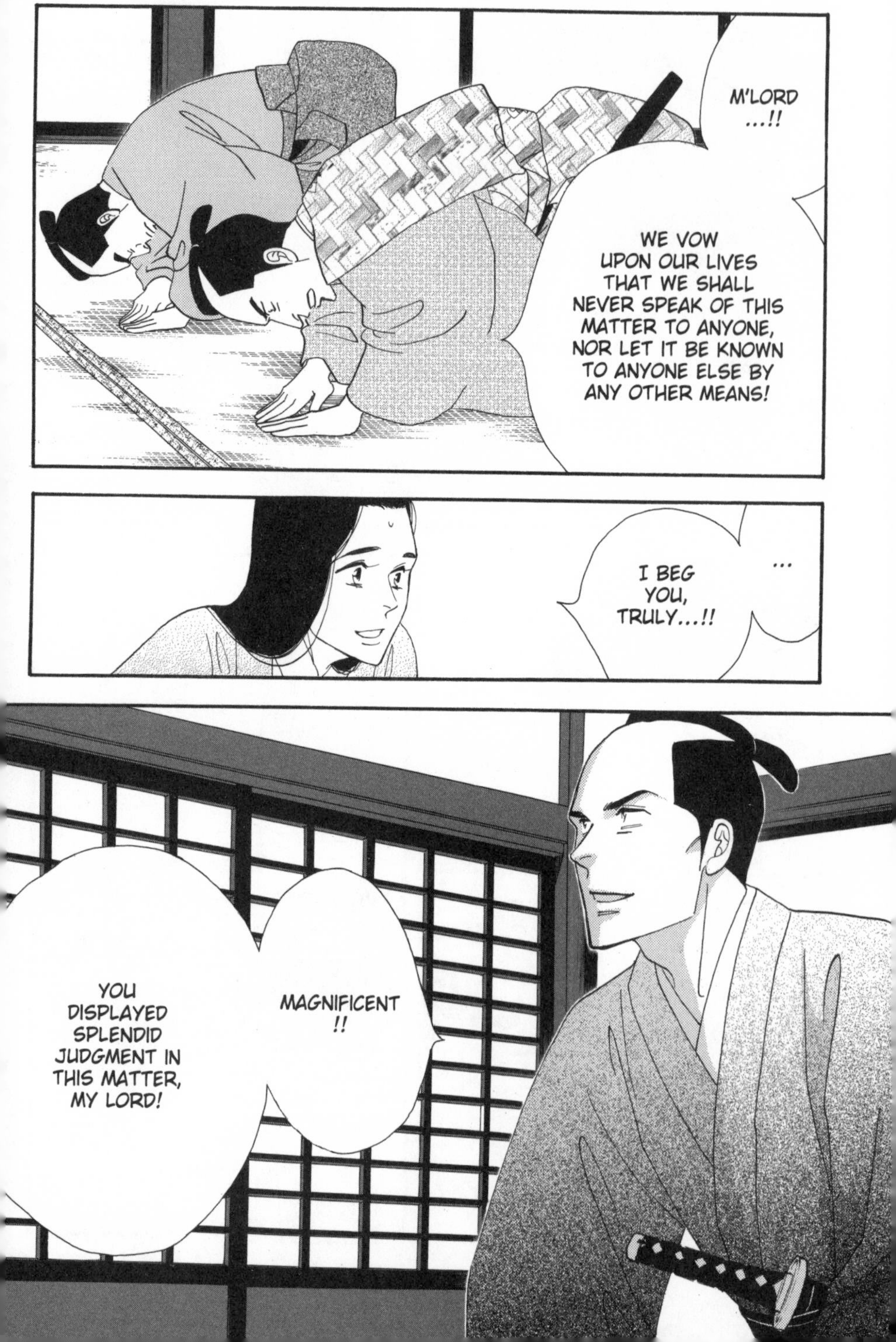
M'LORD ...!!
WE VOW UPON OUR LIVES THAT WE SHALL NEVER SPEAK OF THIS MATTER TO ANYONE, NOR LET IT BE KNOWN TO ANYONE ELSE BY ANY OTHER MEANS!
...
I BEG YOU, TRULY...!!
MAGNIFICENT !!
YOU DISPLAYED SPLENDID JUDGMENT IN THIS MATTER, MY LORD!

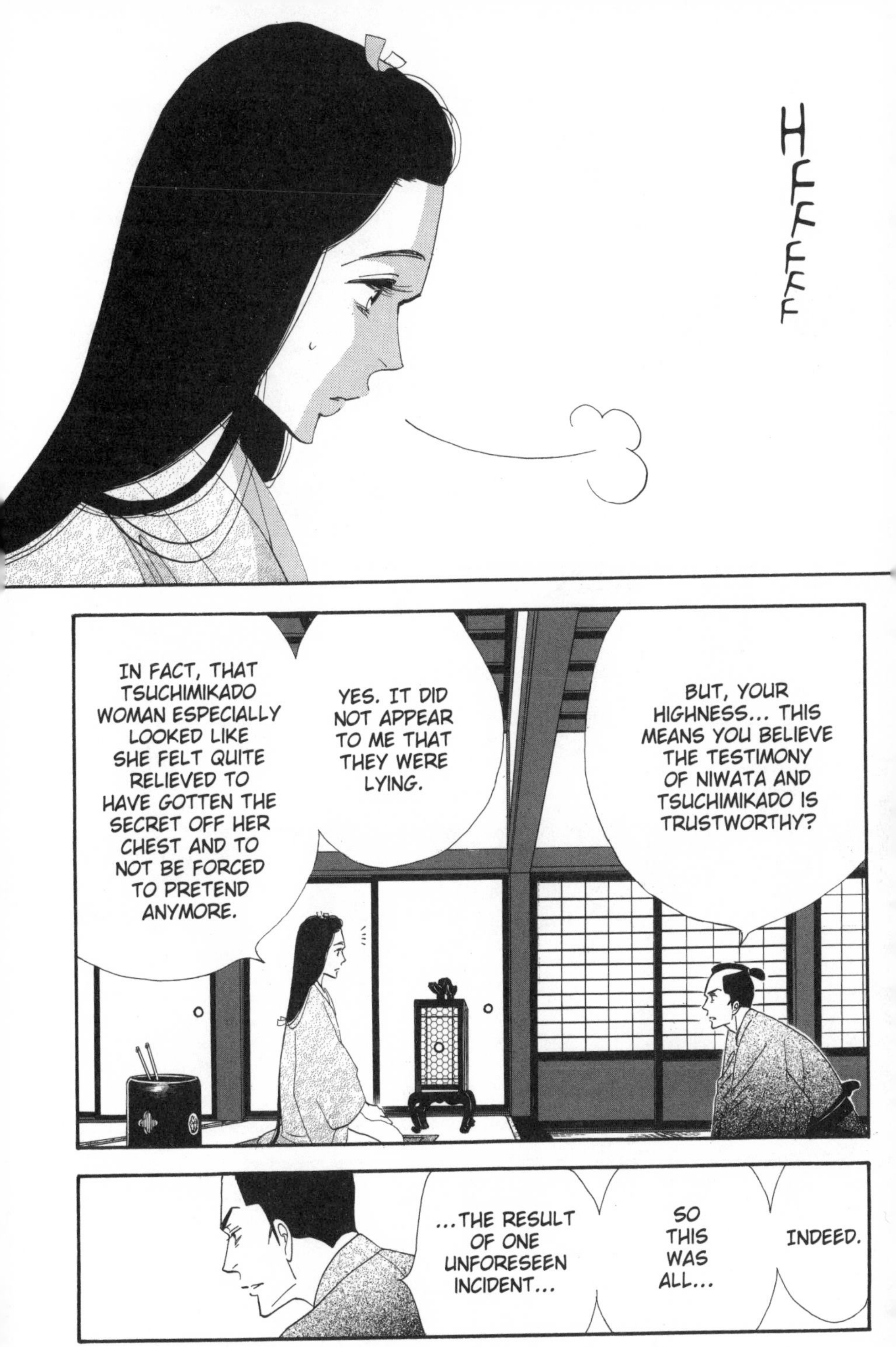
HFFFFF
BUT, YOUR HIGHNESS... THIS MEANS YOU BELIEVE THE TESTIMONY OF NIWATA AND TSUCHIMIKADO IS TRUSTWORTHY?
YES. IT DID NOT APPEAR TO ME THAT THEY WERE LYING.
IN FACT, THAT TSUCHIMIKADO WOMAN ESPECIALLY LOOKED LIKE SHE FELT QUITE RELIEVED TO HAVE GOTTEN THE SECRET OFF HER CHEST AND TO NOT BE FORCED TO PRETEND ANYMORE.
INDEED.
SO THIS WAS ALL...
...THE RESULT OF ONE UNFORESEEN INCIDENT...

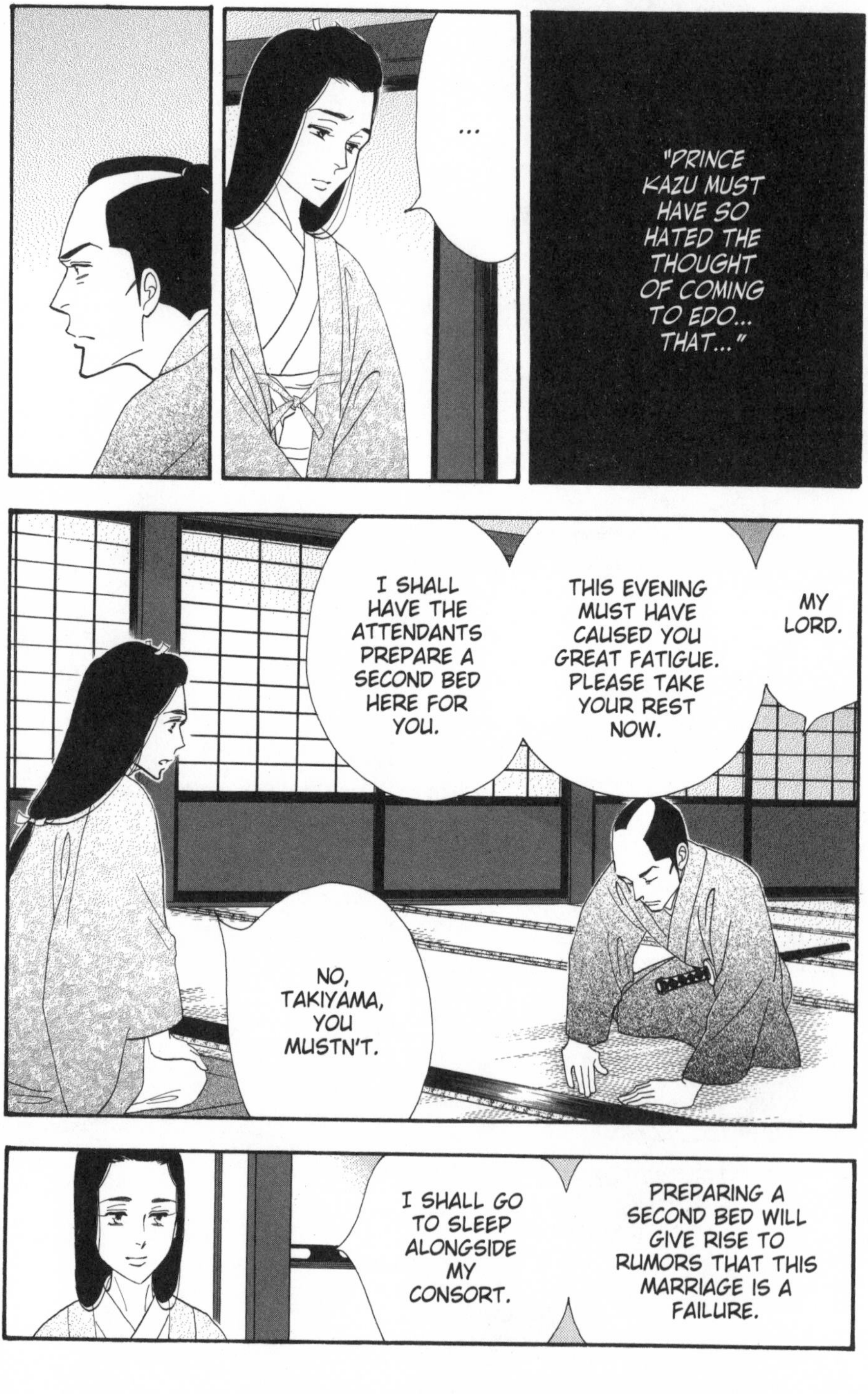
"PRINCE KAZU MUST HAVE SO HATED THE THOUGHT OF COMING TO EDO... THAT..."
...
MY LORD.
THIS EVENING MUST HAVE CAUSED YOU GREAT FATIGUE. PLEASE TAKE YOUR REST NOW.
I SHALL HAVE THE ATTENDANTS PREPARE A SECOND BED HERE FOR YOU.
NO, TAKIYAMA, YOU MUSTN'T.
PREPARING A SECOND BED WILL GIVE RISE TO RUMORS THAT THIS MARRIAGE IS A FAILURE.
I SHALL GO TO SLEEP ALONGSIDE MY CONSORT.

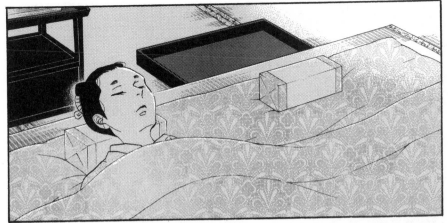

FWAH

ZZZ
ZZZ
ZZZ

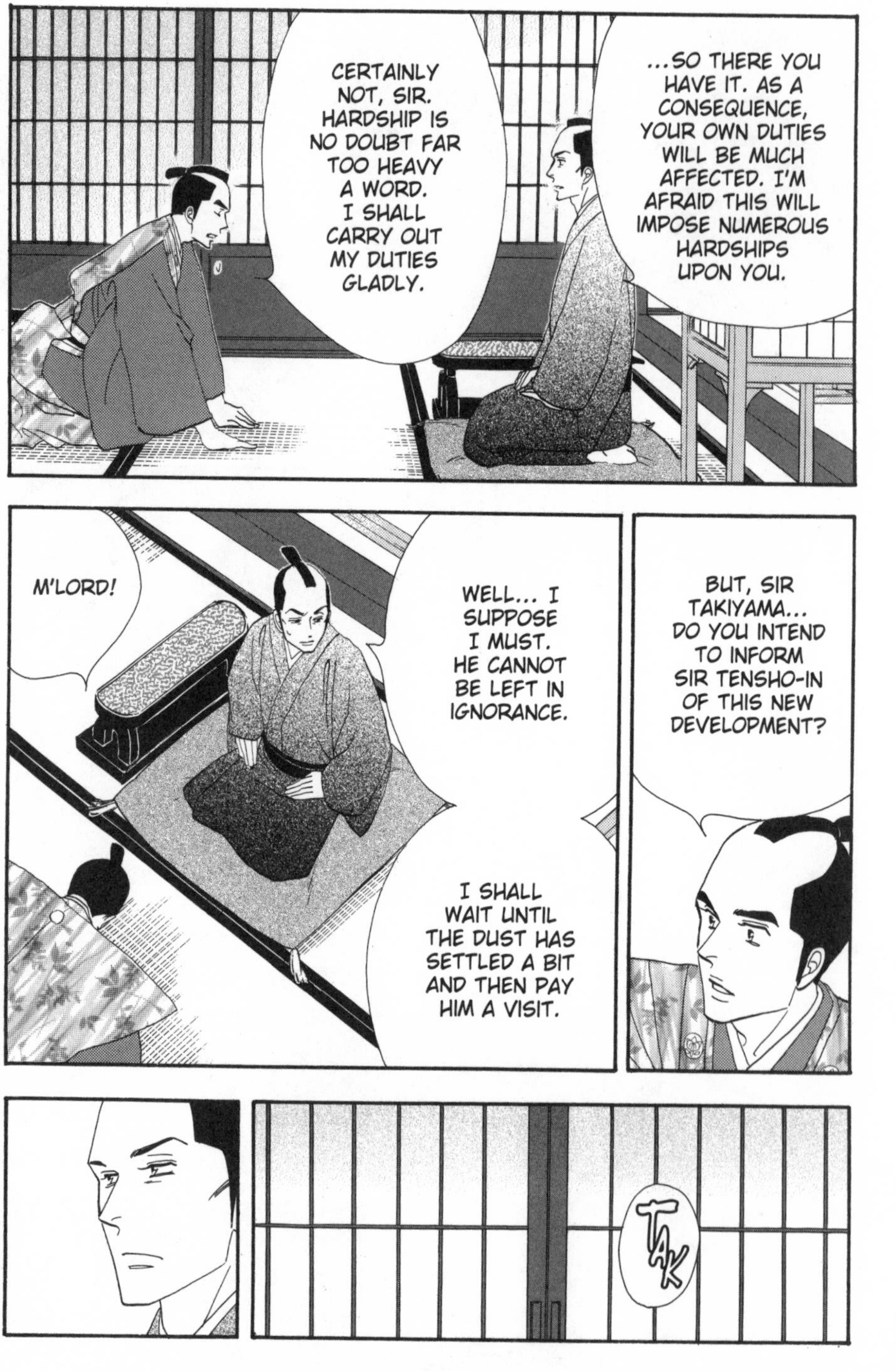
...SO THERE YOU HAVE IT. AS A CONSEQUENCE, YOUR OWN DUTIES WILL BE MUCH AFFECTED. I'M AFRAID THIS WILL IMPOSE NUMEROUS HARDSHIPS UPON YOU.
CERTAINLY NOT, SIR. HARDSHIP IS NO DOUBT FAR TOO HEAVY A WORD. I SHALL CARRY OUT MY DUTIES GLADLY.
BUT, SIR TAKIYAMA... DO YOU INTEND TO INFORM SIR TENSHO-IN OF THIS NEW DEVELOPMENT?
WELL... I SUPPOSE I MUST. HE CANNOT BE LEFT IN IGNORANCE.
I SHALL WAIT UNTIL THE DUST HAS SETTLED A BIT AND THEN PAY HIM A VISIT.
M'LORD!
TAK

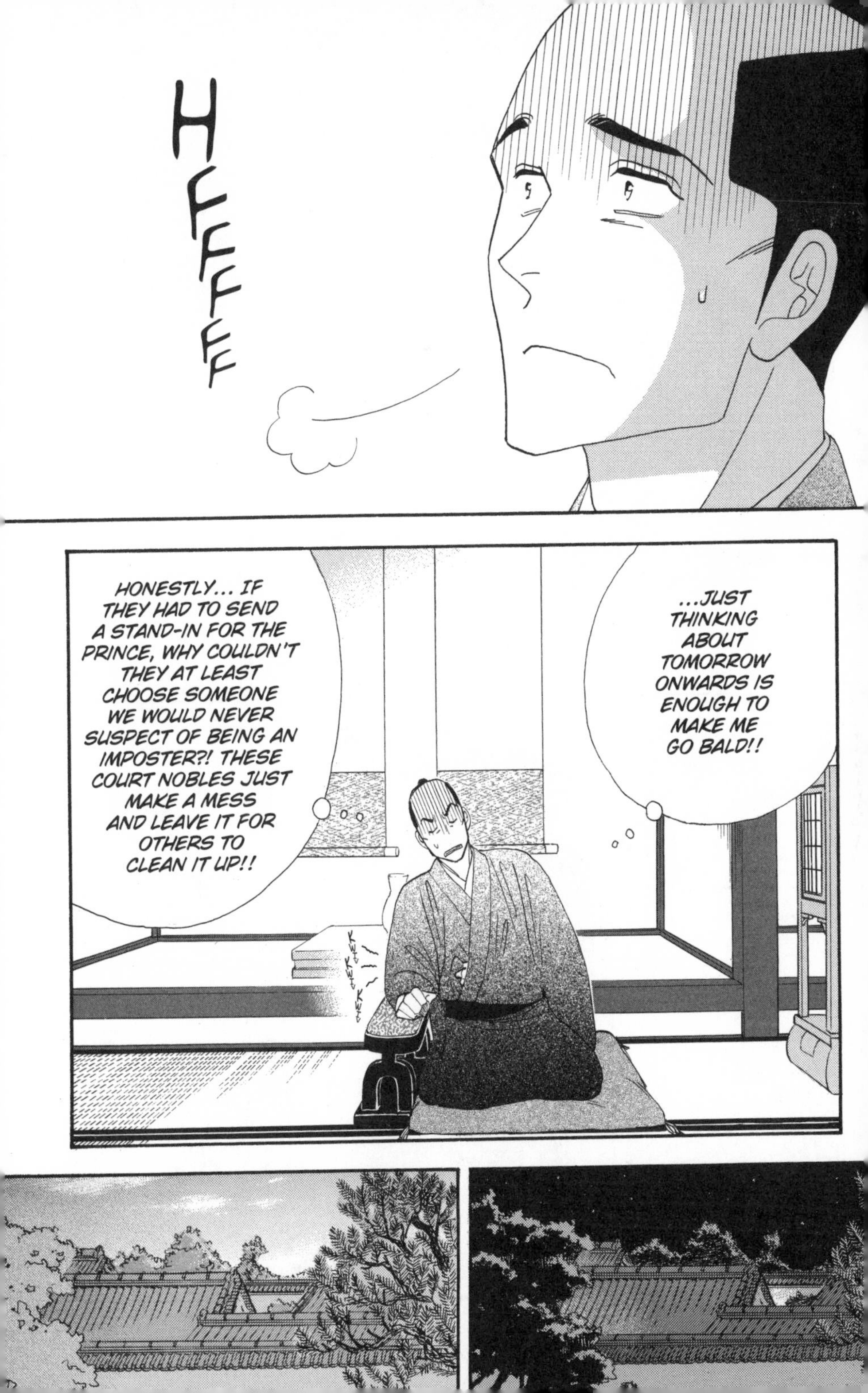
HFFFFFF
...JUST THINKING ABOUT TOMORROW ONWARDS IS ENOUGH TO MAKE ME GO BALD!!
HONESTLY... IF THEY HAD TO SEND A STAND-IN FOR THE PRINCE, WHY COULDN'T THEY AT LEAST CHOOSE SOMEONE WE WOULD NEVER SUSPECT OF BEING AN IMPOSTER?! THESE COURT NOBLES JUST MAKE A MESS AND LEAVE IT FOR OTHERS TO CLEAN IT UP!!

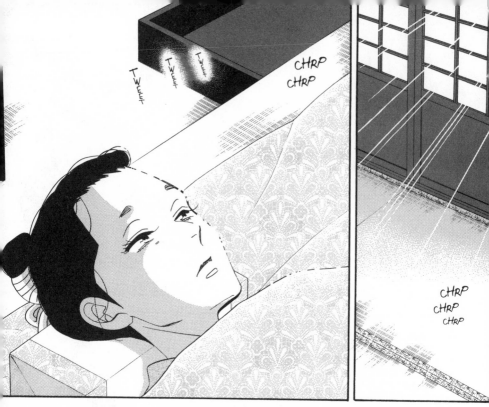

TWEET TWEET TWEET

CHRP
CHRP

CHRP
CHRP
CHRP

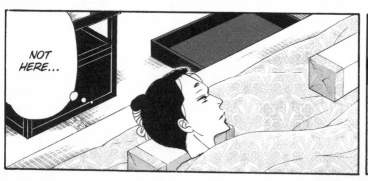

NOT HERE...

FWAP

!

I AM HAPPY TO SEE THAT YOU ARE AWAKE.

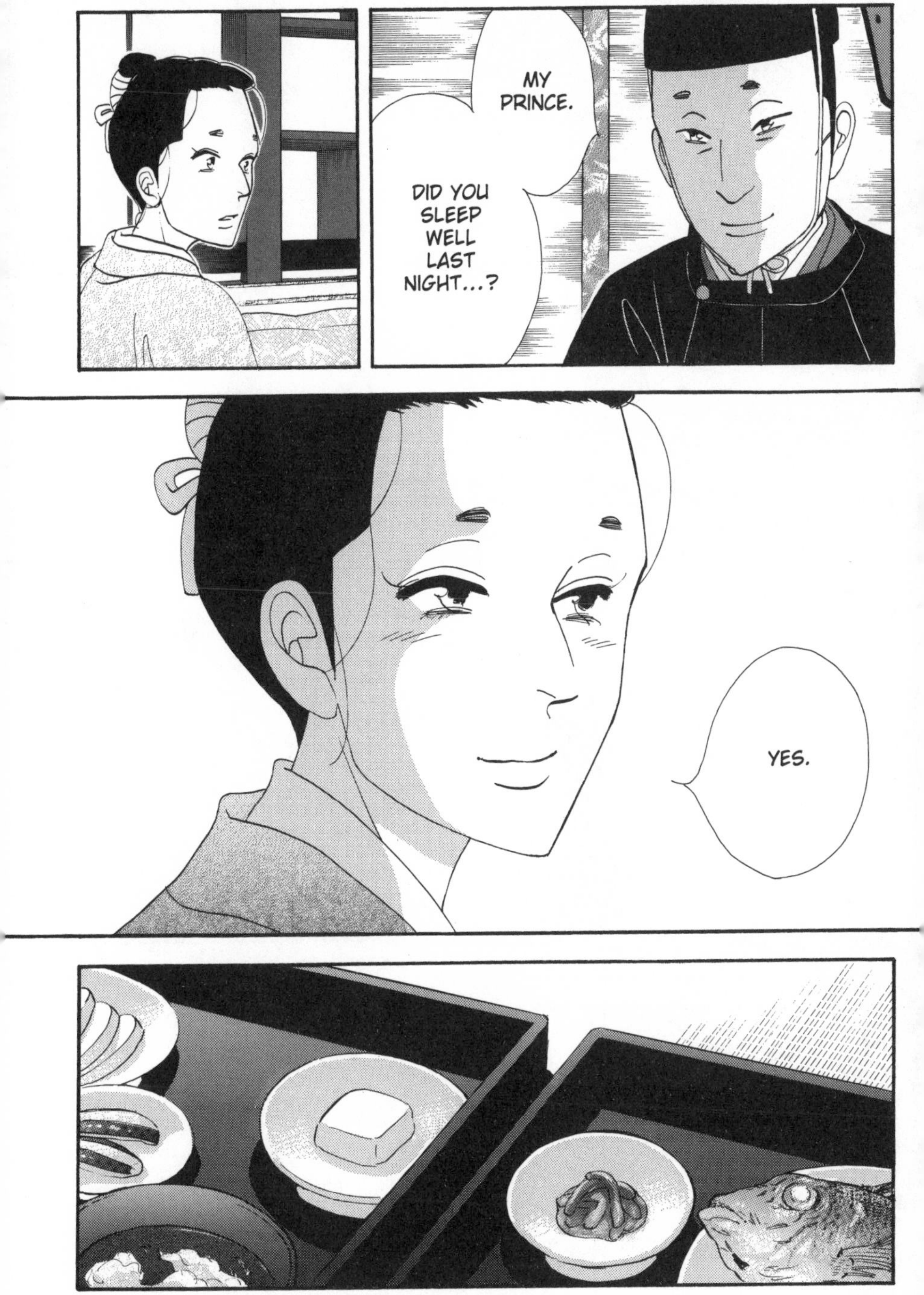
MY PRINCE.
DID YOU SLEEP WELL LAST NIGHT...?
YES.

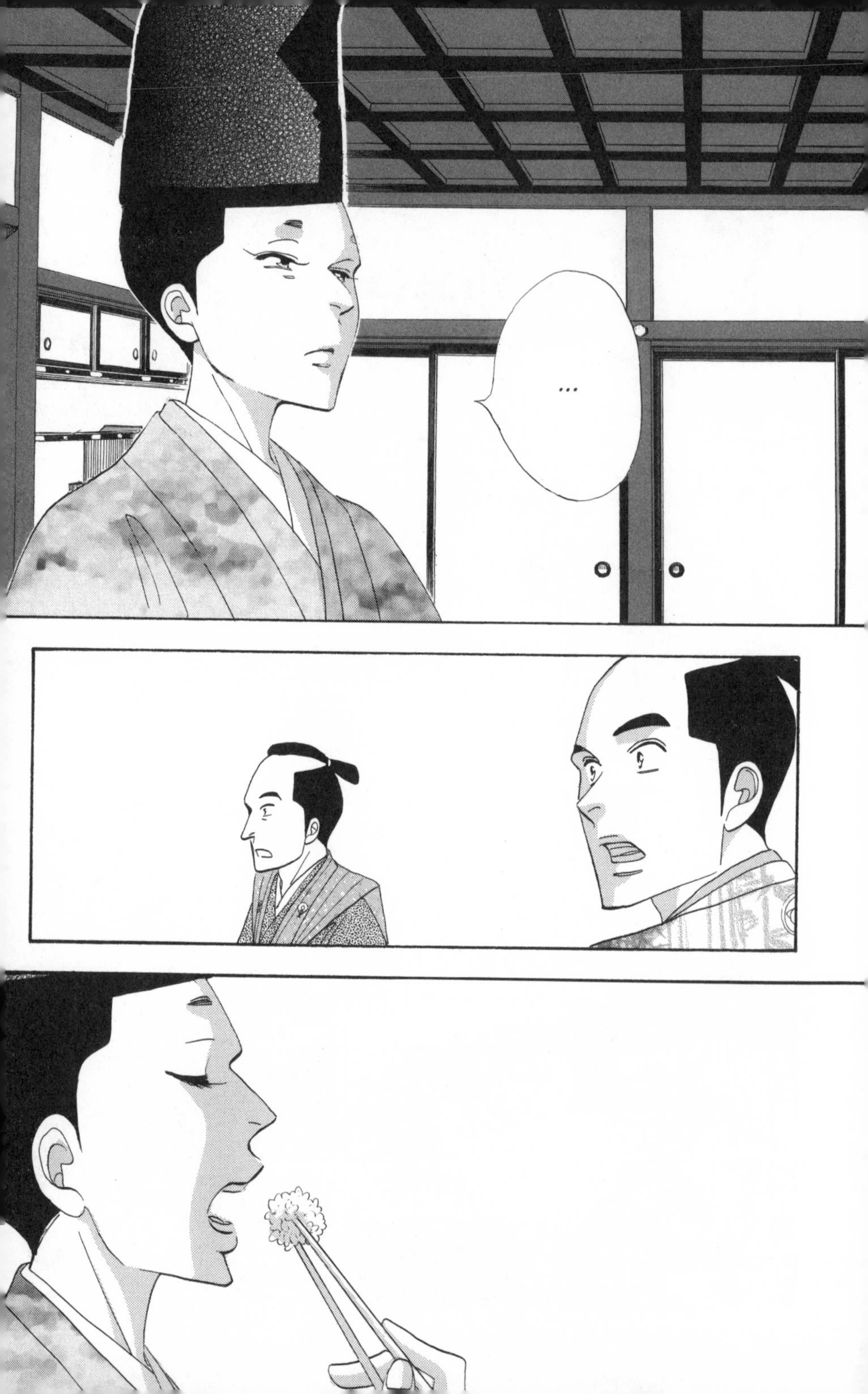
...

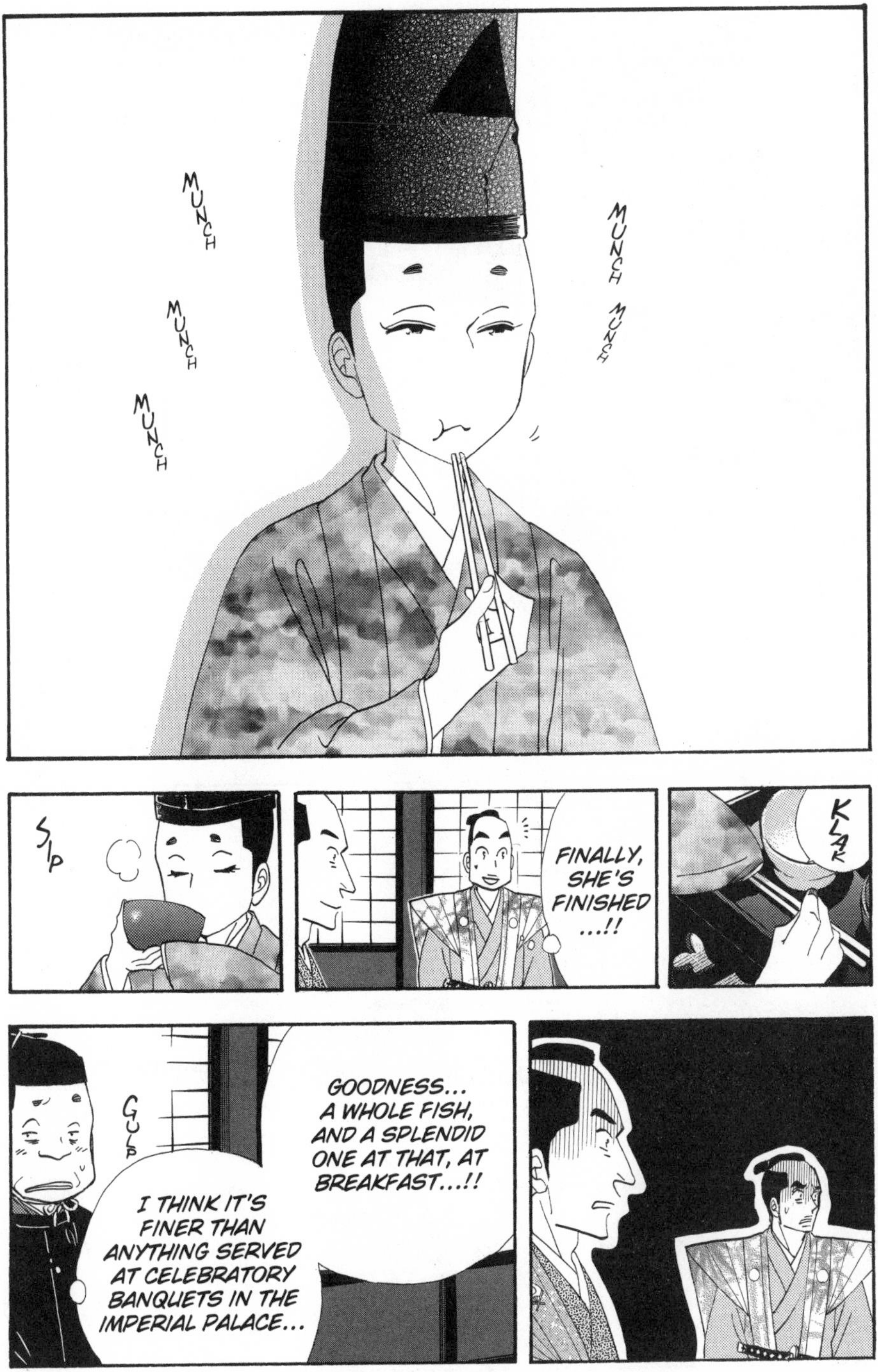
MUNCH MUNCH
MUNCH
MUNCH
MUNCH
KLAK
FINALLY, SHE'S FINISHED ...!!
SIP
GOODNESS... A WHOLE FISH, AND A SPLENDID ONE AT THAT, AT BREAKFAST...!!
I THINK IT'S FINER THAN ANYTHING SERVED AT CELEBRATORY BANQUETS IN THE IMPERIAL PALACE...
GULP

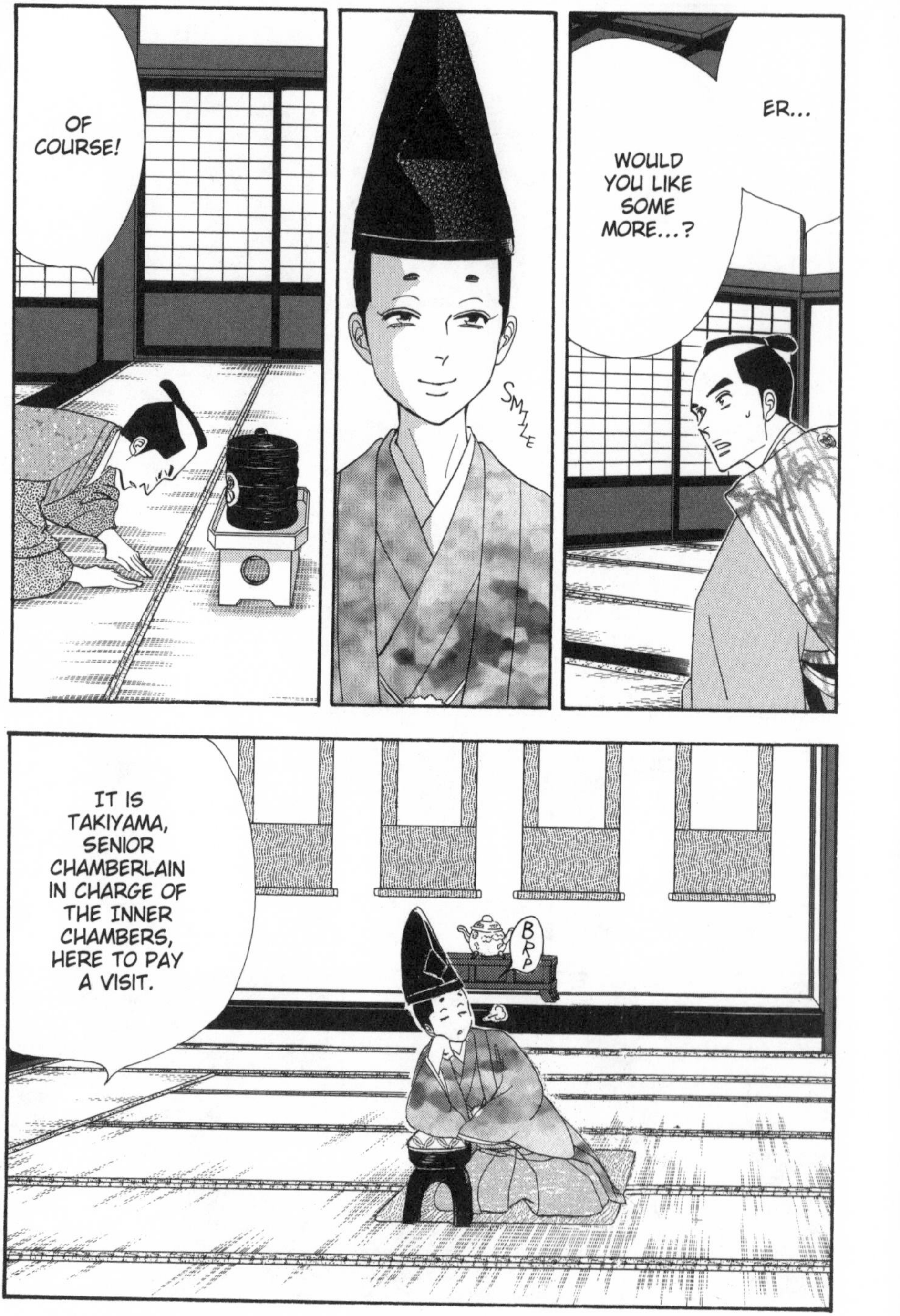
ER...
WOULD YOU LIKE SOME MORE...?
SMILE
OF COURSE!
IT IS TAKIYAMA, SENIOR CHAMBERLAIN IN CHARGE OF THE INNER CHAMBERS, HERE TO PAY A VISIT.
BRP

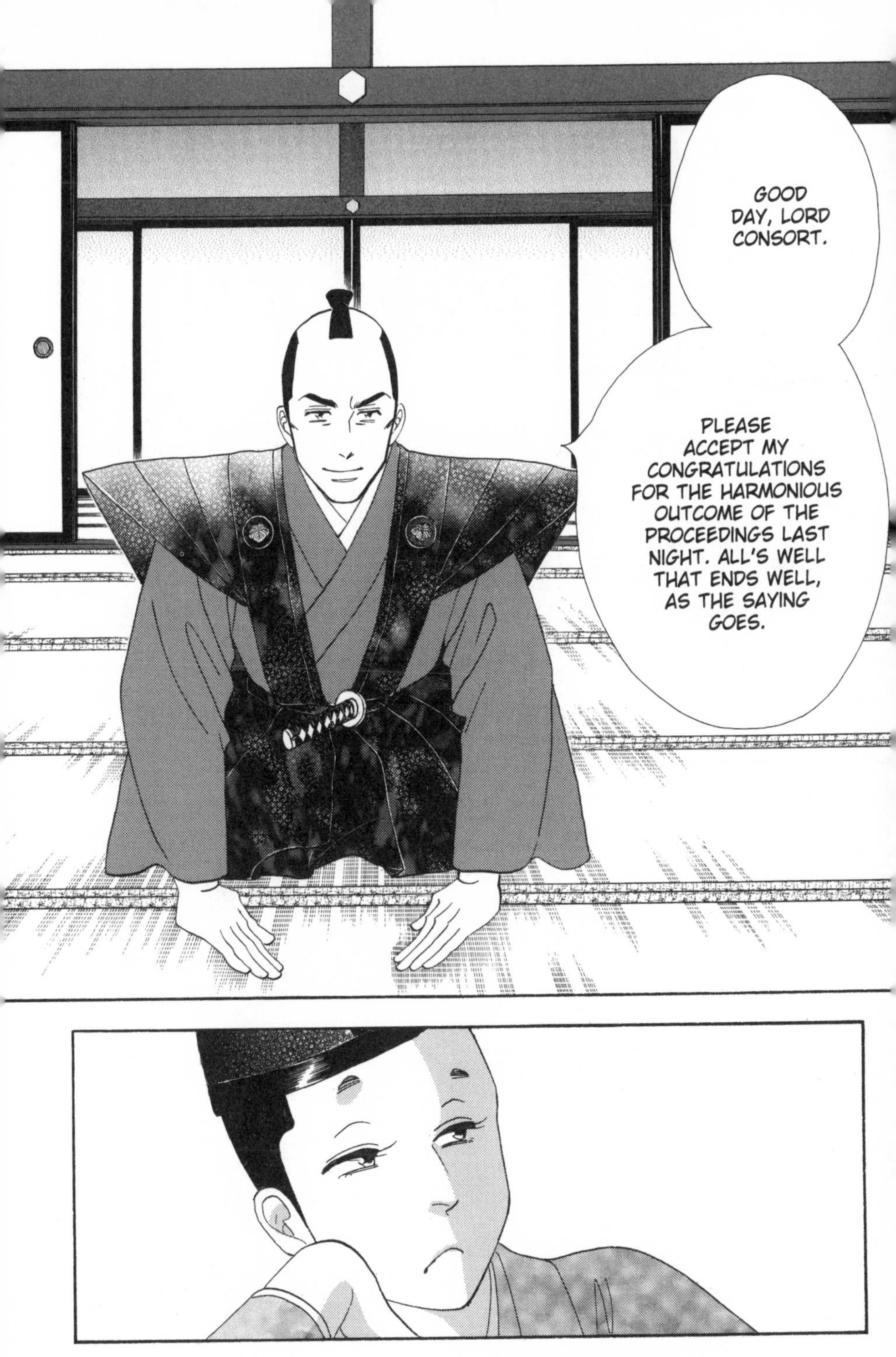
GOOD DAY, LORD CONSORT.
PLEASE ACCEPT MY CONGRATULATIONS FOR THE HARMONIOUS OUTCOME OF THE PROCEEDINGS LAST NIGHT. ALL'S WELL THAT ENDS WELL, AS THE SAYING GOES.

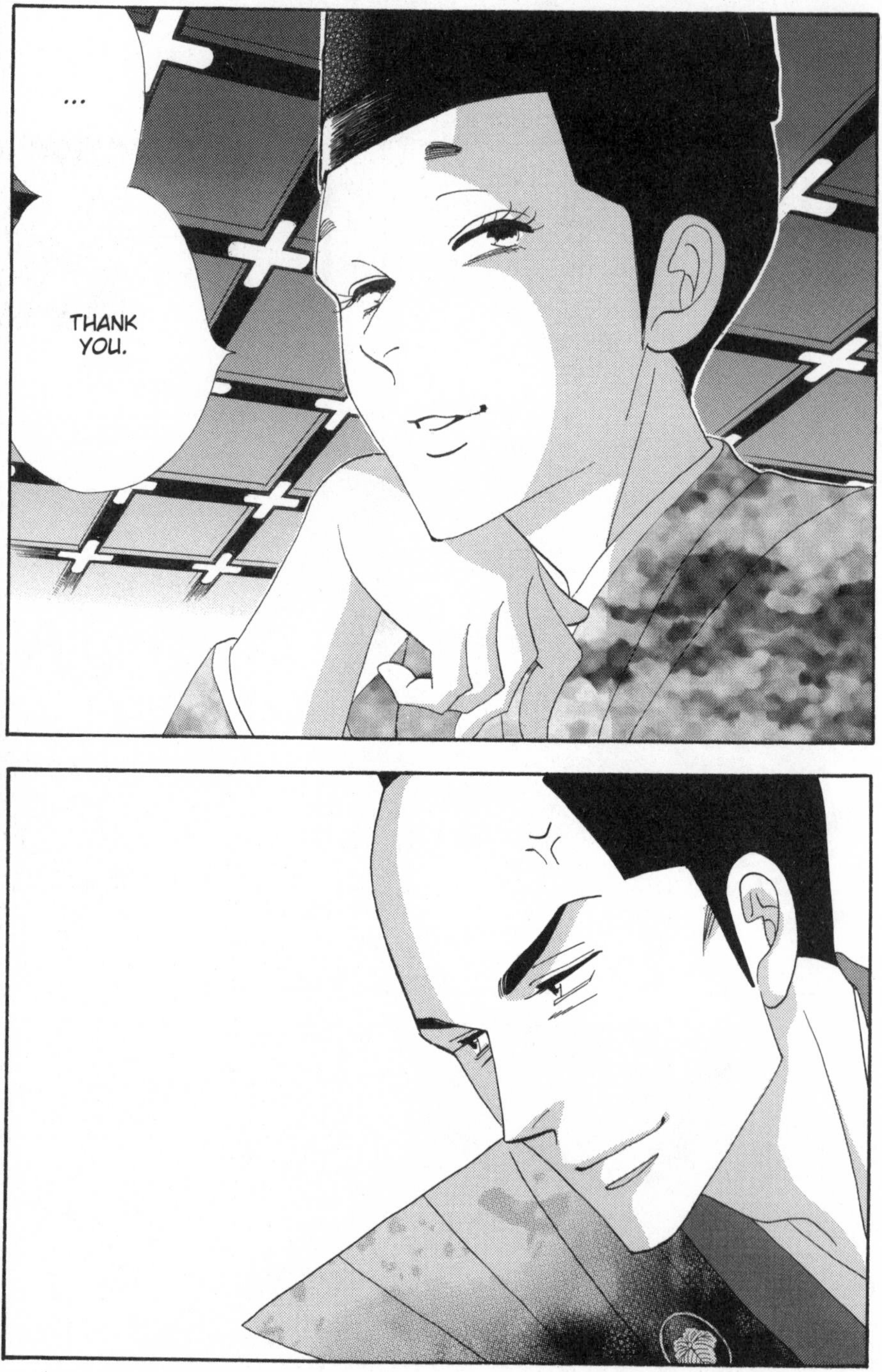
...
THANK YOU.

CHRP
CHRP
CHRP

Ōoku

THE INNER CHAMBERS

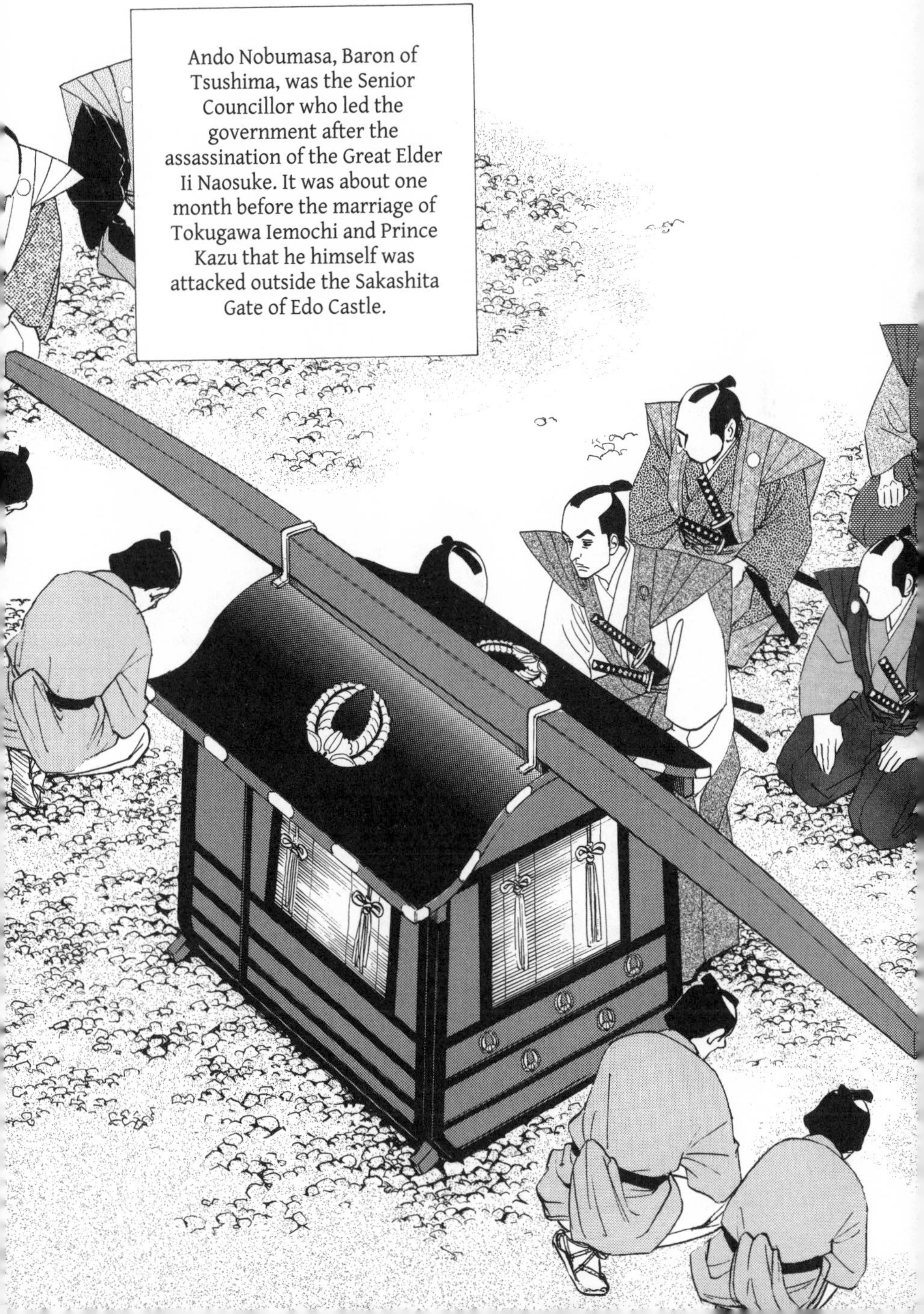
Ando Nobumasa, Baron of Tsushima, was the Senior Councillor who led the government after the assassination of the Great Elder Ii Naosuke. It was about one month before the marriage of Tokugawa Iemochi and Prince Kazu that he himself was attacked outside the Sakashita Gate of Edo Castle.

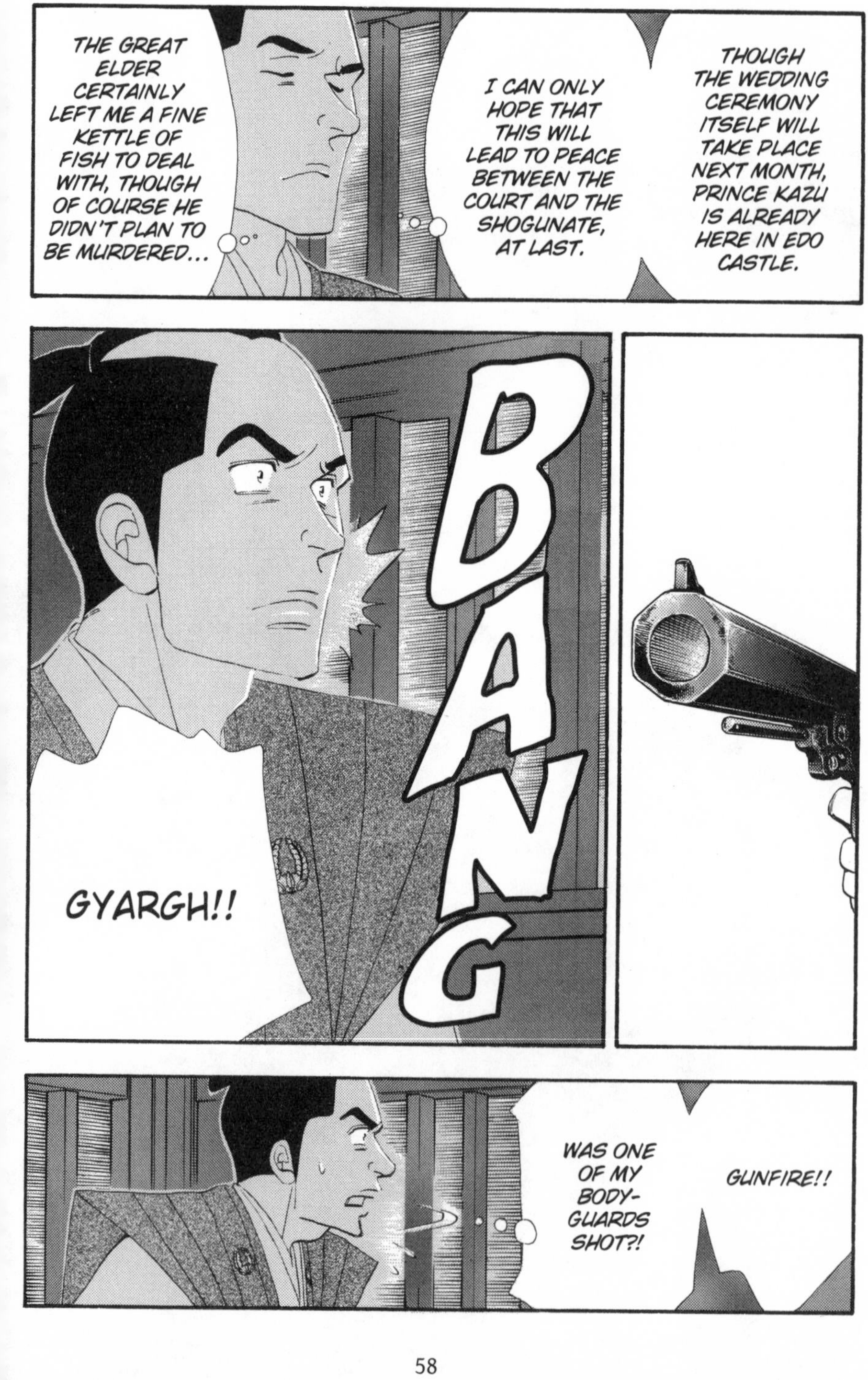
THOUGH THE WEDDING CEREMONY ITSELF WILL TAKE PLACE NEXT MONTH, PRINCE KAZU IS ALREADY HERE IN EDO CASTLE.
I CAN ONLY HOPE THAT THIS WILL LEAD TO PEACE BETWEEN THE COURT AND THE SHOGUNATE, AT LAST.
THE GREAT ELDER CERTAINLY LEFT ME A FINE KETTLE OF FISH TO DEAL WITH, THOUGH OF COURSE HE DIDN'T PLAN TO BE MURDERED...
BANG
GYARGH!!
GUNFIRE!!
WAS ONE OF MY BODY-GUARDS SHOT?!

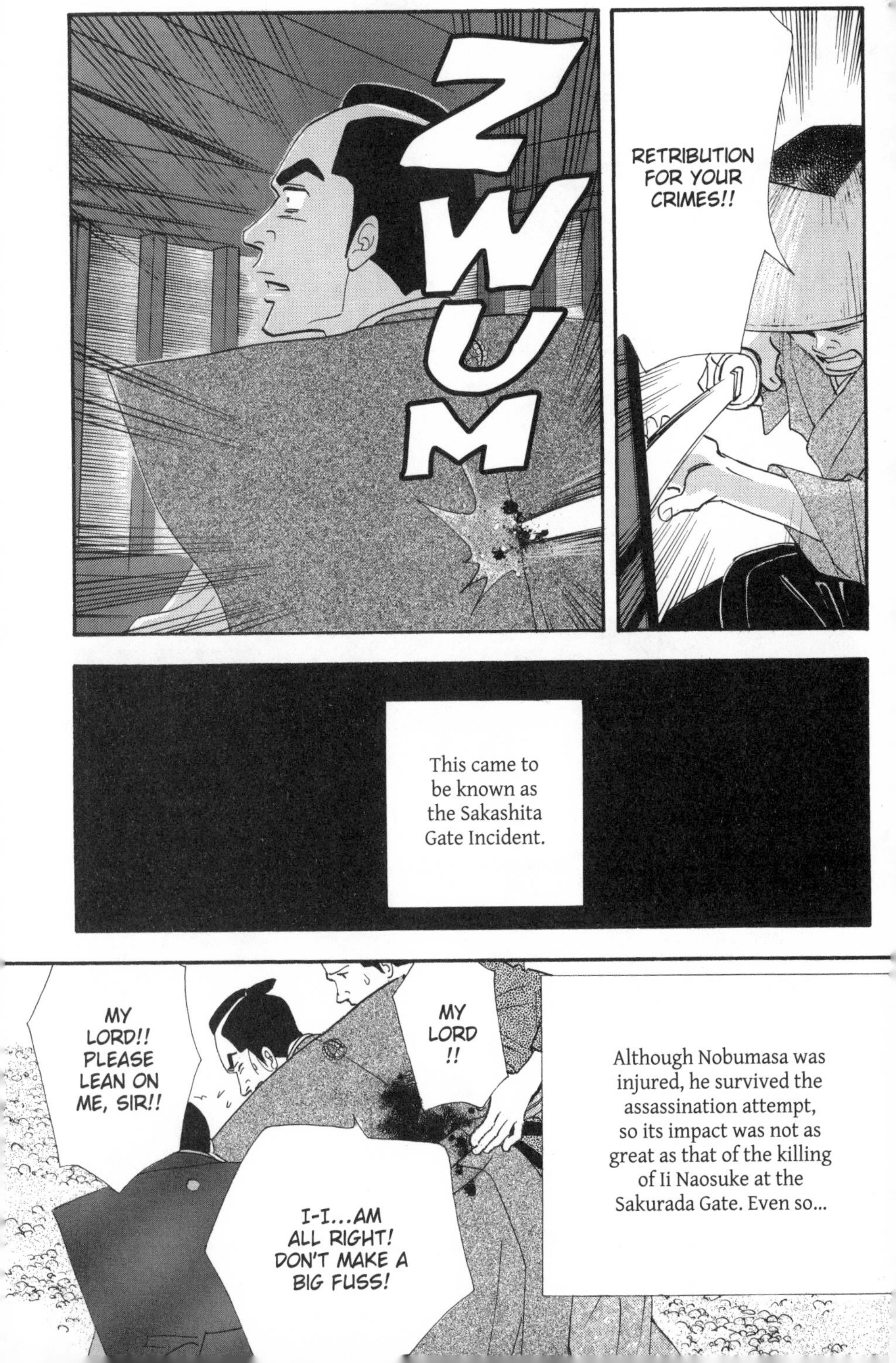
RETRIBUTION FOR YOUR CRIMES!!
ZWUM
This came to be known as the Sakashita Gate Incident.
Although Nobumasa was injured, he survived the assassination attempt, so its impact was not as great as that of the killing of Ii Naosuke at the Sakurada Gate. Even so...
MY LORD !!
MY LORD!! PLEASE LEAN ON ME, SIR!!
I-I...AM ALL RIGHT! DON'T MAKE A BIG FUSS!

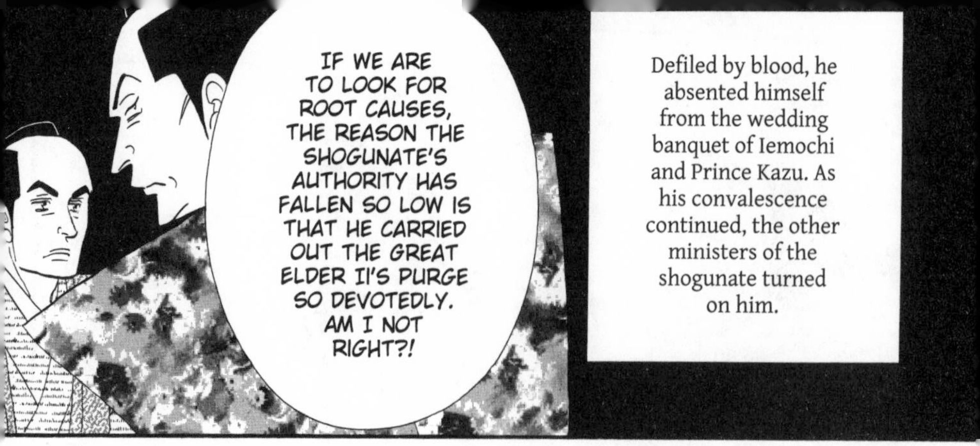
Defiled by blood, he absented himself from the wedding banquet of Iemochi and Prince Kazu. As his convalescence continued, the other ministers of the shogunate turned on him.
IF WE ARE TO LOOK FOR ROOT CAUSES, THE REASON THE SHOGUNATE'S AUTHORITY HAS FALLEN SO LOW IS THAT HE CARRIED OUT THE GREAT ELDER II'S PURGE SO DEVOTEDLY. AM I NOT RIGHT?!
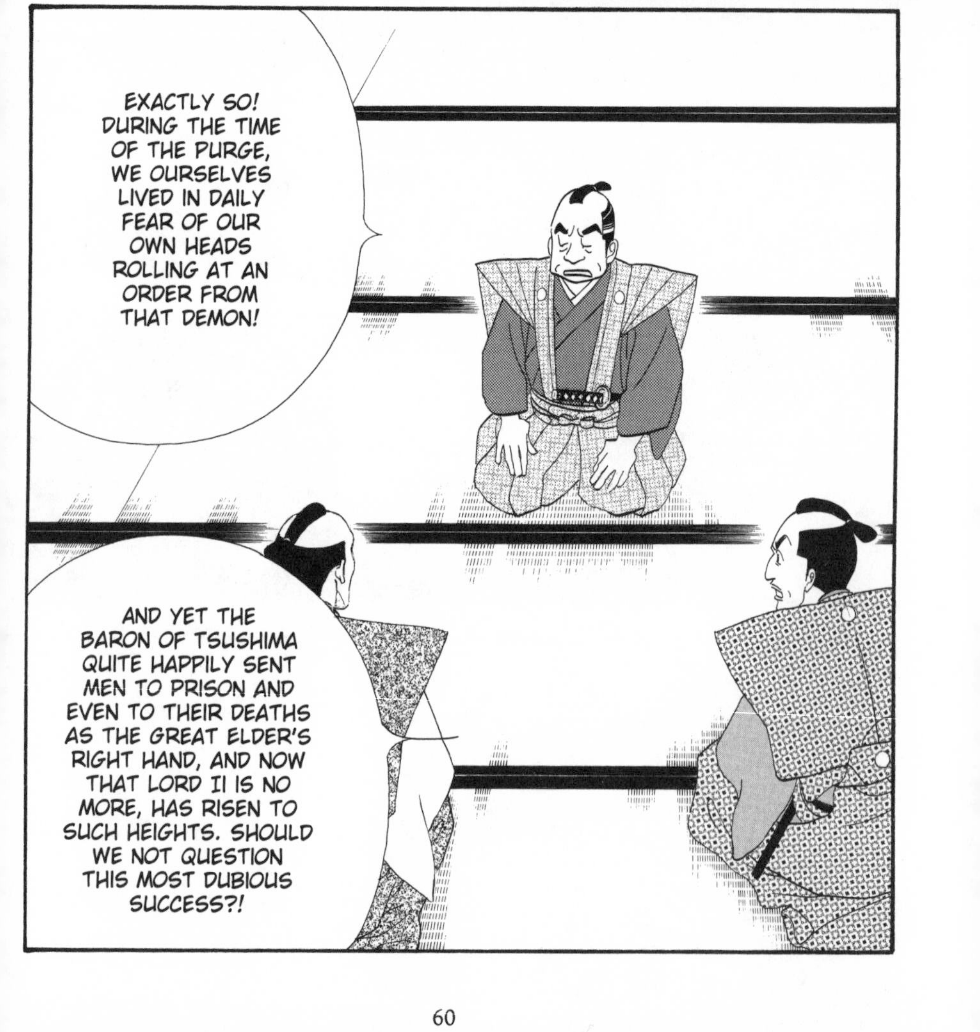
EXACTLY SO! DURING THE TIME OF THE PURGE, WE OURSELVES LIVED IN DAILY FEAR OF OUR OWN HEADS ROLLING AT AN ORDER FROM THAT DEMON!
AND YET THE BARON OF TSUSHIMA QUITE HAPPILY SENT MEN TO PRISON AND EVEN TO THEIR DEATHS AS THE GREAT ELDER'S RIGHT HAND, AND NOW THAT LORD II IS NO MORE, HAS RISEN TO SUCH HEIGHTS. SHOULD WE NOT QUESTION THIS MOST DUBIOUS SUCCESS?!

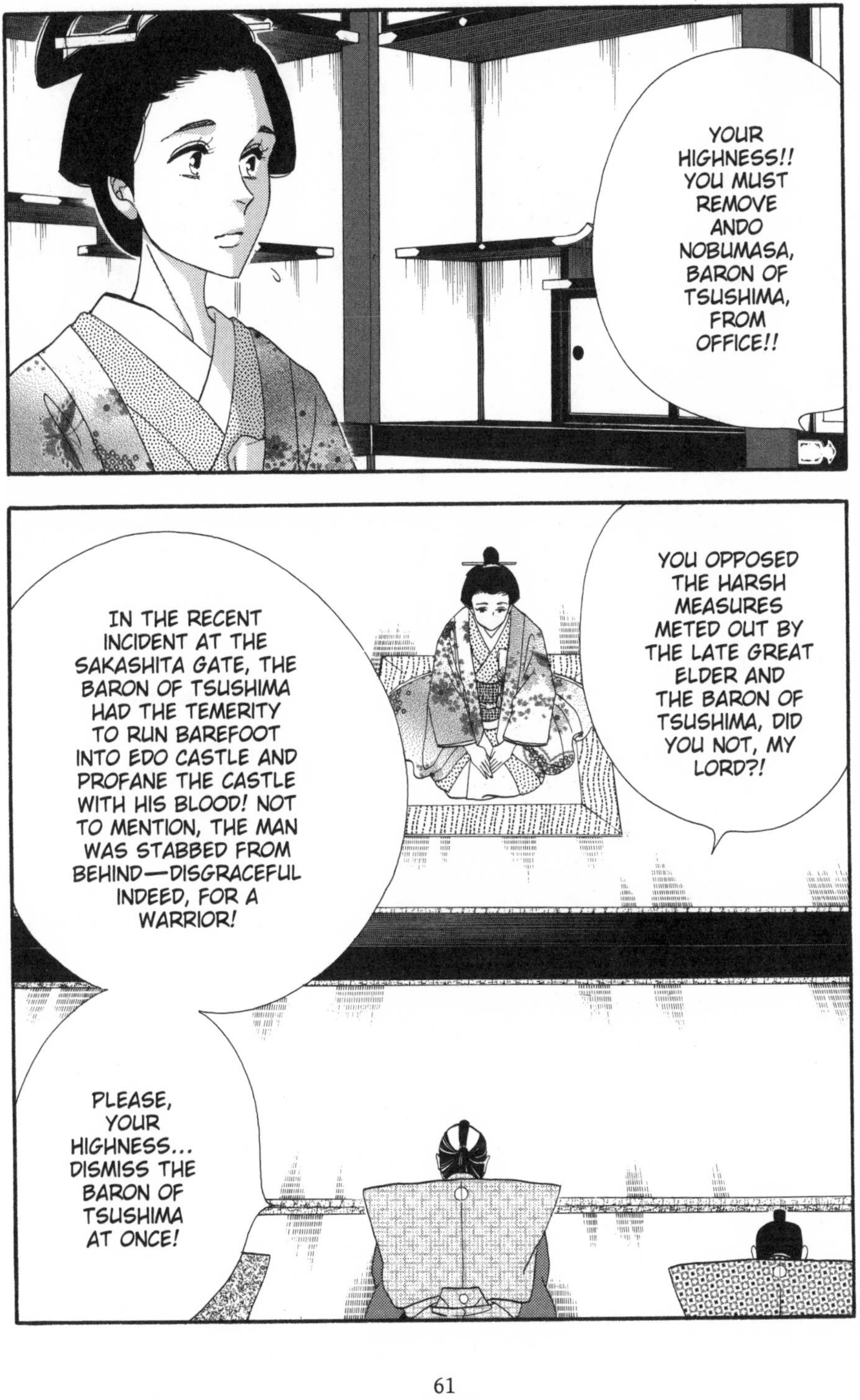
YOUR HIGHNESS!! YOU MUST REMOVE ANDO NOBUMASA, BARON OF TSUSHIMA, FROM OFFICE!!
YOU OPPOSED THE HARSH MEASURES METED OUT BY THE LATE GREAT ELDER AND THE BARON OF TSUSHIMA, DID YOU NOT, MY LORD?!
IN THE RECENT INCIDENT AT THE SAKASHITA GATE, THE BARON OF TSUSHIMA HAD THE TEMERITY TO RUN BAREFOOT INTO EDO CASTLE AND PROFANE THE CASTLE WITH HIS BLOOD! NOT TO MENTION, THE MAN WAS STABBED FROM BEHIND—DISGRACEFUL INDEED, FOR A WARRIOR!
PLEASE, YOUR HIGHNESS... DISMISS THE BARON OF TSUSHIMA AT ONCE!

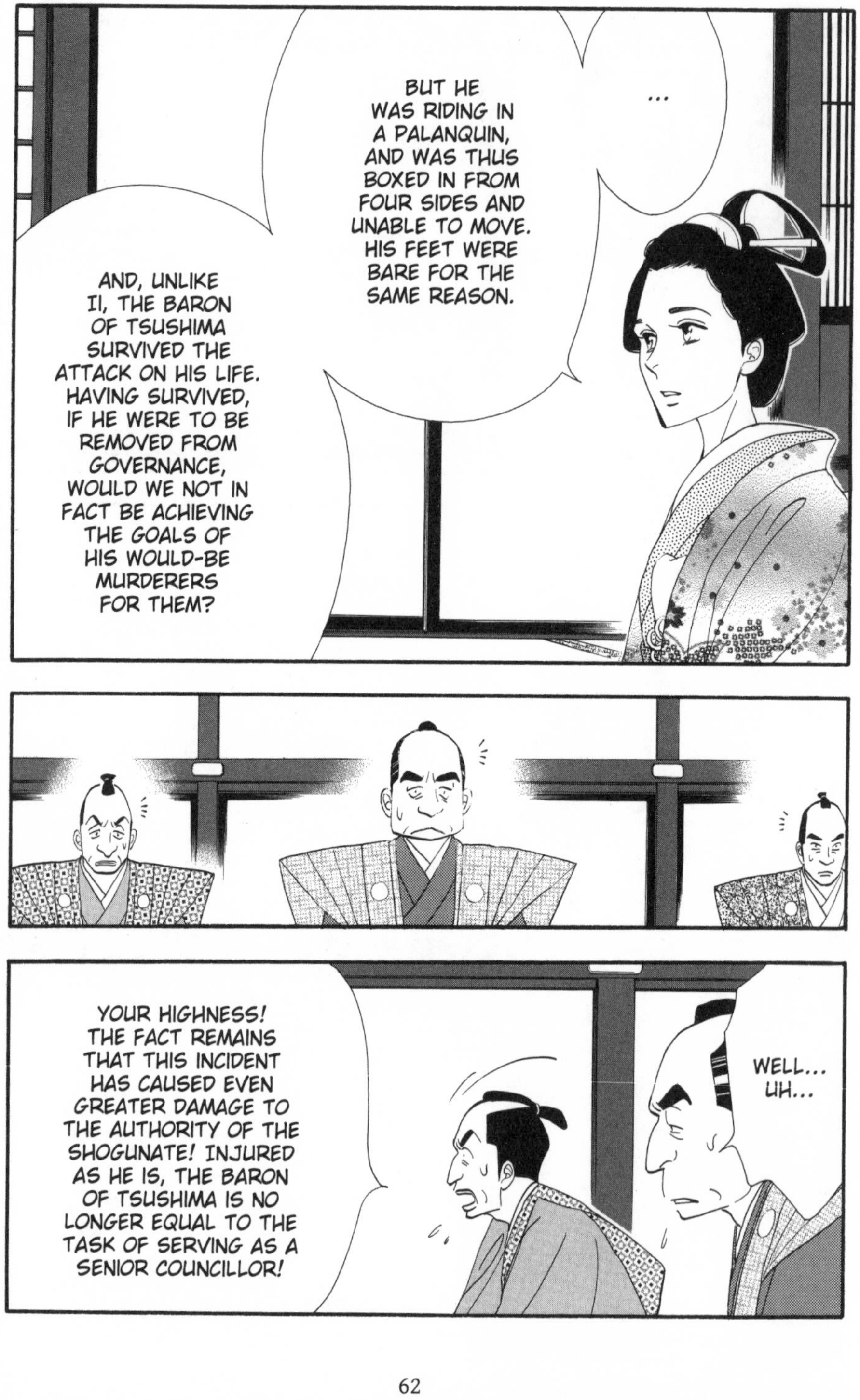
...
BUT HE WAS RIDING IN A PALANQUIN, AND WAS THUS BOXED IN FROM FOUR SIDES AND UNABLE TO MOVE. HIS FEET WERE BARE FOR THE SAME REASON.
AND, UNLIKE II, THE BARON OF TSUSHIMA SURVIVED THE ATTACK ON HIS LIFE. HAVING SURVIVED, IF HE WERE TO BE REMOVED FROM GOVERNANCE, WOULD WE NOT IN FACT BE ACHIEVING THE GOALS OF HIS WOULD-BE MURDERERS FOR THEM?
WELL... UH...
YOUR HIGHNESS! THE FACT REMAINS THAT THIS INCIDENT HAS CAUSED EVEN GREATER DAMAGE TO THE AUTHORITY OF THE SHOGUNATE! INJURED AS HE IS, THE BARON OF TSUSHIMA IS NO LONGER EQUAL TO THE TASK OF SERVING AS A SENIOR COUNCILLOR!

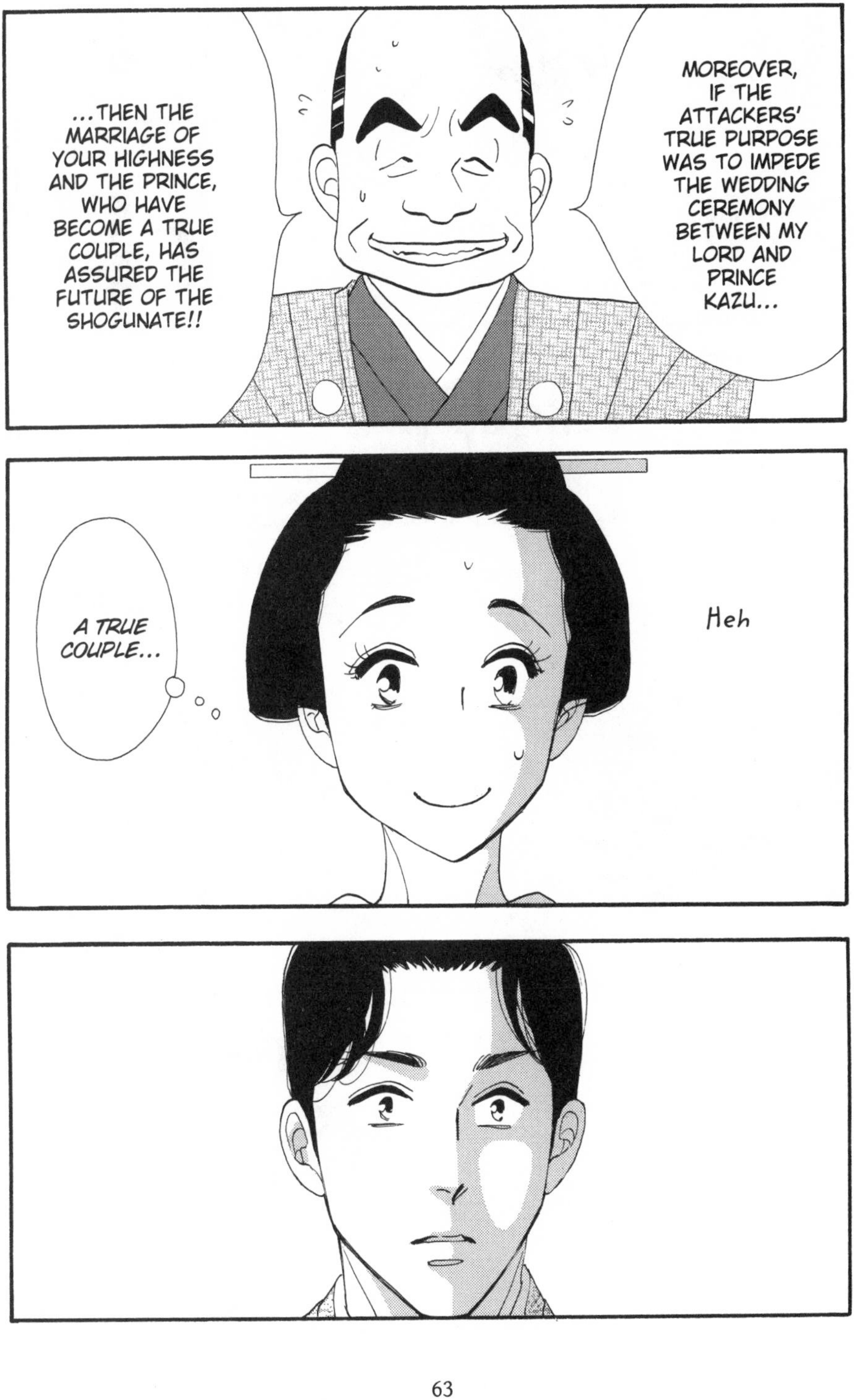
MOREOVER, IF THE ATTACKERS' TRUE PURPOSE WAS TO IMPEDE THE WEDDING CEREMONY BETWEEN MY LORD AND PRINCE KAZU...
...THEN THE MARRIAGE OF YOUR HIGHNESS AND THE PRINCE, WHO HAVE BECOME A TRUE COUPLE, HAS ASSURED THE FUTURE OF THE SHOGUNATE!!
Heh
A TRUE COUPLE...

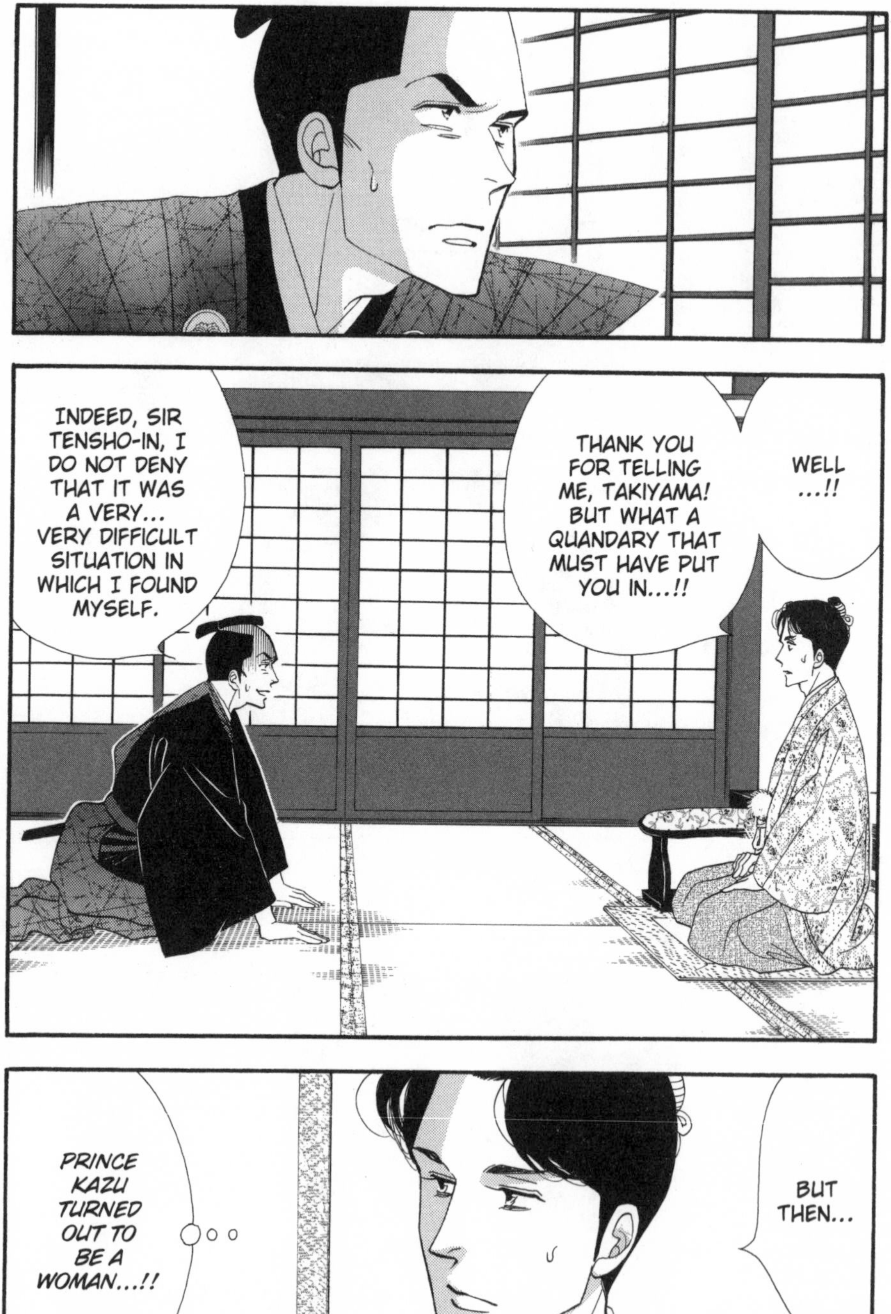
WELL...!!
THANK YOU FOR TELLING ME, TAKIYAMA! BUT WHAT A QUANDARY THAT MUST HAVE PUT YOU IN...!!
INDEED, SIR TENSHO-IN, I DO NOT DENY THAT IT WAS A VERY... VERY DIFFICULT SITUATION IN WHICH I FOUND MYSELF.
BUT THEN...
PRINCE KAZU TURNED OUT TO BE A WOMAN...!!

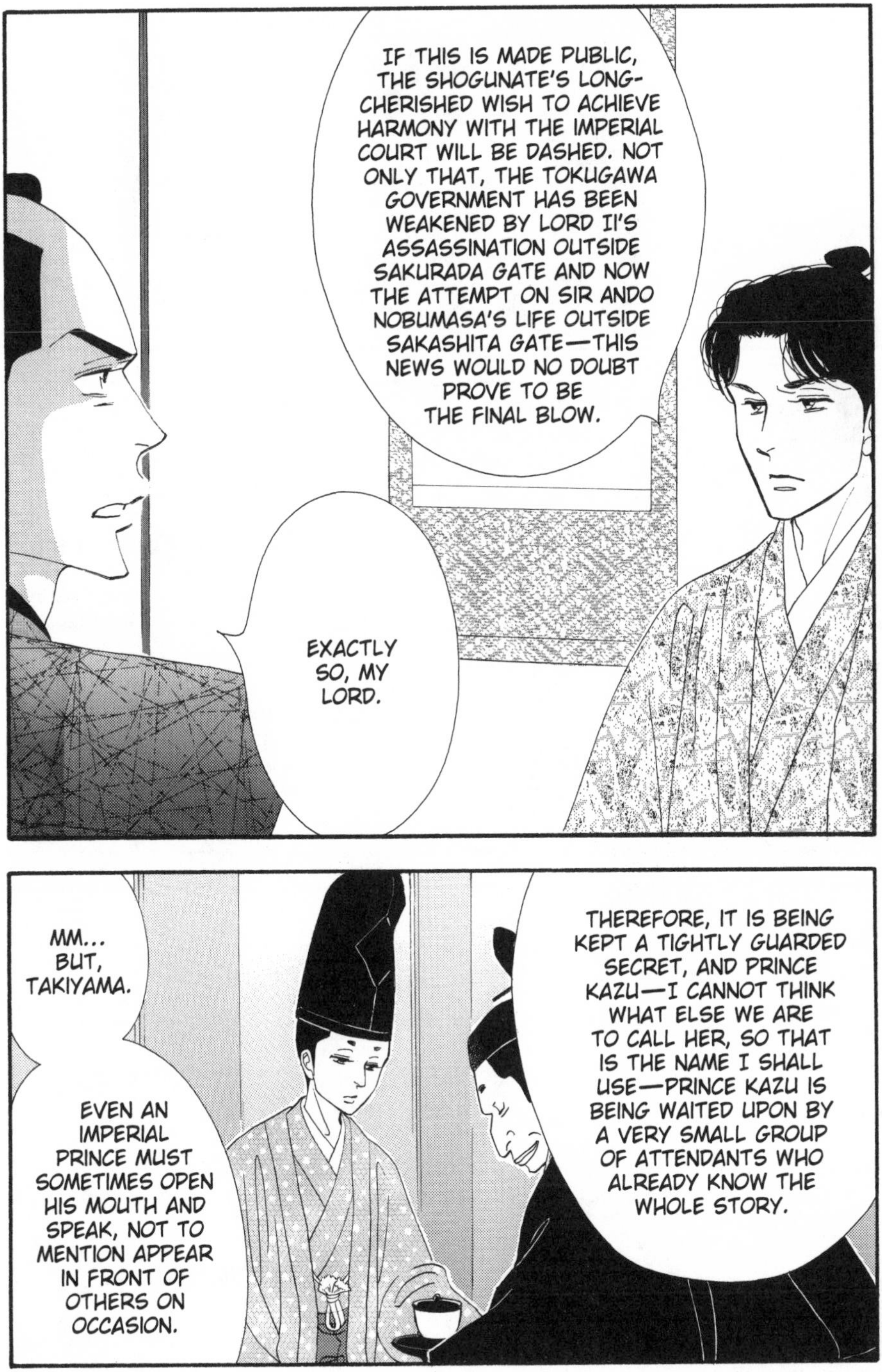
IF THIS IS MADE PUBLIC, THE SHOGUNATE'S LONG-CHERISHED WISH TO ACHIEVE HARMONY WITH THE IMPERIAL COURT WILL BE DASHED. NOT ONLY THAT, THE TOKUGAWA GOVERNMENT HAS BEEN WEAKENED BY LORD II'S ASSASSINATION OUTSIDE SAKURADA GATE AND NOW THE ATTEMPT ON SIR ANDO NOBUMASA'S LIFE OUTSIDE SAKASHITA GATE—THIS NEWS WOULD NO DOUBT PROVE TO BE THE FINAL BLOW.
EXACTLY SO, MY LORD.
THEREFORE, IT IS BEING KEPT A TIGHTLY GUARDED SECRET, AND PRINCE KAZU—I CANNOT THINK WHAT ELSE WE ARE TO CALL HER, SO THAT IS THE NAME I SHALL USE—PRINCE KAZU IS BEING WAITED UPON BY A VERY SMALL GROUP OF ATTENDANTS WHO ALREADY KNOW THE WHOLE STORY.
MM... BUT, TAKIYAMA.
EVEN AN IMPERIAL PRINCE MUST SOMETIMES OPEN HIS MOUTH AND SPEAK, NOT TO MENTION APPEAR IN FRONT OF OTHERS ON OCCASION.

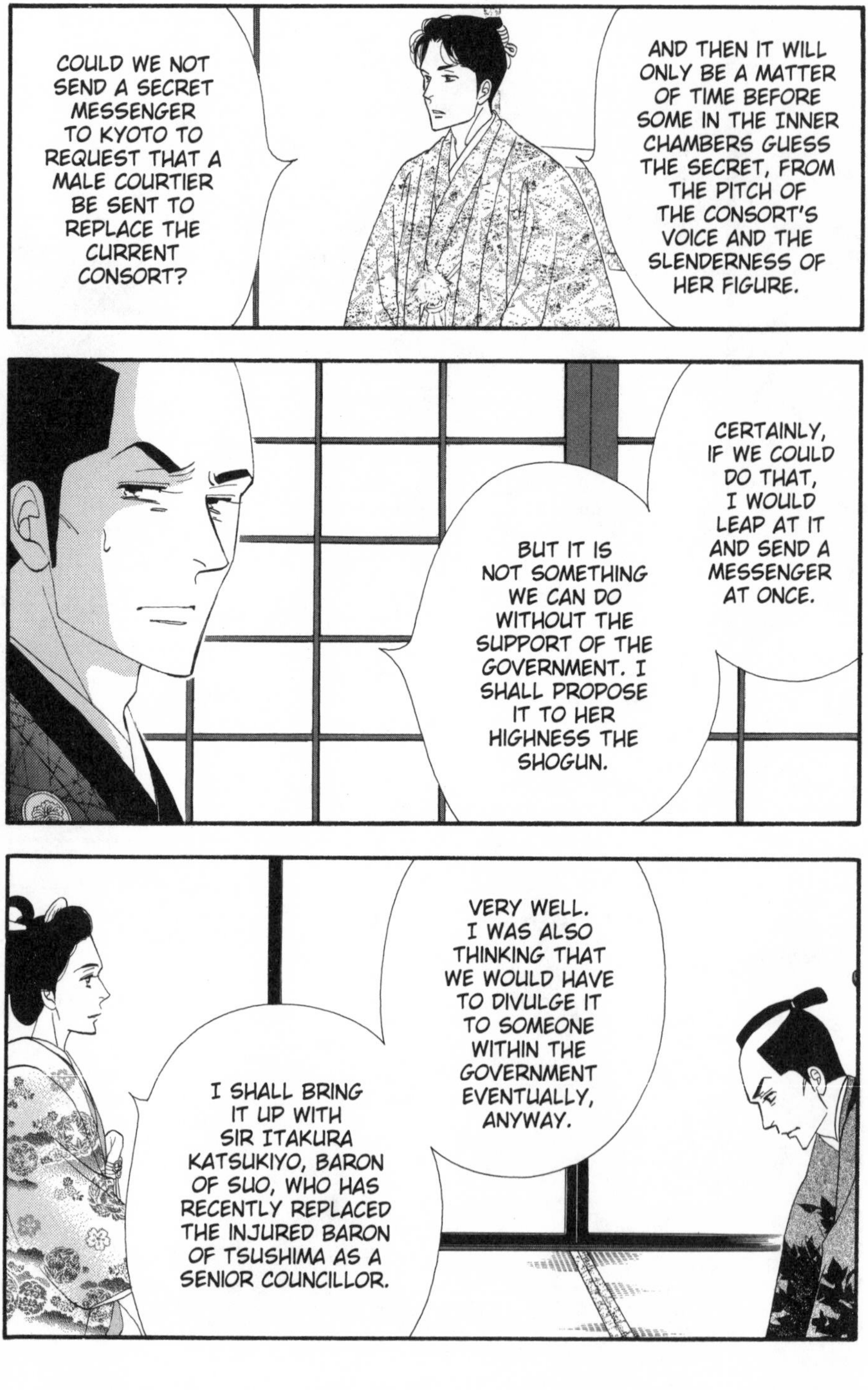
AND THEN IT WILL ONLY BE A MATTER OF TIME BEFORE SOME IN THE INNER CHAMBERS GUESS THE SECRET, FROM THE PITCH OF THE CONSORT'S VOICE AND THE SLENDERNESS OF HER FIGURE.
COULD WE NOT SEND A SECRET MESSENGER TO KYOTO TO REQUEST THAT A MALE COURTIER BE SENT TO REPLACE THE CURRENT CONSORT?
CERTAINLY, IF WE COULD DO THAT, I WOULD LEAP AT IT AND SEND A MESSENGER AT ONCE.
BUT IT IS NOT SOMETHING WE CAN DO WITHOUT THE SUPPORT OF THE GOVERNMENT. I SHALL PROPOSE IT TO HER HIGHNESS THE SHOGUN.
VERY WELL. I WAS ALSO THINKING THAT WE WOULD HAVE TO DIVULGE IT TO SOMEONE WITHIN THE GOVERNMENT EVENTUALLY, ANYWAY.
I SHALL BRING IT UP WITH SIR ITAKURA KATSUKIYO, BARON OF SUO, WHO HAS RECENTLY REPLACED THE INJURED BARON OF TSUSHIMA AS A SENIOR COUNCILLOR.

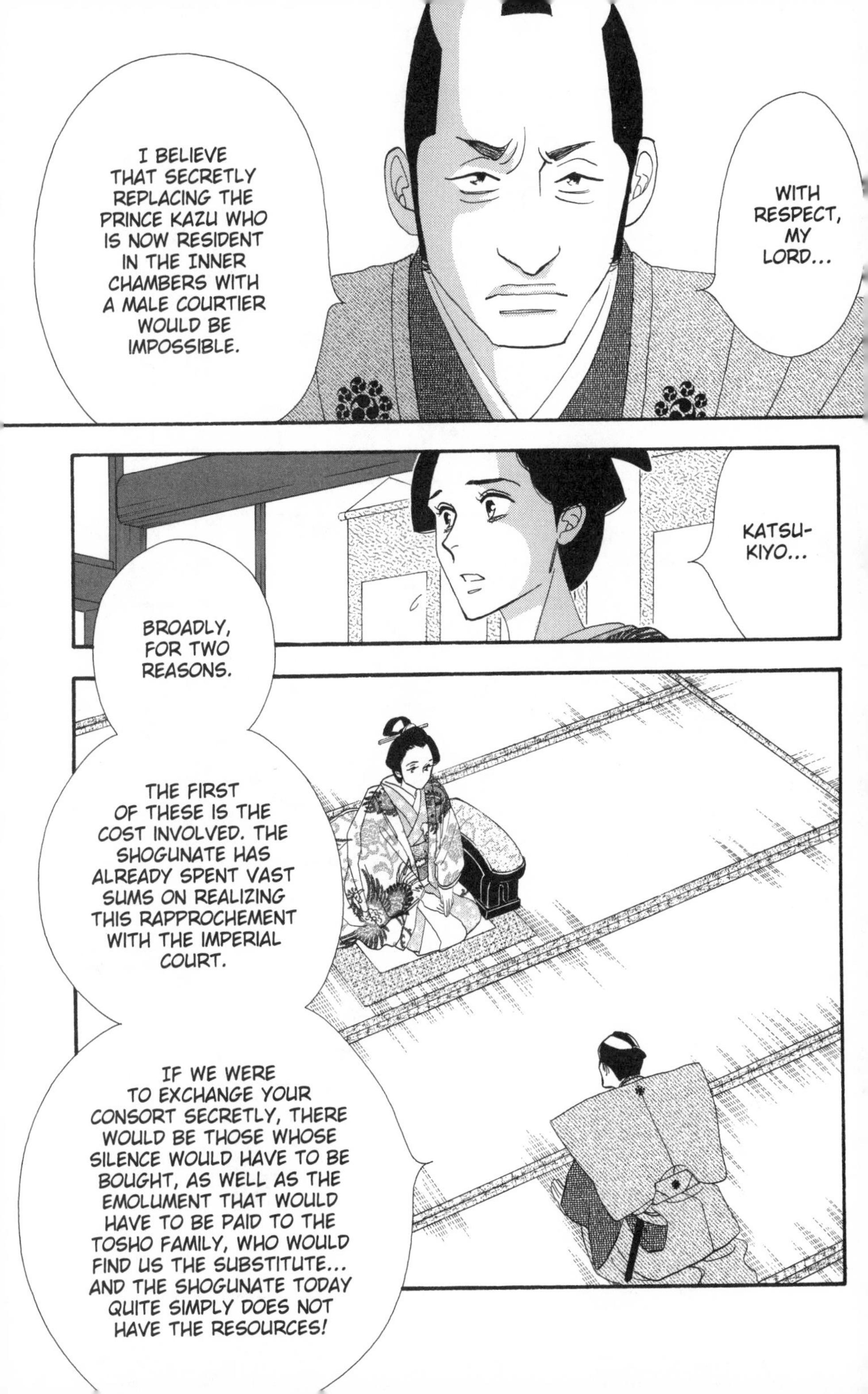
WITH RESPECT, MY LORD...
I BELIEVE THAT SECRETLY REPLACING THE PRINCE KAZU WHO IS NOW RESIDENT IN THE INNER CHAMBERS WITH A MALE COURTIER WOULD BE IMPOSSIBLE.
KATSU-KIYO...
BROADLY, FOR TWO REASONS.
THE FIRST OF THESE IS THE COST INVOLVED. THE SHOGUNATE HAS ALREADY SPENT VAST SUMS ON REALIZING THIS RAPPROCHEMENT WITH THE IMPERIAL COURT.
IF WE WERE TO EXCHANGE YOUR CONSORT SECRETLY, THERE WOULD BE THOSE WHOSE SILENCE WOULD HAVE TO BE BOUGHT, AS WELL AS THE EMOLUMENT THAT WOULD HAVE TO BE PAID TO THE TOSHO FAMILY, WHO WOULD FIND US THE SUBSTITUTE... AND THE SHOGUNATE TODAY QUITE SIMPLY DOES NOT HAVE THE RESOURCES!

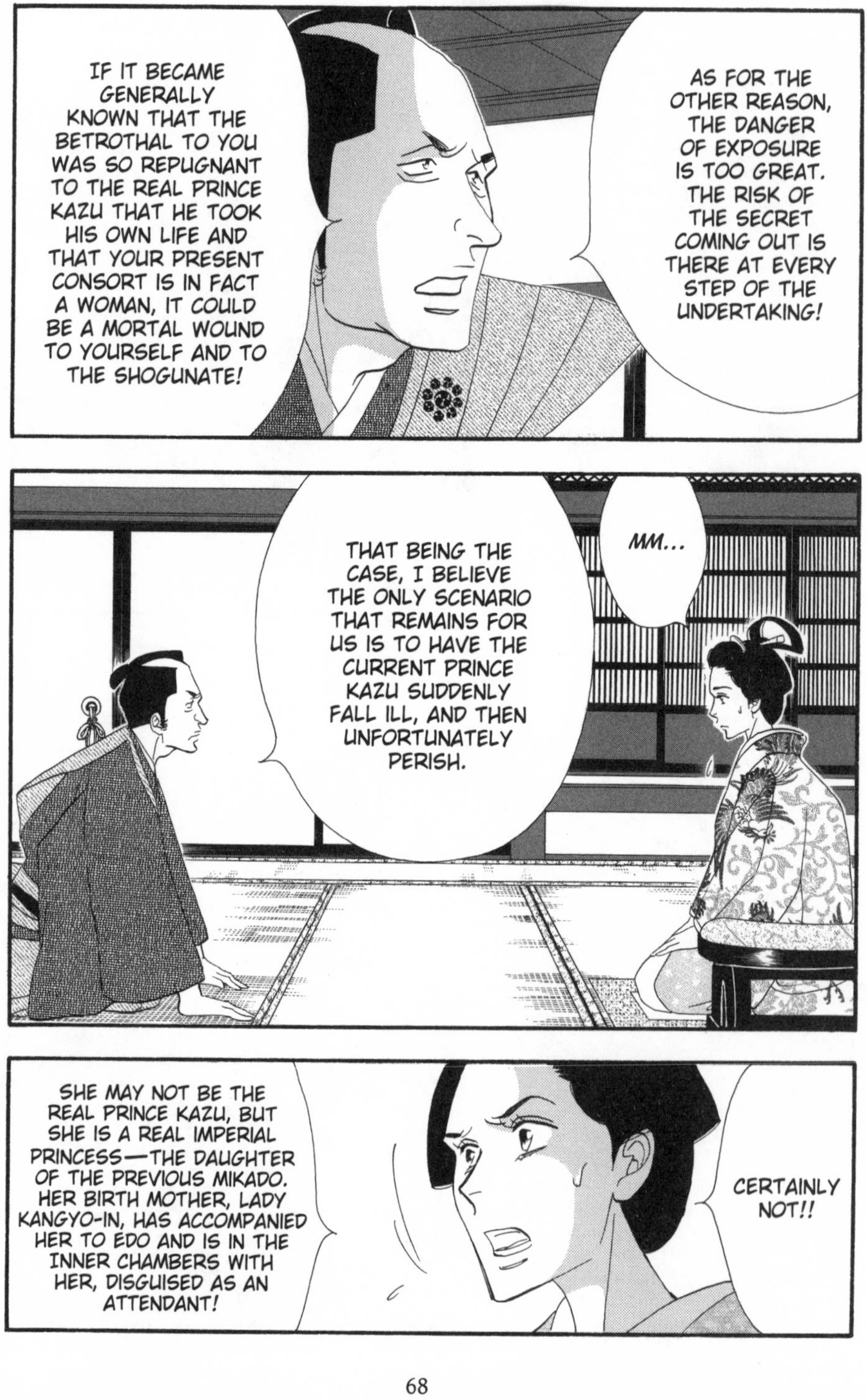
AS FOR THE OTHER REASON, THE DANGER OF EXPOSURE IS TOO GREAT. THE RISK OF THE SECRET COMING OUT IS THERE AT EVERY STEP OF THE UNDERTAKING!
IF IT BECAME GENERALLY KNOWN THAT THE BETROTHAL TO YOU WAS SO REPUGNANT TO THE REAL PRINCE KAZU THAT HE TOOK HIS OWN LIFE AND THAT YOUR PRESENT CONSORT IS IN FACT A WOMAN, IT COULD BE A MORTAL WOUND TO YOURSELF AND TO THE SHOGUNATE!
MM...
THAT BEING THE CASE, I BELIEVE THE ONLY SCENARIO THAT REMAINS FOR US IS TO HAVE THE CURRENT PRINCE KAZU SUDDENLY FALL ILL, AND THEN UNFORTUNATELY PERISH.
CERTAINLY NOT!!
SHE MAY NOT BE THE REAL PRINCE KAZU, BUT SHE IS A REAL IMPERIAL PRINCESS—THE DAUGHTER OF THE PREVIOUS MIKADO. HER BIRTH MOTHER, LADY KANGYO-IN, HAS ACCOMPANIED HER TO EDO AND IS IN THE INNER CHAMBERS WITH HER, DISGUISED AS AN ATTENDANT!

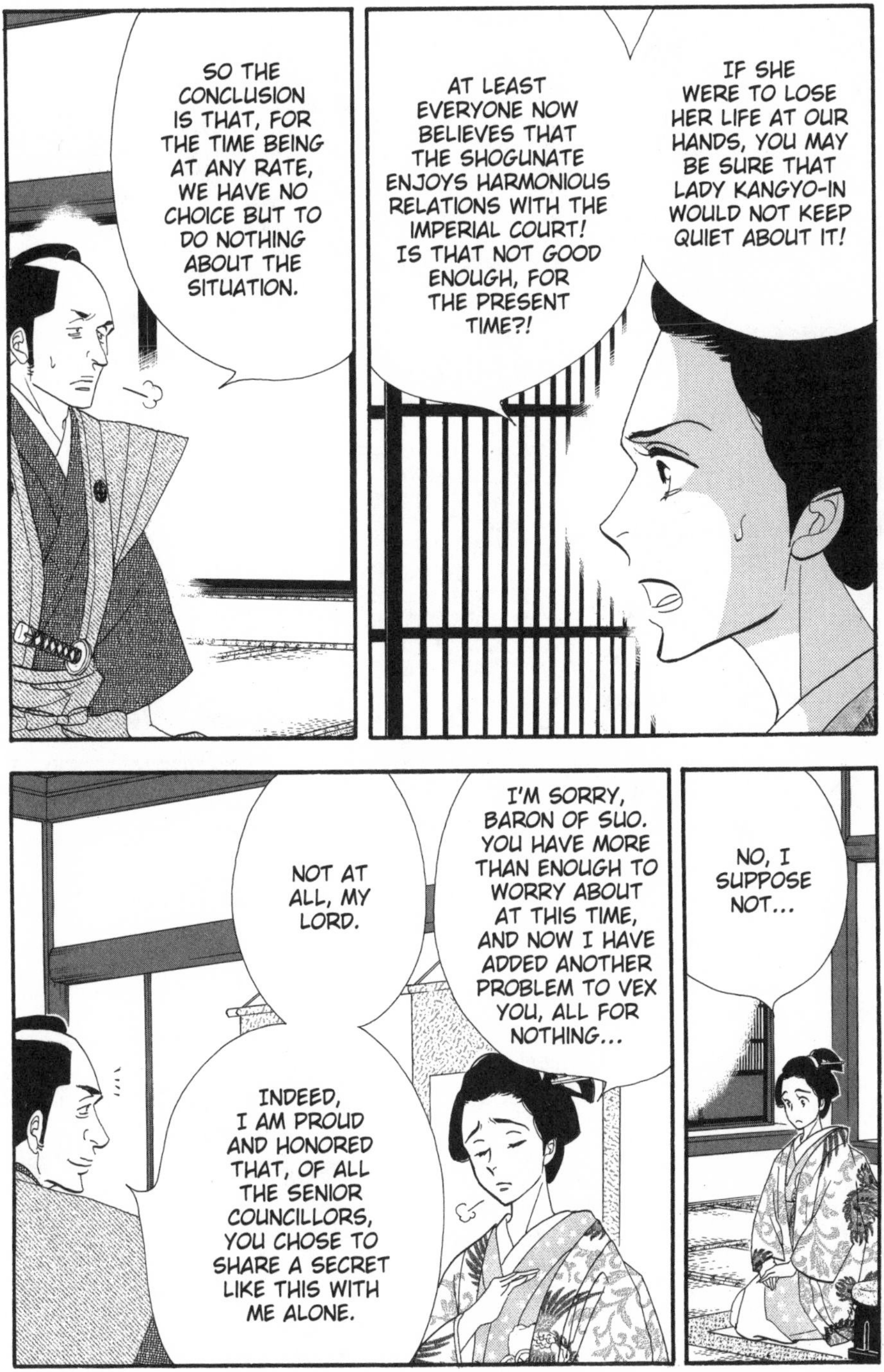
IF SHE WERE TO LOSE HER LIFE AT OUR HANDS, YOU MAY BE SURE THAT LADY KANGYO-IN WOULD NOT KEEP QUIET ABOUT IT!
AT LEAST EVERYONE NOW BELIEVES THAT THE SHOGUNATE ENJOYS HARMONIOUS RELATIONS WITH THE IMPERIAL COURT! IS THAT NOT GOOD ENOUGH, FOR THE PRESENT TIME?!
SO THE CONCLUSION IS THAT, FOR THE TIME BEING AT ANY RATE, WE HAVE NO CHOICE BUT TO DO NOTHING ABOUT THE SITUATION.
NO, I SUPPOSE NOT...
I'M SORRY, BARON OF SUO. YOU HAVE MORE THAN ENOUGH TO WORRY ABOUT AT THIS TIME, AND NOW I HAVE ADDED ANOTHER PROBLEM TO VEX YOU, ALL FOR NOTHING...
NOT AT ALL, MY LORD.
INDEED, I AM PROUD AND HONORED THAT, OF ALL THE SENIOR COUNCILLORS, YOU CHOSE TO SHARE A SECRET LIKE THIS WITH ME ALONE.

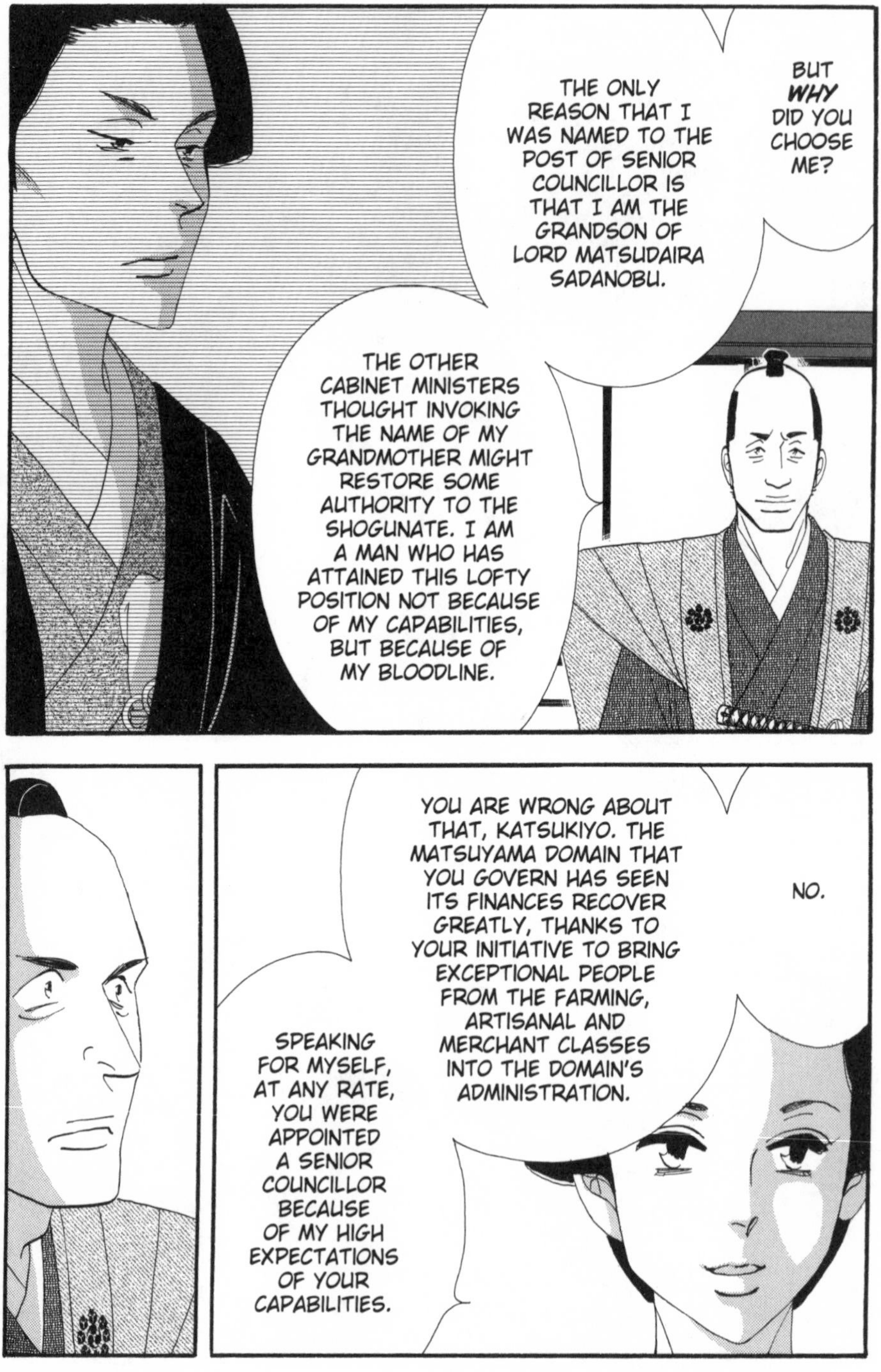
BUT *WHY* DID YOU CHOOSE ME?
THE ONLY REASON THAT I WAS NAMED TO THE POST OF SENIOR COUNCILLOR IS THAT I AM THE GRANDSON OF LORD MATSUDAIRA SADANOBU.
THE OTHER CABINET MINISTERS THOUGHT INVOKING THE NAME OF MY GRANDMOTHER MIGHT RESTORE SOME AUTHORITY TO THE SHOGUNATE. I AM A MAN WHO HAS ATTAINED THIS LOFTY POSITION NOT BECAUSE OF MY CAPABILITIES, BUT BECAUSE OF MY BLOODLINE.
NO.
YOU ARE WRONG ABOUT THAT, KATSUKIYO. THE MATSUYAMA DOMAIN THAT YOU GOVERN HAS SEEN ITS FINANCES RECOVER GREATLY, THANKS TO YOUR INITIATIVE TO BRING EXCEPTIONAL PEOPLE FROM THE FARMING, ARTISANAL AND MERCHANT CLASSES INTO THE DOMAIN'S ADMINISTRATION.
SPEAKING FOR MYSELF, AT ANY RATE, YOU WERE APPOINTED A SENIOR COUNCILLOR BECAUSE OF MY HIGH EXPECTATIONS OF YOUR CAPABILITIES.

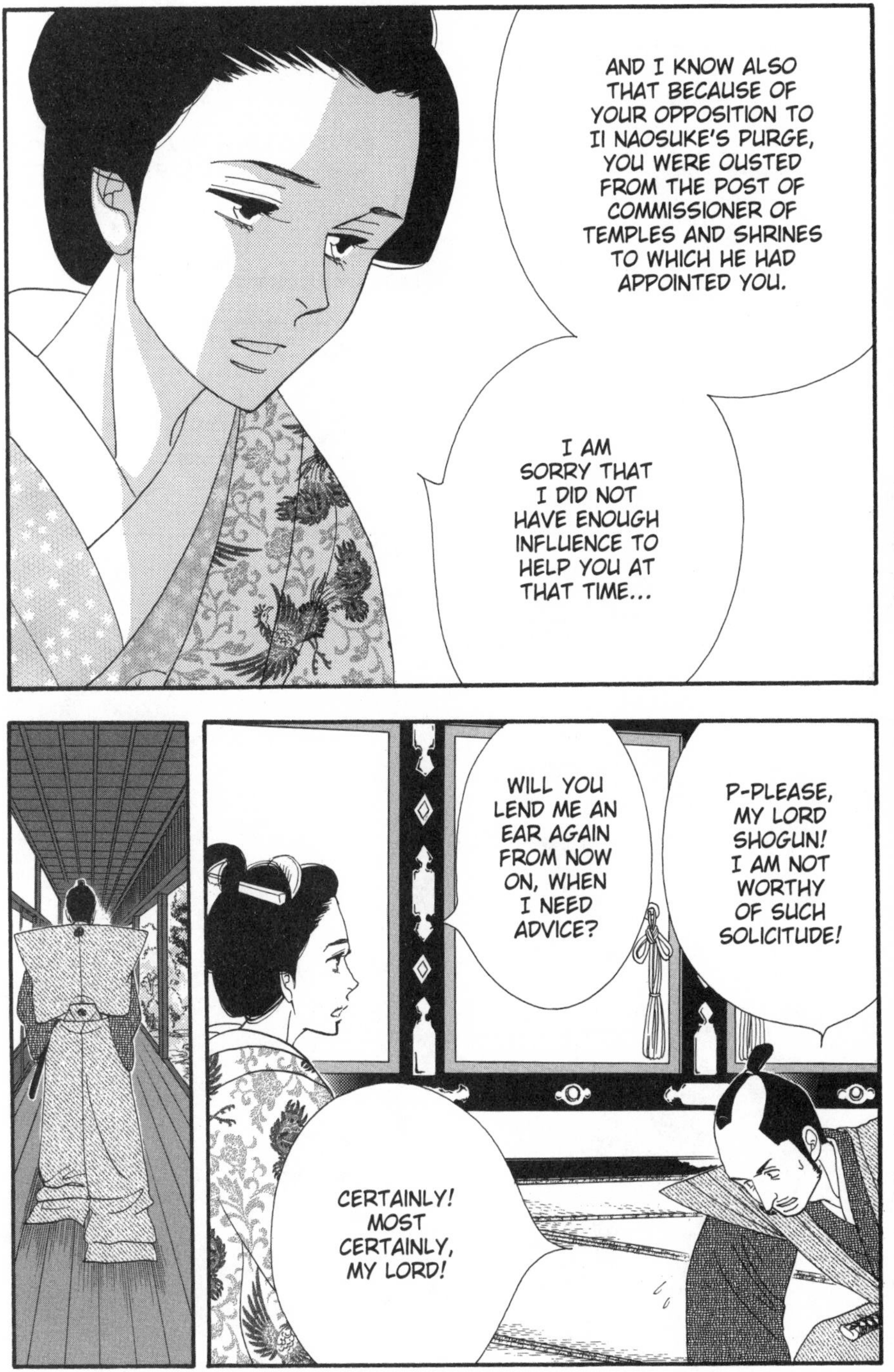
AND I KNOW ALSO THAT BECAUSE OF YOUR OPPOSITION TO II NAOSUKE'S PURGE, YOU WERE OUSTED FROM THE POST OF COMMISSIONER OF TEMPLES AND SHRINES TO WHICH HE HAD APPOINTED YOU.
I AM SORRY THAT I DID NOT HAVE ENOUGH INFLUENCE TO HELP YOU AT THAT TIME...
P-PLEASE, MY LORD SHOGUN! I AM NOT WORTHY OF SUCH SOLICITUDE!
WILL YOU LEND ME AN EAR AGAIN FROM NOW ON, WHEN I NEED ADVICE?
CERTAINLY! MOST CERTAINLY, MY LORD!

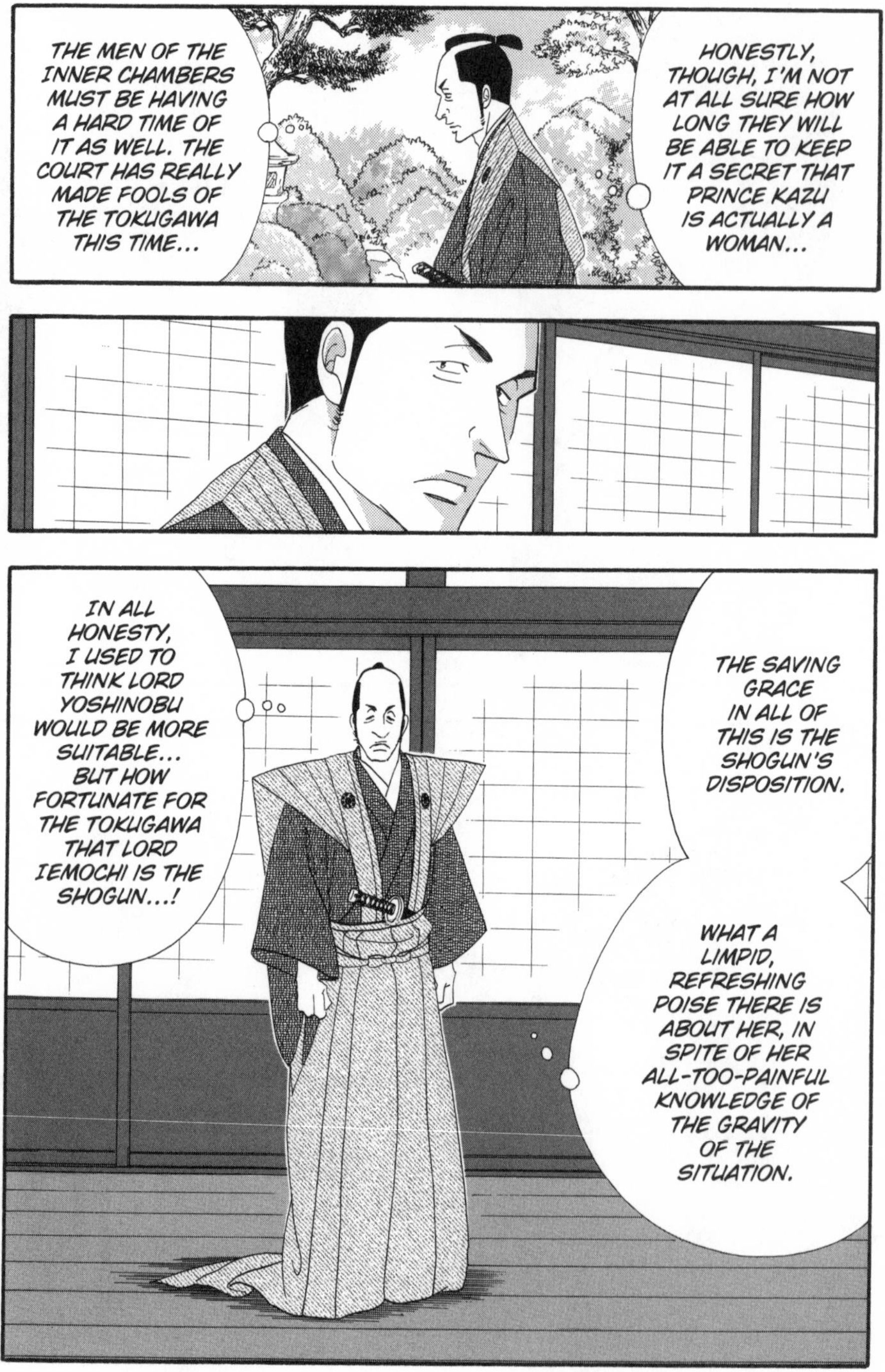
HONESTLY, THOUGH, I'M NOT AT ALL SURE HOW LONG THEY WILL BE ABLE TO KEEP IT A SECRET THAT PRINCE KAZU IS ACTUALLY A WOMAN...
THE MEN OF THE INNER CHAMBERS MUST BE HAVING A HARD TIME OF IT AS WELL. THE COURT HAS REALLY MADE FOOLS OF THE TOKUGAWA THIS TIME...
THE SAVING GRACE IN ALL OF THIS IS THE SHOGUN'S DISPOSITION.
WHAT A LIMPID, REFRESHING POISE THERE IS ABOUT HER, IN SPITE OF HER ALL-TOO-PAINFUL KNOWLEDGE OF THE GRAVITY OF THE SITUATION.
IN ALL HONESTY, I USED TO THINK LORD YOSHINOBU WOULD BE MORE SUITABLE... BUT HOW FORTUNATE FOR THE TOKUGAWA THAT LORD IEMOCHI IS THE SHOGUN...!

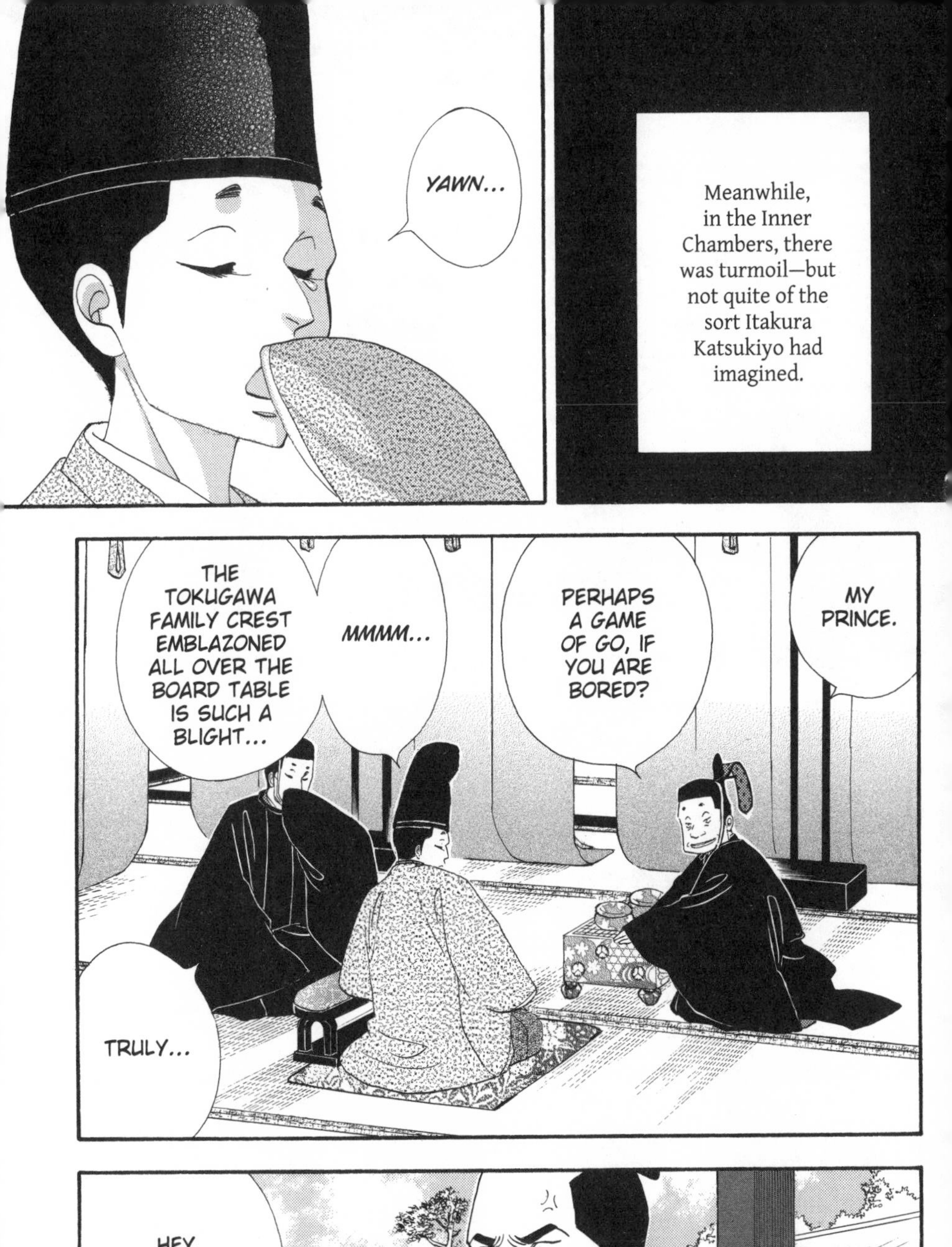
Meanwhile, in the Inner Chambers, there was turmoil—but not quite of the sort Itakura Katsukiyo had imagined.
YAWN...
MY PRINCE.
PERHAPS A GAME OF GO, IF YOU ARE BORED?
MMMM...
THE TOKUGAWA FAMILY CREST EMBLAZONED ALL OVER THE BOARD TABLE IS SUCH A BLIGHT...
TRULY...
HEY, KUROKI. DID YOU HEAR?!

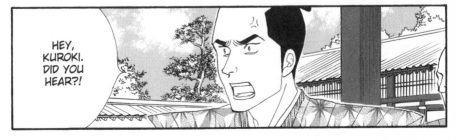

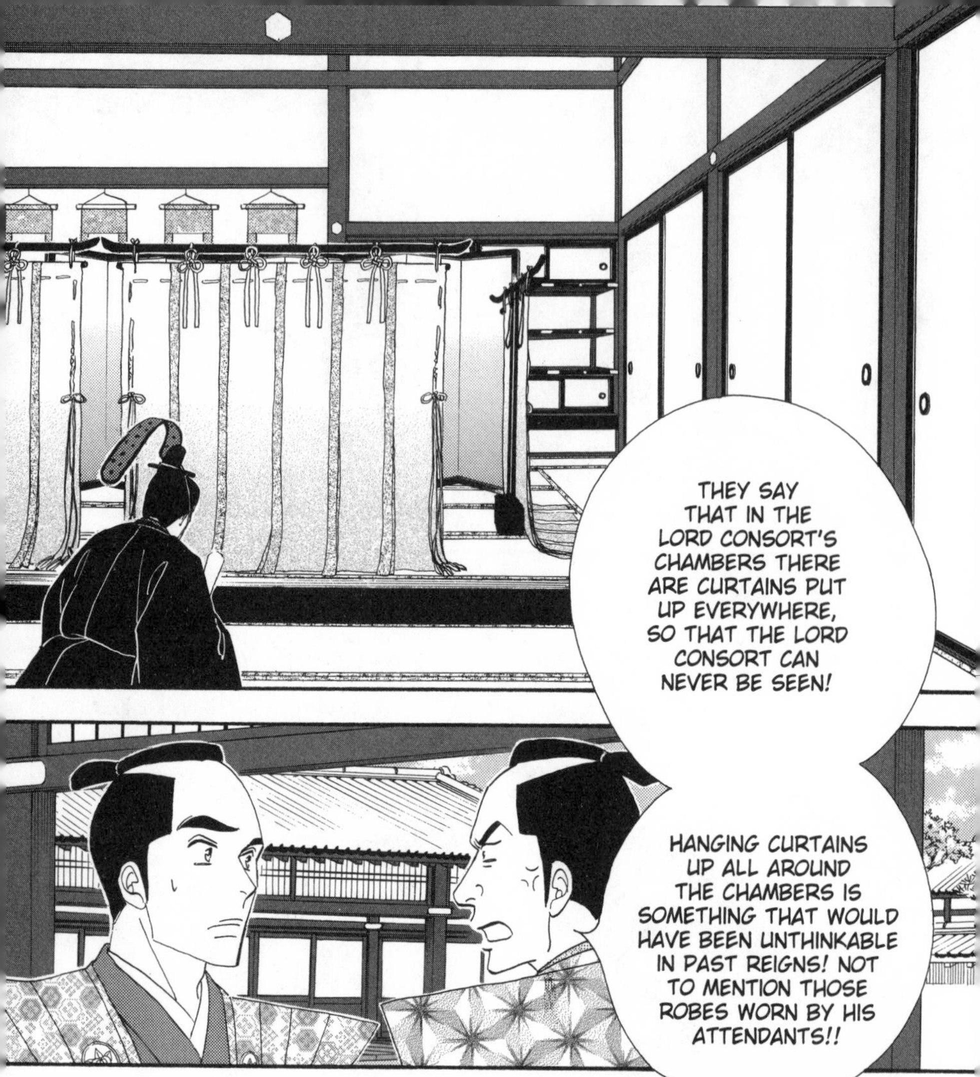
THEY SAY THAT IN THE LORD CONSORT'S CHAMBERS THERE ARE CURTAINS PUT UP EVERYWHERE, SO THAT THE LORD CONSORT CAN NEVER BE SEEN!
HANGING CURTAINS UP ALL AROUND THE CHAMBERS IS SOMETHING THAT WOULD HAVE BEEN UNTHINKABLE IN PAST REIGNS! NOT TO MENTION THOSE ROBES WORN BY HIS ATTENDANTS!!
THIS IS HARDLY THE FIRST TIME THE SHOGUN'S CONSORT HAS BEEN A COURT NOBLE—IN FACT, MOST OF THEM HAVE BEEN KYOTO ARISTOCRATS. BUT WHEN THEY ARRIVED IN EDO CASTLE, THEY EXCHANGED THEIR COURTLY ATTIRE FOR THE SAMURAI STYLE OF EDO, THE LORD CONSORT INCLUDED!
BUT NOW? LOOK AT HOW THEY ARROGANTLY PARADE AROUND EDO CASTLE IN THEIR KYOTO COURTIER CLOTHES! WHO DO THEY THINK THEY ARE?!

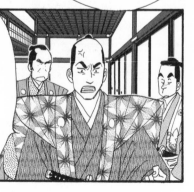

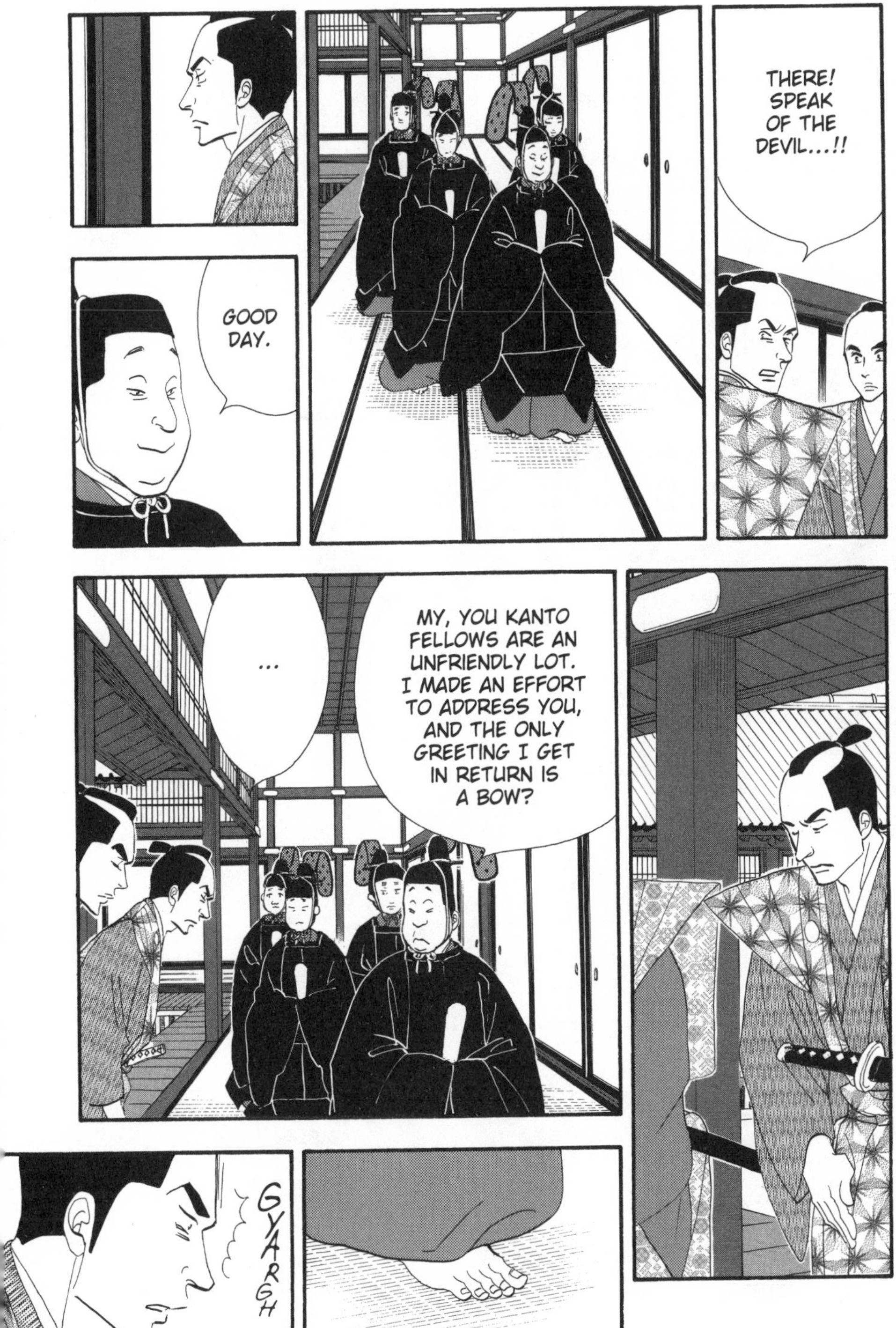
THERE! SPEAK OF THE DEVIL...!!
GOOD DAY.
MY, YOU KANTO FELLOWS ARE AN UNFRIENDLY LOT. I MADE AN EFFORT TO ADDRESS YOU, AND THE ONLY GREETING I GET IN RETURN IS A BOW?
...
GYARGH

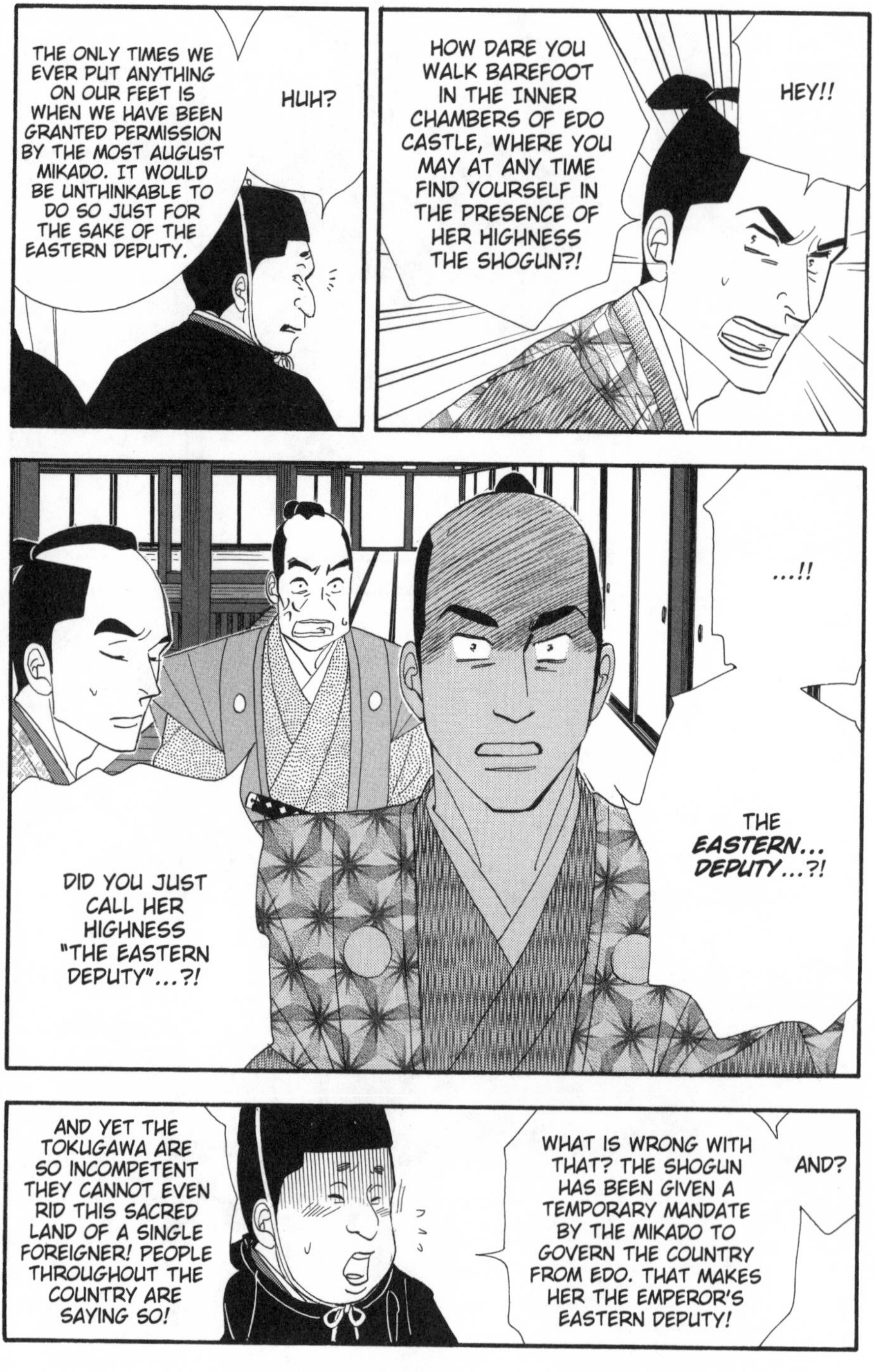
HEY!!
HOW DARE YOU WALK BAREFOOT IN THE INNER CHAMBERS OF EDO CASTLE, WHERE YOU MAY AT ANY TIME FIND YOURSELF IN THE PRESENCE OF HER HIGHNESS THE SHOGUN?!
HUH?
THE ONLY TIMES WE EVER PUT ANYTHING ON OUR FEET IS WHEN WE HAVE BEEN GRANTED PERMISSION BY THE MOST AUGUST MIKADO. IT WOULD BE UNTHINKABLE TO DO SO JUST FOR THE SAKE OF THE EASTERN DEPUTY.
...!!
THE *EASTERN... DEPUTY*...?!
DID YOU JUST CALL HER HIGHNESS "THE EASTERN DEPUTY"...?!
AND?
WHAT IS WRONG WITH THAT? THE SHOGUN HAS BEEN GIVEN A TEMPORARY MANDATE BY THE MIKADO TO GOVERN THE COUNTRY FROM EDO. THAT MAKES HER THE EMPEROR'S EASTERN DEPUTY!
AND YET THE TOKUGAWA ARE SO INCOMPETENT THEY CANNOT EVEN RID THIS SACRED LAND OF A SINGLE FOREIGNER! PEOPLE THROUGHOUT THE COUNTRY ARE SAYING SO!

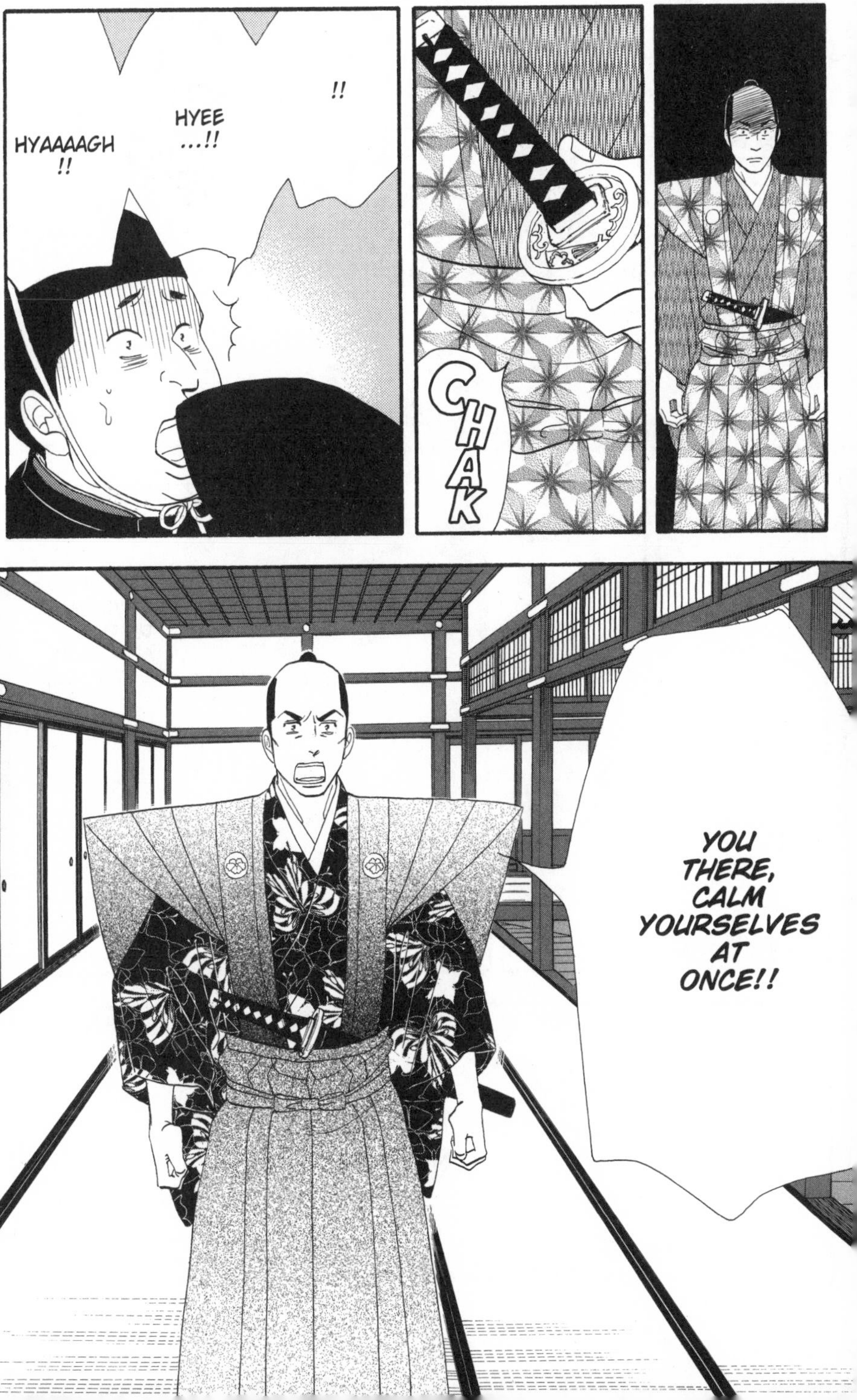
CHAK
!!
HYEE ...!!
HYAAAAGH !!
YOU THERE, CALM YOURSELVES AT ONCE!!

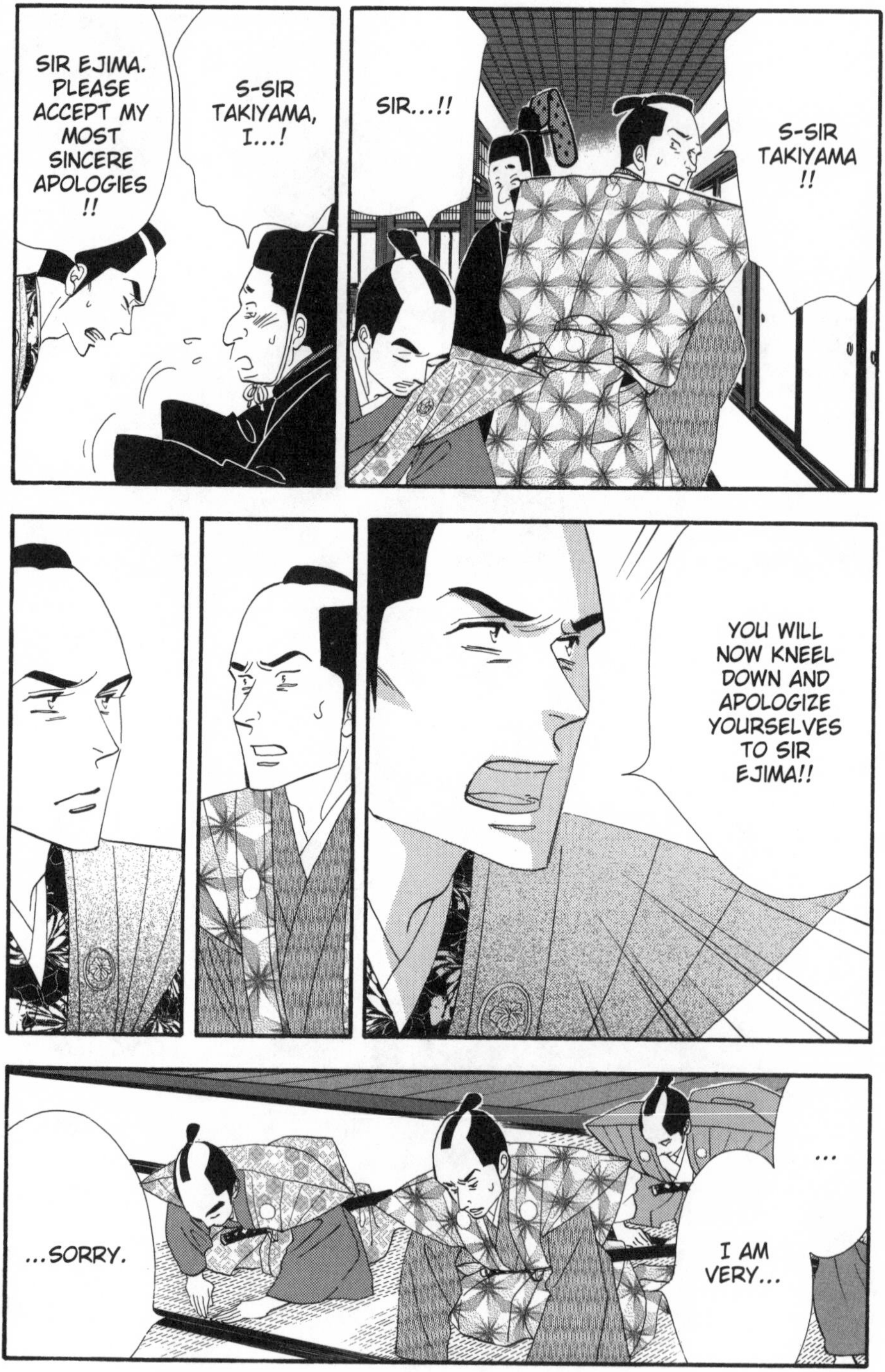
S-SIR TAKIYAMA !!
SIR...!!
S-SIR TAKIYAMA, I...!
SIR EJIMA. PLEASE ACCEPT MY MOST SINCERE APOLOGIES !!
YOU WILL NOW KNEEL DOWN AND APOLOGIZE YOURSELVES TO SIR EJIMA!!
...
I AM VERY...
...SORRY.

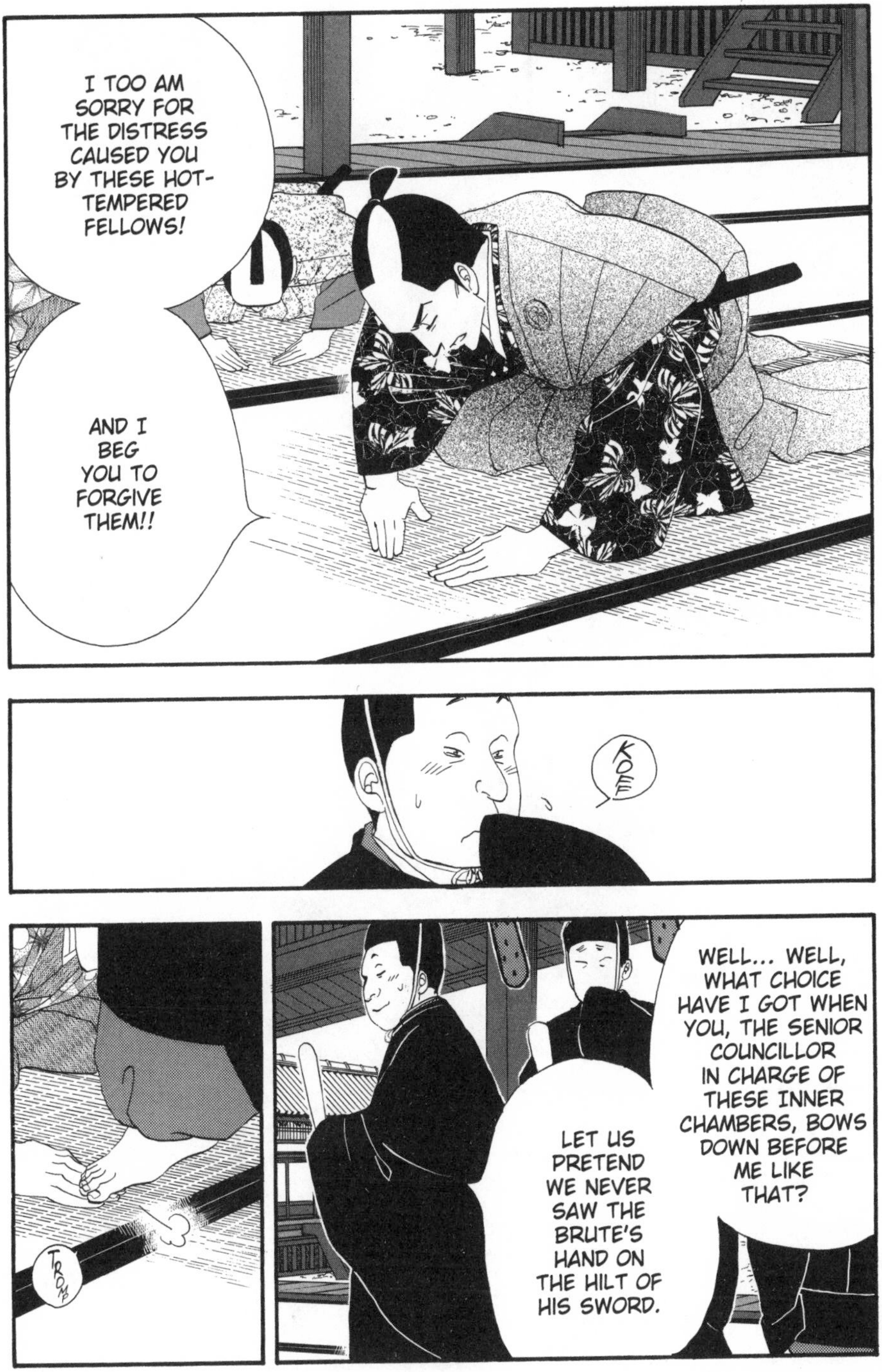
I TOO AM SORRY FOR THE DISTRESS CAUSED YOU BY THESE HOT-TEMPERED FELLOWS!
AND I BEG YOU TO FORGIVE THEM!!
KOFF
WELL... WELL, WHAT CHOICE HAVE I GOT WHEN YOU, THE SENIOR COUNCILLOR IN CHARGE OF THESE INNER CHAMBERS, BOWS DOWN BEFORE ME LIKE THAT?
LET US PRETEND WE NEVER SAW THE BRUTE'S HAND ON THE HILT OF HIS SWORD.
TROMP

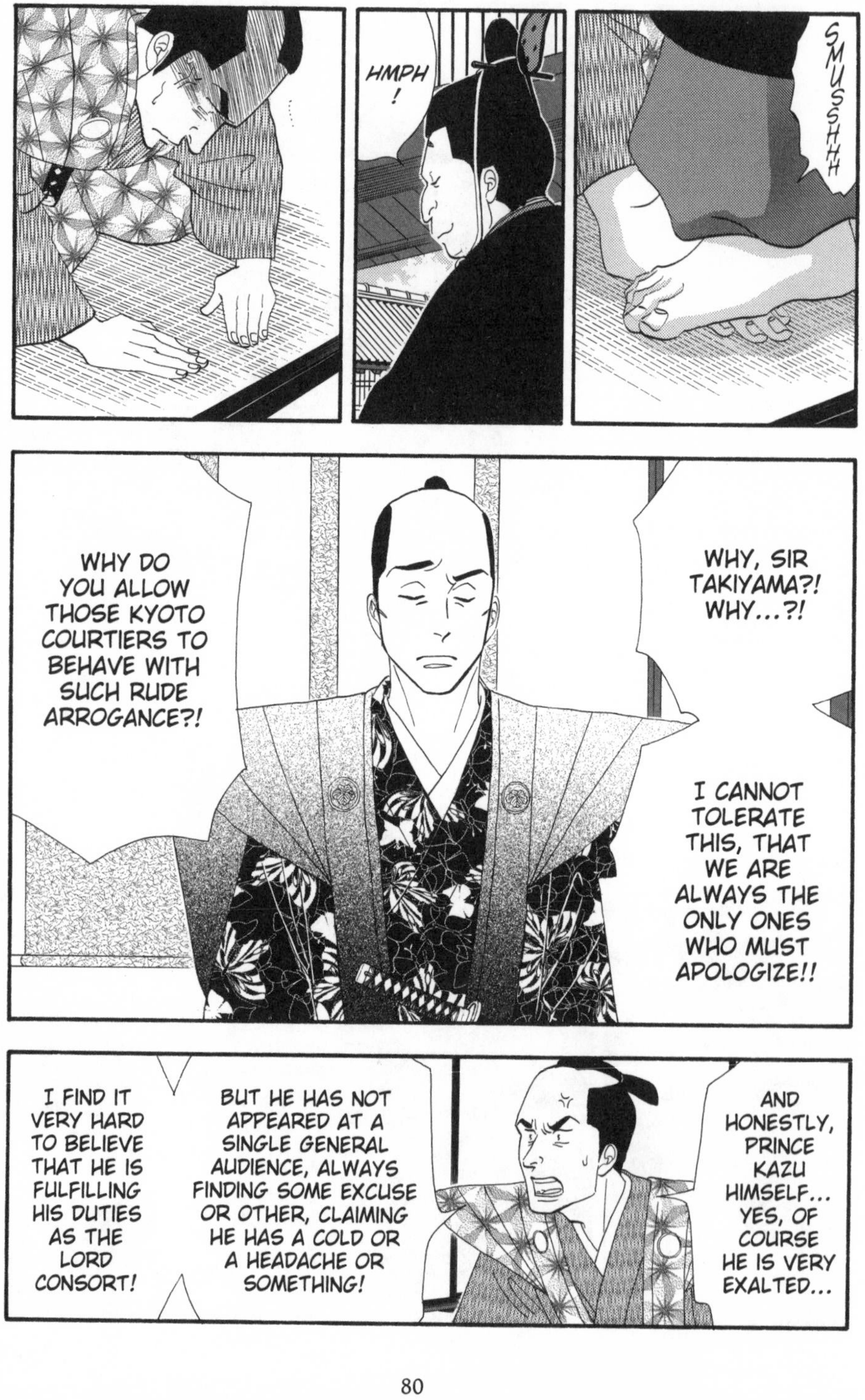
SMUSSHHH
HMPH!
......
WHY, SIR TAKIYAMA?! WHY...?!
WHY DO YOU ALLOW THOSE KYOTO COURTIERS TO BEHAVE WITH SUCH RUDE ARROGANCE?!
I CANNOT TOLERATE THIS, THAT WE ARE ALWAYS THE ONLY ONES WHO MUST APOLOGIZE!!
AND HONESTLY, PRINCE KAZU HIMSELF... YES, OF COURSE HE IS VERY EXALTED...
BUT HE HAS NOT APPEARED AT A SINGLE GENERAL AUDIENCE, ALWAYS FINDING SOME EXCUSE OR OTHER, CLAIMING HE HAS A COLD OR A HEADACHE OR SOMETHING!
I FIND IT VERY HARD TO BELIEVE THAT HE IS FULFILLING HIS DUTIES AS THE LORD CONSORT!

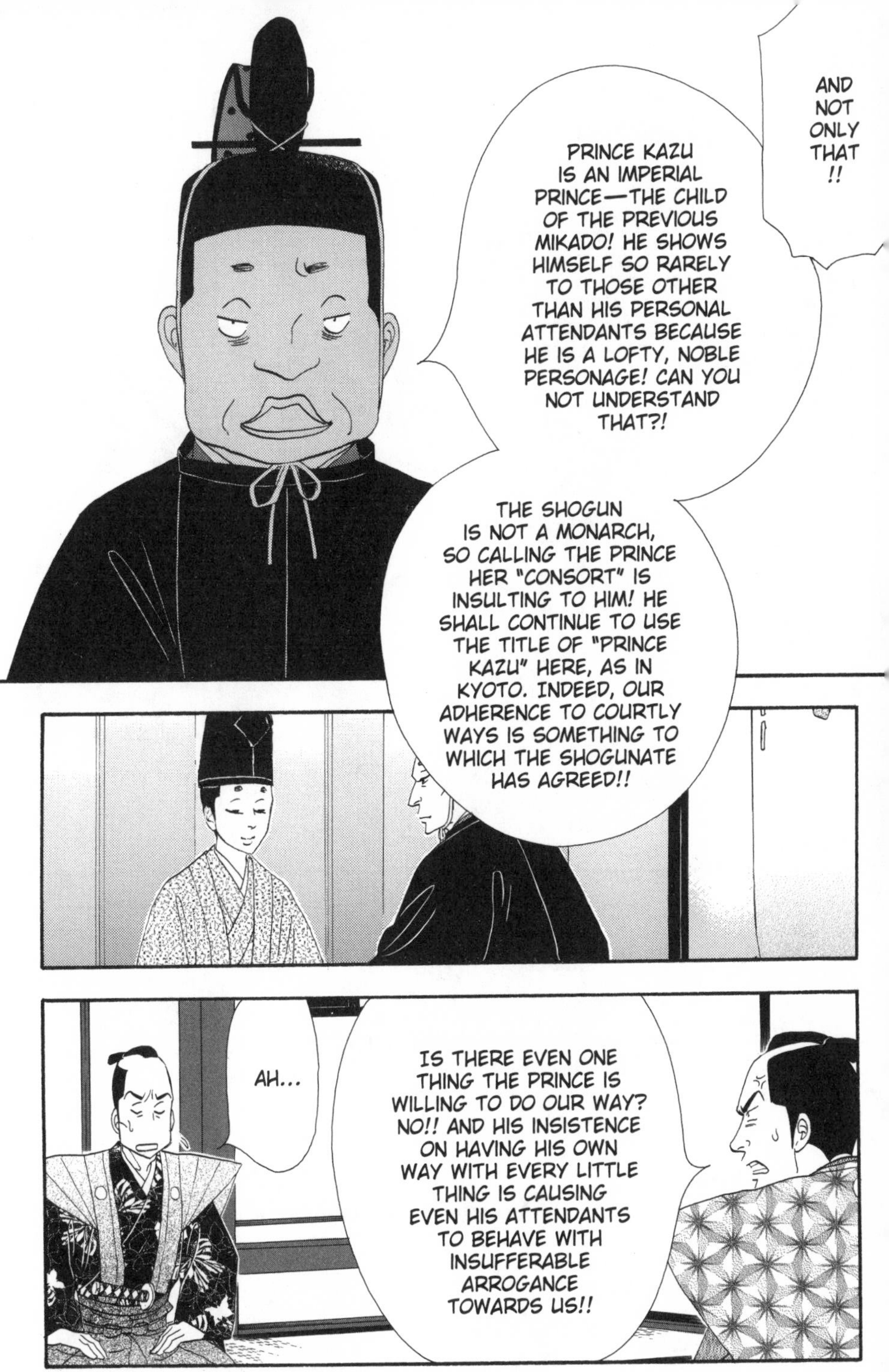
AND NOT ONLY THAT!!
PRINCE KAZU IS AN IMPERIAL PRINCE—THE CHILD OF THE PREVIOUS MIKADO! HE SHOWS HIMSELF SO RARELY TO THOSE OTHER THAN HIS PERSONAL ATTENDANTS BECAUSE HE IS A LOFTY, NOBLE PERSONAGE! CAN YOU NOT UNDERSTAND THAT?!
THE SHOGUN IS NOT A MONARCH, SO CALLING THE PRINCE HER "CONSORT" IS INSULTING TO HIM! HE SHALL CONTINUE TO USE THE TITLE OF "PRINCE KAZU" HERE, AS IN KYOTO. INDEED, OUR ADHERENCE TO COURTLY WAYS IS SOMETHING TO WHICH THE SHOGUNATE HAS AGREED!!
IS THERE EVEN ONE THING THE PRINCE IS WILLING TO DO OUR WAY? NO!! AND HIS INSISTENCE ON HAVING HIS OWN WAY WITH EVERY LITTLE THING IS CAUSING EVEN HIS ATTENDANTS TO BEHAVE WITH INSUFFERABLE ARROGANCE TOWARDS US!!
AH...

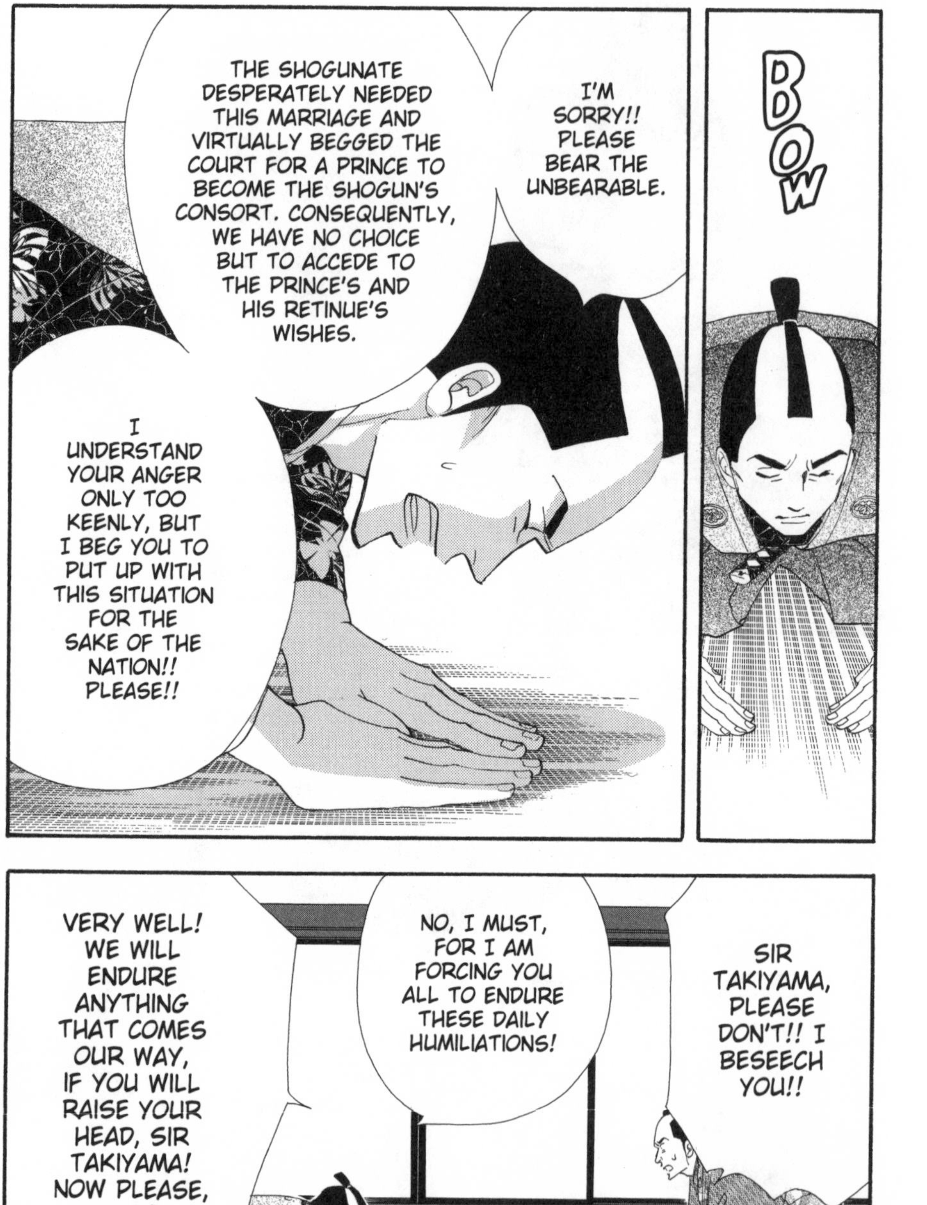
BOW
I'M SORRY!! PLEASE BEAR THE UNBEARABLE.
THE SHOGUNATE DESPERATELY NEEDED THIS MARRIAGE AND VIRTUALLY BEGGED THE COURT FOR A PRINCE TO BECOME THE SHOGUN'S CONSORT. CONSEQUENTLY, WE HAVE NO CHOICE BUT TO ACCEDE TO THE PRINCE'S AND HIS RETINUE'S WISHES.
I UNDERSTAND YOUR ANGER ONLY TOO KEENLY, BUT I BEG YOU TO PUT UP WITH THIS SITUATION FOR THE SAKE OF THE NATION!! PLEASE!!
SIR TAKIYAMA, PLEASE DON'T!! I BESEECH YOU!!
NO, I MUST, FOR I AM FORCING YOU ALL TO ENDURE THESE DAILY HUMILIATIONS!
VERY WELL! WE WILL ENDURE ANYTHING THAT COMES OUR WAY, IF YOU WILL RAISE YOUR HEAD, SIR TAKIYAMA! NOW PLEASE, SIR!

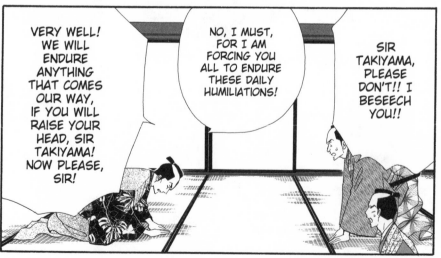

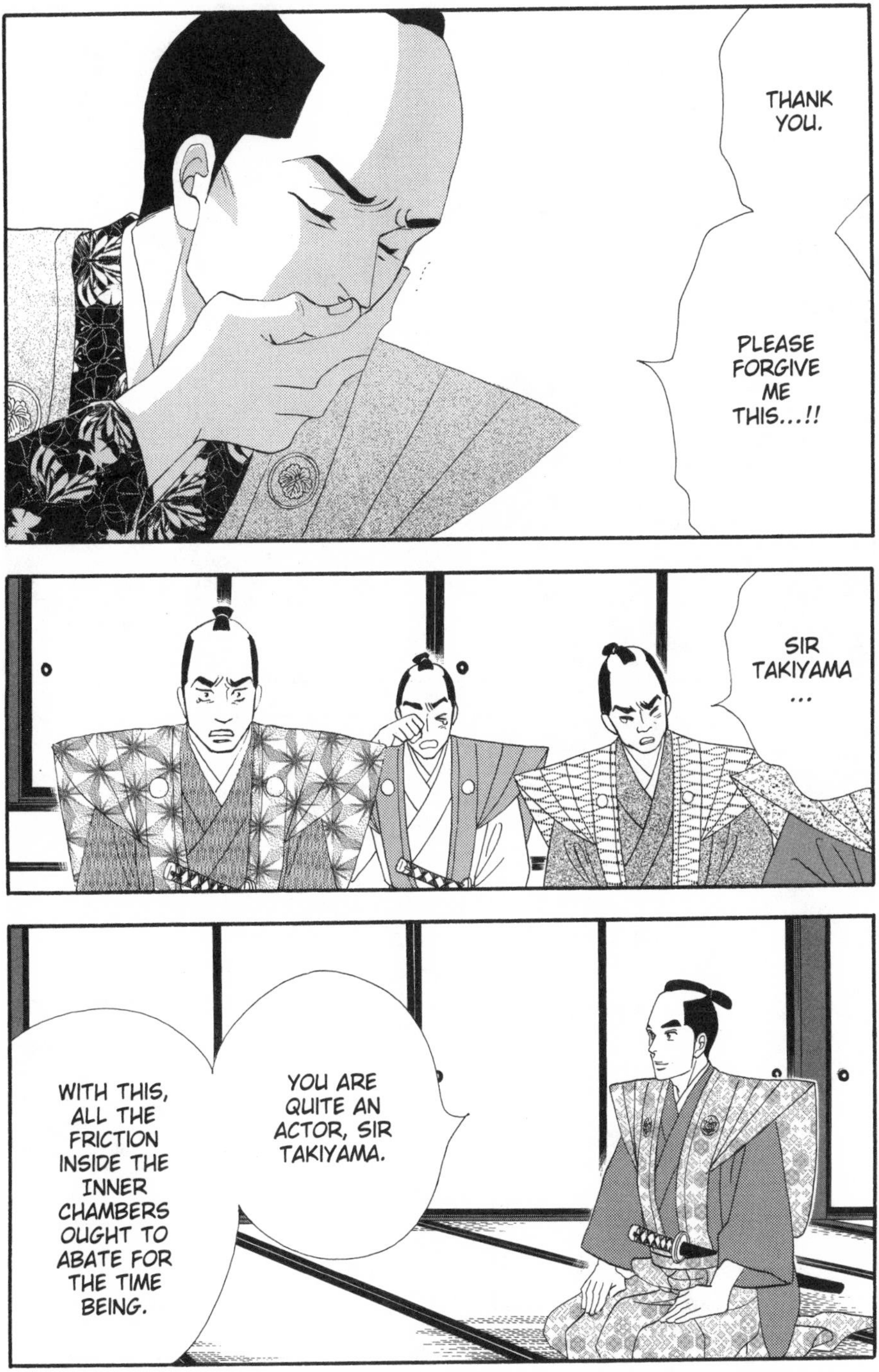
THANK YOU.
PLEASE FORGIVE ME THIS...!!
SIR TAKIYAMA...
YOU ARE QUITE AN ACTOR, SIR TAKIYAMA.
WITH THIS, ALL THE FRICTION INSIDE THE INNER CHAMBERS OUGHT TO ABATE FOR THE TIME BEING.

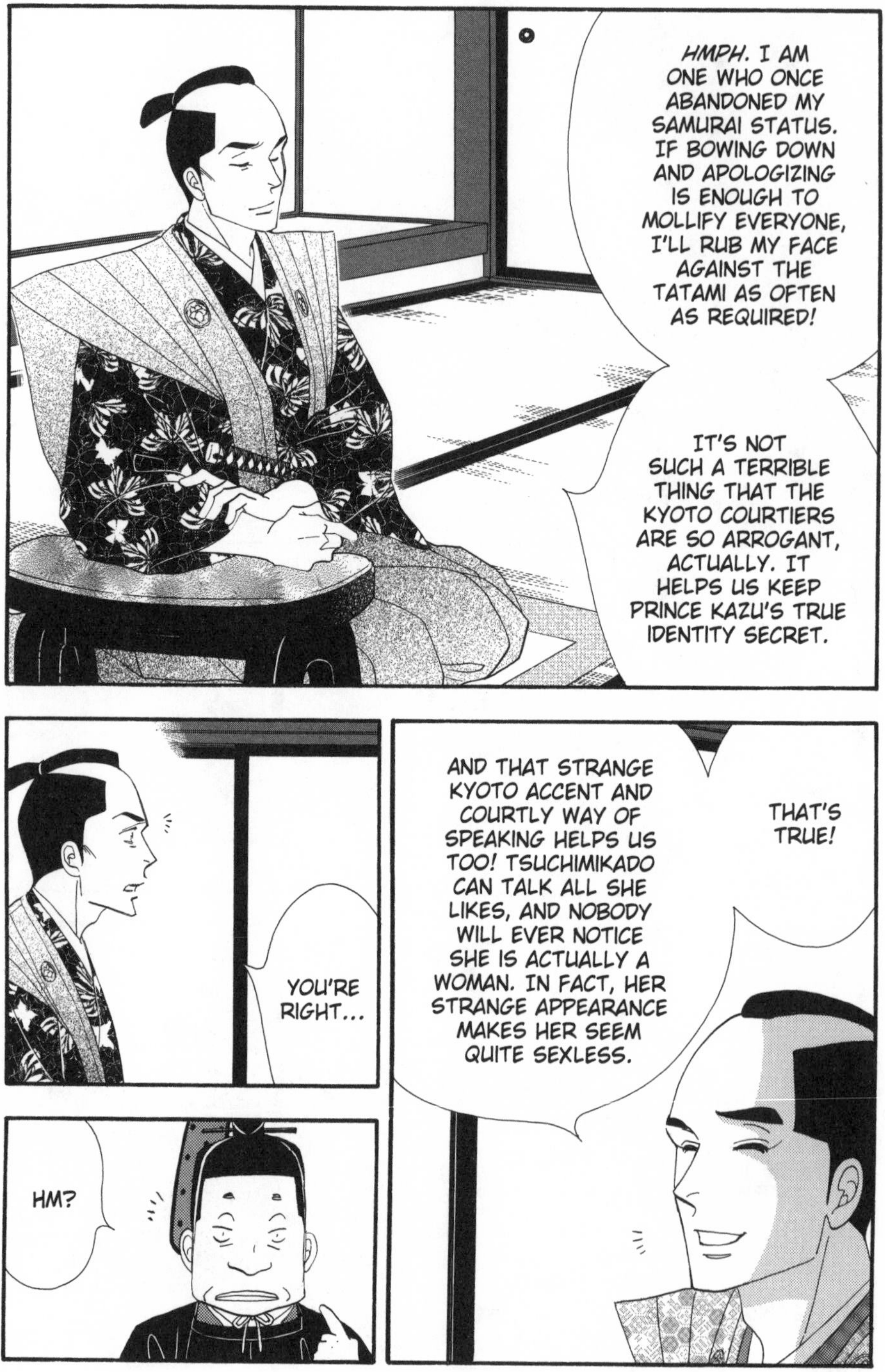
HMPH. I AM ONE WHO ONCE ABANDONED MY SAMURAI STATUS. IF BOWING DOWN AND APOLOGIZING IS ENOUGH TO MOLLIFY EVERYONE, I'LL RUB MY FACE AGAINST THE TATAMI AS OFTEN AS REQUIRED!
IT'S NOT SUCH A TERRIBLE THING THAT THE KYOTO COURTIERS ARE SO ARROGANT, ACTUALLY. IT HELPS US KEEP PRINCE KAZU'S TRUE IDENTITY SECRET.
YOU'RE RIGHT...
AND THAT STRANGE KYOTO ACCENT AND COURTLY WAY OF SPEAKING HELPS US TOO! TSUCHIMIKADO CAN TALK ALL SHE LIKES, AND NOBODY WILL EVER NOTICE SHE IS ACTUALLY A WOMAN. IN FACT, HER STRANGE APPEARANCE MAKES HER SEEM QUITE SEXLESS.
THAT'S TRUE!
HM?

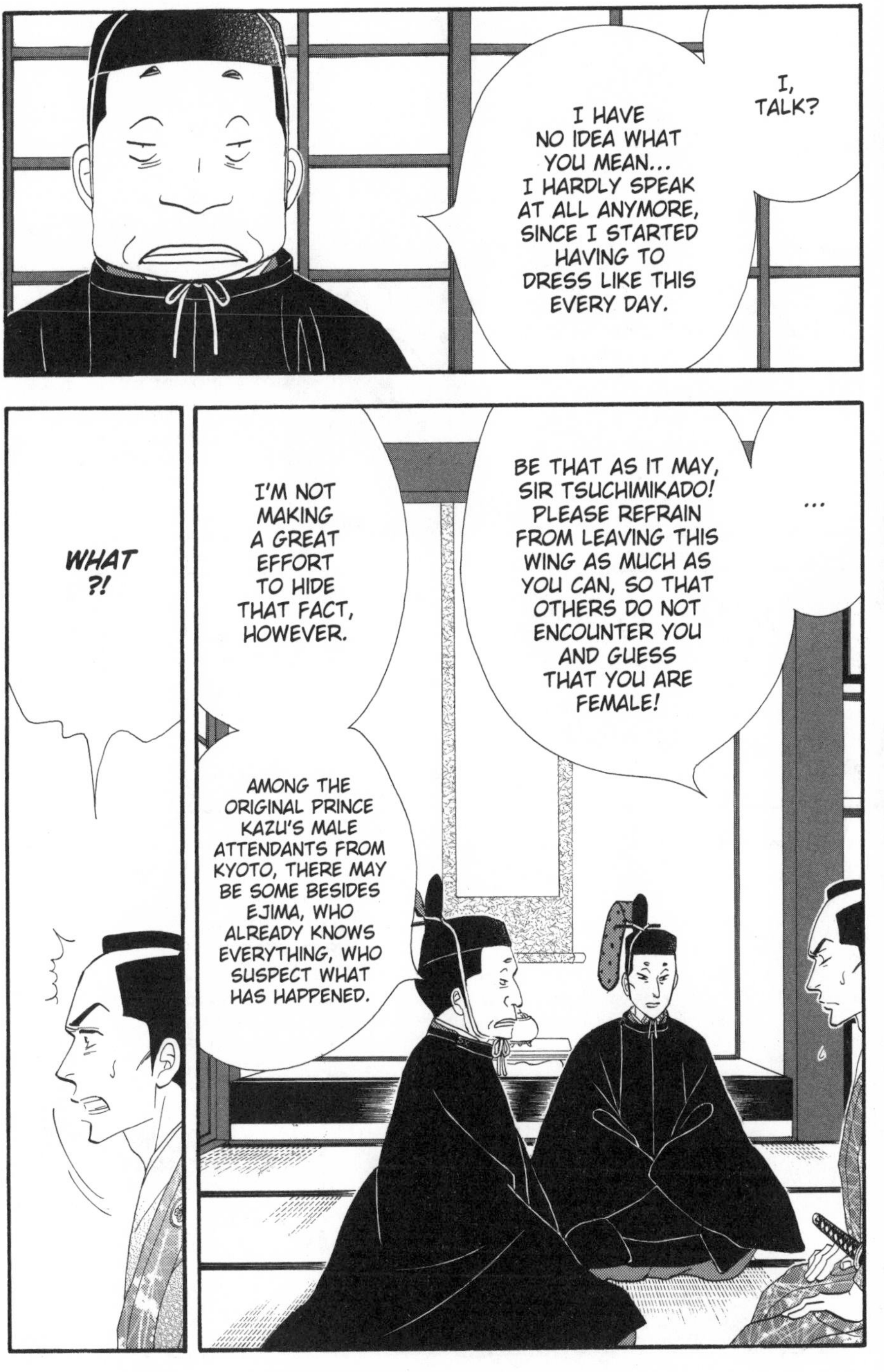
I, TALK?
I HAVE NO IDEA WHAT YOU MEAN... I HARDLY SPEAK AT ALL ANYMORE, SINCE I STARTED HAVING TO DRESS LIKE THIS EVERY DAY.
...
BE THAT AS IT MAY, SIR TSUCHIMIKADO! PLEASE REFRAIN FROM LEAVING THIS WING AS MUCH AS YOU CAN, SO THAT OTHERS DO NOT ENCOUNTER YOU AND GUESS THAT YOU ARE FEMALE!
I'M NOT MAKING A GREAT EFFORT TO HIDE THAT FACT, HOWEVER.
AMONG THE ORIGINAL PRINCE KAZU'S MALE ATTENDANTS FROM KYOTO, THERE MAY BE SOME BESIDES EJIMA, WHO ALREADY KNOWS EVERYTHING, WHO SUSPECT WHAT HAS HAPPENED.
WHAT?!

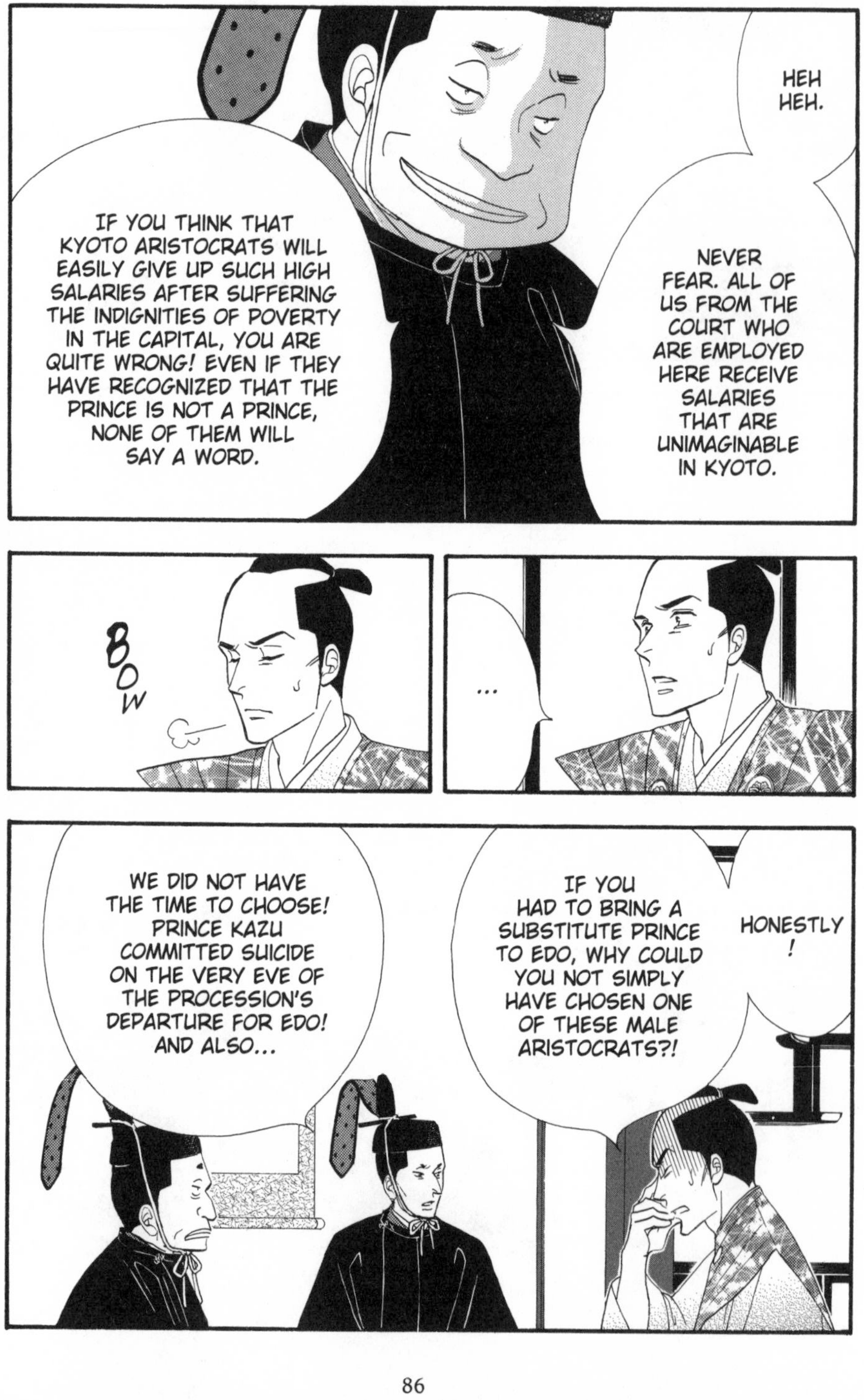
HEH HEH.
NEVER FEAR. ALL OF US FROM THE COURT WHO ARE EMPLOYED HERE RECEIVE SALARIES THAT ARE UNIMAGINABLE IN KYOTO.
IF YOU THINK THAT KYOTO ARISTOCRATS WILL EASILY GIVE UP SUCH HIGH SALARIES AFTER SUFFERING THE INDIGNITIES OF POVERTY IN THE CAPITAL, YOU ARE QUITE WRONG! EVEN IF THEY HAVE RECOGNIZED THAT THE PRINCE IS NOT A PRINCE, NONE OF THEM WILL SAY A WORD.
...
BOW
HONESTLY!
IF YOU HAD TO BRING A SUBSTITUTE PRINCE TO EDO, WHY COULD YOU NOT SIMPLY HAVE CHOSEN ONE OF THESE MALE ARISTOCRATS?!
WE DID NOT HAVE THE TIME TO CHOOSE! PRINCE KAZU COMMITTED SUICIDE ON THE VERY EVE OF THE PROCESSION'S DEPARTURE FOR EDO! AND ALSO...

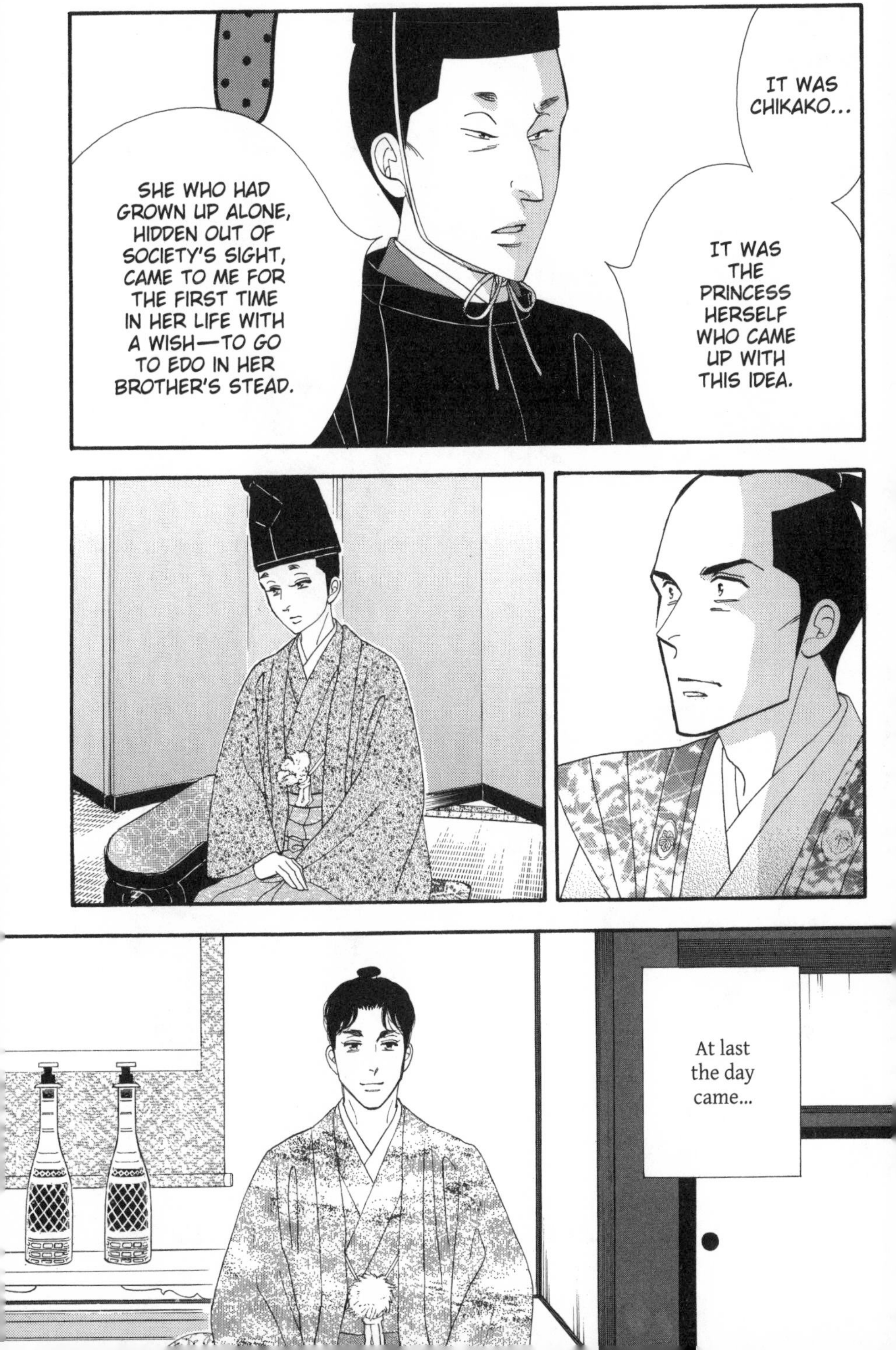
IT WAS CHIKAKO...
IT WAS THE PRINCESS HERSELF WHO CAME UP WITH THIS IDEA.
SHE WHO HAD GROWN UP ALONE, HIDDEN OUT OF SOCIETY'S SIGHT, CAME TO ME FOR THE FIRST TIME IN HER LIFE WITH A WISH—TO GO TO EDO IN HER BROTHER'S STEAD.
At last the day came...

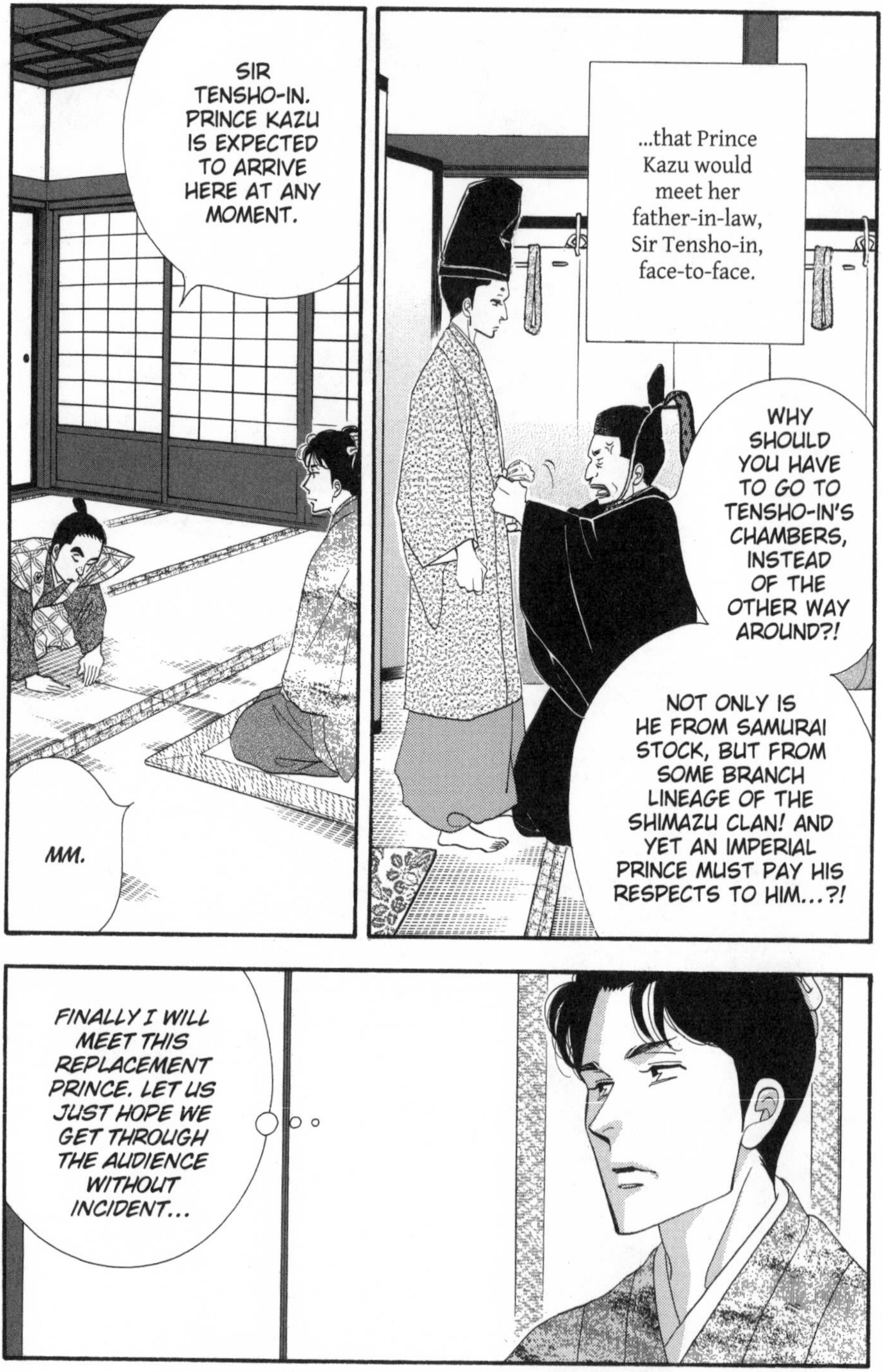

...that Prince Kazu would meet her father-in-law, Sir Tensho-in, face-to-face.
WHY SHOULD YOU HAVE TO GO TO TENSHO-IN'S CHAMBERS, INSTEAD OF THE OTHER WAY AROUND?!
NOT ONLY IS HE FROM SAMURAI STOCK, BUT FROM SOME BRANCH LINEAGE OF THE SHIMAZU CLAN! AND YET AN IMPERIAL PRINCE MUST PAY HIS RESPECTS TO HIM...?!
SIR TENSHO-IN. PRINCE KAZU IS EXPECTED TO ARRIVE HERE AT ANY MOMENT.
MM.
FINALLY I WILL MEET THIS REPLACEMENT PRINCE. LET US JUST HOPE WE GET THROUGH THE AUDIENCE WITHOUT INCIDENT...

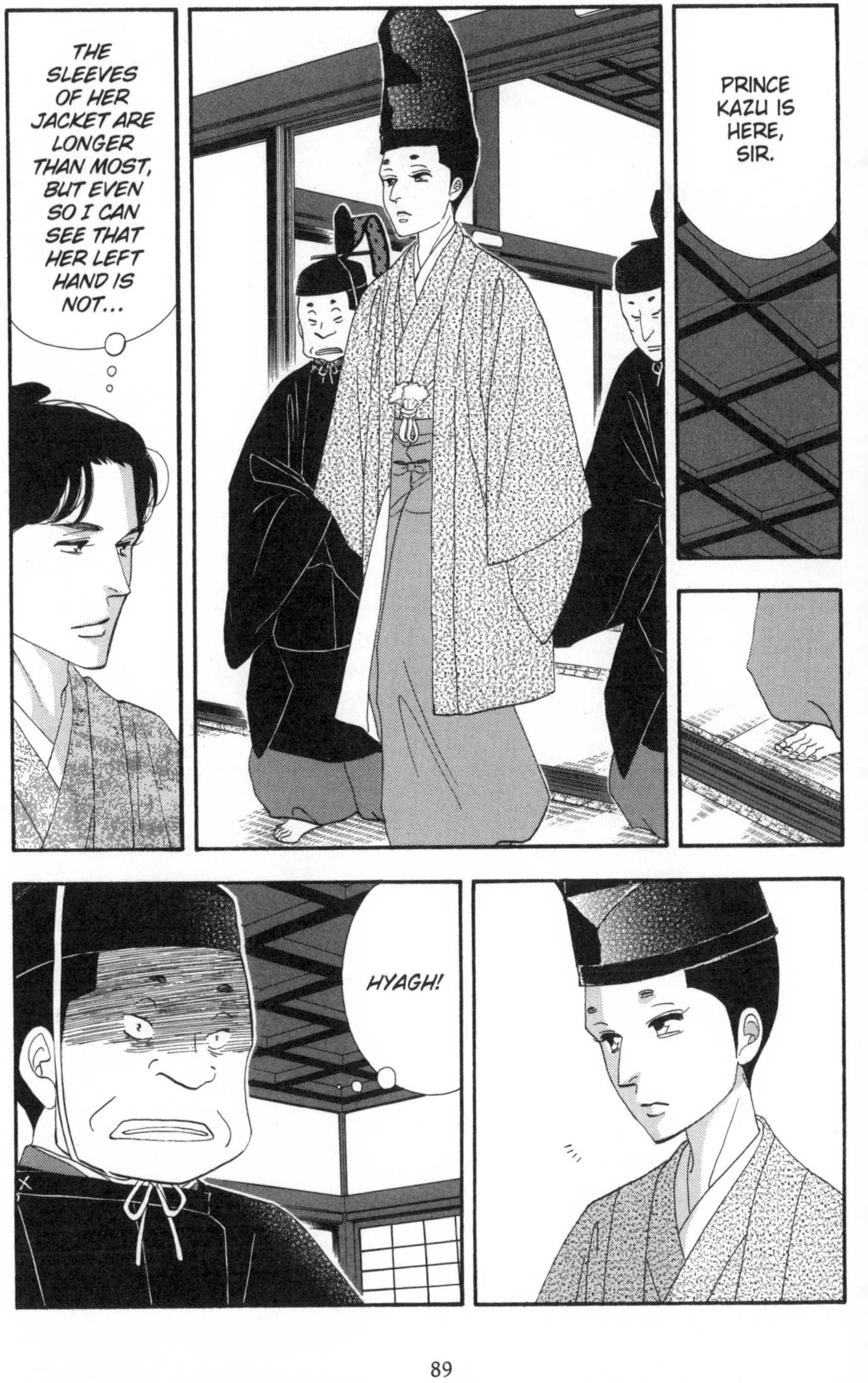
PRINCE KAZU IS HERE, SIR.
THE SLEEVES OF HER JACKET ARE LONGER THAN MOST, BUT EVEN SO I CAN SEE THAT HER LEFT HAND IS NOT...
HYAGH!

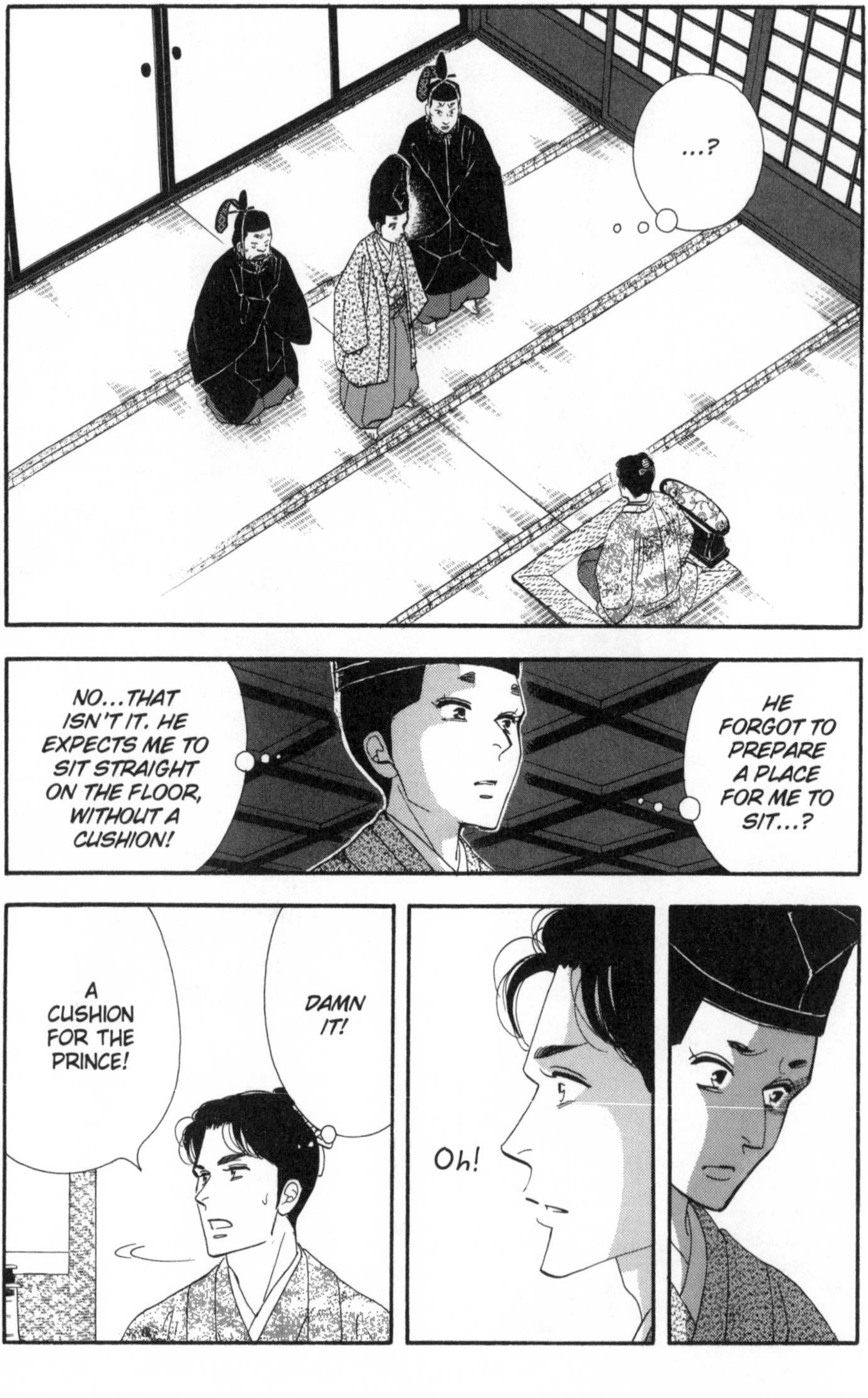
...?
HE FORGOT TO PREPARE A PLACE FOR ME TO SIT...?
NO...THAT ISN'T IT. HE EXPECTS ME TO SIT STRAIGHT ON THE FLOOR, WITHOUT A CUSHION!
Oh!
DAMN IT!
A CUSHION FOR THE PRINCE!

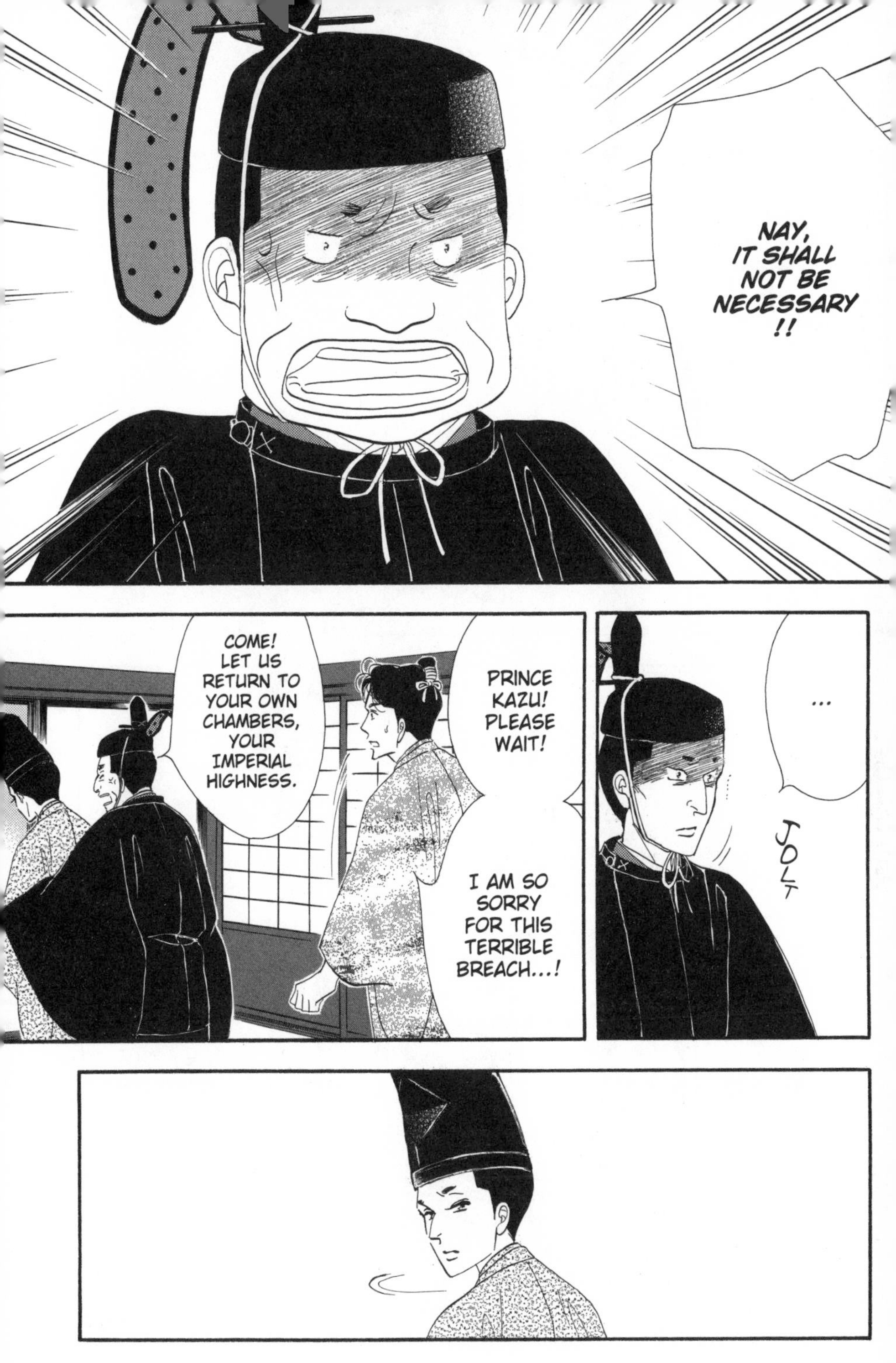
NAY, IT SHALL NOT BE NECESSARY!!
...
JOLT
PRINCE KAZU! PLEASE WAIT!
COME! LET US RETURN TO YOUR OWN CHAMBERS, YOUR IMPERIAL HIGHNESS.
I AM SO SORRY FOR THIS TERRIBLE BREACH...!

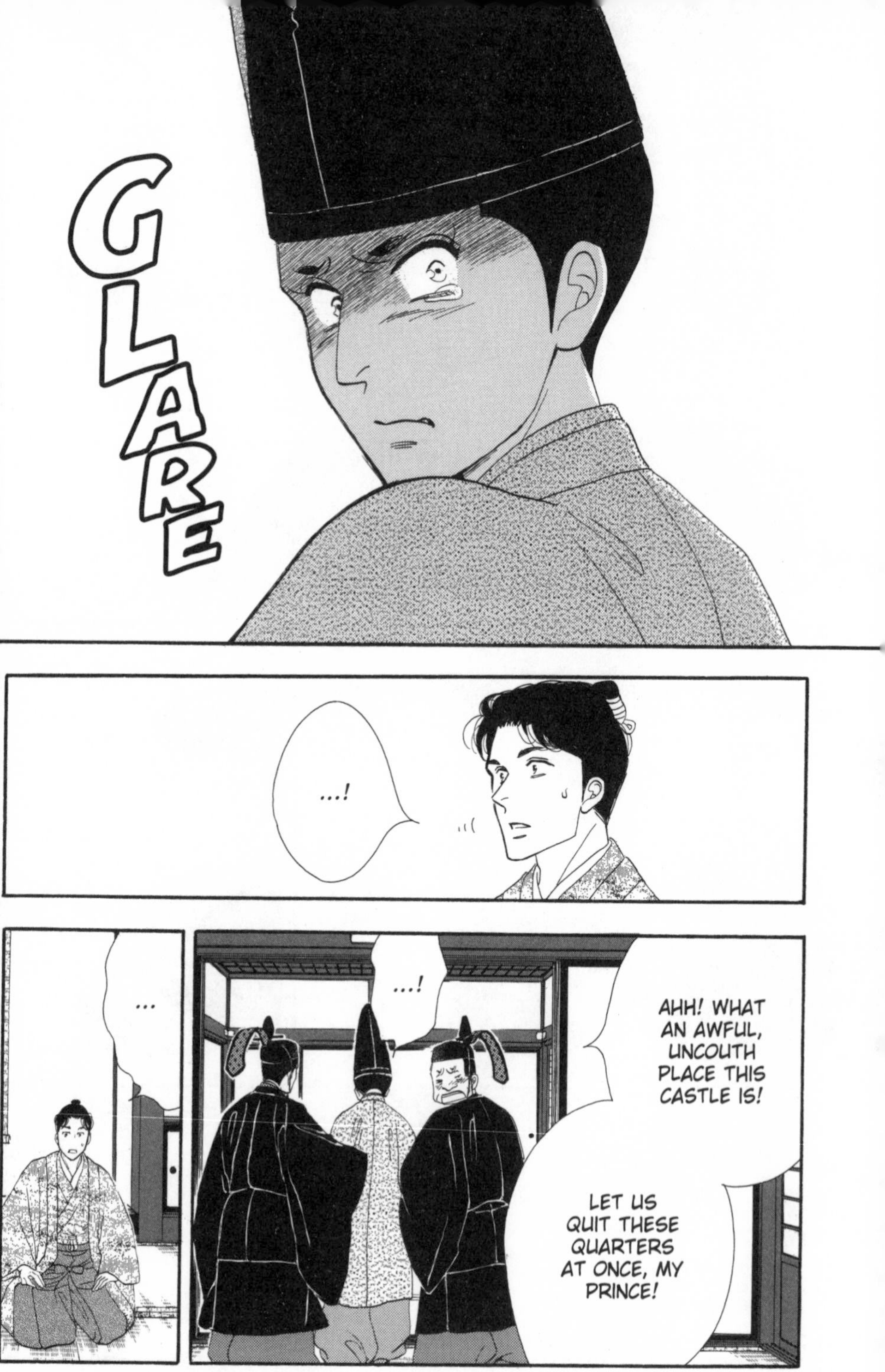
GLARE
...!
AHH! WHAT AN AWFUL, UNCOUTH PLACE THIS CASTLE IS!
LET US QUIT THESE QUARTERS AT ONCE, MY PRINCE!
...!
...

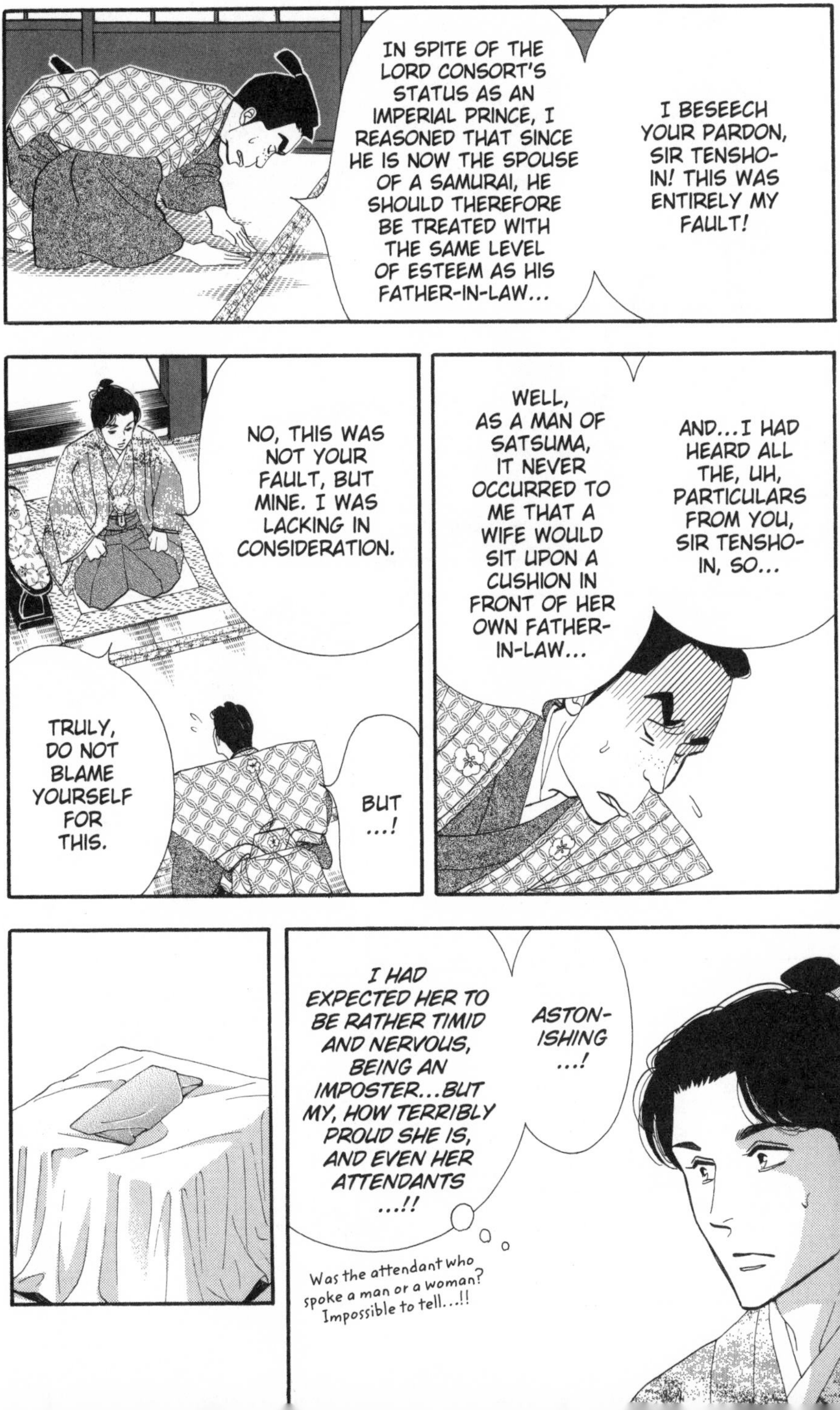
I BESEECH YOUR PARDON, SIR TENSHO-IN! THIS WAS ENTIRELY MY FAULT!
IN SPITE OF THE LORD CONSORT'S STATUS AS AN IMPERIAL PRINCE, I REASONED THAT SINCE HE IS NOW THE SPOUSE OF A SAMURAI, HE SHOULD THEREFORE BE TREATED WITH THE SAME LEVEL OF ESTEEM AS HIS FATHER-IN-LAW...
WELL, AS A MAN OF SATSUMA, IT NEVER OCCURRED TO ME THAT A WIFE WOULD SIT UPON A CUSHION IN FRONT OF HER OWN FATHER-IN-LAW...
AND...I HAD HEARD ALL THE, UH, PARTICULARS FROM YOU, SIR TENSHO-IN, SO...
NO, THIS WAS NOT YOUR FAULT, BUT MINE. I WAS LACKING IN CONSIDERATION.
BUT ...!
TRULY, DO NOT BLAME YOURSELF FOR THIS.
ASTON-ISHING ...!
I HAD EXPECTED HER TO BE RATHER TIMID AND NERVOUS, BEING AN IMPOSTER...BUT MY, HOW TERRIBLY PROUD SHE IS, AND EVEN HER ATTENDANTS ...!!
Was the attendant who spoke a man or a woman? Impossible to tell...!!

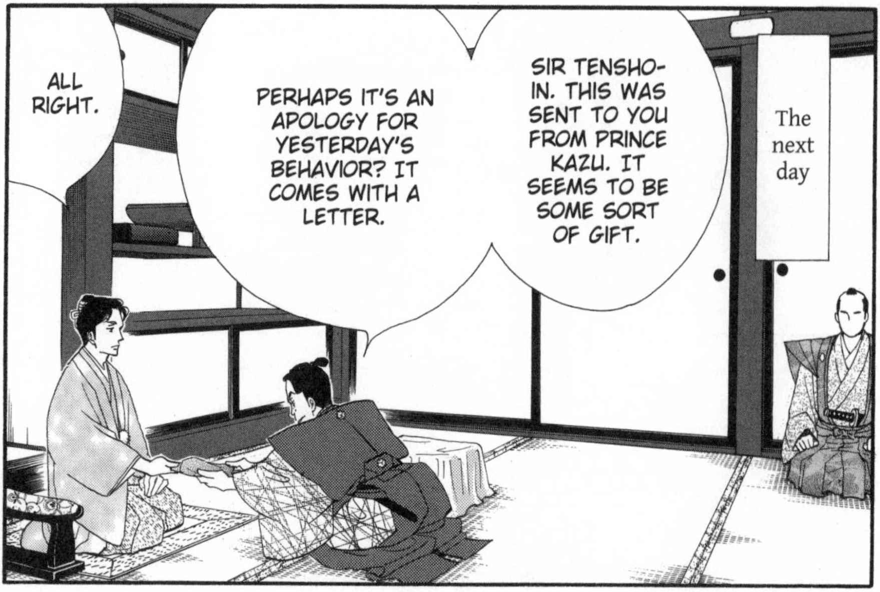
The next day
SIR TENSHO-IN. THIS WAS SENT TO YOU FROM PRINCE KAZU. IT SEEMS TO BE SOME SORT OF GIFT.
PERHAPS IT'S AN APOLOGY FOR YESTERDAY'S BEHAVIOR? IT COMES WITH A LETTER.
ALL RIGHT.

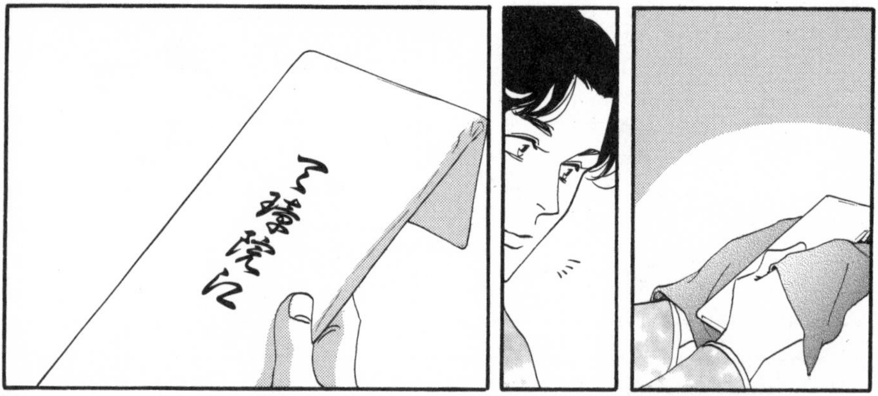

Letter: For Tensho-in

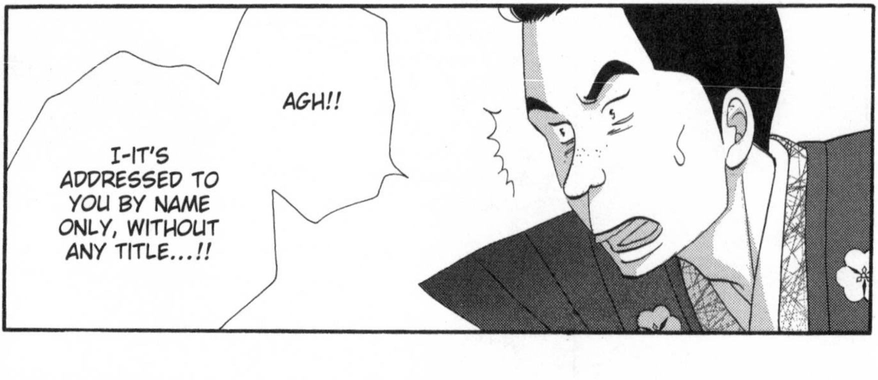
AGH!!
I-IT'S ADDRESSED TO YOU BY NAME ONLY, WITHOUT ANY TITLE...!!

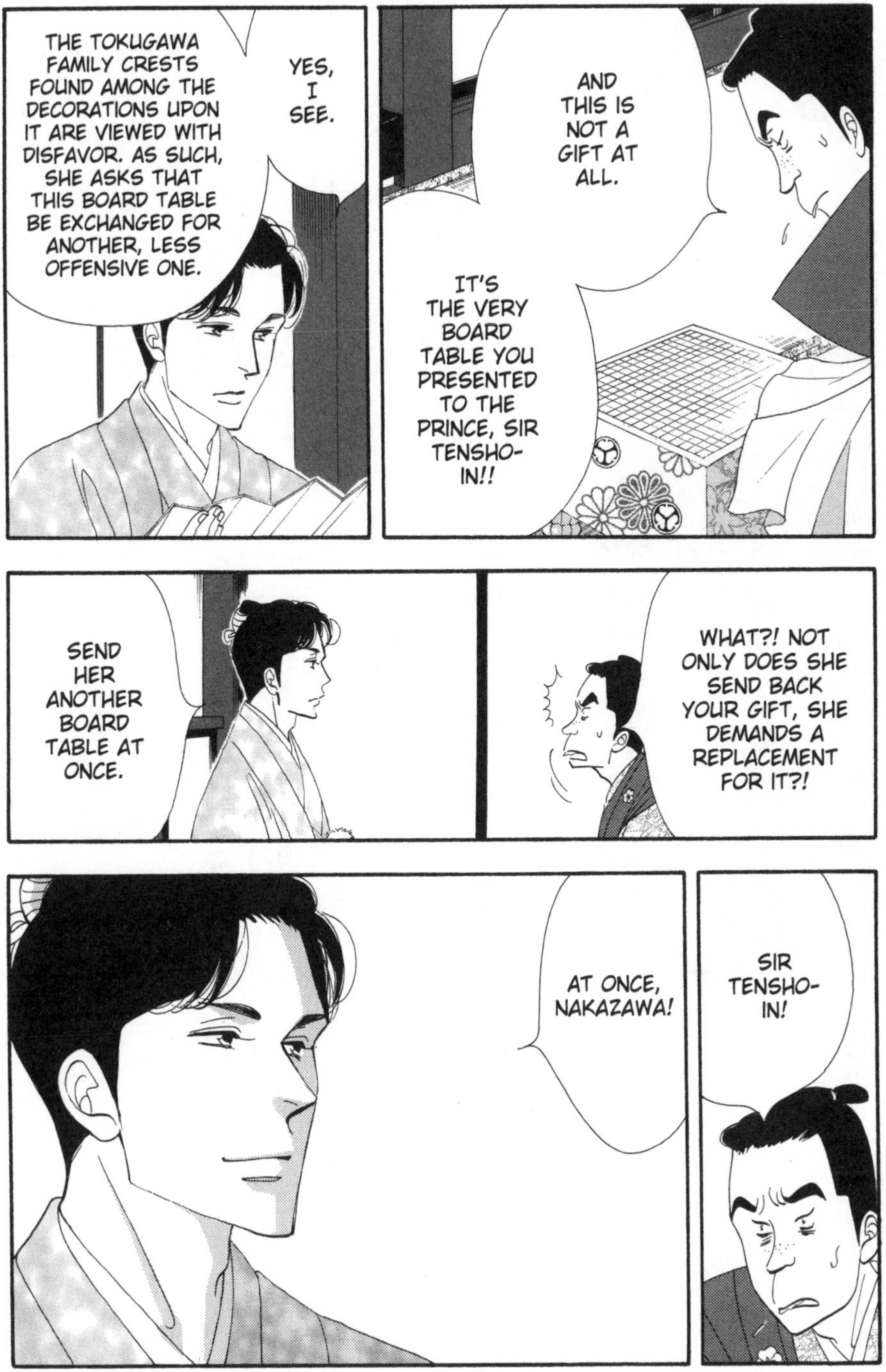
AND THIS IS NOT A GIFT AT ALL.
IT'S THE VERY BOARD TABLE YOU PRESENTED TO THE PRINCE, SIR TENSHO-IN!!
YES, I SEE.
THE TOKUGAWA FAMILY CRESTS FOUND AMONG THE DECORATIONS UPON IT ARE VIEWED WITH DISFAVOR. AS SUCH, SHE ASKS THAT THIS BOARD TABLE BE EXCHANGED FOR ANOTHER, LESS OFFENSIVE ONE.
WHAT?! NOT ONLY DOES SHE SEND BACK YOUR GIFT, SHE DEMANDS A REPLACEMENT FOR IT?!
SEND HER ANOTHER BOARD TABLE AT ONCE.
SIR TENSHO-IN!
AT ONCE, NAKAZAWA!

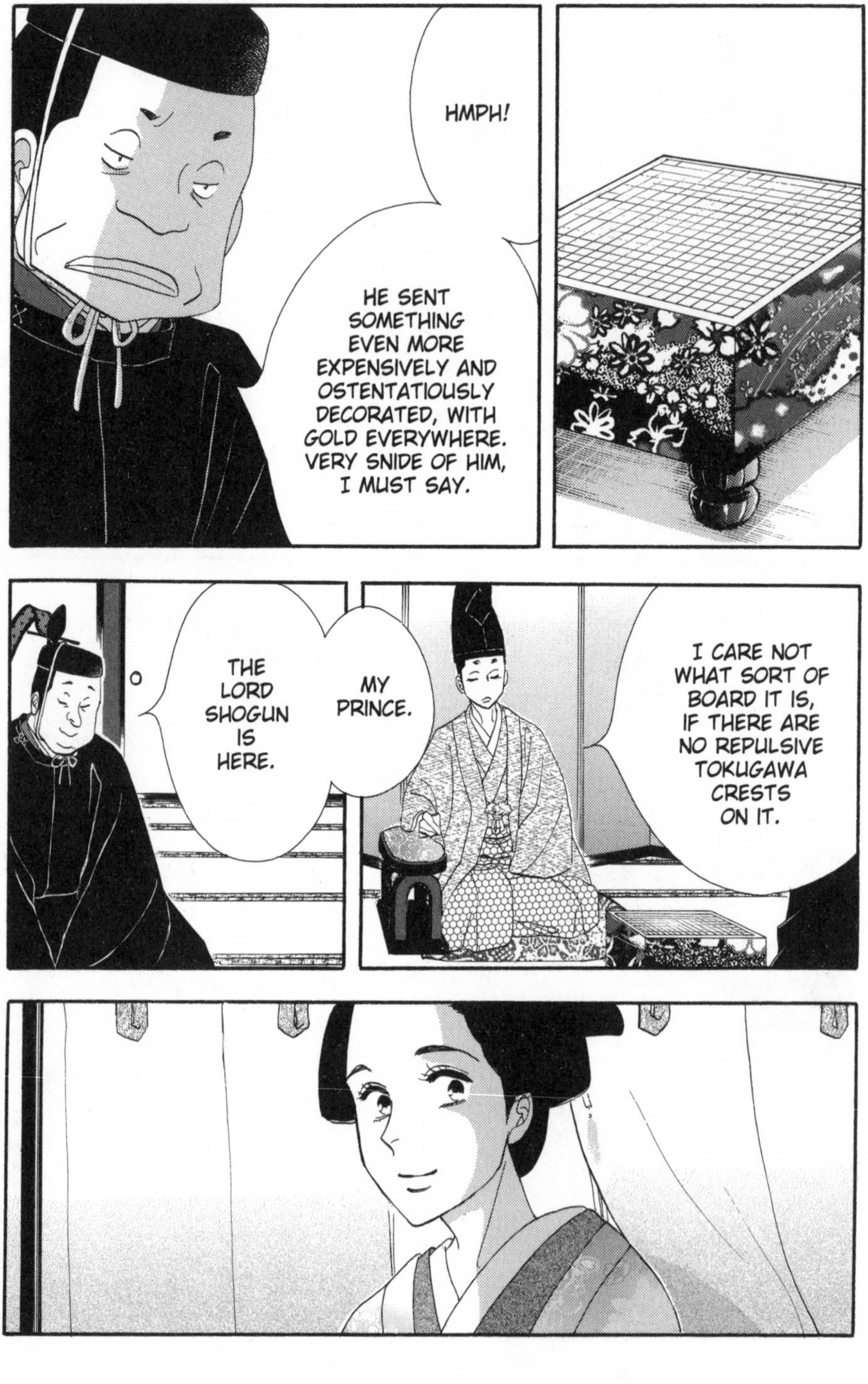
HMPH!
HE SENT SOMETHING EVEN MORE EXPENSIVELY AND OSTENTATIOUSLY DECORATED, WITH GOLD EVERYWHERE. VERY SNIDE OF HIM, I MUST SAY.
I CARE NOT WHAT SORT OF BOARD IT IS, IF THERE ARE NO REPULSIVE TOKUGAWA CRESTS ON IT.
MY PRINCE.
THE LORD SHOGUN IS HERE.

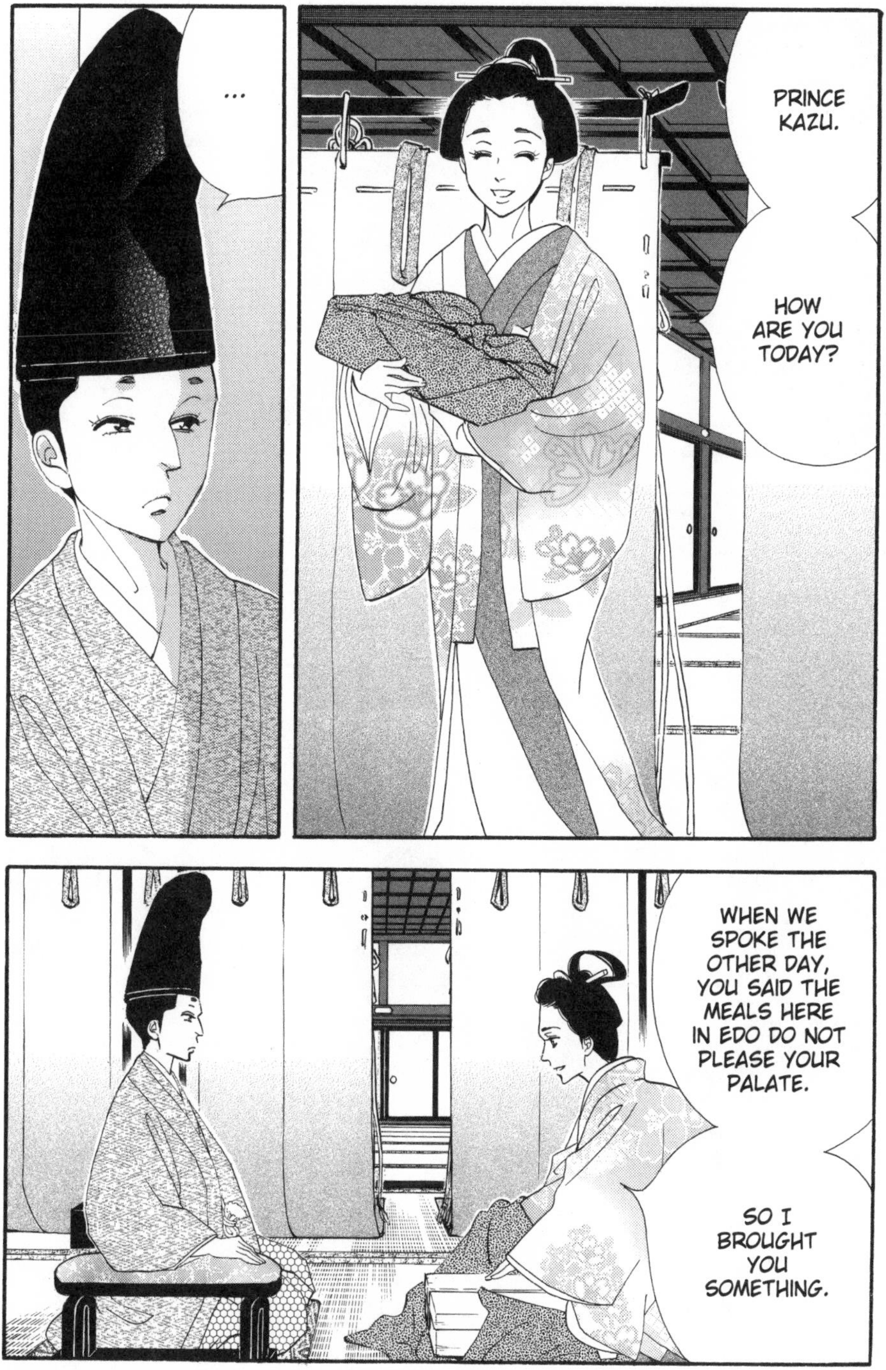
PRINCE KAZU.
HOW ARE YOU TODAY?
...
WHEN WE SPOKE THE OTHER DAY, YOU SAID THE MEALS HERE IN EDO DO NOT PLEASE YOUR PALATE.
SO I BROUGHT YOU SOMETHING.

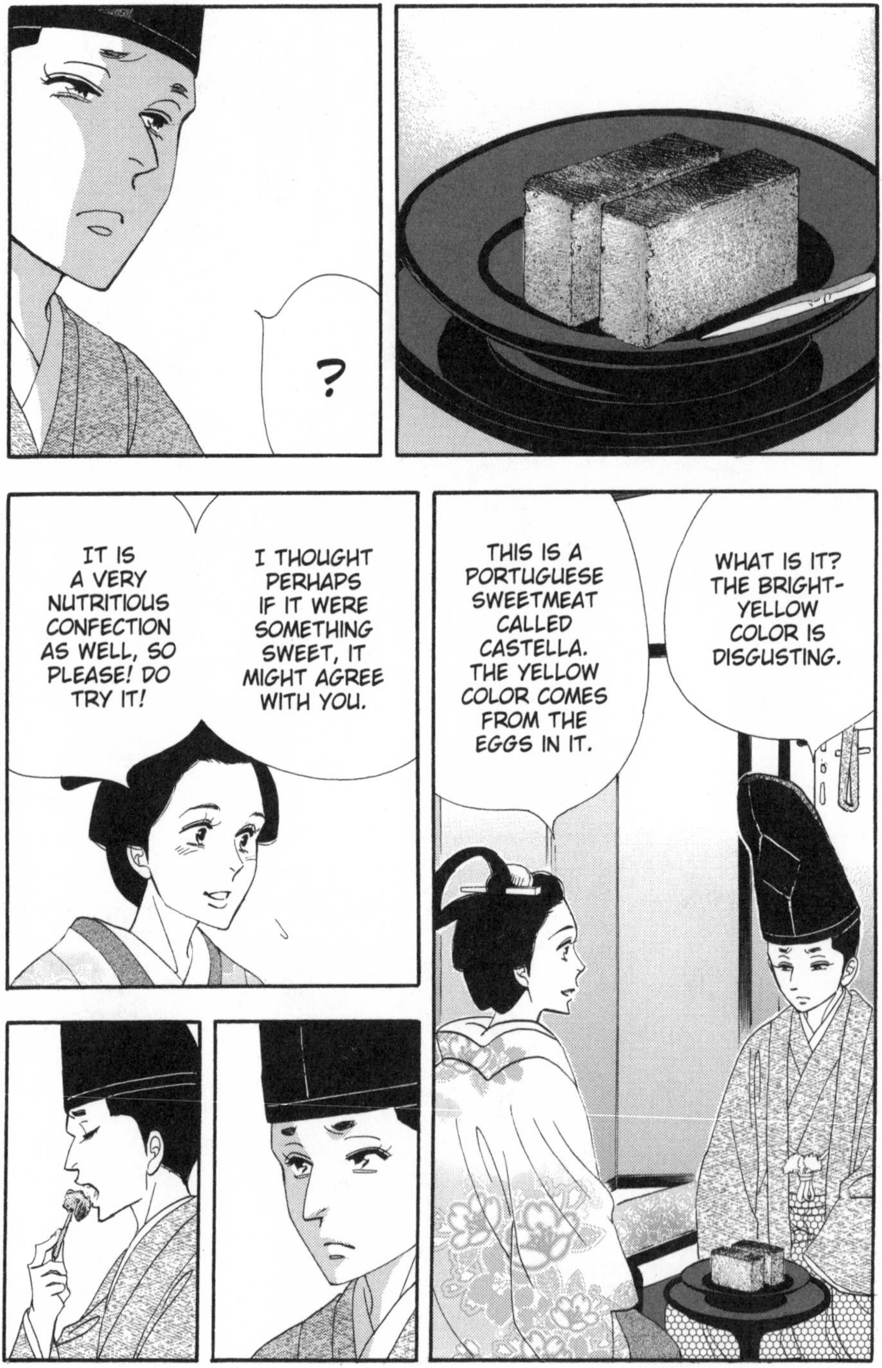
?
WHAT IS IT? THE BRIGHT-YELLOW COLOR IS DISGUSTING.
THIS IS A PORTUGUESE SWEETMEAT CALLED CASTELLA. THE YELLOW COLOR COMES FROM THE EGGS IN IT.
I THOUGHT PERHAPS IF IT WERE SOMETHING SWEET, IT MIGHT AGREE WITH YOU.
IT IS A VERY NUTRITIOUS CONFECTION AS WELL, SO PLEASE! DO TRY IT!

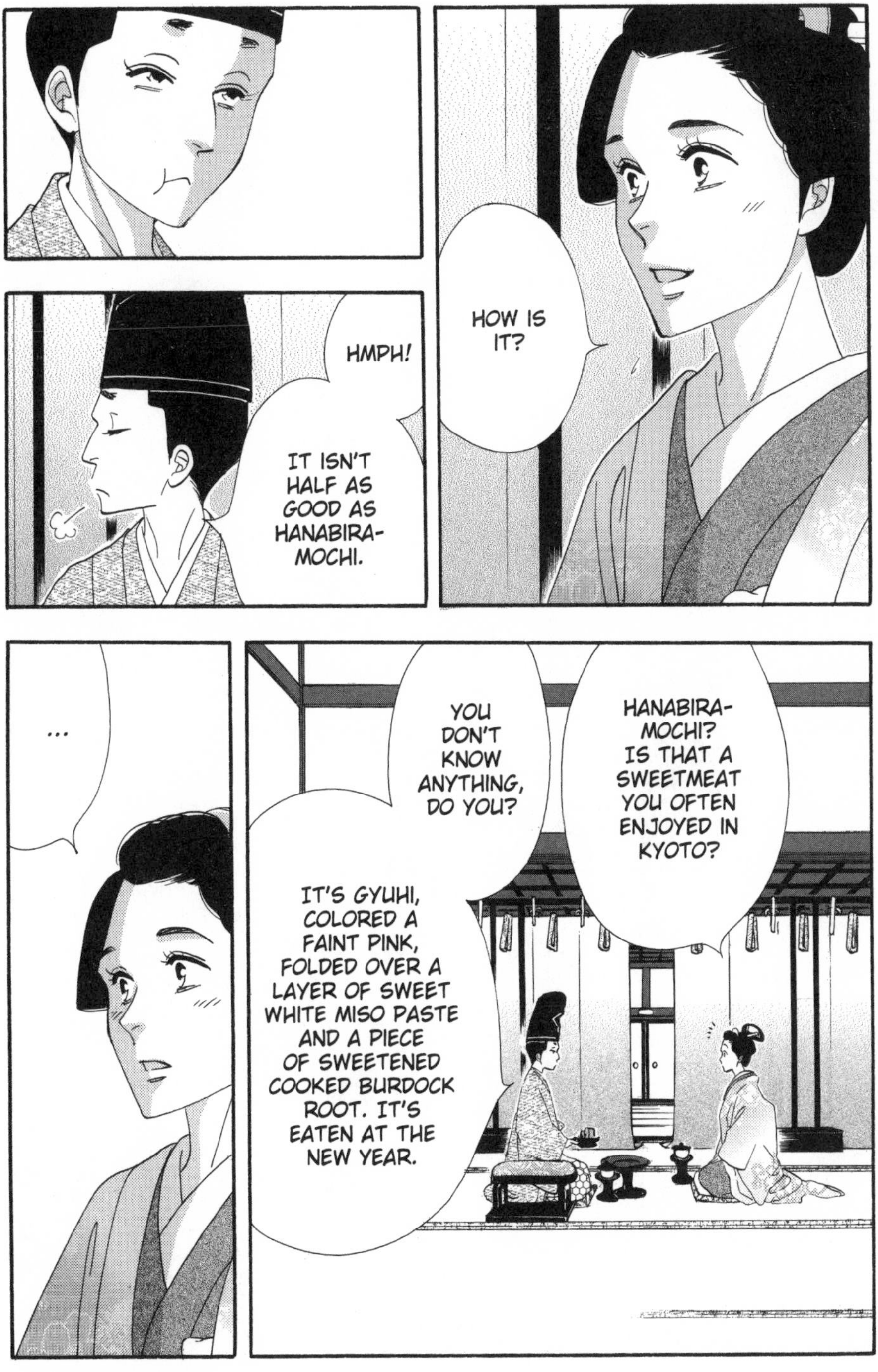
HOW IS IT?
HMPH!
IT ISN'T HALF AS GOOD AS HANABIRA-MOCHI.
HANABIRA-MOCHI? IS THAT A SWEETMEAT YOU OFTEN ENJOYED IN KYOTO?
YOU DON'T KNOW ANYTHING, DO YOU?
IT'S GYUHI, COLORED A FAINT PINK, FOLDED OVER A LAYER OF SWEET WHITE MISO PASTE AND A PIECE OF SWEETENED COOKED BURDOCK ROOT. IT'S EATEN AT THE NEW YEAR.
...

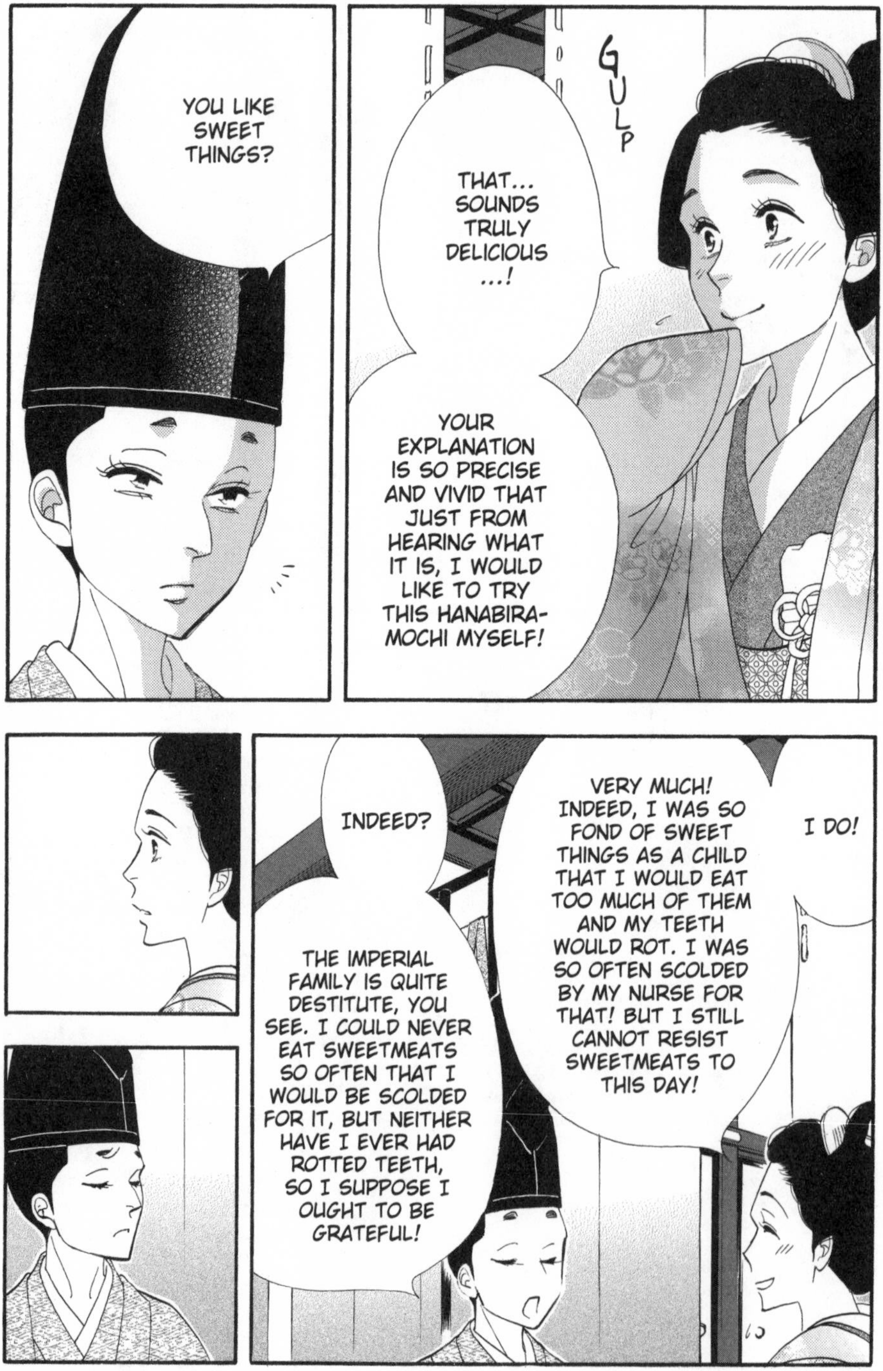
GULP
THAT... SOUNDS TRULY DELICIOUS ...!
YOUR EXPLANATION IS SO PRECISE AND VIVID THAT JUST FROM HEARING WHAT IT IS, I WOULD LIKE TO TRY THIS HANABIRA-MOCHI MYSELF!
YOU LIKE SWEET THINGS?
I DO!
VERY MUCH! INDEED, I WAS SO FOND OF SWEET THINGS AS A CHILD THAT I WOULD EAT TOO MUCH OF THEM AND MY TEETH WOULD ROT. I WAS SO OFTEN SCOLDED BY MY NURSE FOR THAT! BUT I STILL CANNOT RESIST SWEETMEATS TO THIS DAY!
INDEED?
THE IMPERIAL FAMILY IS QUITE DESTITUTE, YOU SEE. I COULD NEVER EAT SWEETMEATS SO OFTEN THAT I WOULD BE SCOLDED FOR IT, BUT NEITHER HAVE I EVER HAD ROTTED TEETH, SO I SUPPOSE I OUGHT TO BE GRATEFUL!

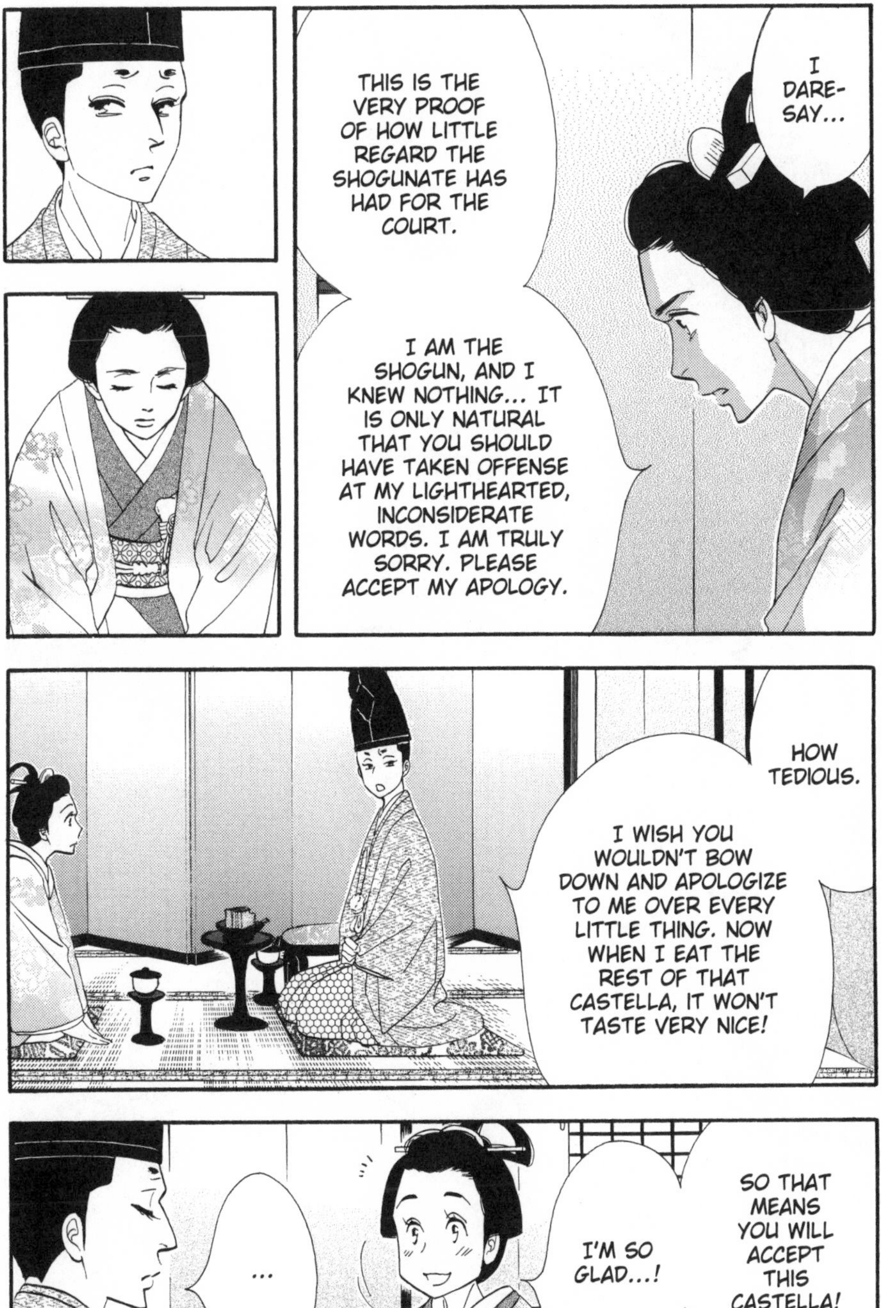
I DARE-SAY...
THIS IS THE VERY PROOF OF HOW LITTLE REGARD THE SHOGUNATE HAS HAD FOR THE COURT.
I AM THE SHOGUN, AND I KNEW NOTHING... IT IS ONLY NATURAL THAT YOU SHOULD HAVE TAKEN OFFENSE AT MY LIGHTHEARTED, INCONSIDERATE WORDS. I AM TRULY SORRY. PLEASE ACCEPT MY APOLOGY.
HOW TEDIOUS.
I WISH YOU WOULDN'T BOW DOWN AND APOLOGIZE TO ME OVER EVERY LITTLE THING. NOW WHEN I EAT THE REST OF THAT CASTELLA, IT WON'T TASTE VERY NICE!
SO THAT MEANS YOU WILL ACCEPT THIS CASTELLA!
I'M SO GLAD...!
...

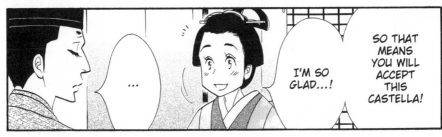

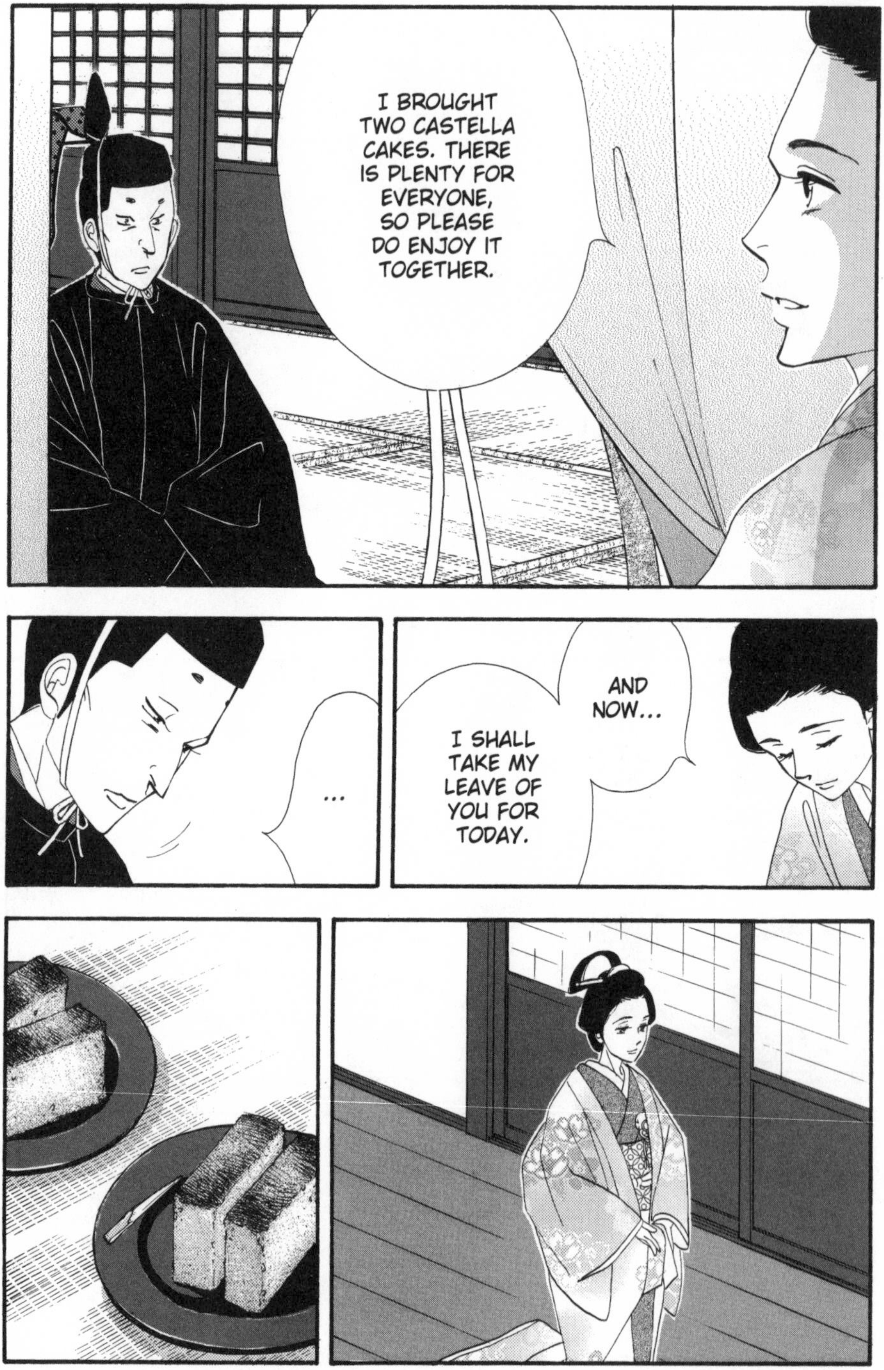
I BROUGHT TWO CASTELLA CAKES. THERE IS PLENTY FOR EVERYONE, SO PLEASE DO ENJOY IT TOGETHER.
AND NOW...
I SHALL TAKE MY LEAVE OF YOU FOR TODAY.
...

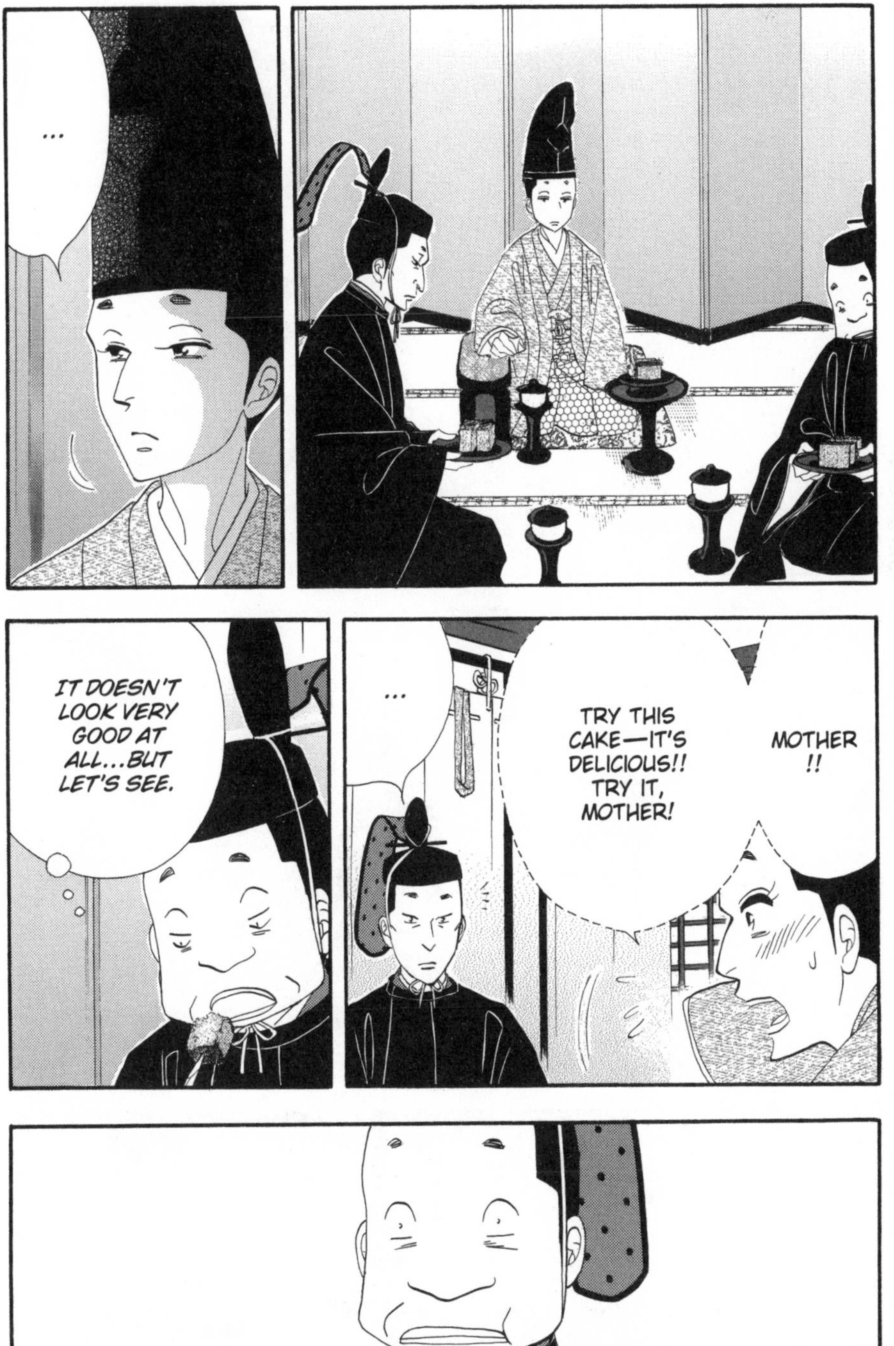
...
MOTHER !!
TRY THIS CAKE—IT'S DELICIOUS!! TRY IT, MOTHER!
...
IT DOESN'T LOOK VERY GOOD AT ALL...BUT LET'S SEE.

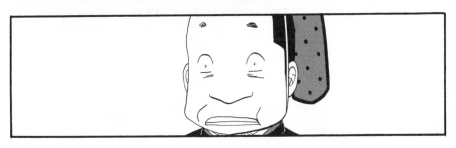

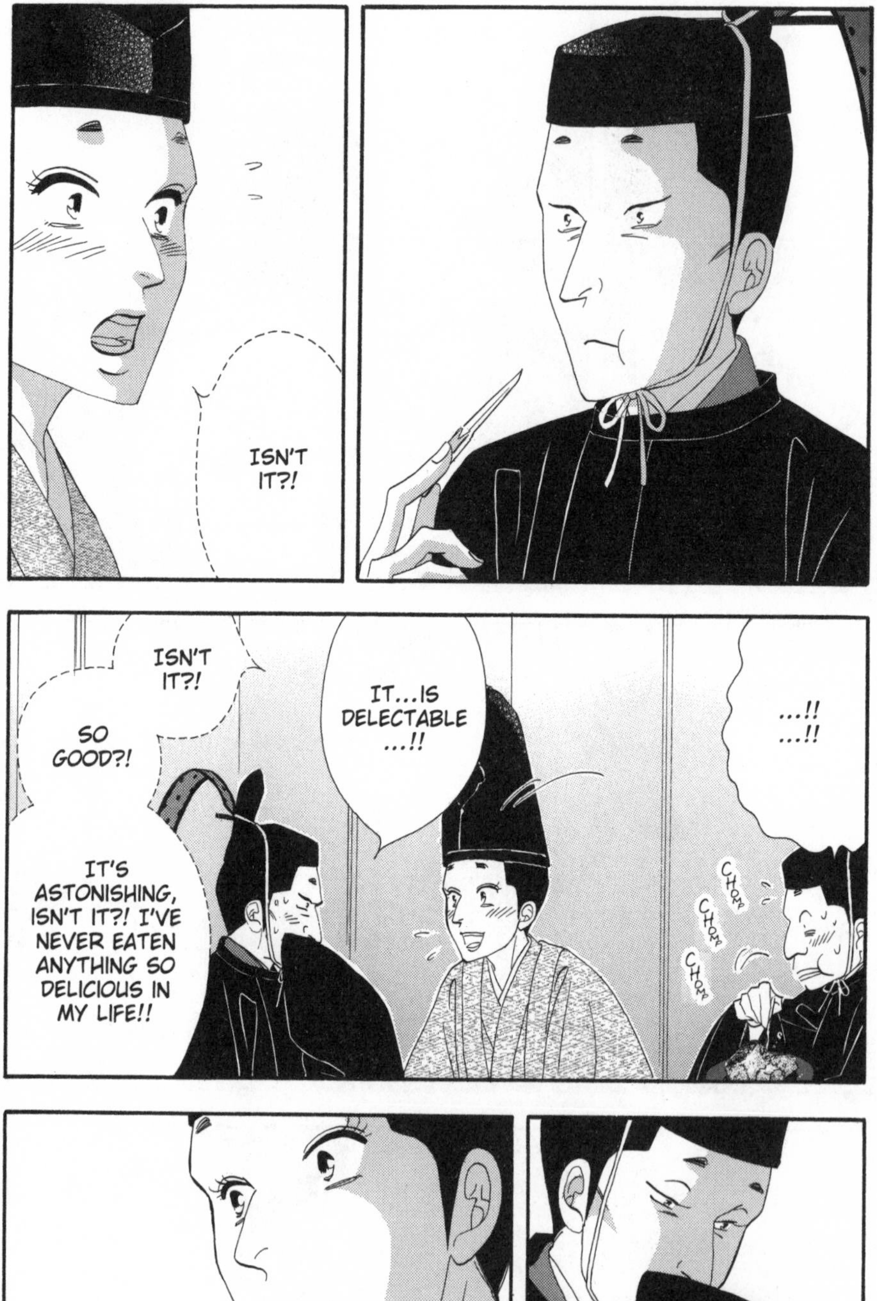
ISN'T IT?!
...!! ...!!
CHOMP CHOMP CHOMP
IT...IS DELECTABLE ...!!
ISN'T IT?!
SO GOOD?!
IT'S ASTONISHING, ISN'T IT?! I'VE NEVER EATEN ANYTHING SO DELICIOUS IN MY LIFE!!

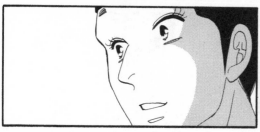

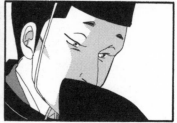

HOW I WISH THE REAL PRINCE KAZU...

...COULD HAVE PARTAKEN OF THIS...

...

PRINCE KAZU...

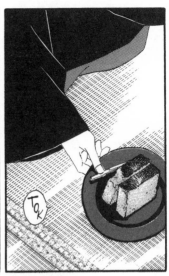

TOK

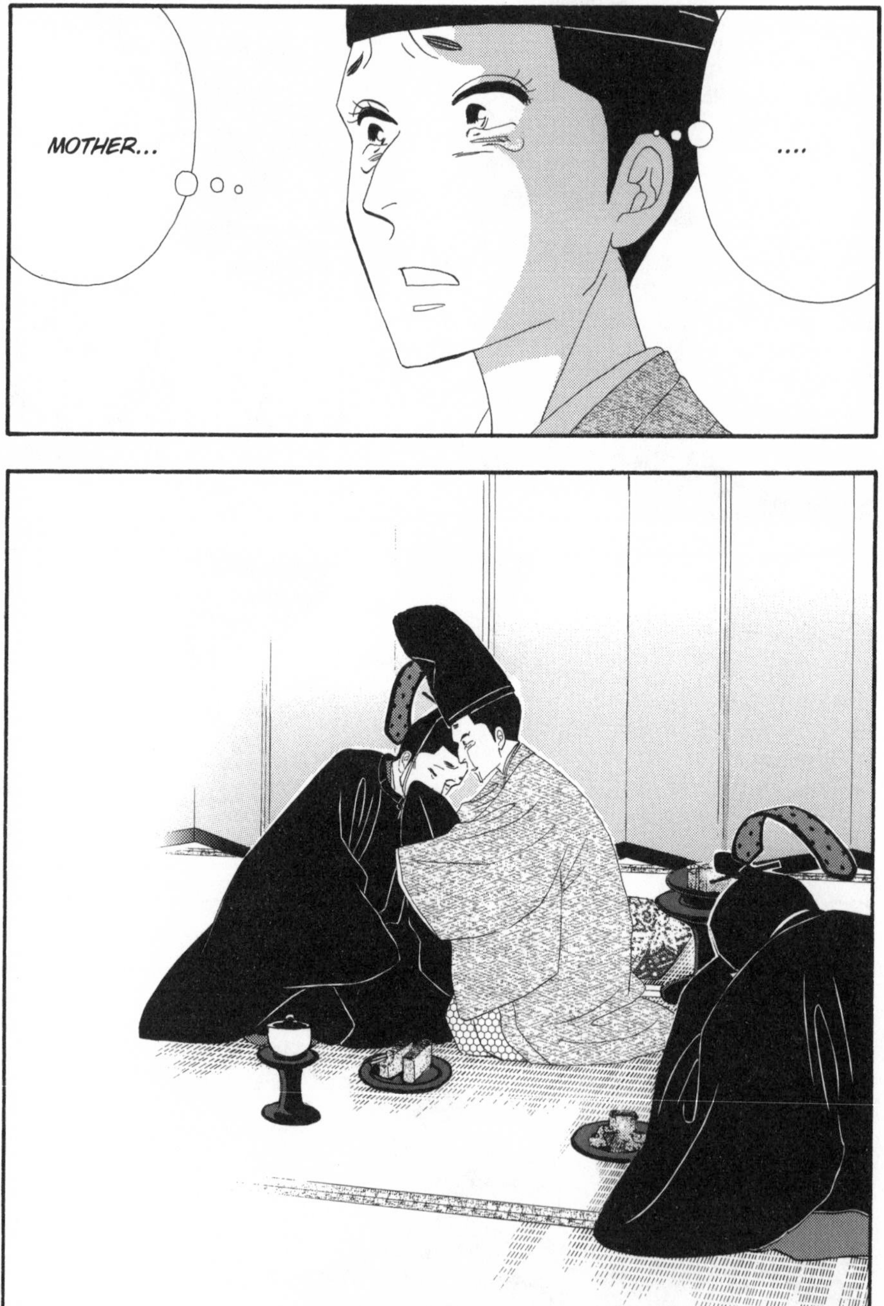
....
MOTHER...

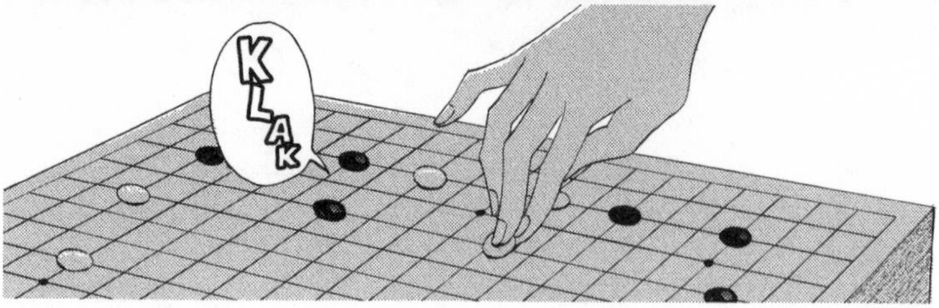
KLAK

Ōoku

THE INNER CHAMBERS

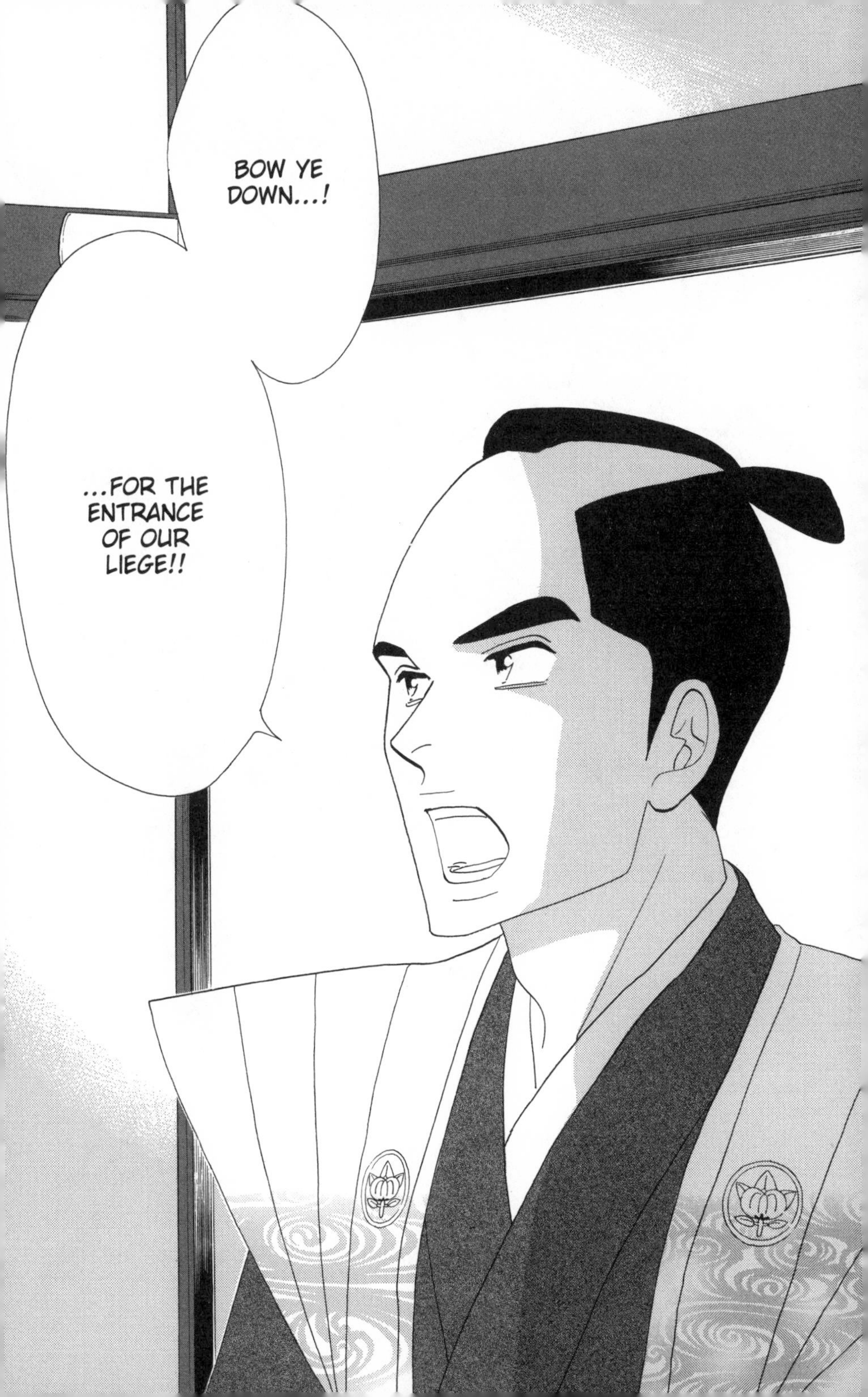
BOW YE DOWN...!
...FOR THE ENTRANCE OF OUR LIEGE!!

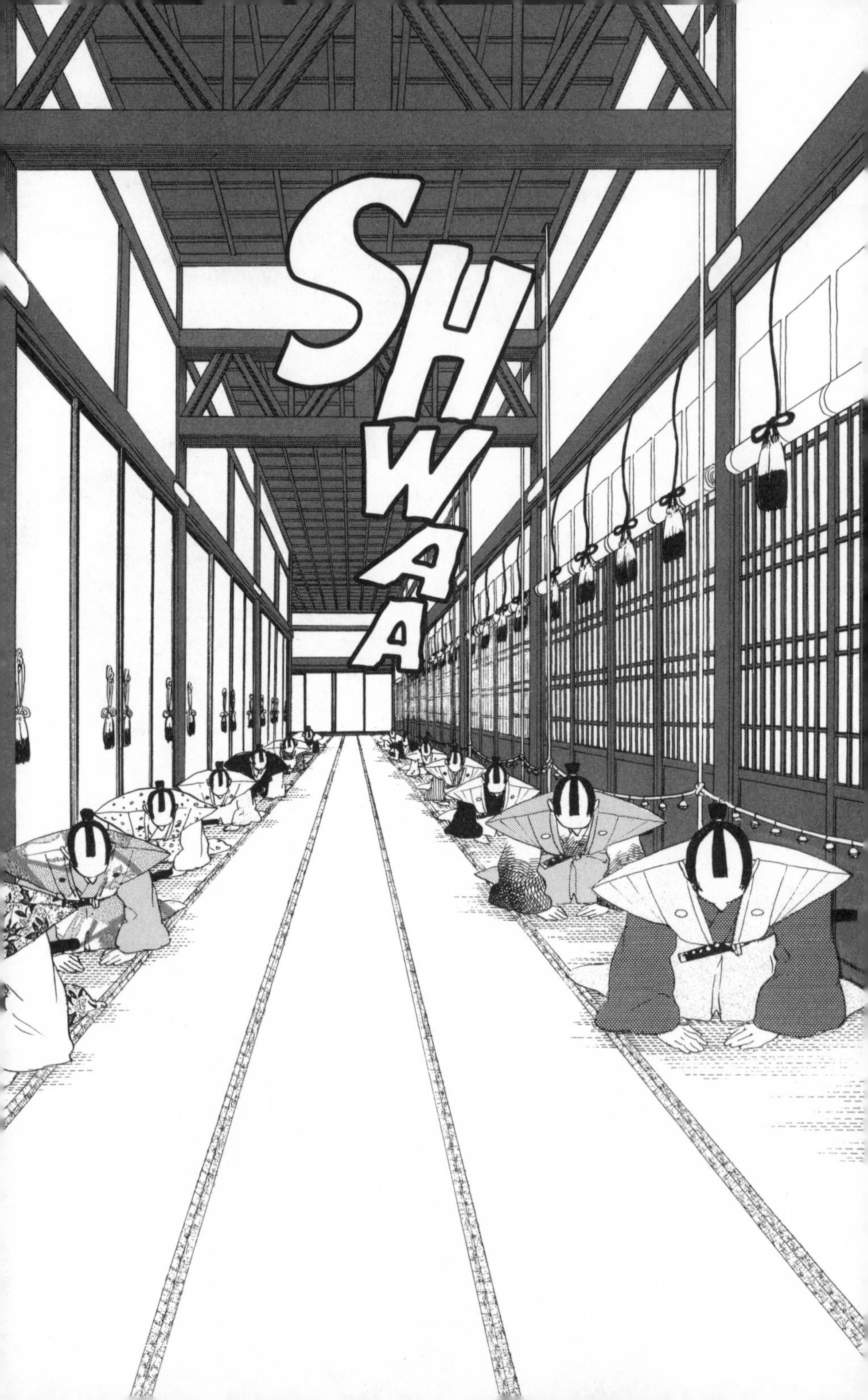
SHWAA

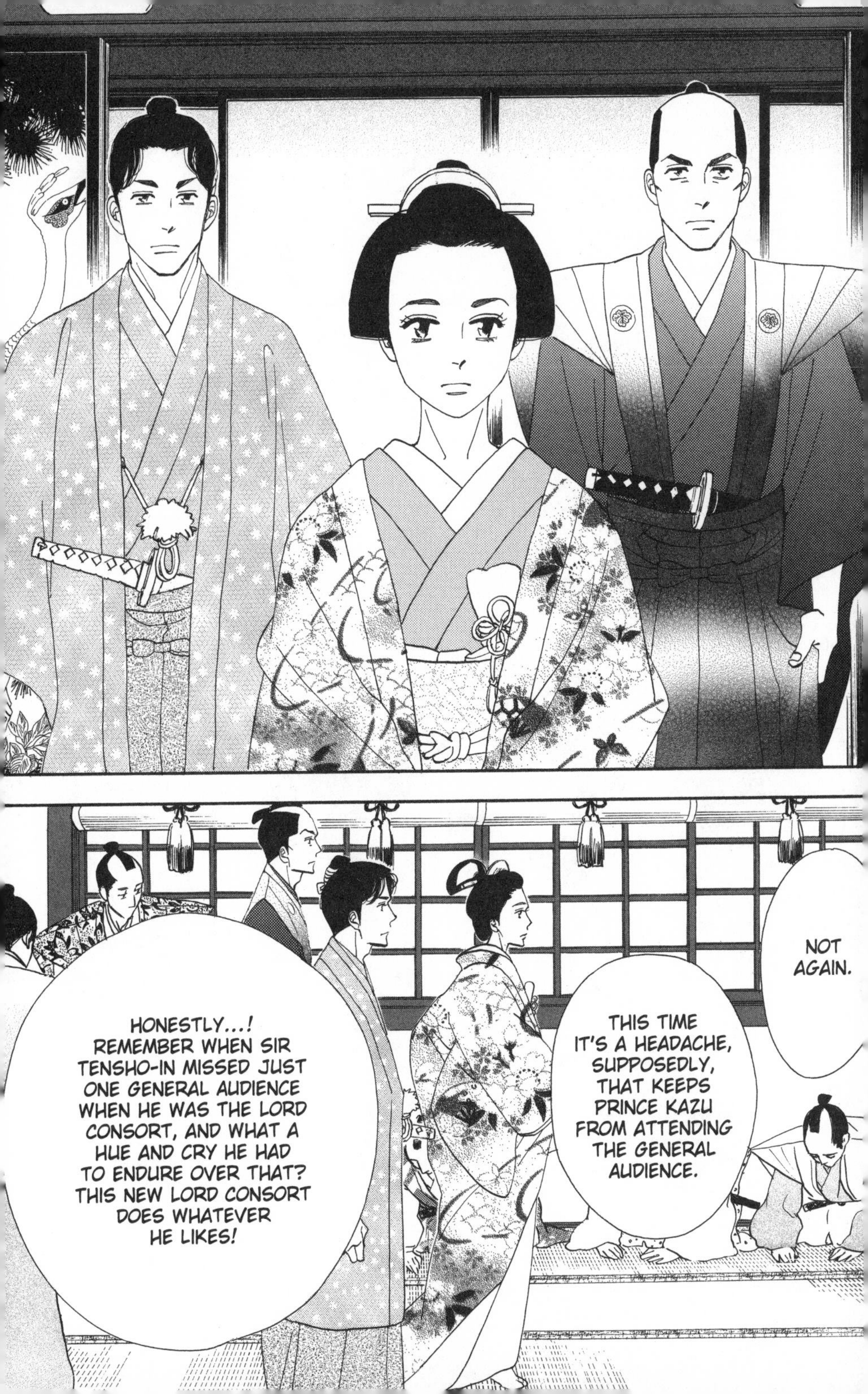
NOT AGAIN.
THIS TIME IT'S A HEADACHE, SUPPOSEDLY, THAT KEEPS PRINCE KAZU FROM ATTENDING THE GENERAL AUDIENCE.
HONESTLY...! REMEMBER WHEN SIR TENSHO-IN MISSED JUST ONE GENERAL AUDIENCE WHEN HE WAS THE LORD CONSORT, AND WHAT A HUE AND CRY HE HAD TO ENDURE OVER THAT? THIS NEW LORD CONSORT DOES WHATEVER HE LIKES!

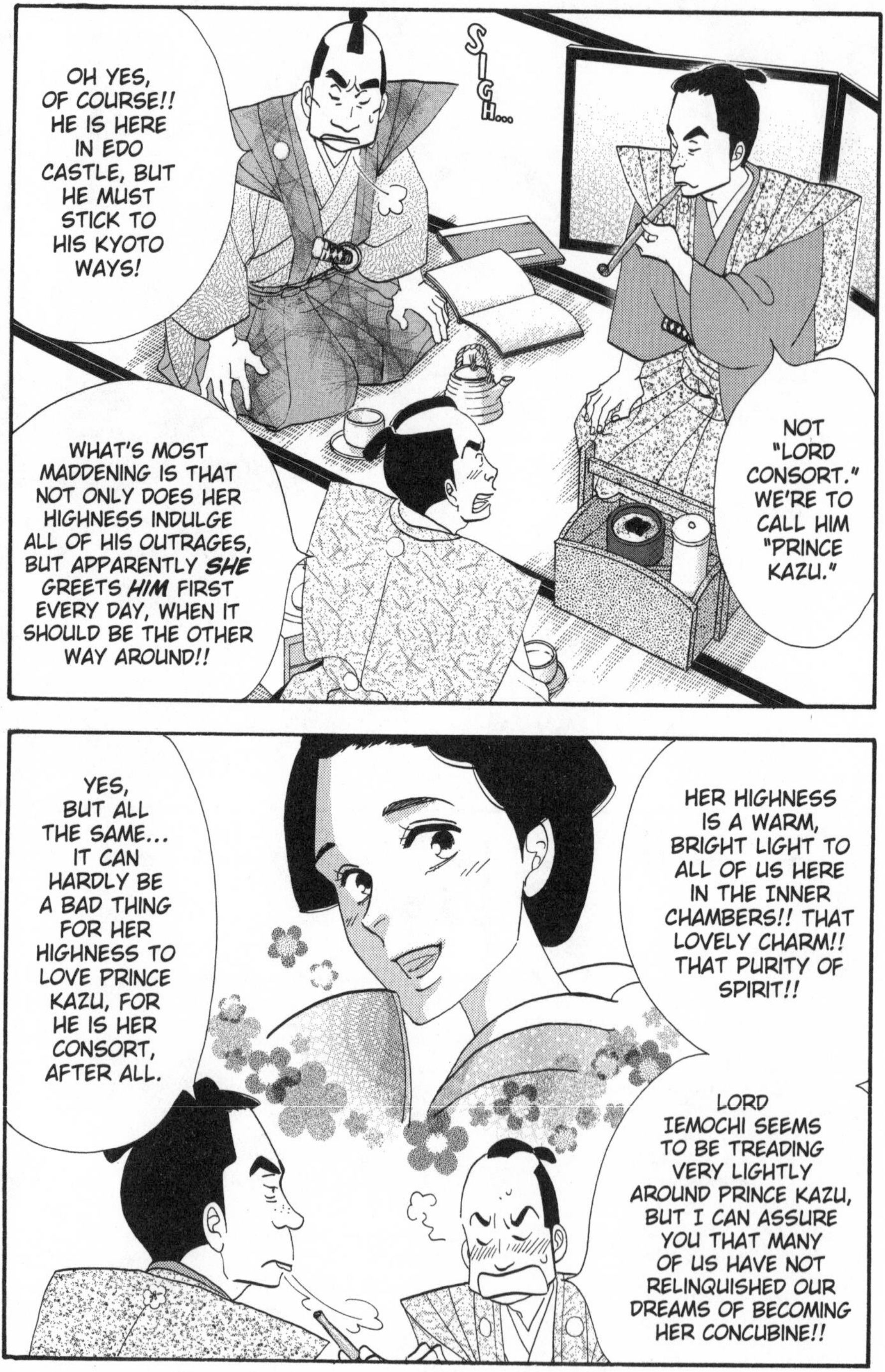
OH YES, OF COURSE!! HE IS HERE IN EDO CASTLE, BUT HE MUST STICK TO HIS KYOTO WAYS!
SIGH...
NOT "LORD CONSORT." WE'RE TO CALL HIM "PRINCE KAZU."
WHAT'S MOST MADDENING IS THAT NOT ONLY DOES HER HIGHNESS INDULGE ALL OF HIS OUTRAGES, BUT APPARENTLY ***SHE*** GREETS ***HIM*** FIRST EVERY DAY, WHEN IT SHOULD BE THE OTHER WAY AROUND!!
HER HIGHNESS IS A WARM, BRIGHT LIGHT TO ALL OF US HERE IN THE INNER CHAMBERS!! THAT LOVELY CHARM!! THAT PURITY OF SPIRIT!!
YES, BUT ALL THE SAME... IT CAN HARDLY BE A BAD THING FOR HER HIGHNESS TO LOVE PRINCE KAZU, FOR HE IS HER CONSORT, AFTER ALL.
LORD IEMOCHI SEEMS TO BE TREADING VERY LIGHTLY AROUND PRINCE KAZU, BUT I CAN ASSURE YOU THAT MANY OF US HAVE NOT RELINQUISHED OUR DREAMS OF BECOMING HER CONCUBINE!!

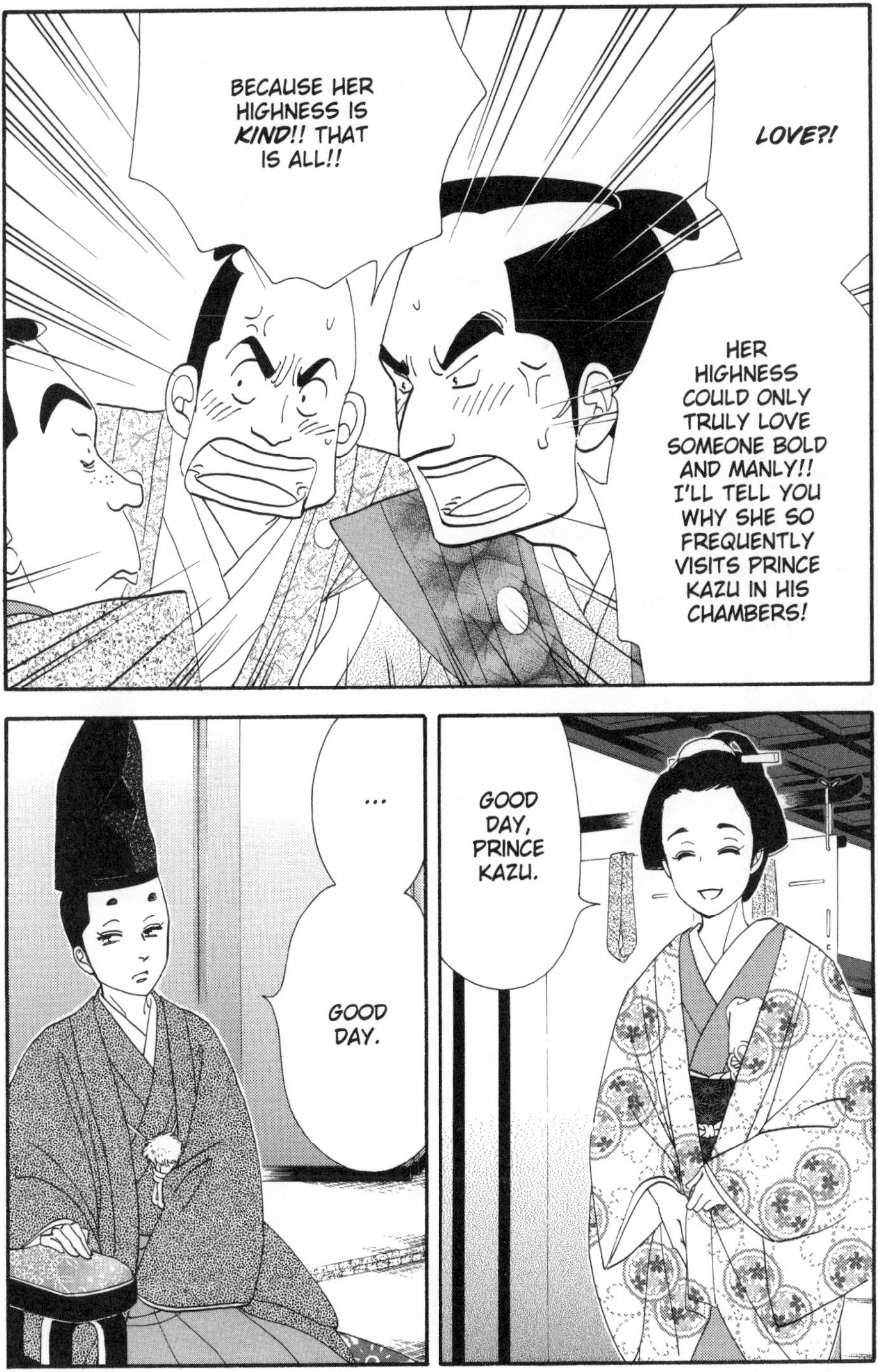

LOVE?!
HER HIGHNESS COULD ONLY TRULY LOVE SOMEONE BOLD AND MANLY!! I'LL TELL YOU WHY SHE SO FREQUENTLY VISITS PRINCE KAZU IN HIS CHAMBERS!
BECAUSE HER HIGHNESS IS *KIND*!! THAT IS ALL!!
GOOD DAY, PRINCE KAZU.
...
GOOD DAY.

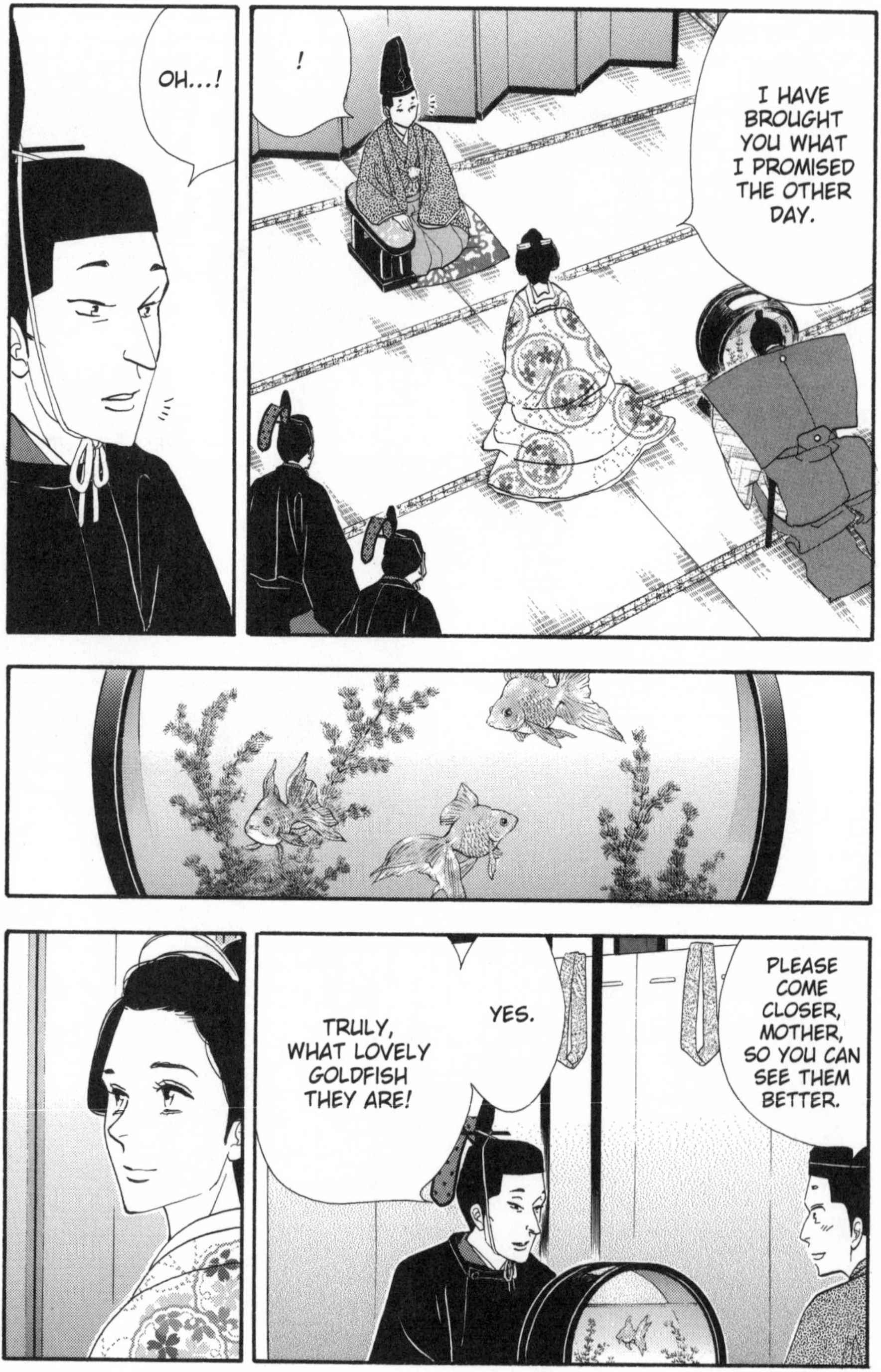
I HAVE BROUGHT YOU WHAT I PROMISED THE OTHER DAY.
!
OH...!
PLEASE COME CLOSER, MOTHER, SO YOU CAN SEE THEM BETTER.
YES.
TRULY, WHAT LOVELY GOLDFISH THEY ARE!

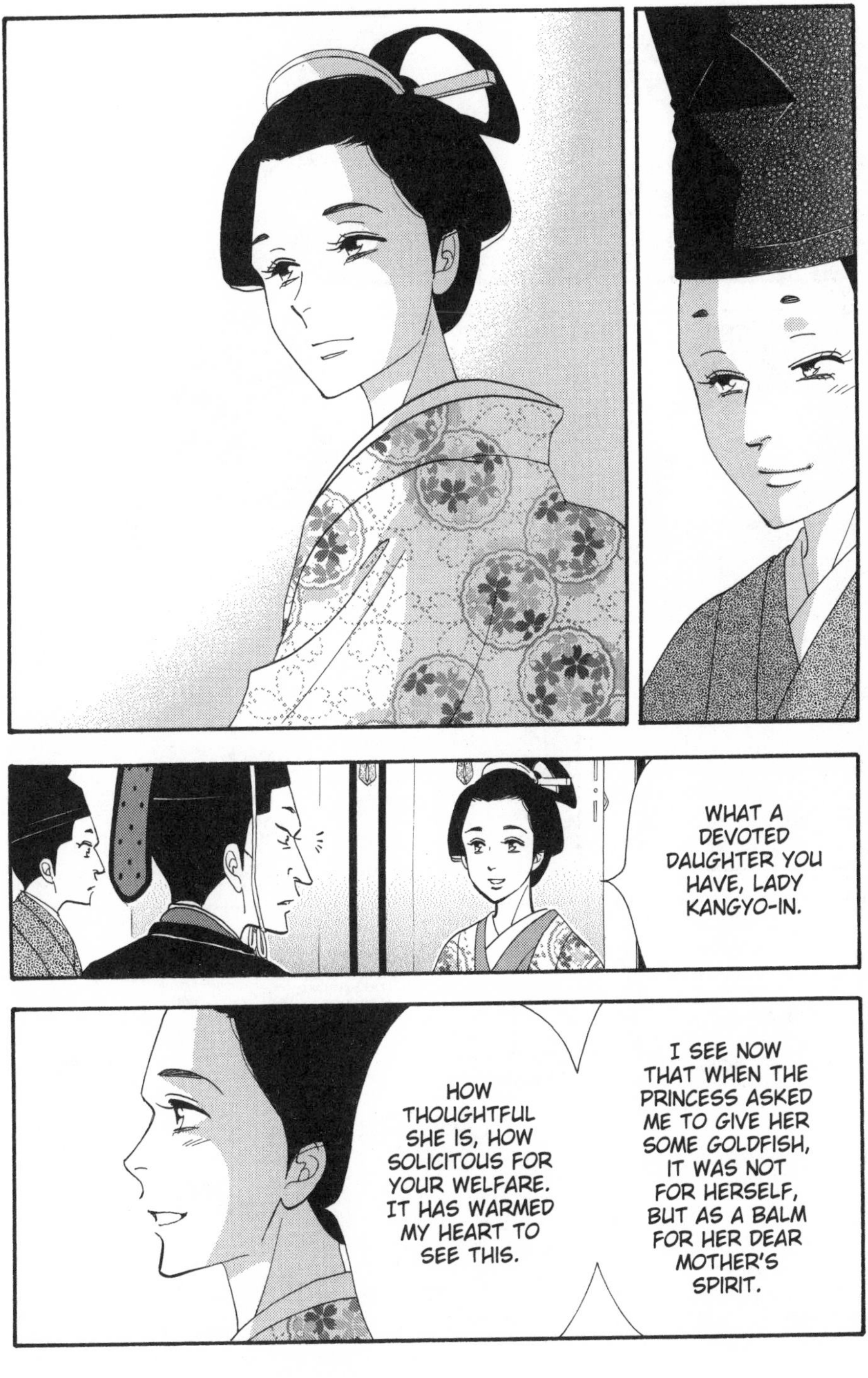
WHAT A DEVOTED DAUGHTER YOU HAVE, LADY KANGYO-IN.
I SEE NOW THAT WHEN THE PRINCESS ASKED ME TO GIVE HER SOME GOLDFISH, IT WAS NOT FOR HERSELF, BUT AS A BALM FOR HER DEAR MOTHER'S SPIRIT.
HOW THOUGHTFUL SHE IS, HOW SOLICITOUS FOR YOUR WELFARE. IT HAS WARMED MY HEART TO SEE THIS.

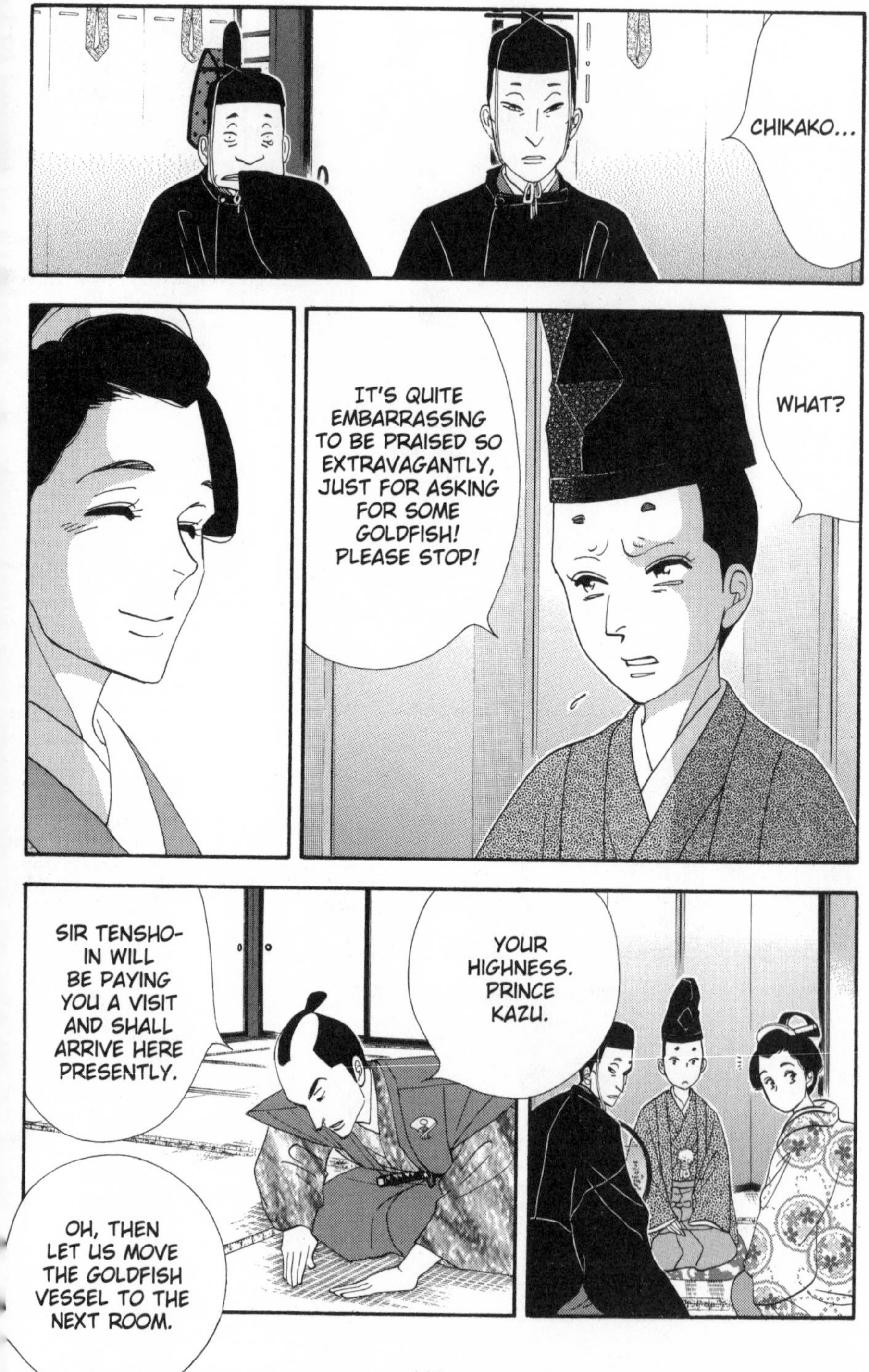
CHIKAKO...
WHAT?
IT'S QUITE EMBARRASSING TO BE PRAISED SO EXTRAVAGANTLY, JUST FOR ASKING FOR SOME GOLDFISH! PLEASE STOP!
YOUR HIGHNESS. PRINCE KAZU.
SIR TENSHO-IN WILL BE PAYING YOU A VISIT AND SHALL ARRIVE HERE PRESENTLY.
OH, THEN LET US MOVE THE GOLDFISH VESSEL TO THE NEXT ROOM.

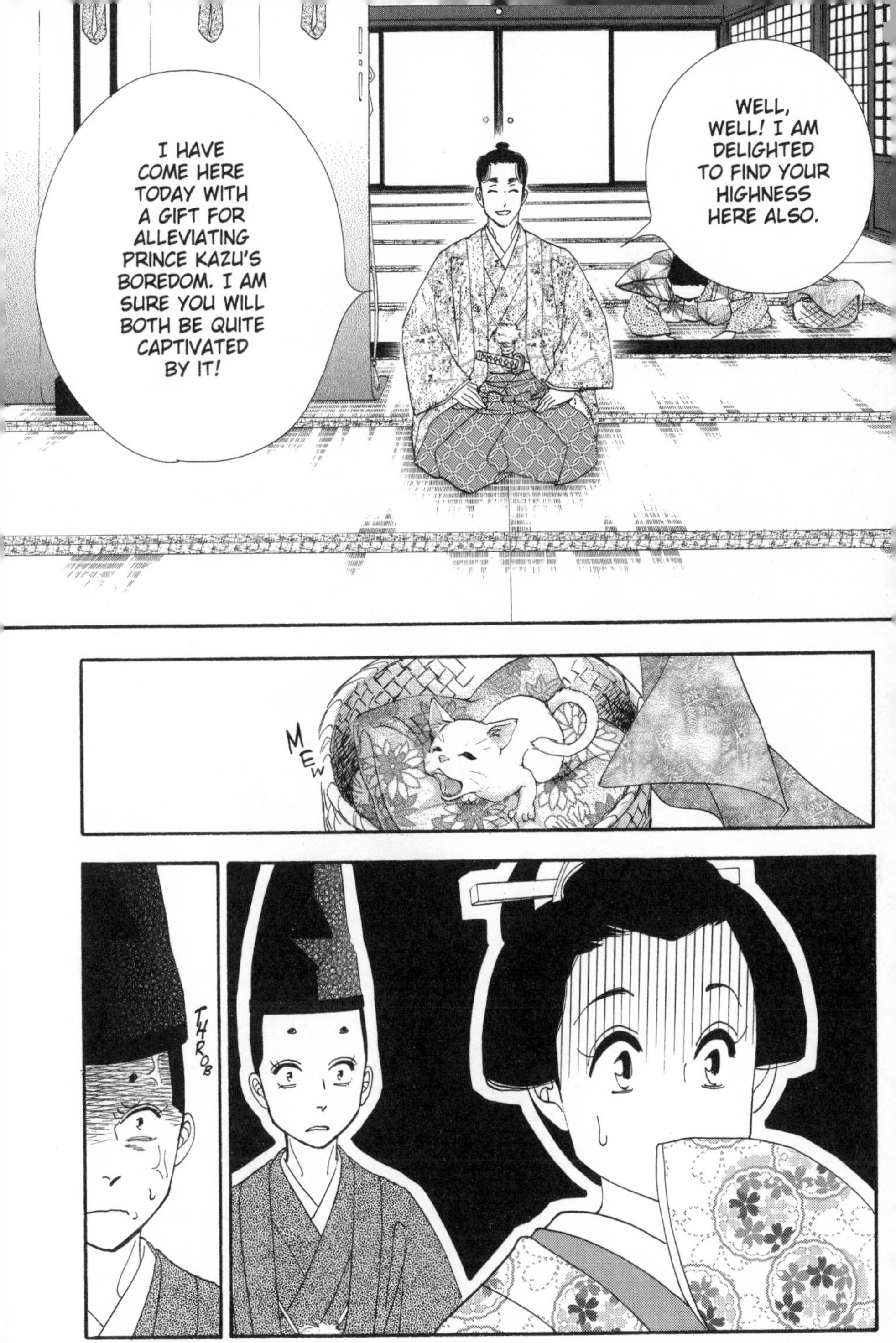
WELL, WELL! I AM DELIGHTED TO FIND YOUR HIGHNESS HERE ALSO.
I HAVE COME HERE TODAY WITH A GIFT FOR ALLEVIATING PRINCE KAZU'S BOREDOM. I AM SURE YOU WILL BOTH BE QUITE CAPTIVATED BY IT!
MEW
THROB

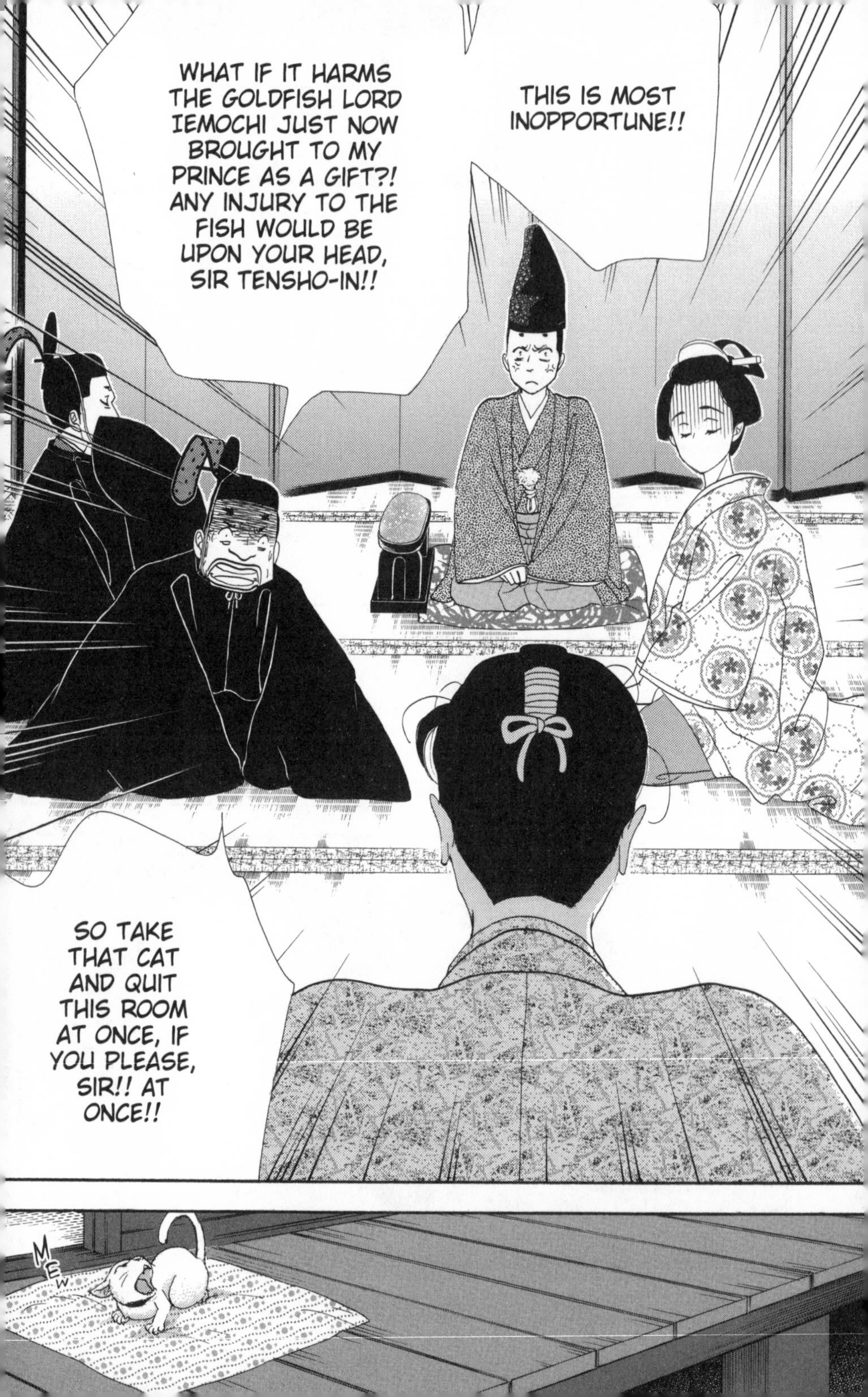
THIS IS MOST INOPPORTUNE!!
WHAT IF IT HARMS THE GOLDFISH LORD IEMOCHI JUST NOW BROUGHT TO MY PRINCE AS A GIFT?! ANY INJURY TO THE FISH WOULD BE UPON YOUR HEAD, SIR TENSHO-IN!!
SO TAKE THAT CAT AND QUIT THIS ROOM AT ONCE, IF YOU PLEASE, SIR!! AT ONCE!!
MEW

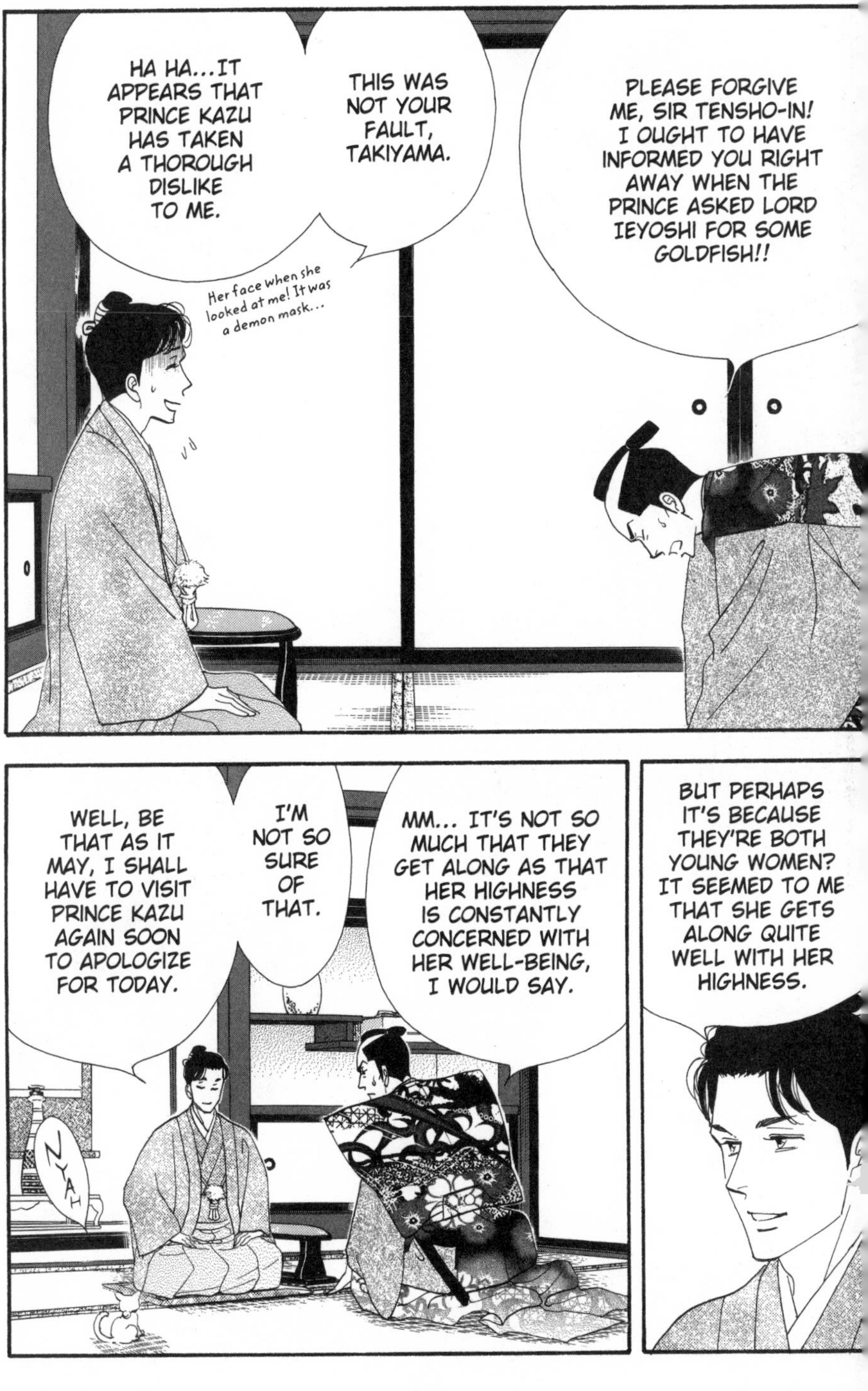
PLEASE FORGIVE ME, SIR TENSHO-IN! I OUGHT TO HAVE INFORMED YOU RIGHT AWAY WHEN THE PRINCE ASKED LORD IEYOSHI FOR SOME GOLDFISH!!
THIS WAS NOT YOUR FAULT, TAKIYAMA.
HA HA...IT APPEARS THAT PRINCE KAZU HAS TAKEN A THOROUGH DISLIKE TO ME.
Her face when she looked at me! It was a demon mask...
BUT PERHAPS IT'S BECAUSE THEY'RE BOTH YOUNG WOMEN? IT SEEMED TO ME THAT SHE GETS ALONG QUITE WELL WITH HER HIGHNESS.
MM... IT'S NOT SO MUCH THAT THEY GET ALONG AS THAT HER HIGHNESS IS CONSTANTLY CONCERNED WITH HER WELL-BEING, I WOULD SAY.
I'M NOT SO SURE OF THAT.
WELL, BE THAT AS IT MAY, I SHALL HAVE TO VISIT PRINCE KAZU AGAIN SOON TO APOLOGIZE FOR TODAY.
NYAH

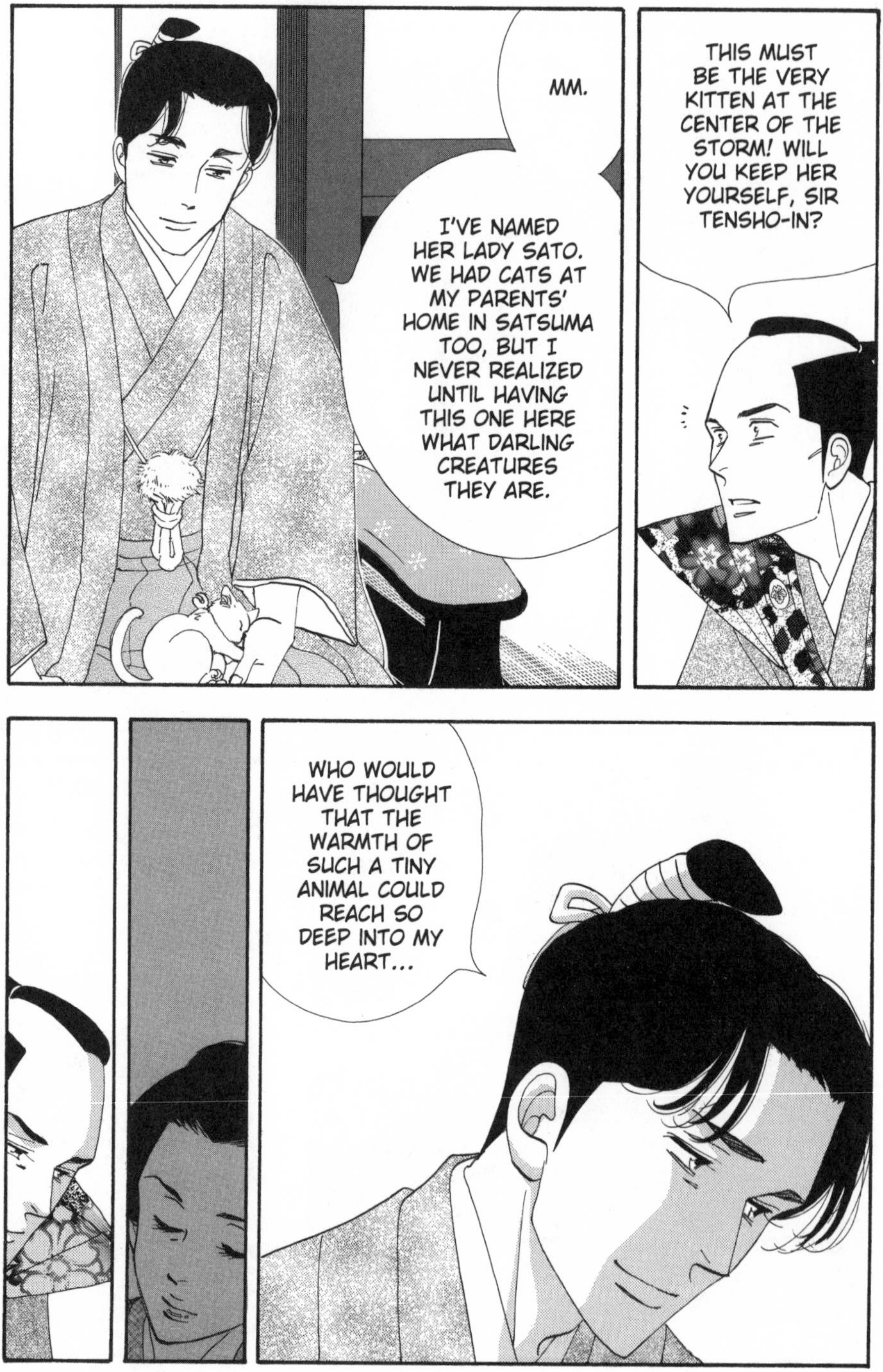
THIS MUST BE THE VERY KITTEN AT THE CENTER OF THE STORM! WILL YOU KEEP HER YOURSELF, SIR TENSHO-IN?
MM.
I'VE NAMED HER LADY SATO. WE HAD CATS AT MY PARENTS' HOME IN SATSUMA TOO, BUT I NEVER REALIZED UNTIL HAVING THIS ONE HERE WHAT DARLING CREATURES THEY ARE.
WHO WOULD HAVE THOUGHT THAT THE WARMTH OF SUCH A TINY ANIMAL COULD REACH SO DEEP INTO MY HEART...

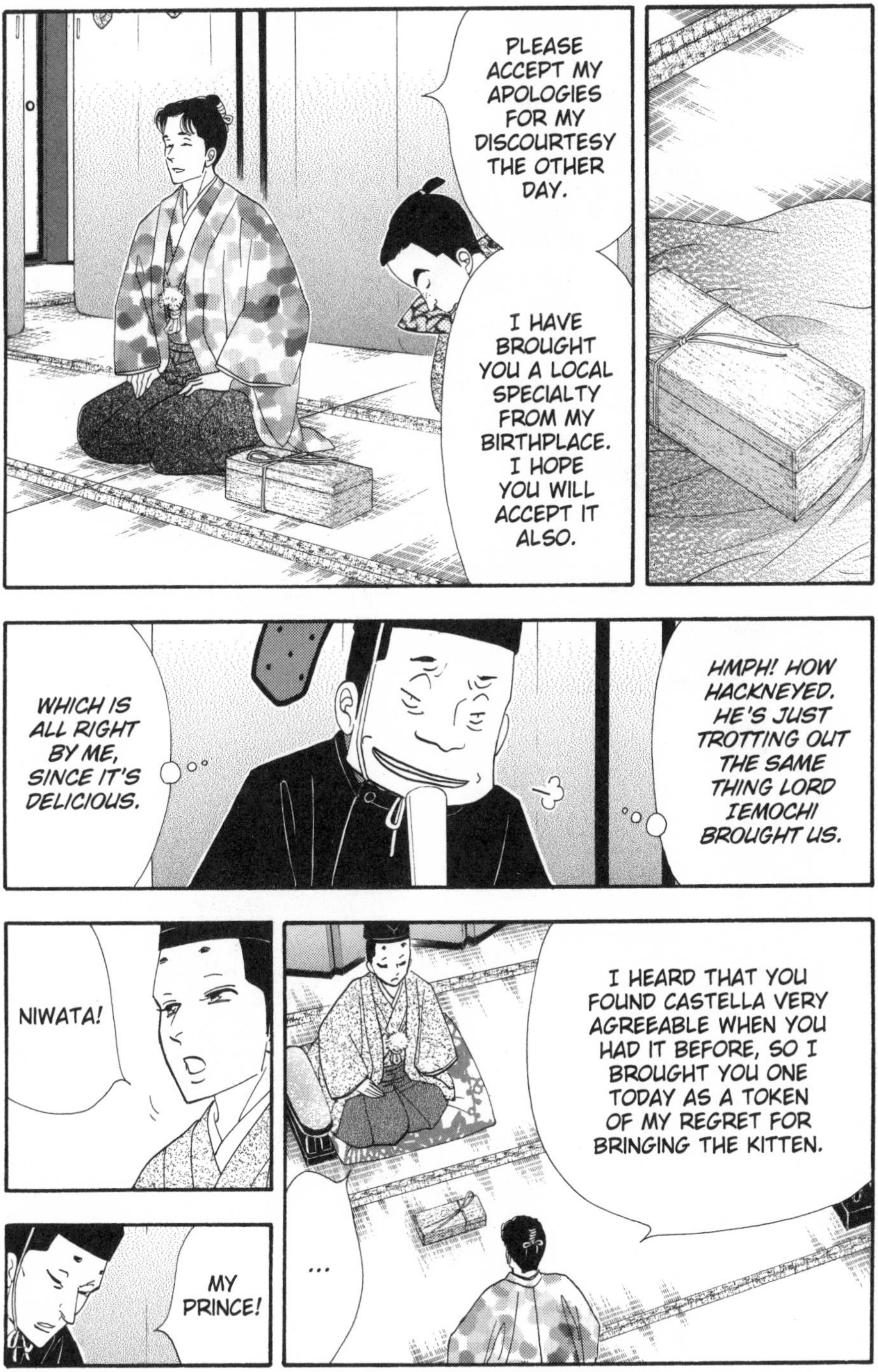
PLEASE ACCEPT MY APOLOGIES FOR MY DISCOURTESY THE OTHER DAY.
I HAVE BROUGHT YOU A LOCAL SPECIALTY FROM MY BIRTHPLACE. I HOPE YOU WILL ACCEPT IT ALSO.
HMPH! HOW HACKNEYED. HE'S JUST TROTTING OUT THE SAME THING LORD IEMOCHI BROUGHT US.
WHICH IS ALL RIGHT BY ME, SINCE IT'S DELICIOUS.
I HEARD THAT YOU FOUND CASTELLA VERY AGREEABLE WHEN YOU HAD IT BEFORE, SO I BROUGHT YOU ONE TODAY AS A TOKEN OF MY REGRET FOR BRINGING THE KITTEN.
...
NIWATA!
MY PRINCE!

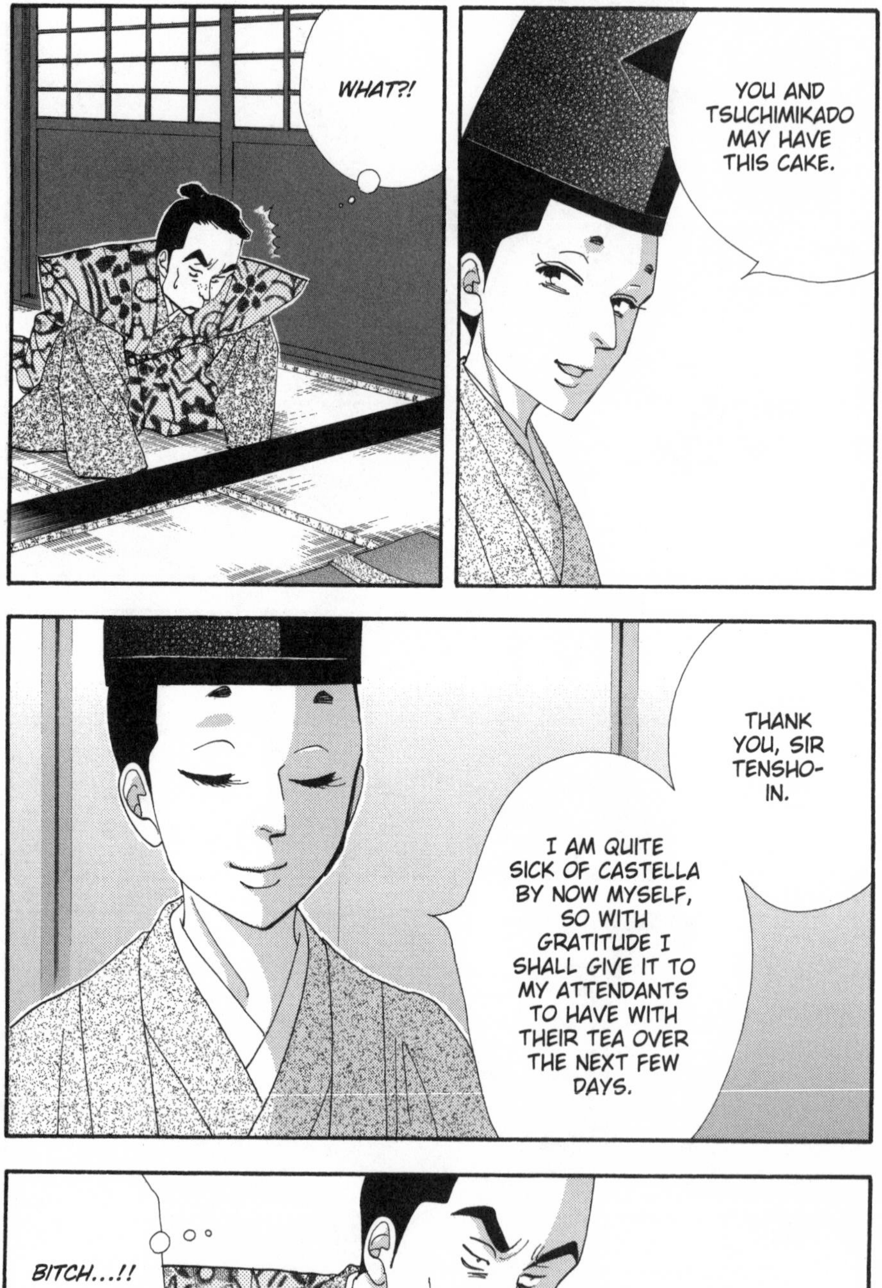
YOU AND TSUCHIMIKADO MAY HAVE THIS CAKE.
WHAT?!
THANK YOU, SIR TENSHO-IN.
I AM QUITE SICK OF CASTELLA BY NOW MYSELF, SO WITH GRATITUDE I SHALL GIVE IT TO MY ATTENDANTS TO HAVE WITH THEIR TEA OVER THE NEXT FEW DAYS.
BITCH...!!

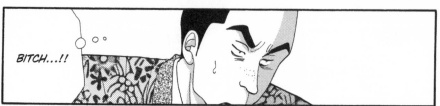

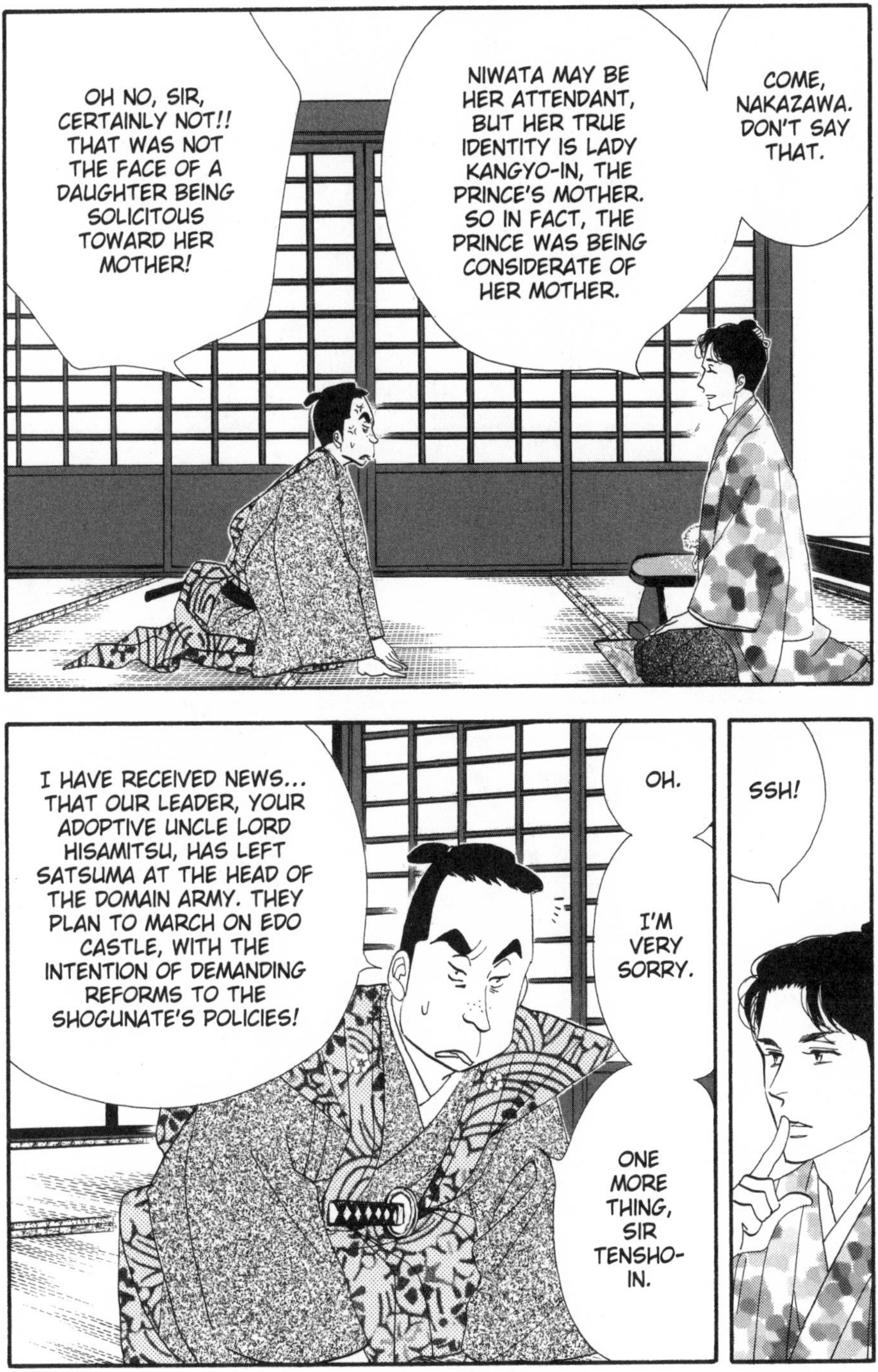
COME, NAKAZAWA. DON'T SAY THAT.
NIWATA MAY BE HER ATTENDANT, BUT HER TRUE IDENTITY IS LADY KANGYO-IN, THE PRINCE'S MOTHER. SO IN FACT, THE PRINCE WAS BEING CONSIDERATE OF HER MOTHER.
OH NO, SIR, CERTAINLY NOT!! THAT WAS NOT THE FACE OF A DAUGHTER BEING SOLICITOUS TOWARD HER MOTHER!
SSH!
OH.
I'M VERY SORRY.
ONE MORE THING, SIR TENSHO-IN.
I HAVE RECEIVED NEWS... THAT OUR LEADER, YOUR ADOPTIVE UNCLE LORD HISAMITSU, HAS LEFT SATSUMA AT THE HEAD OF THE DOMAIN ARMY. THEY PLAN TO MARCH ON EDO CASTLE, WITH THE INTENTION OF DEMANDING REFORMS TO THE SHOGUNATE'S POLICIES!

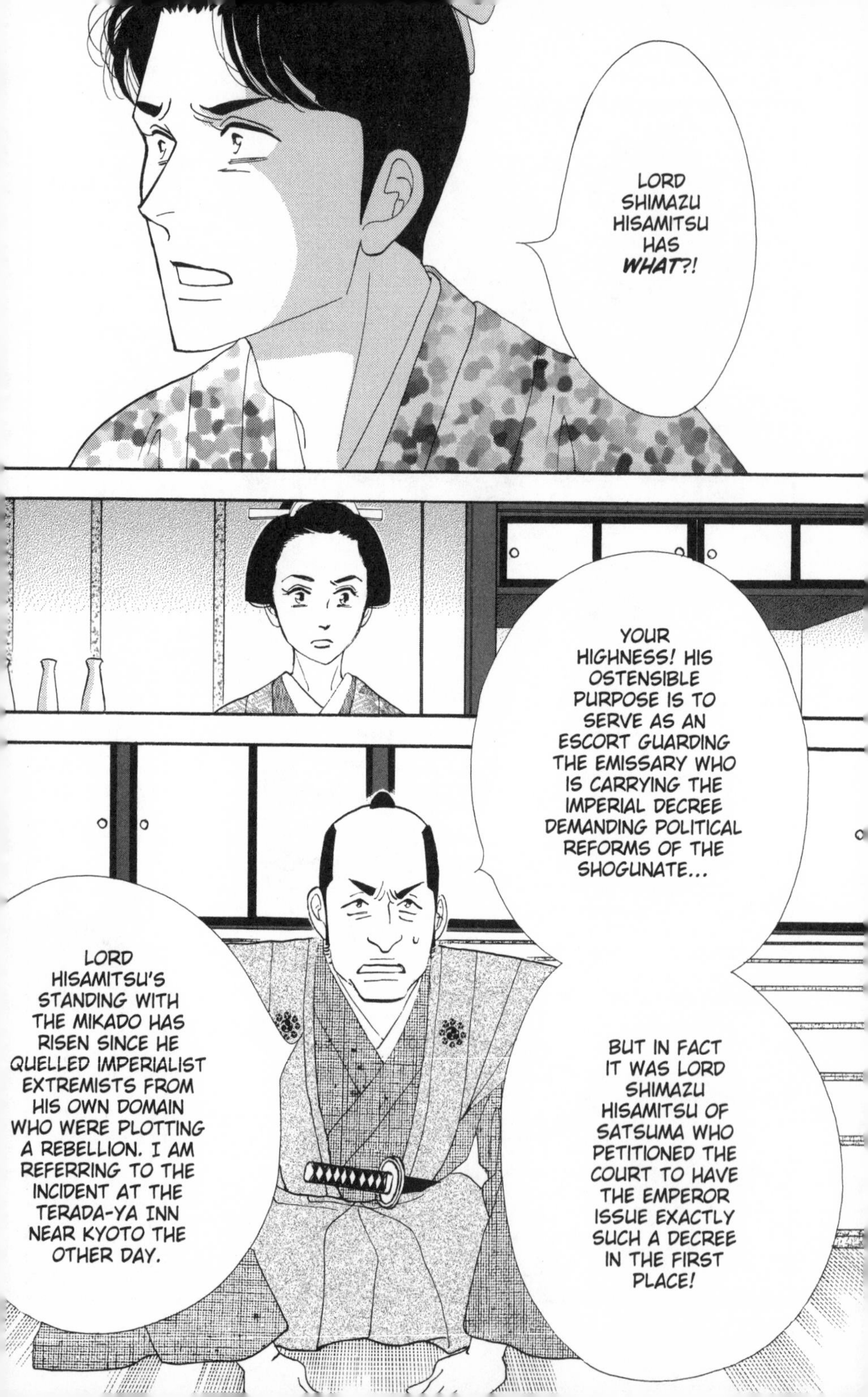
LORD SHIMAZU HISAMITSU HAS ***WHAT***?!
YOUR HIGHNESS! HIS OSTENSIBLE PURPOSE IS TO SERVE AS AN ESCORT GUARDING THE EMISSARY WHO IS CARRYING THE IMPERIAL DECREE DEMANDING POLITICAL REFORMS OF THE SHOGUNATE...
BUT IN FACT IT WAS LORD SHIMAZU HISAMITSU OF SATSUMA WHO PETITIONED THE COURT TO HAVE THE EMPEROR ISSUE EXACTLY SUCH A DECREE IN THE FIRST PLACE!
LORD HISAMITSU'S STANDING WITH THE MIKADO HAS RISEN SINCE HE QUELLED IMPERIALIST EXTREMISTS FROM HIS OWN DOMAIN WHO WERE PLOTTING A REBELLION. I AM REFERRING TO THE INCIDENT AT THE TERADA-YA INN NEAR KYOTO THE OTHER DAY.

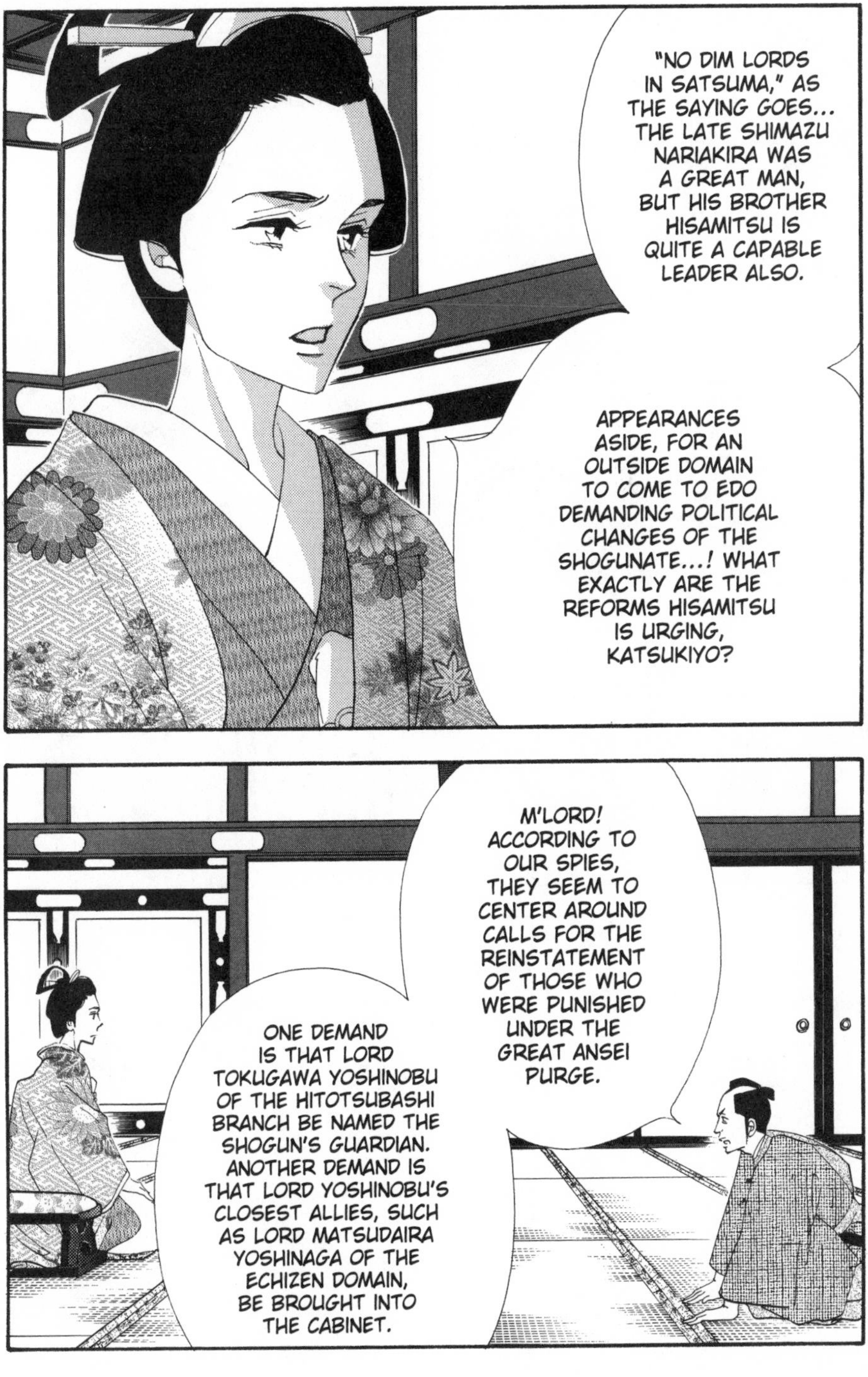
"NO DIM LORDS IN SATSUMA," AS THE SAYING GOES... THE LATE SHIMAZU NARIAKIRA WAS A GREAT MAN, BUT HIS BROTHER HISAMITSU IS QUITE A CAPABLE LEADER ALSO.
APPEARANCES ASIDE, FOR AN OUTSIDE DOMAIN TO COME TO EDO DEMANDING POLITICAL CHANGES OF THE SHOGUNATE...! WHAT EXACTLY ARE THE REFORMS HISAMITSU IS URGING, KATSUKIYO?
M'LORD! ACCORDING TO OUR SPIES, THEY SEEM TO CENTER AROUND CALLS FOR THE REINSTATEMENT OF THOSE WHO WERE PUNISHED UNDER THE GREAT ANSEI PURGE.
ONE DEMAND IS THAT LORD TOKUGAWA YOSHINOBU OF THE HITOTSUBASHI BRANCH BE NAMED THE SHOGUN'S GUARDIAN. ANOTHER DEMAND IS THAT LORD YOSHINOBU'S CLOSEST ALLIES, SUCH AS LORD MATSUDAIRA YOSHINAGA OF THE ECHIZEN DOMAIN, BE BROUGHT INTO THE CABINET.

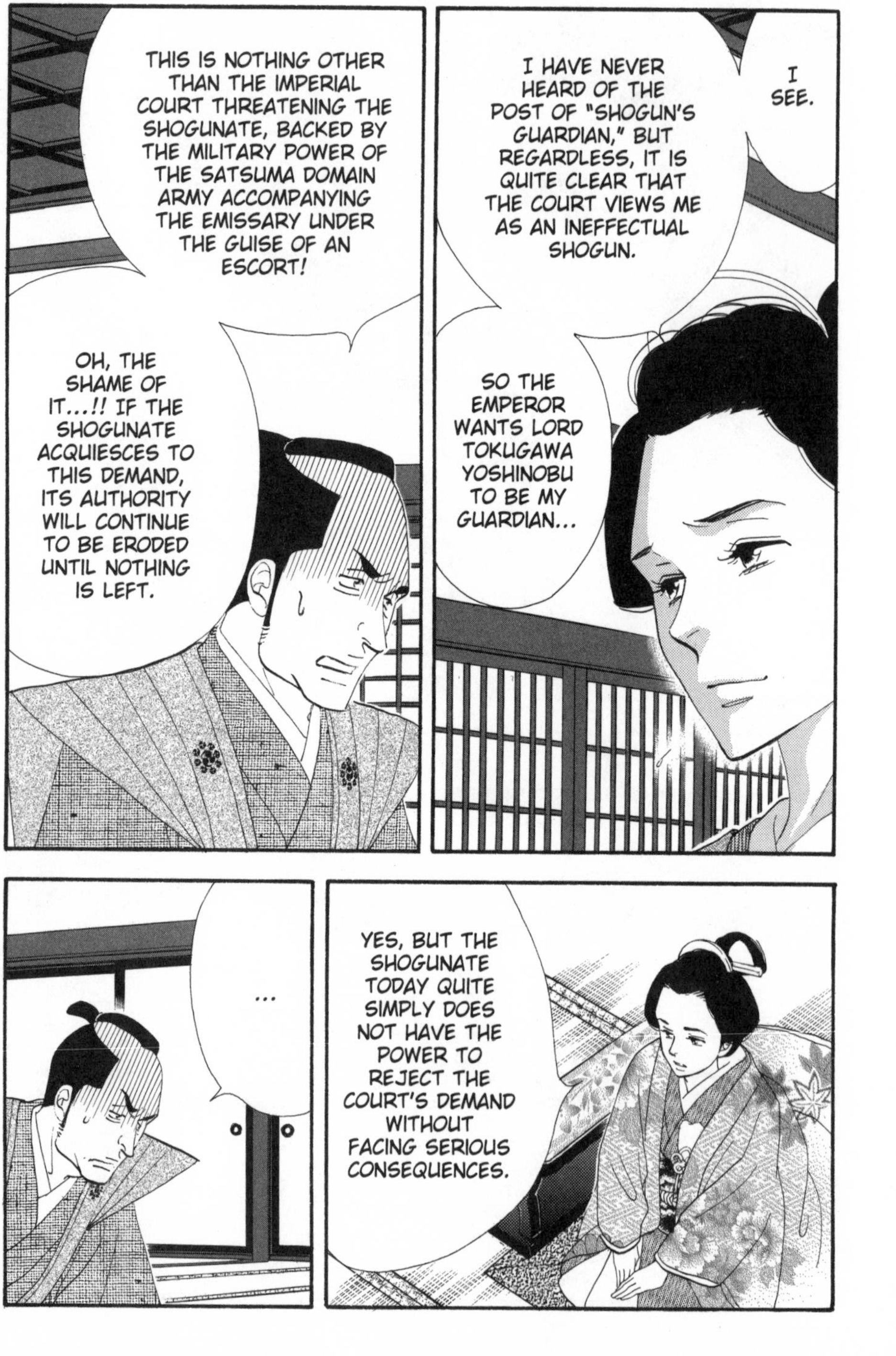
I SEE.
I HAVE NEVER HEARD OF THE POST OF "SHOGUN'S GUARDIAN," BUT REGARDLESS, IT IS QUITE CLEAR THAT THE COURT VIEWS ME AS AN INEFFECTUAL SHOGUN.
SO THE EMPEROR WANTS LORD TOKUGAWA YOSHINOBU TO BE MY GUARDIAN...
THIS IS NOTHING OTHER THAN THE IMPERIAL COURT THREATENING THE SHOGUNATE, BACKED BY THE MILITARY POWER OF THE SATSUMA DOMAIN ARMY ACCOMPANYING THE EMISSARY UNDER THE GUISE OF AN ESCORT!
OH, THE SHAME OF IT...!! IF THE SHOGUNATE ACQUIESCES TO THIS DEMAND, ITS AUTHORITY WILL CONTINUE TO BE ERODED UNTIL NOTHING IS LEFT.
YES, BUT THE SHOGUNATE TODAY QUITE SIMPLY DOES NOT HAVE THE POWER TO REJECT THE COURT'S DEMAND WITHOUT FACING SERIOUS CONSEQUENCES.
...

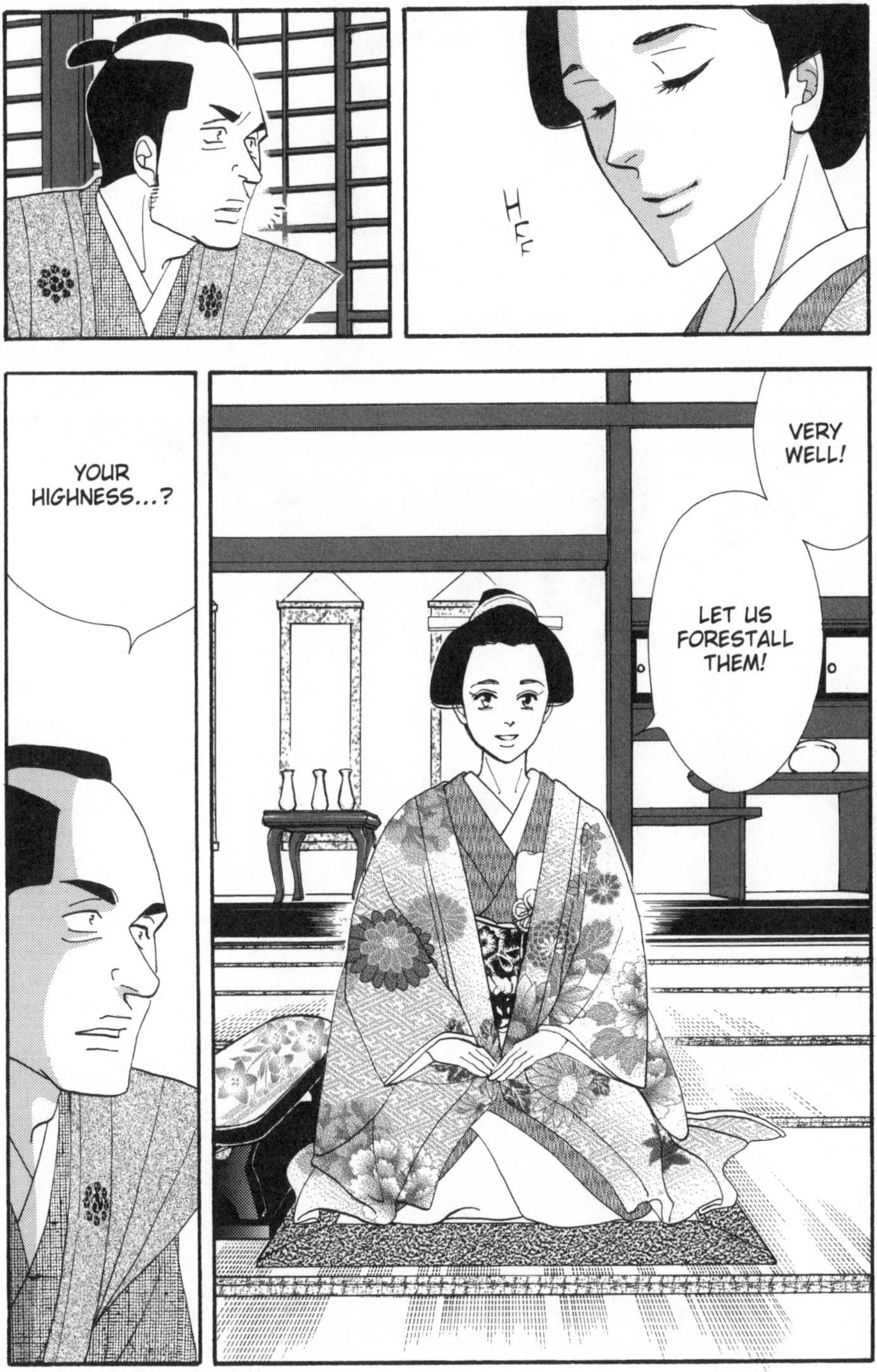
VERY WELL!
LET US FORESTALL THEM!
YOUR HIGHNESS...?

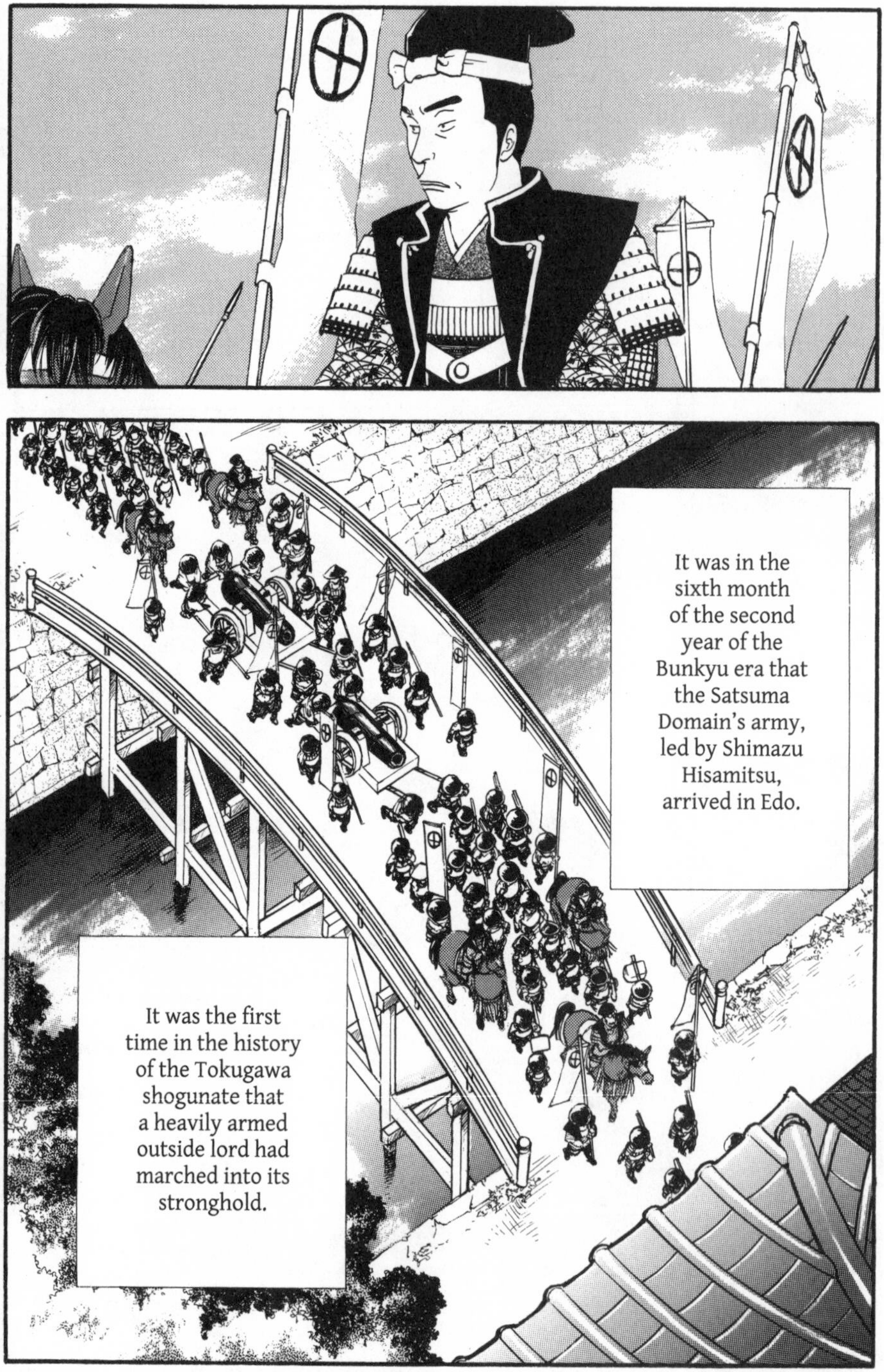
It was in the sixth month of the second year of the Bunkyu era that the Satsuma Domain's army, led by Shimazu Hisamitsu, arrived in Edo.
It was the first time in the history of the Tokugawa shogunate that a heavily armed outside lord had marched into its stronghold.

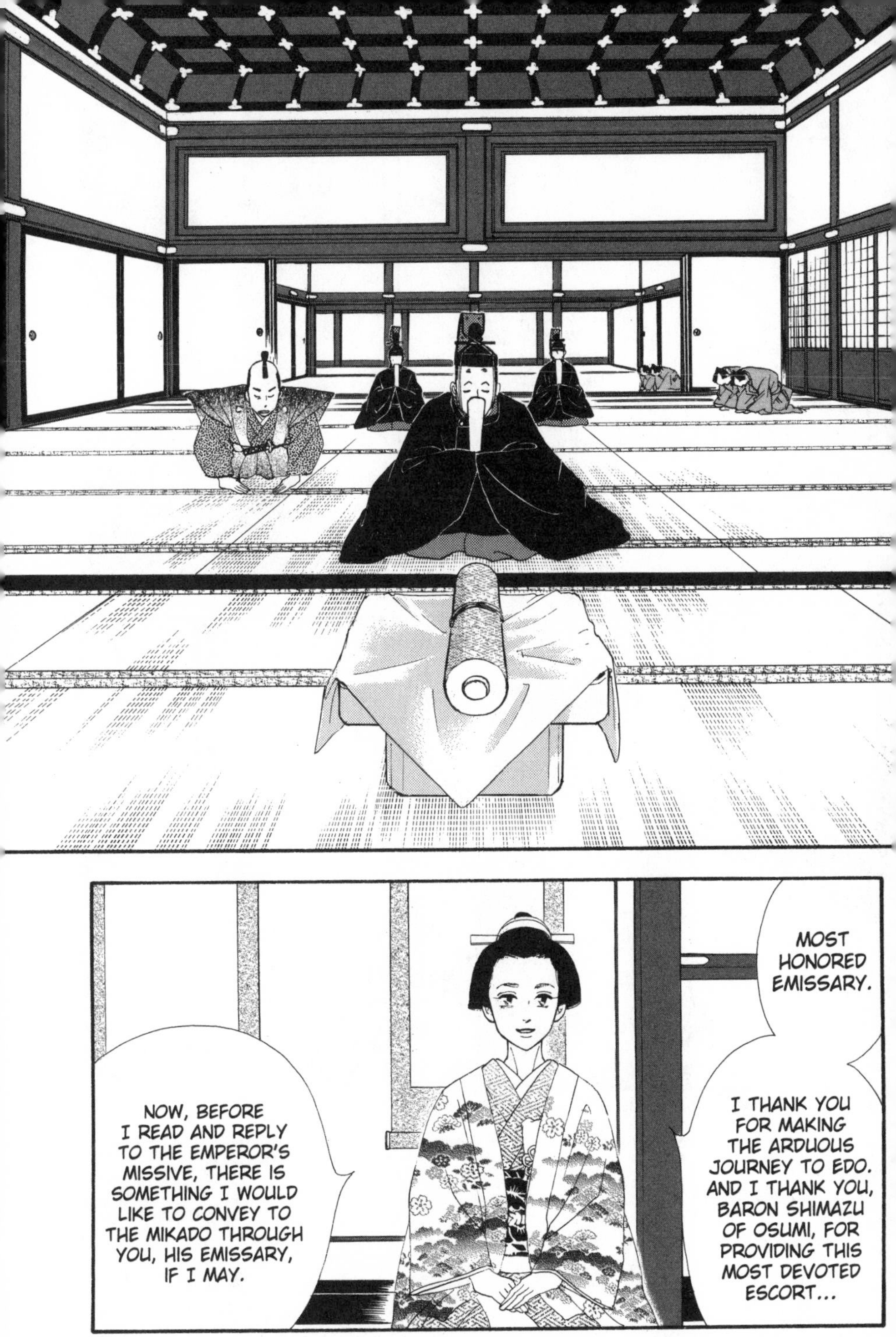
MOST HONORED EMISSARY.
I THANK YOU FOR MAKING THE ARDUOUS JOURNEY TO EDO. AND I THANK YOU, BARON SHIMAZU OF OSUMI, FOR PROVIDING THIS MOST DEVOTED ESCORT...
NOW, BEFORE I READ AND REPLY TO THE EMPEROR'S MISSIVE, THERE IS SOMETHING I WOULD LIKE TO CONVEY TO THE MIKADO THROUGH YOU, HIS EMISSARY, IF I MAY.

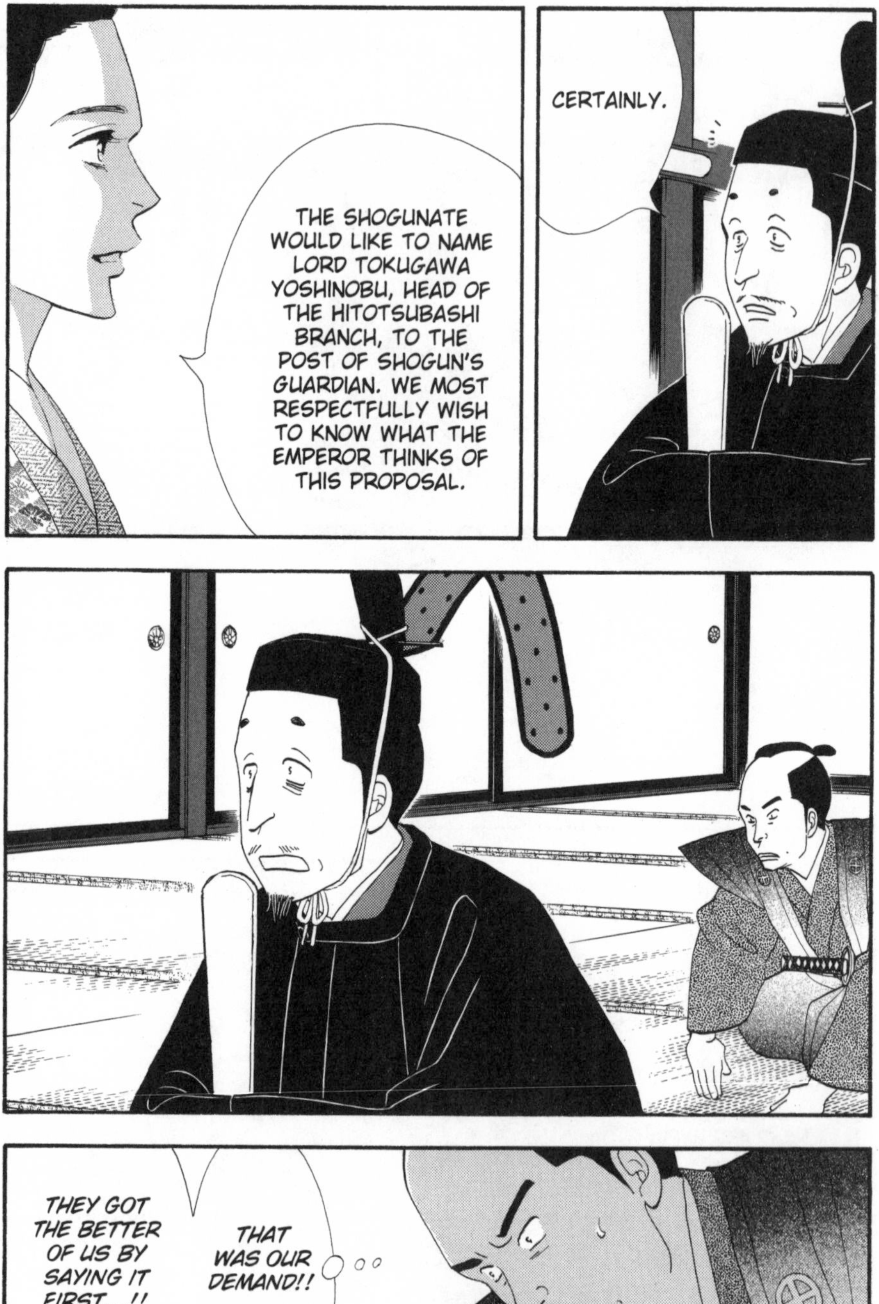
CERTAINLY.
THE SHOGUNATE WOULD LIKE TO NAME LORD TOKUGAWA YOSHINOBU, HEAD OF THE HITOTSUBASHI BRANCH, TO THE POST OF SHOGUN'S GUARDIAN. WE MOST RESPECTFULLY WISH TO KNOW WHAT THE EMPEROR THINKS OF THIS PROPOSAL.
THAT WAS OUR DEMAND!!
THEY GOT THE BETTER OF US BY SAYING IT FIRST...!!

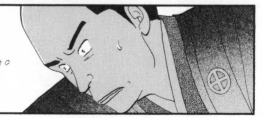

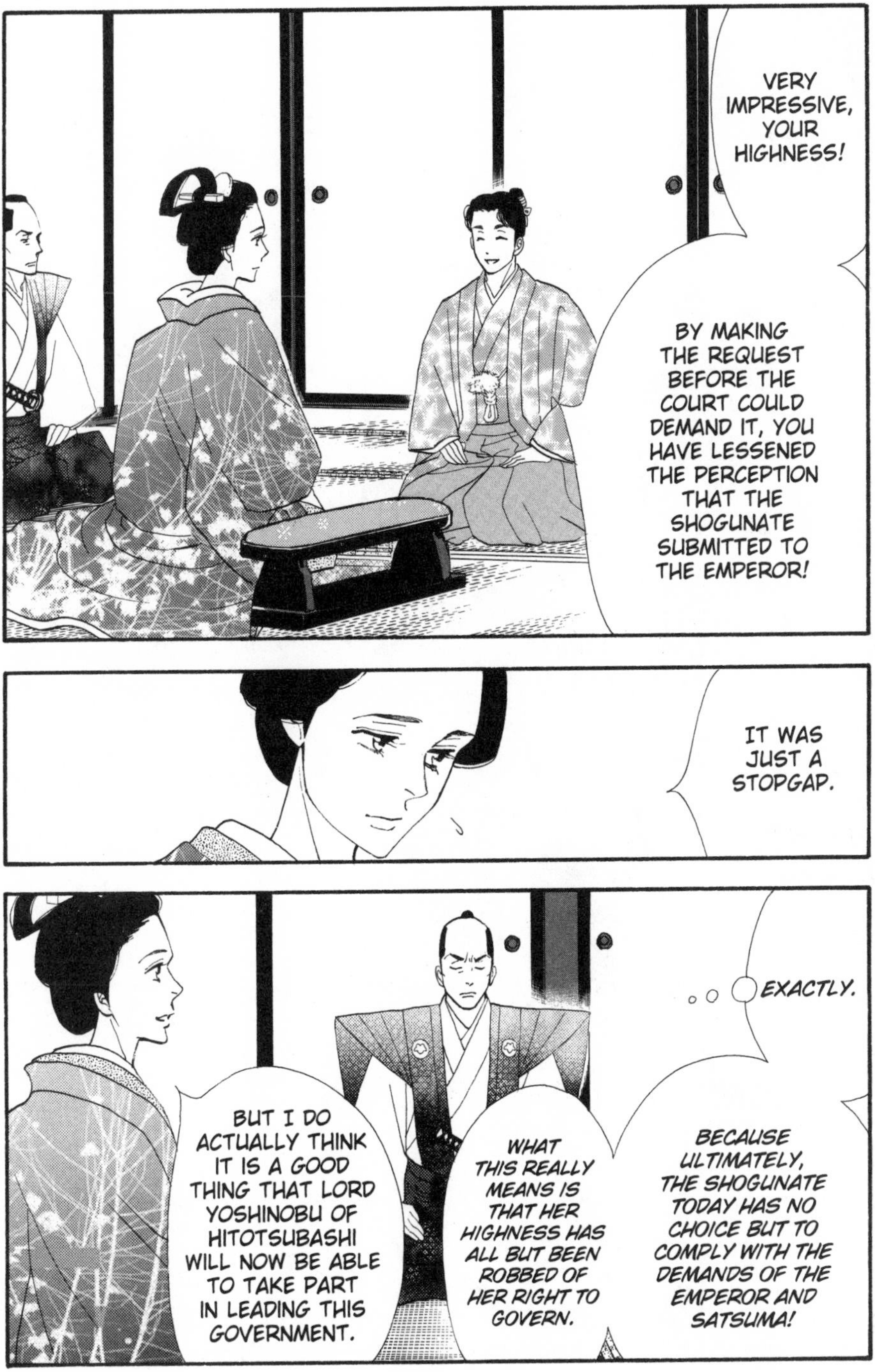
VERY IMPRESSIVE, YOUR HIGHNESS!
BY MAKING THE REQUEST BEFORE THE COURT COULD DEMAND IT, YOU HAVE LESSENED THE PERCEPTION THAT THE SHOGUNATE SUBMITTED TO THE EMPEROR!
IT WAS JUST A STOPGAP.
EXACTLY.
BECAUSE ULTIMATELY, THE SHOGUNATE TODAY HAS NO CHOICE BUT TO COMPLY WITH THE DEMANDS OF THE EMPEROR AND SATSUMA!
WHAT THIS REALLY MEANS IS THAT HER HIGHNESS HAS ALL BUT BEEN ROBBED OF HER RIGHT TO GOVERN.
BUT I DO ACTUALLY THINK IT IS A GOOD THING THAT LORD YOSHINOBU OF HITOTSUBASHI WILL NOW BE ABLE TO TAKE PART IN LEADING THIS GOVERNMENT.

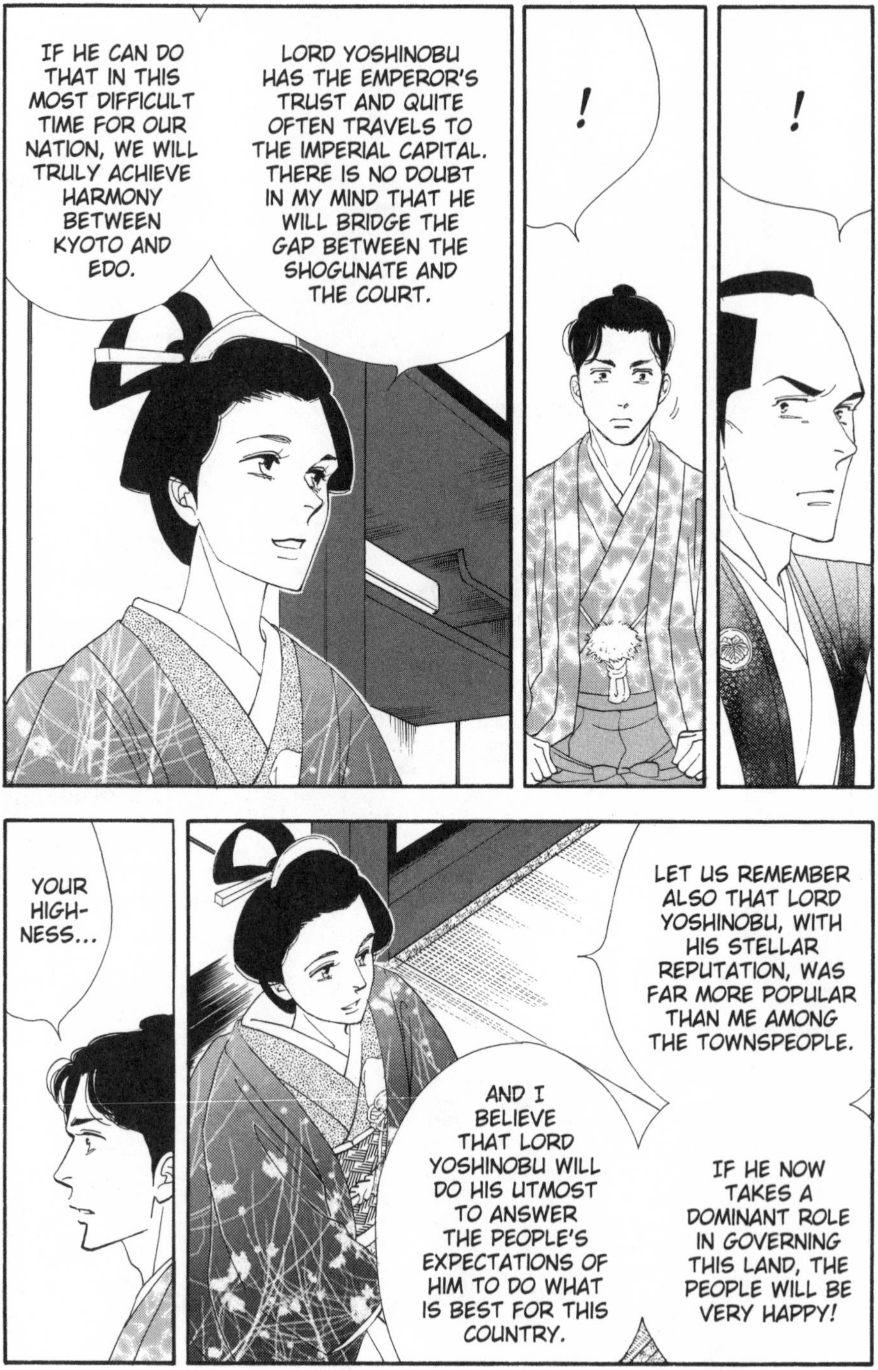
!
!
LORD YOSHINOBU HAS THE EMPEROR'S TRUST AND QUITE OFTEN TRAVELS TO THE IMPERIAL CAPITAL. THERE IS NO DOUBT IN MY MIND THAT HE WILL BRIDGE THE GAP BETWEEN THE SHOGUNATE AND THE COURT.
IF HE CAN DO THAT IN THIS MOST DIFFICULT TIME FOR OUR NATION, WE WILL TRULY ACHIEVE HARMONY BETWEEN KYOTO AND EDO.
LET US REMEMBER ALSO THAT LORD YOSHINOBU, WITH HIS STELLAR REPUTATION, WAS FAR MORE POPULAR THAN ME AMONG THE TOWNSPEOPLE.
IF HE NOW TAKES A DOMINANT ROLE IN GOVERNING THIS LAND, THE PEOPLE WILL BE VERY HAPPY!
AND I BELIEVE THAT LORD YOSHINOBU WILL DO HIS UTMOST TO ANSWER THE PEOPLE'S EXPECTATIONS OF HIM TO DO WHAT IS BEST FOR THIS COUNTRY.
YOUR HIGH-NESS...

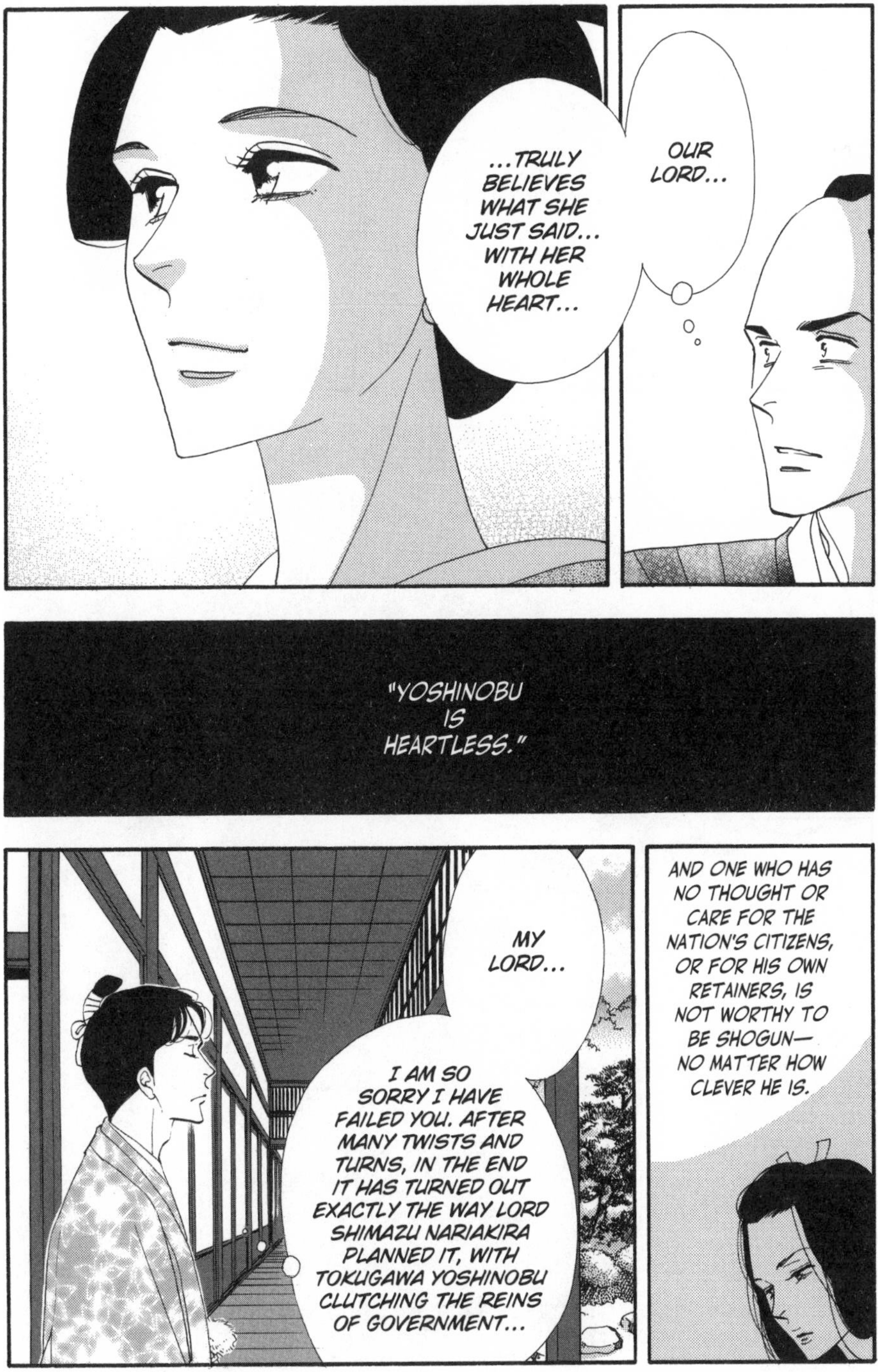
OUR LORD...
...TRULY BELIEVES WHAT SHE JUST SAID... WITH HER WHOLE HEART...
"YOSHINOBU IS HEARTLESS."
AND ONE WHO HAS NO THOUGHT OR CARE FOR THE NATION'S CITIZENS, OR FOR HIS OWN RETAINERS, IS NOT WORTHY TO BE SHOGUN—NO MATTER HOW CLEVER HE IS.
MY LORD...
I AM SO SORRY I HAVE FAILED YOU. AFTER MANY TWISTS AND TURNS, IN THE END IT HAS TURNED OUT EXACTLY THE WAY LORD SHIMAZU NARIAKIRA PLANNED IT, WITH TOKUGAWA YOSHINOBU CLUTCHING THE REINS OF GOVERNMENT...

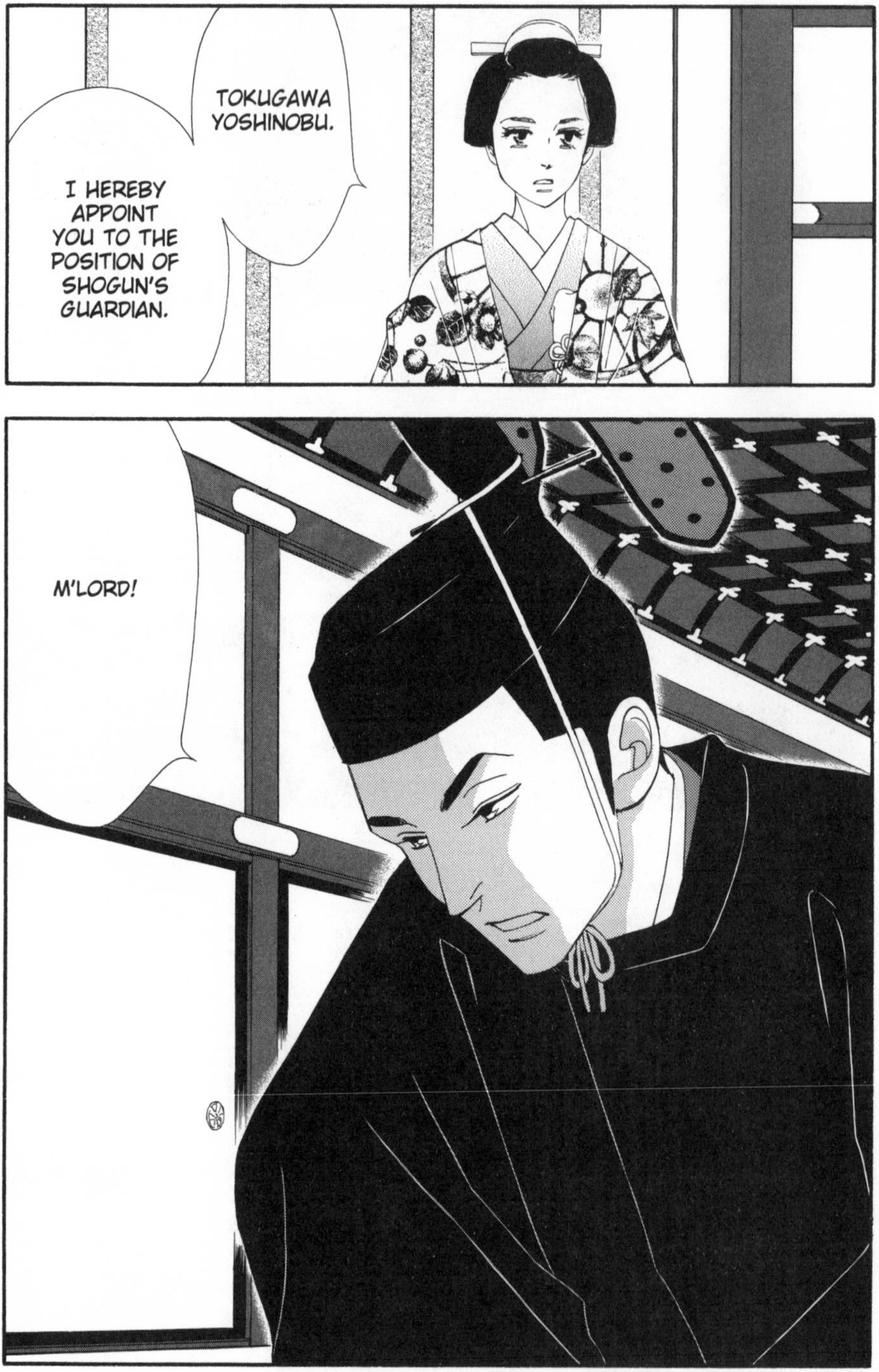
TOKUGAWA YOSHINOBU.
I HEREBY APPOINT YOU TO THE POSITION OF SHOGUN'S GUARDIAN.
M'LORD!

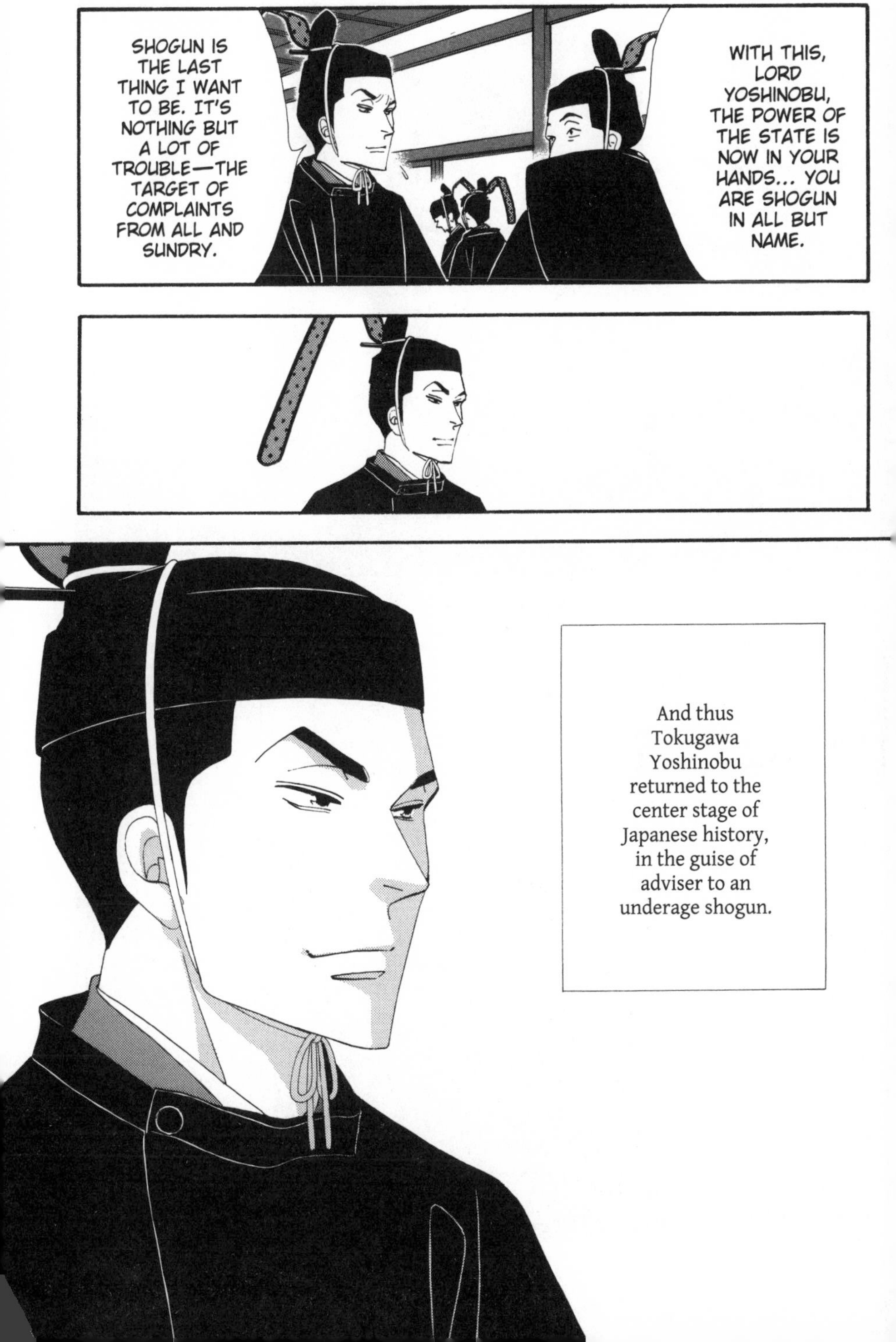
WITH THIS, LORD YOSHINOBU, THE POWER OF THE STATE IS NOW IN YOUR HANDS... YOU ARE SHOGUN IN ALL BUT NAME.
SHOGUN IS THE LAST THING I WANT TO BE. IT'S NOTHING BUT A LOT OF TROUBLE—THE TARGET OF COMPLAINTS FROM ALL AND SUNDRY.
And thus Tokugawa Yoshinobu returned to the center stage of Japanese history, in the guise of adviser to an underage shogun.

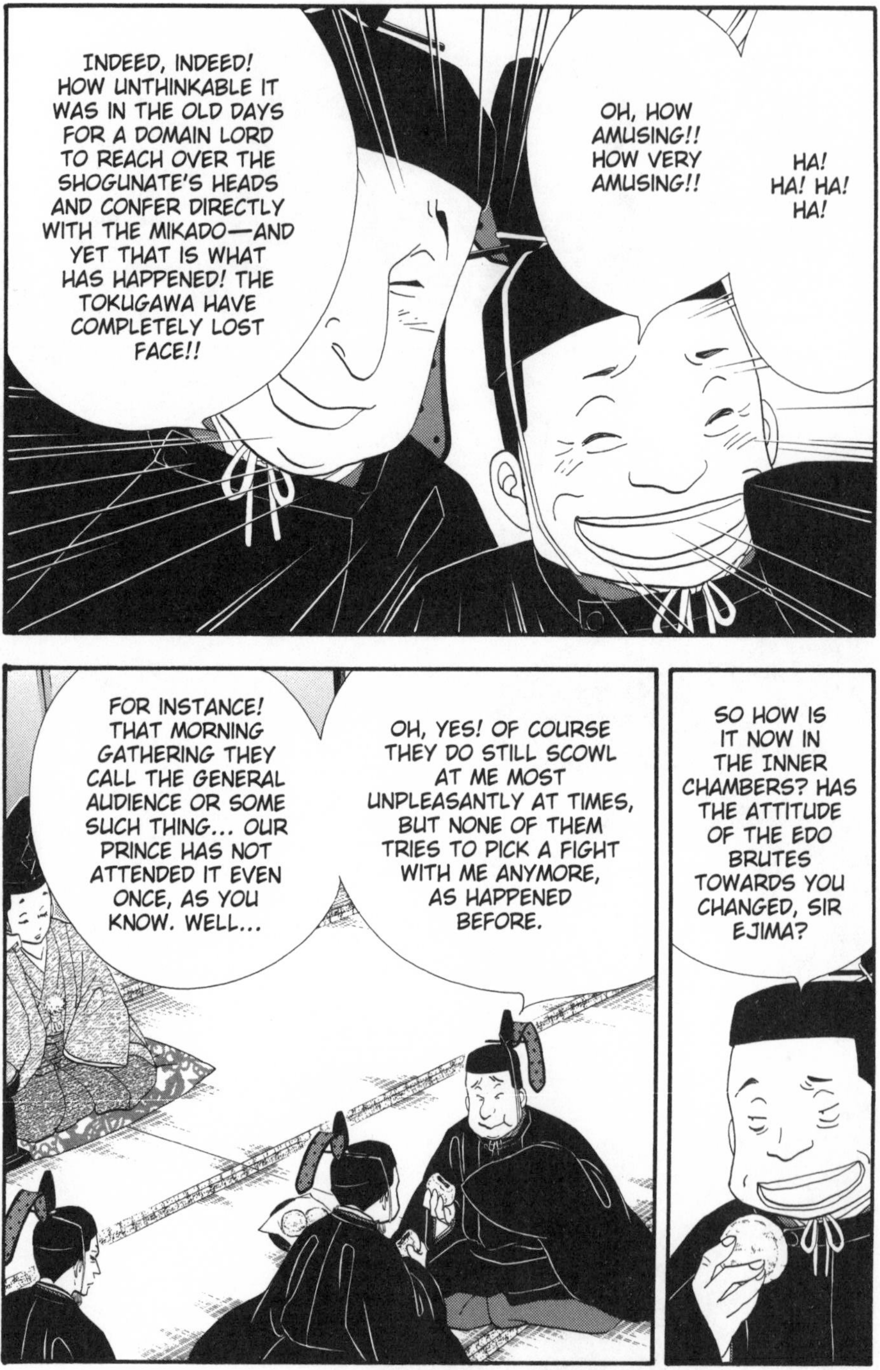
HA! HA! HA! HA!
OH, HOW AMUSING!! HOW VERY AMUSING!!
INDEED, INDEED! HOW UNTHINKABLE IT WAS IN THE OLD DAYS FOR A DOMAIN LORD TO REACH OVER THE SHOGUNATE'S HEADS AND CONFER DIRECTLY WITH THE MIKADO—AND YET THAT IS WHAT HAS HAPPENED! THE TOKUGAWA HAVE COMPLETELY LOST FACE!!
SO HOW IS IT NOW IN THE INNER CHAMBERS? HAS THE ATTITUDE OF THE EDO BRUTES TOWARDS YOU CHANGED, SIR EJIMA?
OH, YES! OF COURSE THEY DO STILL SCOWL AT ME MOST UNPLEASANTLY AT TIMES, BUT NONE OF THEM TRIES TO PICK A FIGHT WITH ME ANYMORE, AS HAPPENED BEFORE.
FOR INSTANCE! THAT MORNING GATHERING THEY CALL THE GENERAL AUDIENCE OR SOME SUCH THING... OUR PRINCE HAS NOT ATTENDED IT EVEN ONCE, AS YOU KNOW. WELL...

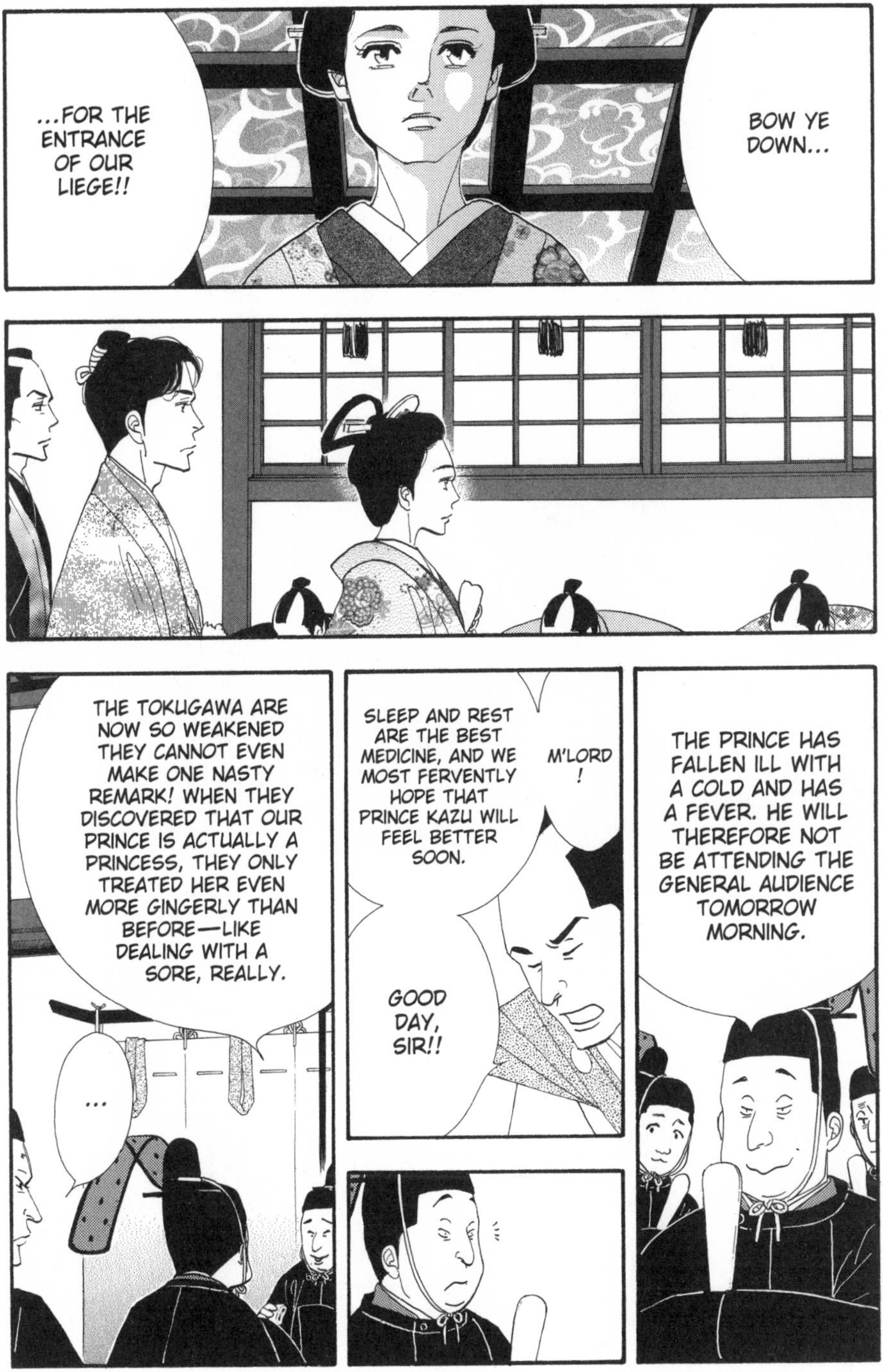
BOW YE DOWN...
...FOR THE ENTRANCE OF OUR LIEGE!!
THE PRINCE HAS FALLEN ILL WITH A COLD AND HAS A FEVER. HE WILL THEREFORE NOT BE ATTENDING THE GENERAL AUDIENCE TOMORROW MORNING.
M'LORD!
SLEEP AND REST ARE THE BEST MEDICINE, AND WE MOST FERVENTLY HOPE THAT PRINCE KAZU WILL FEEL BETTER SOON.
GOOD DAY, SIR!!
THE TOKUGAWA ARE NOW SO WEAKENED THEY CANNOT EVEN MAKE ONE NASTY REMARK! WHEN THEY DISCOVERED THAT OUR PRINCE IS ACTUALLY A PRINCESS, THEY ONLY TREATED HER EVEN MORE GINGERLY THAN BEFORE—LIKE DEALING WITH A SORE, REALLY.
...

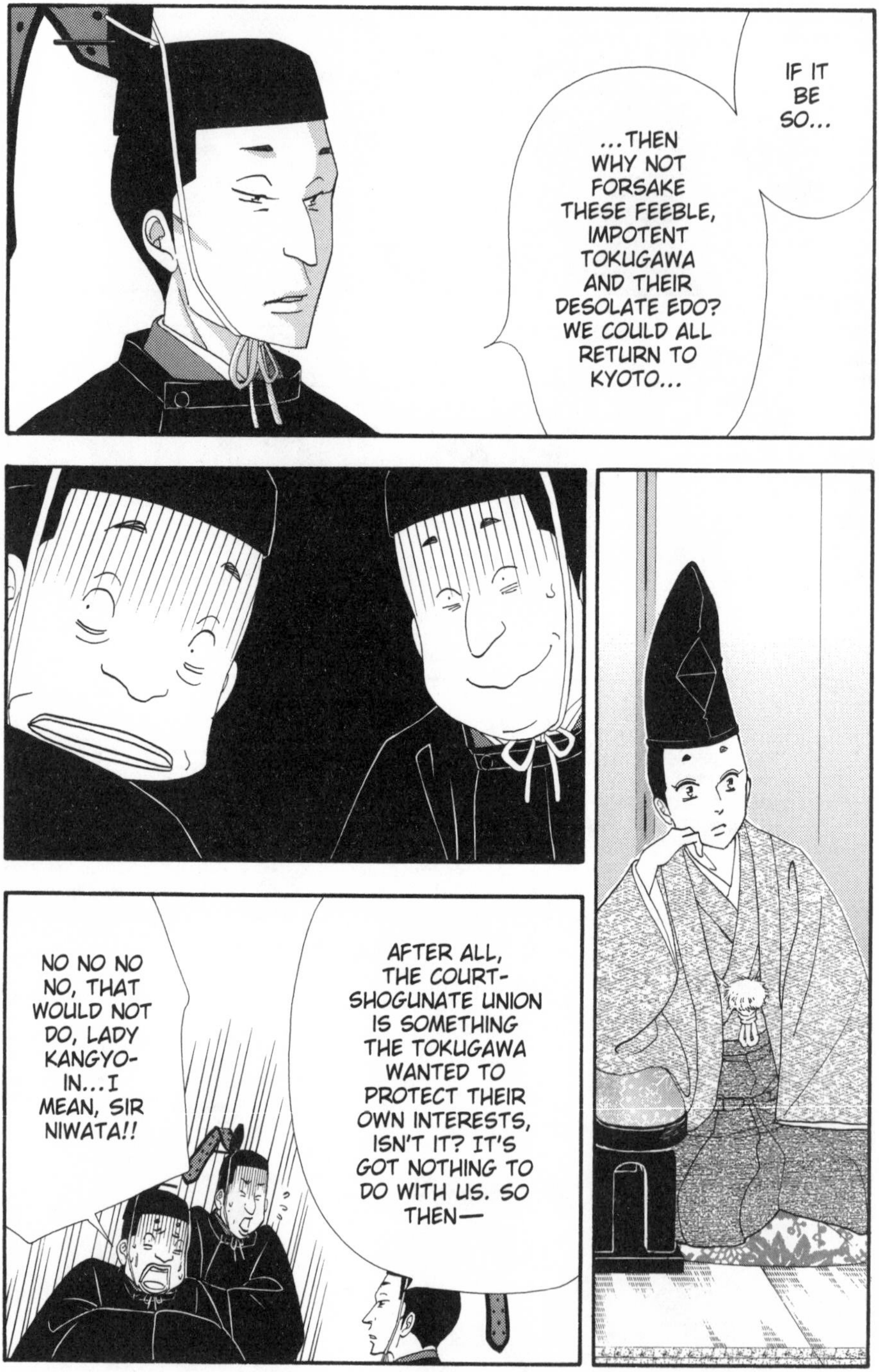
IF IT BE SO...
...THEN WHY NOT FORSAKE THESE FEEBLE, IMPOTENT TOKUGAWA AND THEIR DESOLATE EDO? WE COULD ALL RETURN TO KYOTO...
AFTER ALL, THE COURT-SHOGUNATE UNION IS SOMETHING THE TOKUGAWA WANTED TO PROTECT THEIR OWN INTERESTS, ISN'T IT? IT'S GOT NOTHING TO DO WITH US. SO THEN—
NO NO NO NO, THAT WOULD NOT DO, LADY KANGYO-IN...I MEAN, SIR NIWATA!!

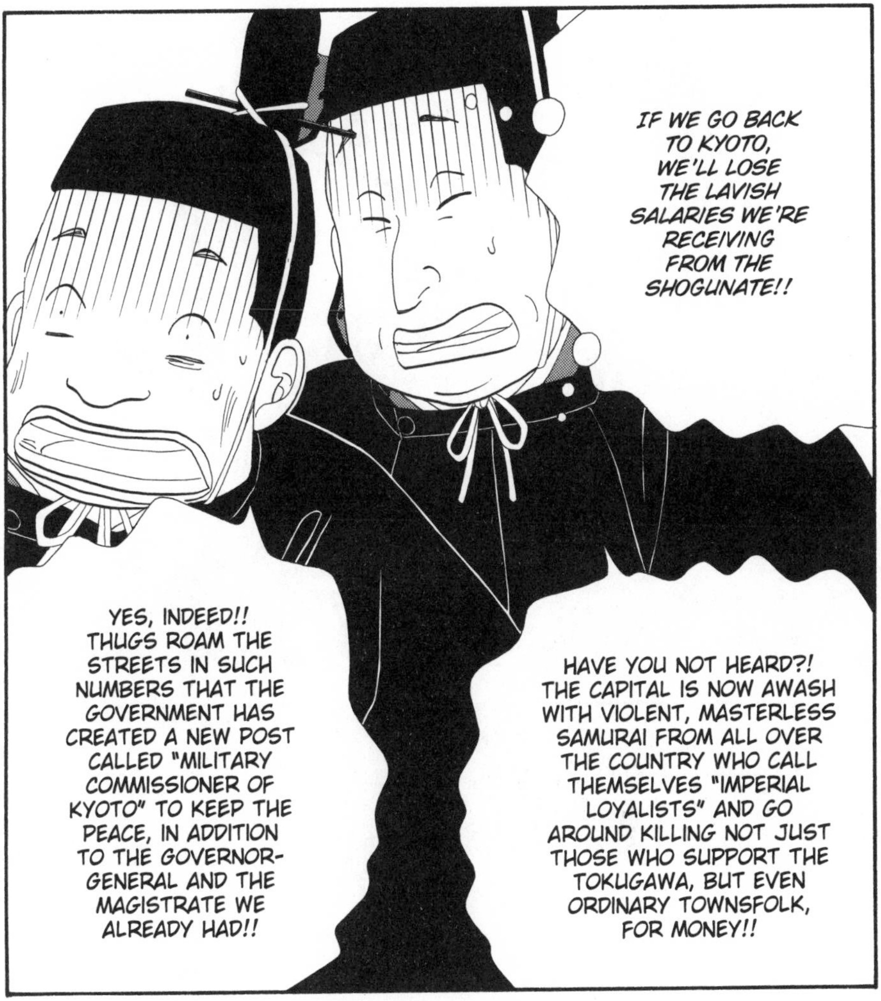
IF WE GO BACK TO KYOTO, WE'LL LOSE THE LAVISH SALARIES WE'RE RECEIVING FROM THE SHOGUNATE!!
HAVE YOU NOT HEARD?! THE CAPITAL IS NOW AWASH WITH VIOLENT, MASTERLESS SAMURAI FROM ALL OVER THE COUNTRY WHO CALL THEMSELVES "IMPERIAL LOYALISTS" AND GO AROUND KILLING NOT JUST THOSE WHO SUPPORT THE TOKUGAWA, BUT EVEN ORDINARY TOWNSFOLK, FOR MONEY!!
YES, INDEED!! THUGS ROAM THE STREETS IN SUCH NUMBERS THAT THE GOVERNMENT HAS CREATED A NEW POST CALLED "MILITARY COMMISSIONER OF KYOTO" TO KEEP THE PEACE, IN ADDITION TO THE GOVERNOR-GENERAL AND THE MAGISTRATE WE ALREADY HAD!!

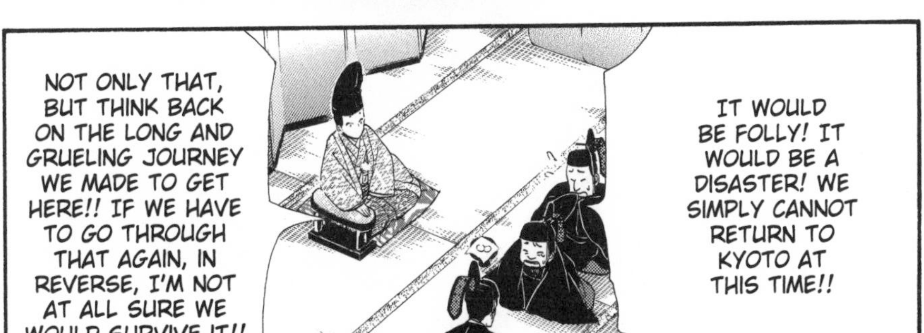
IT WOULD BE FOLLY! IT WOULD BE A DISASTER! WE SIMPLY CANNOT RETURN TO KYOTO AT THIS TIME!!
NOT ONLY THAT, BUT THINK BACK ON THE LONG AND GRUELING JOURNEY WE MADE TO GET HERE!! IF WE HAVE TO GO THROUGH THAT AGAIN, IN REVERSE, I'M NOT AT ALL SURE WE WOULD SURVIVE IT!!

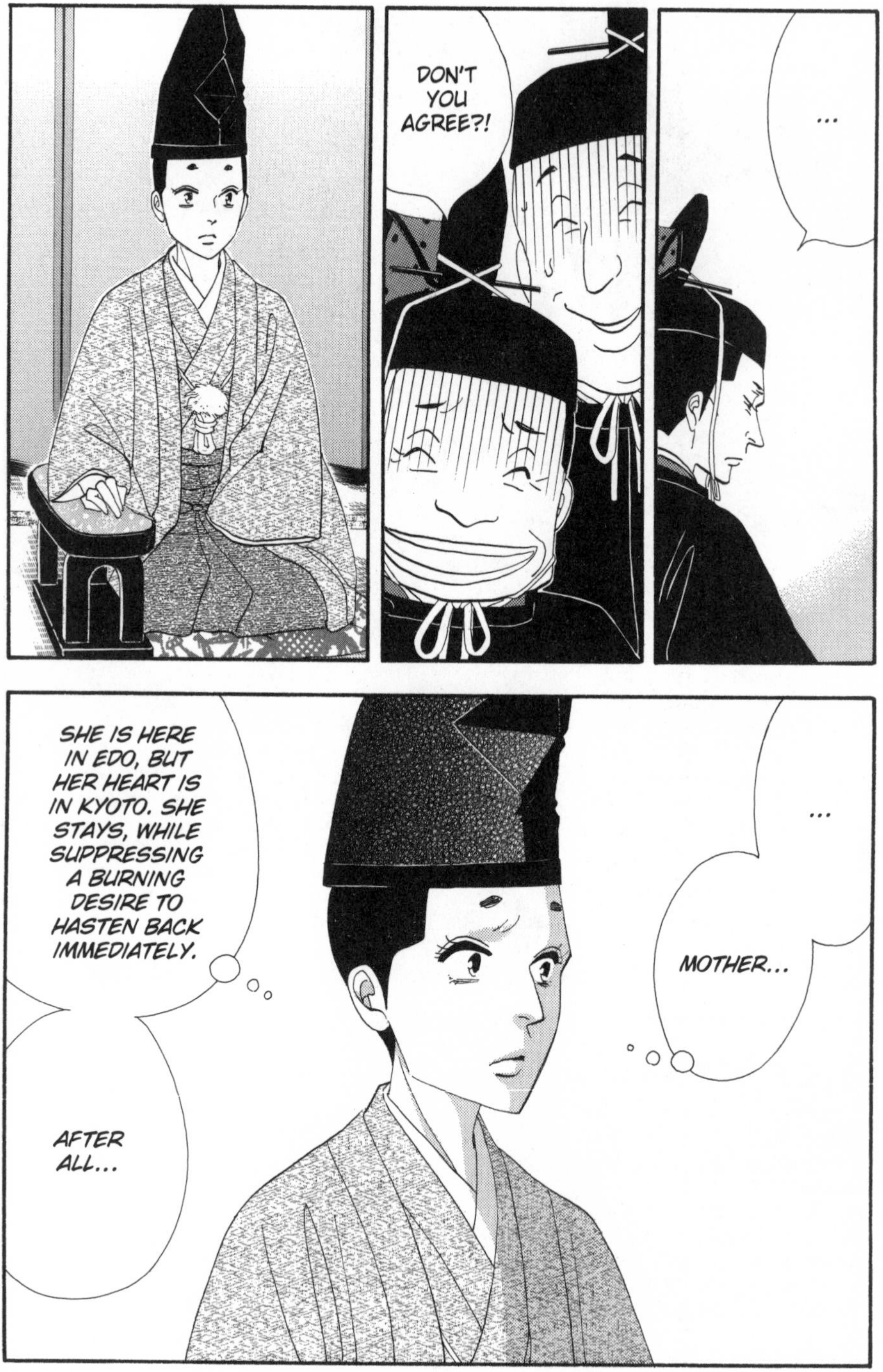
...
DON'T YOU AGREE?!
...
MOTHER...
SHE IS HERE IN EDO, BUT HER HEART IS IN KYOTO. SHE STAYS, WHILE SUPPRESSING A BURNING DESIRE TO HASTEN BACK IMMEDIATELY.
AFTER ALL...

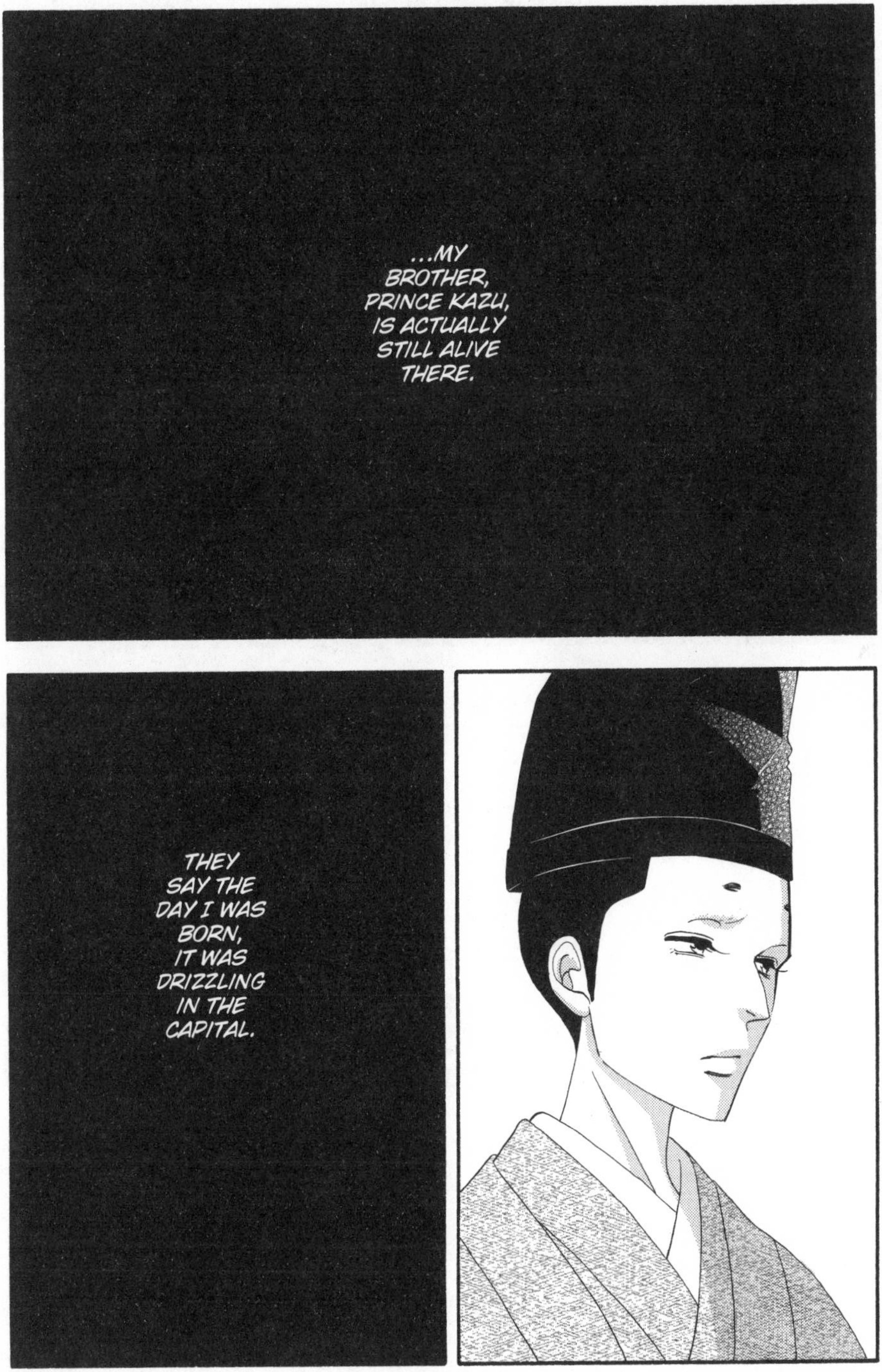

...MY BROTHER, PRINCE KAZU, IS ACTUALLY STILL ALIVE THERE.
THEY SAY THE DAY I WAS BORN, IT WAS DRIZZLING IN THE CAPITAL.

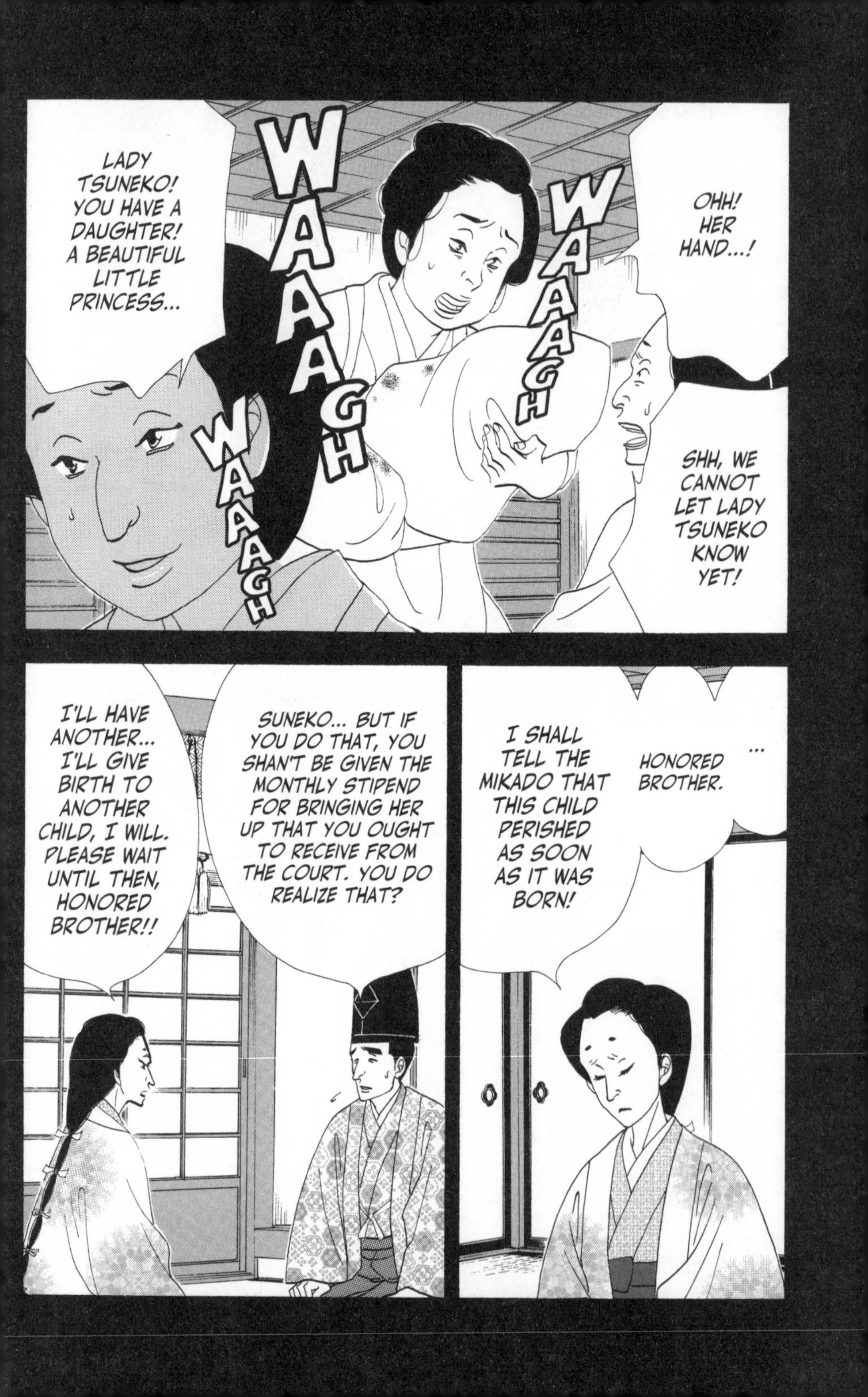
OHH! HER HAND...!
WAAAAGH
WAAAGH
LADY TSUNEKO! YOU HAVE A DAUGHTER! A BEAUTIFUL LITTLE PRINCESS...
SHH, WE CANNOT LET LADY TSUNEKO KNOW YET!
WAAAAGH
...
HONORED BROTHER.
I SHALL TELL THE MIKADO THAT THIS CHILD PERISHED AS SOON AS IT WAS BORN!
SUNEKO... BUT IF YOU DO THAT, YOU SHAN'T BE GIVEN THE MONTHLY STIPEND FOR BRINGING HER UP THAT YOU OUGHT TO RECEIVE FROM THE COURT. YOU DO REALIZE THAT?
I'LL HAVE ANOTHER... I'LL GIVE BIRTH TO ANOTHER CHILD, I WILL. PLEASE WAIT UNTIL THEN, HONORED BROTHER!!

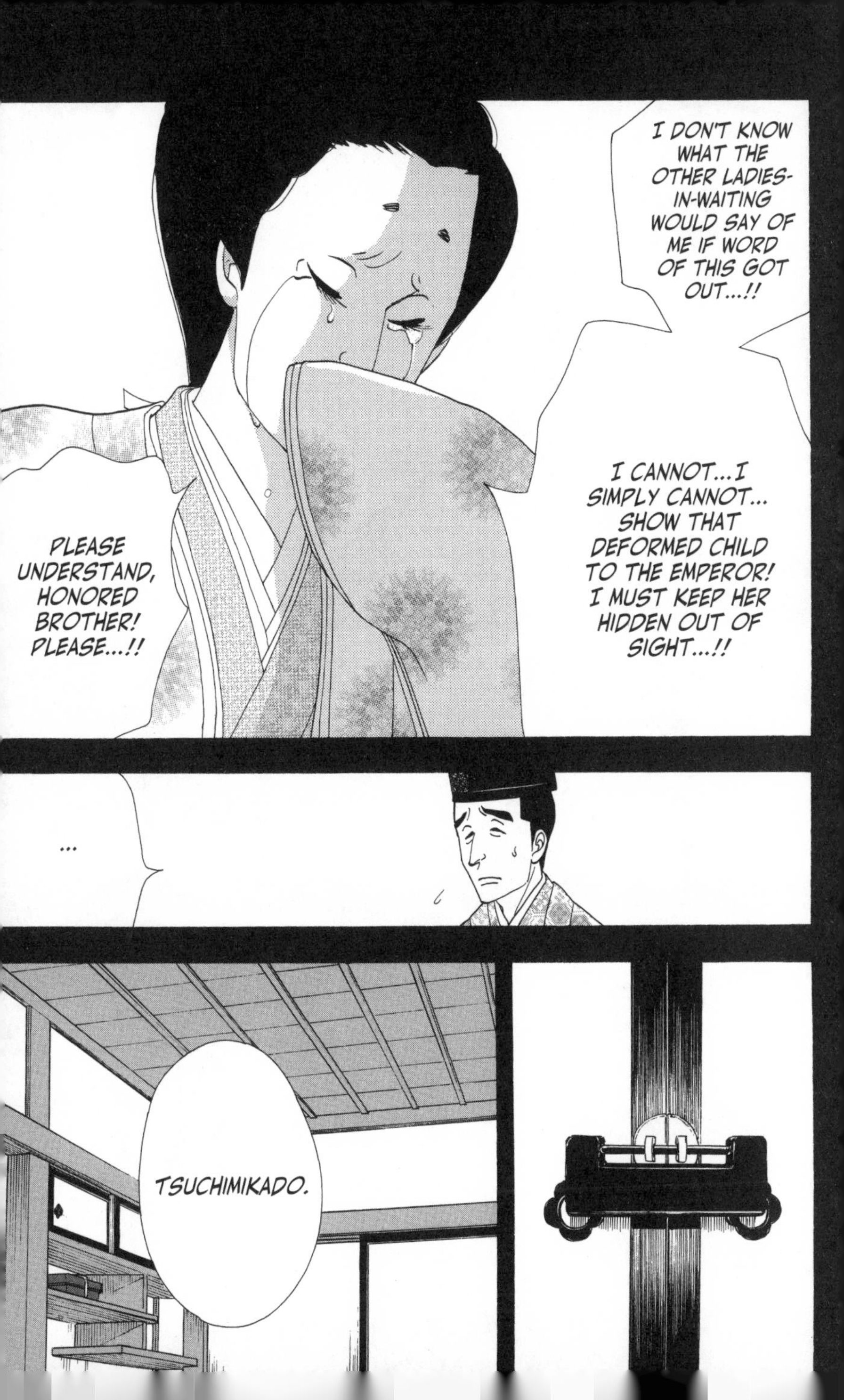
I DON'T KNOW WHAT THE OTHER LADIES-IN-WAITING WOULD SAY OF ME IF WORD OF THIS GOT OUT...!!
I CANNOT...I SIMPLY CANNOT... SHOW THAT DEFORMED CHILD TO THE EMPEROR! I MUST KEEP HER HIDDEN OUT OF SIGHT...!!
PLEASE UNDERSTAND, HONORED BROTHER! PLEASE...!!
...
TSUCHIMIKADO.

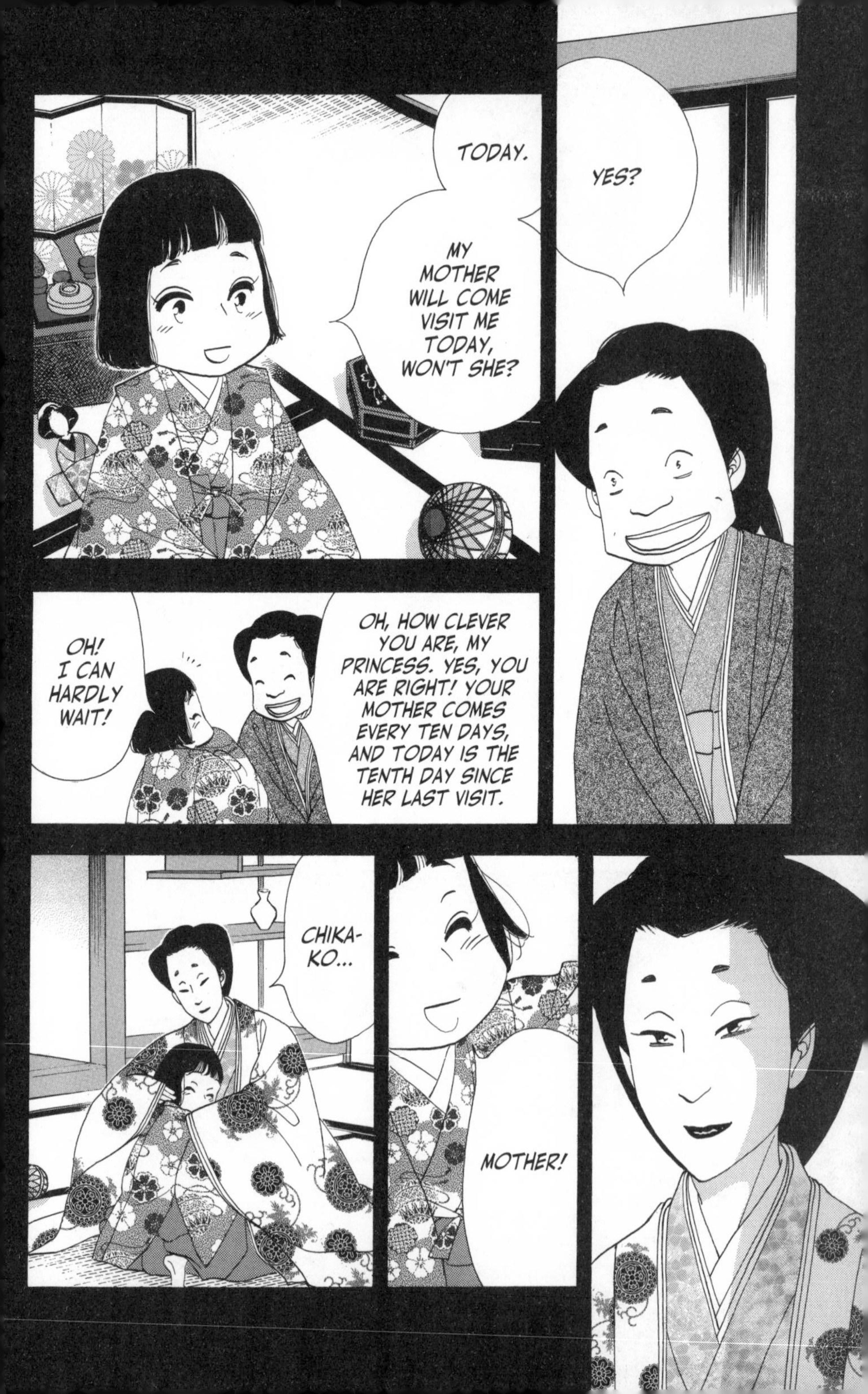
YES?
TODAY.
MY MOTHER WILL COME VISIT ME TODAY, WON'T SHE?
OH, HOW CLEVER YOU ARE, MY PRINCESS. YES, YOU ARE RIGHT! YOUR MOTHER COMES EVERY TEN DAYS, AND TODAY IS THE TENTH DAY SINCE HER LAST VISIT.
OH! I CAN HARDLY WAIT!
MOTHER!
CHIKA-KO...

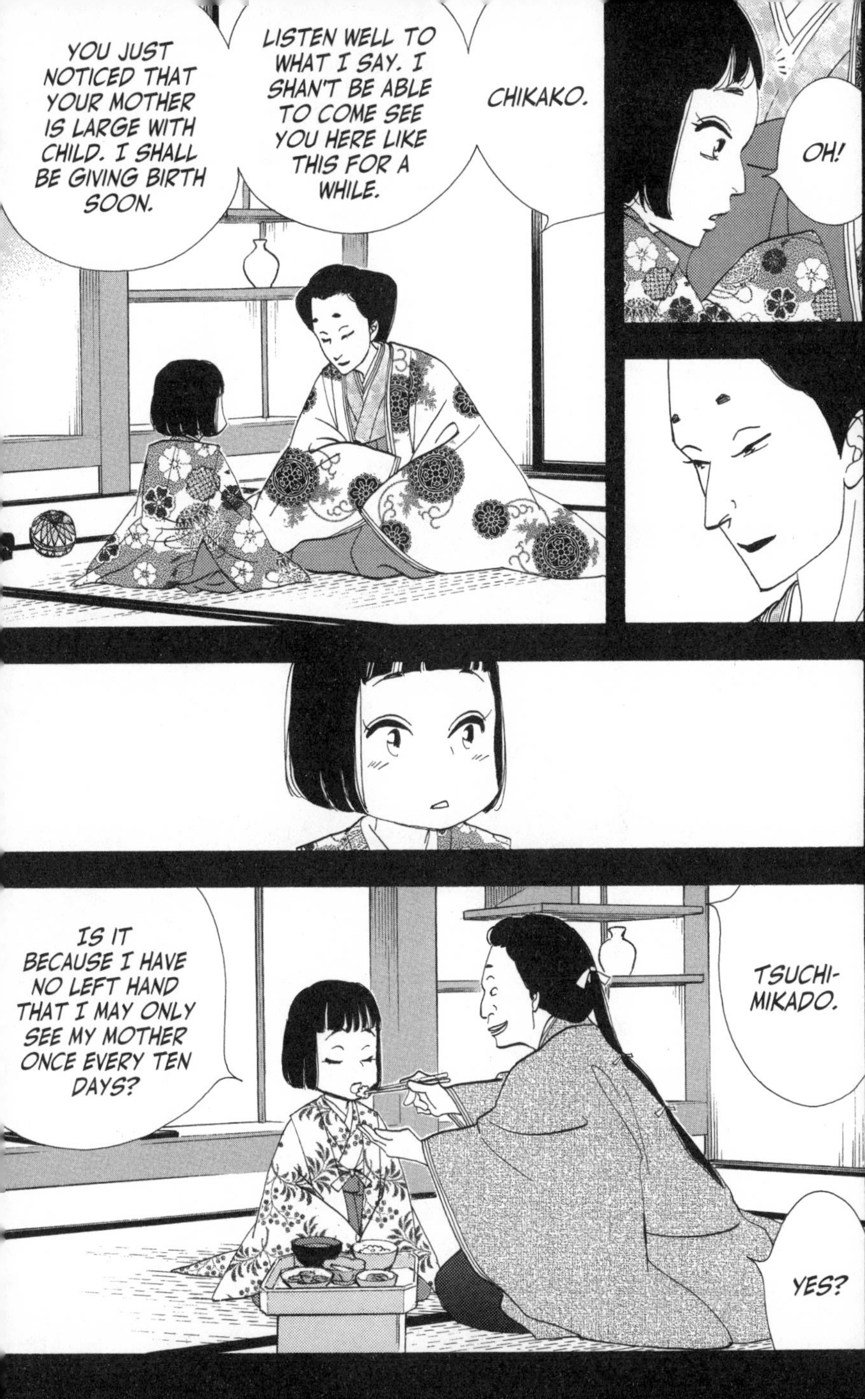
OH!
CHIKAKO.
LISTEN WELL TO WHAT I SAY. I SHAN'T BE ABLE TO COME SEE YOU HERE LIKE THIS FOR A WHILE.
YOU JUST NOTICED THAT YOUR MOTHER IS LARGE WITH CHILD. I SHALL BE GIVING BIRTH SOON.
TSUCHI-MIKADO.
YES?
IS IT BECAUSE I HAVE NO LEFT HAND THAT I MAY ONLY SEE MY MOTHER ONCE EVERY TEN DAYS?

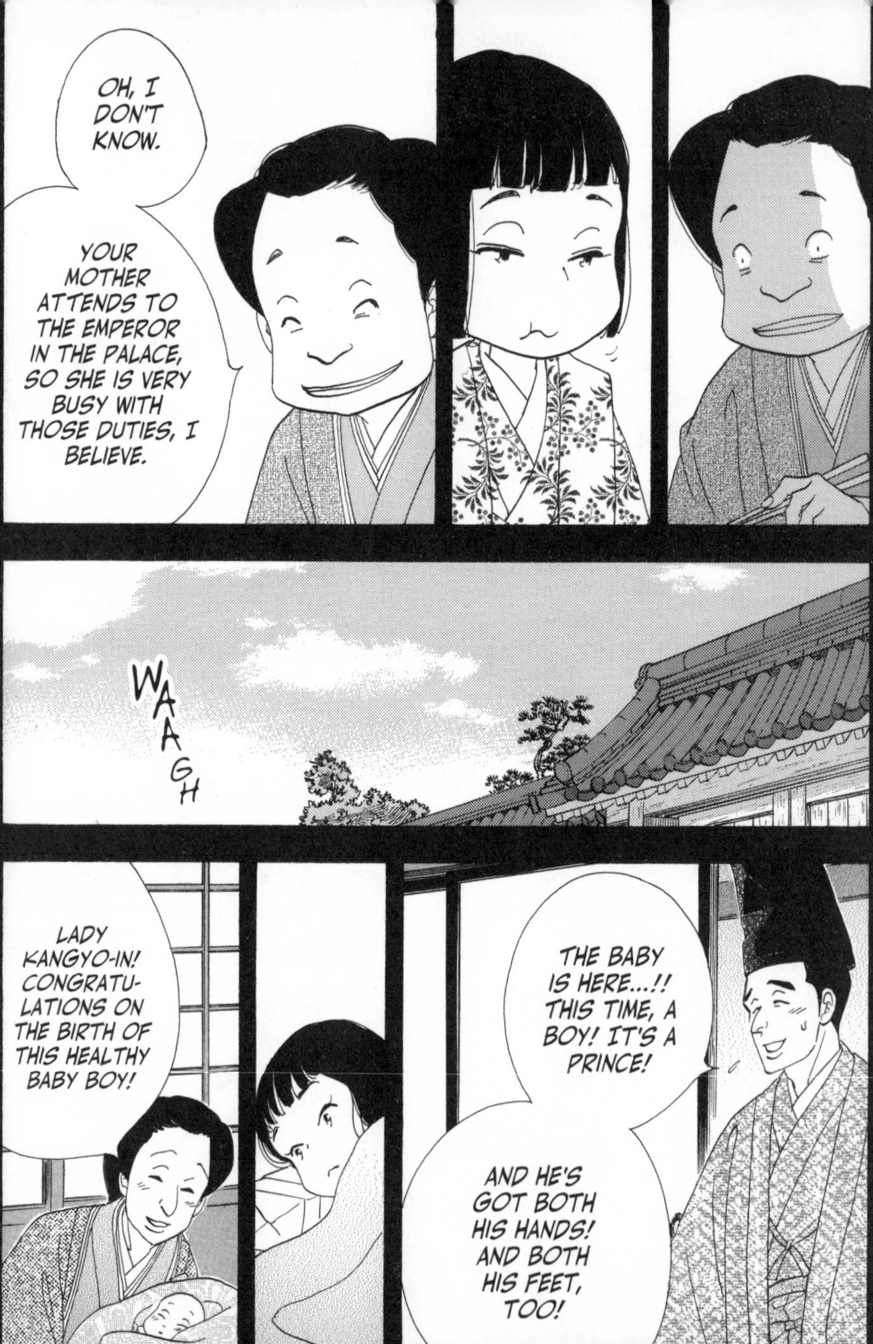
OH, I DON'T KNOW.
YOUR MOTHER ATTENDS TO THE EMPEROR IN THE PALACE, SO SHE IS VERY BUSY WITH THOSE DUTIES, I BELIEVE.
WAAAGH
THE BABY IS HERE...!! THIS TIME, A BOY! IT'S A PRINCE!
AND HE'S GOT BOTH HIS HANDS! AND BOTH HIS FEET, TOO!
LADY KANGYO-IN! CONGRATU-LATIONS ON THE BIRTH OF THIS HEALTHY BABY BOY!

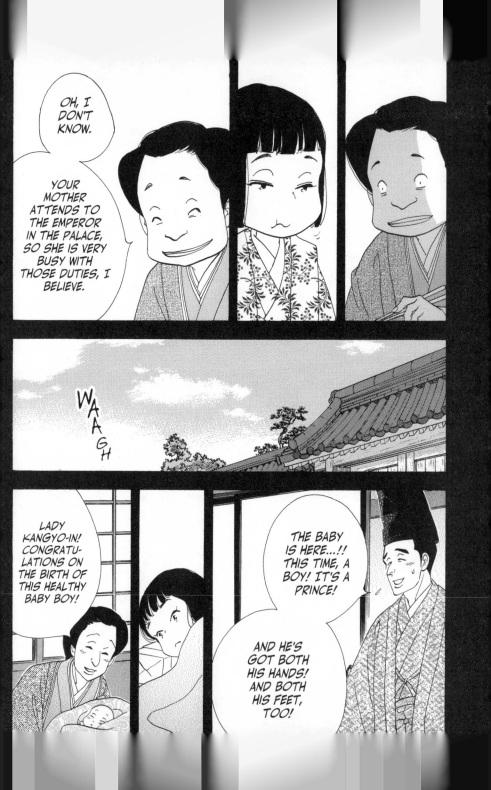

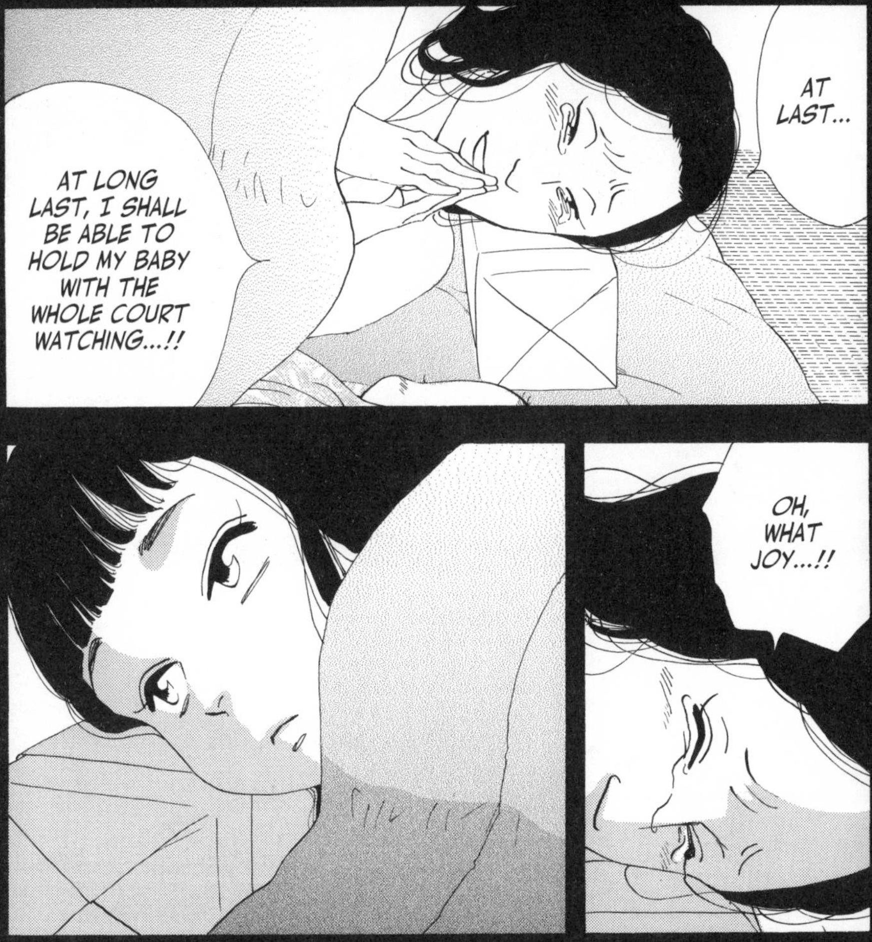
AT LAST...
AT LONG LAST, I SHALL BE ABLE TO HOLD MY BABY WITH THE WHOLE COURT WATCHING...!!
OH, WHAT JOY...!!

THE BABY BOY WAS NAMED PRINCE KAZU, AND AFTER THE DAY HE WAS BORN, MY MOTHER'S VISITS TO MY CHAMBER BECAME VERY RARE.

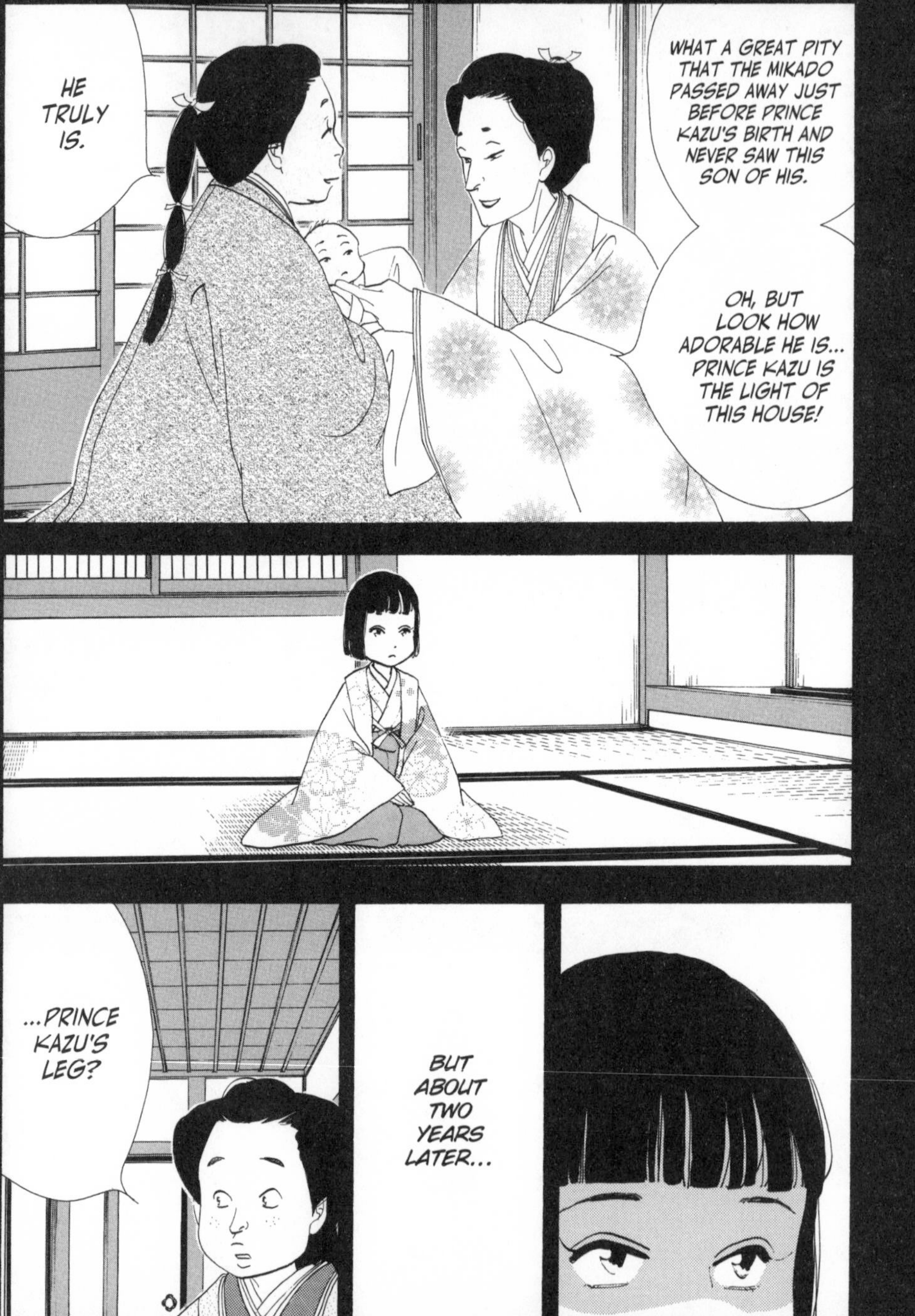
WHAT A GREAT PITY THAT THE MIKADO PASSED AWAY JUST BEFORE PRINCE KAZU'S BIRTH AND NEVER SAW THIS SON OF HIS.
OH, BUT LOOK HOW ADORABLE HE IS... PRINCE KAZU IS THE LIGHT OF THIS HOUSE!
HE TRULY IS.
BUT ABOUT TWO YEARS LATER...
...PRINCE KAZU'S LEG?

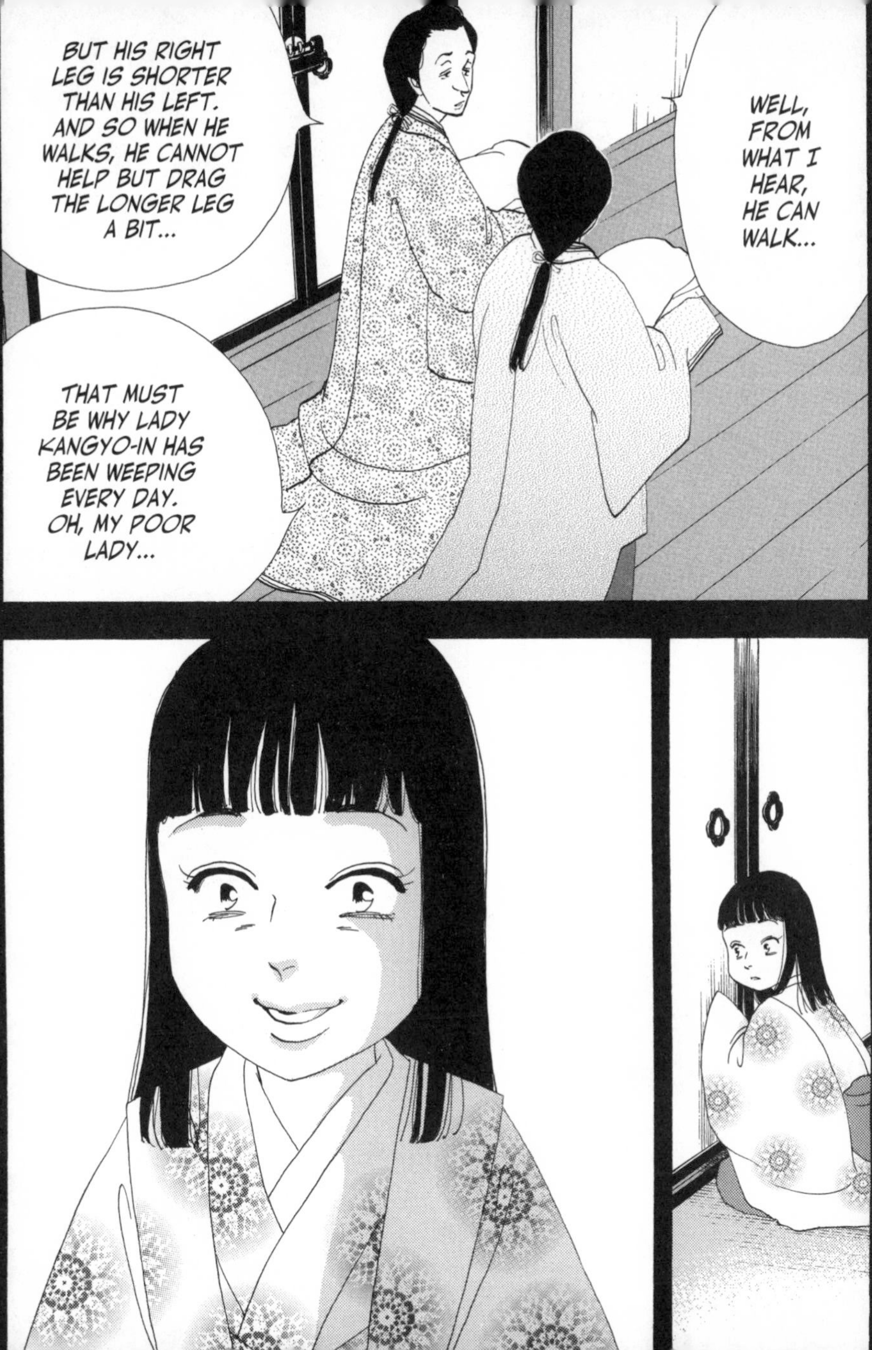
WELL, FROM WHAT I HEAR, HE CAN WALK...
BUT HIS RIGHT LEG IS SHORTER THAN HIS LEFT. AND SO WHEN HE WALKS, HE CANNOT HELP BUT DRAG THE LONGER LEG A BIT...
THAT MUST BE WHY LADY KANGYO-IN HAS BEEN WEEPING EVERY DAY. OH, MY POOR LADY...

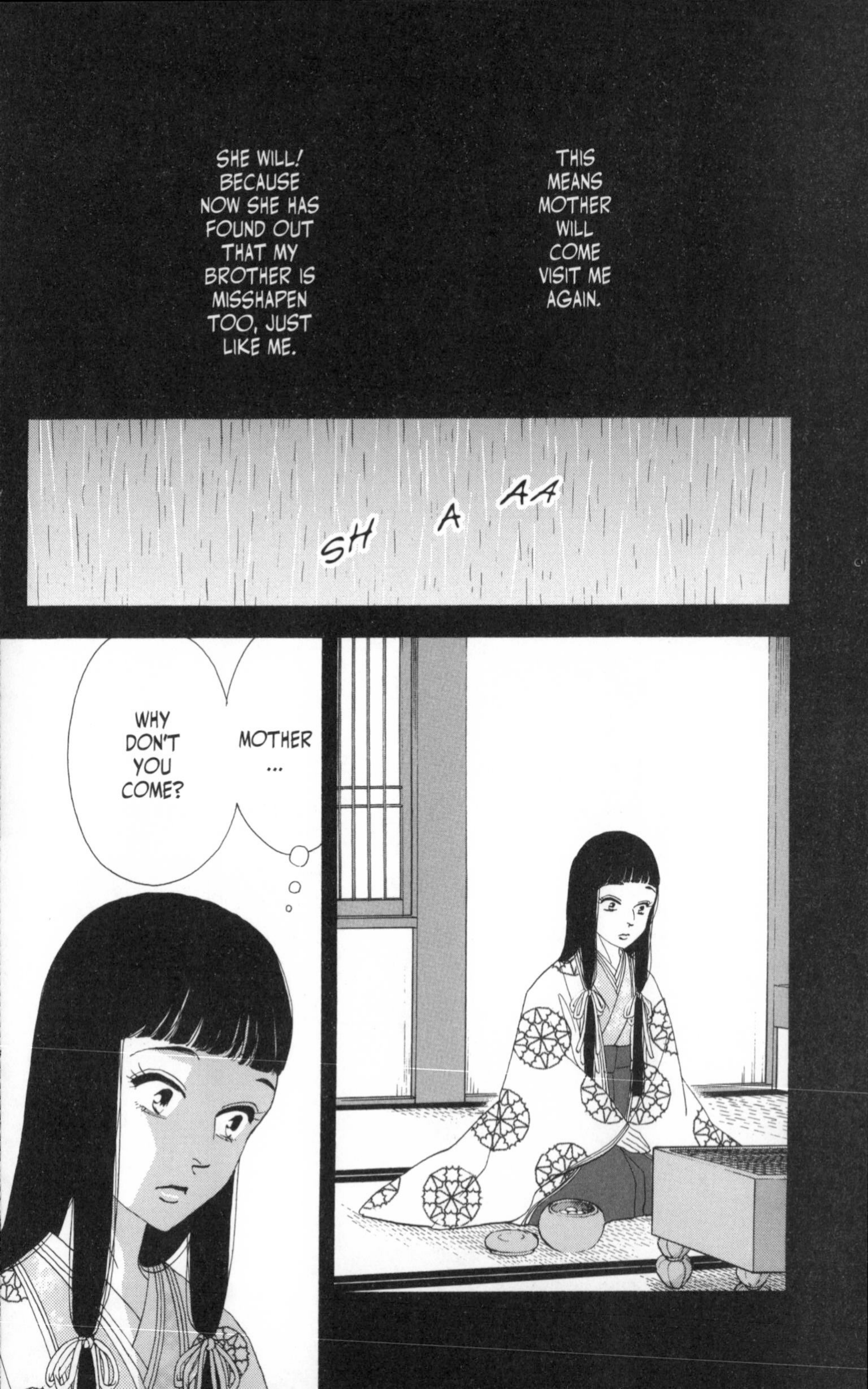
THIS MEANS MOTHER WILL COME VISIT ME AGAIN.
SHE WILL! BECAUSE NOW SHE HAS FOUND OUT THAT MY BROTHER IS MISSHAPEN TOO, JUST LIKE ME.
SH A AA
MOTHER ...
WHY DON'T YOU COME?

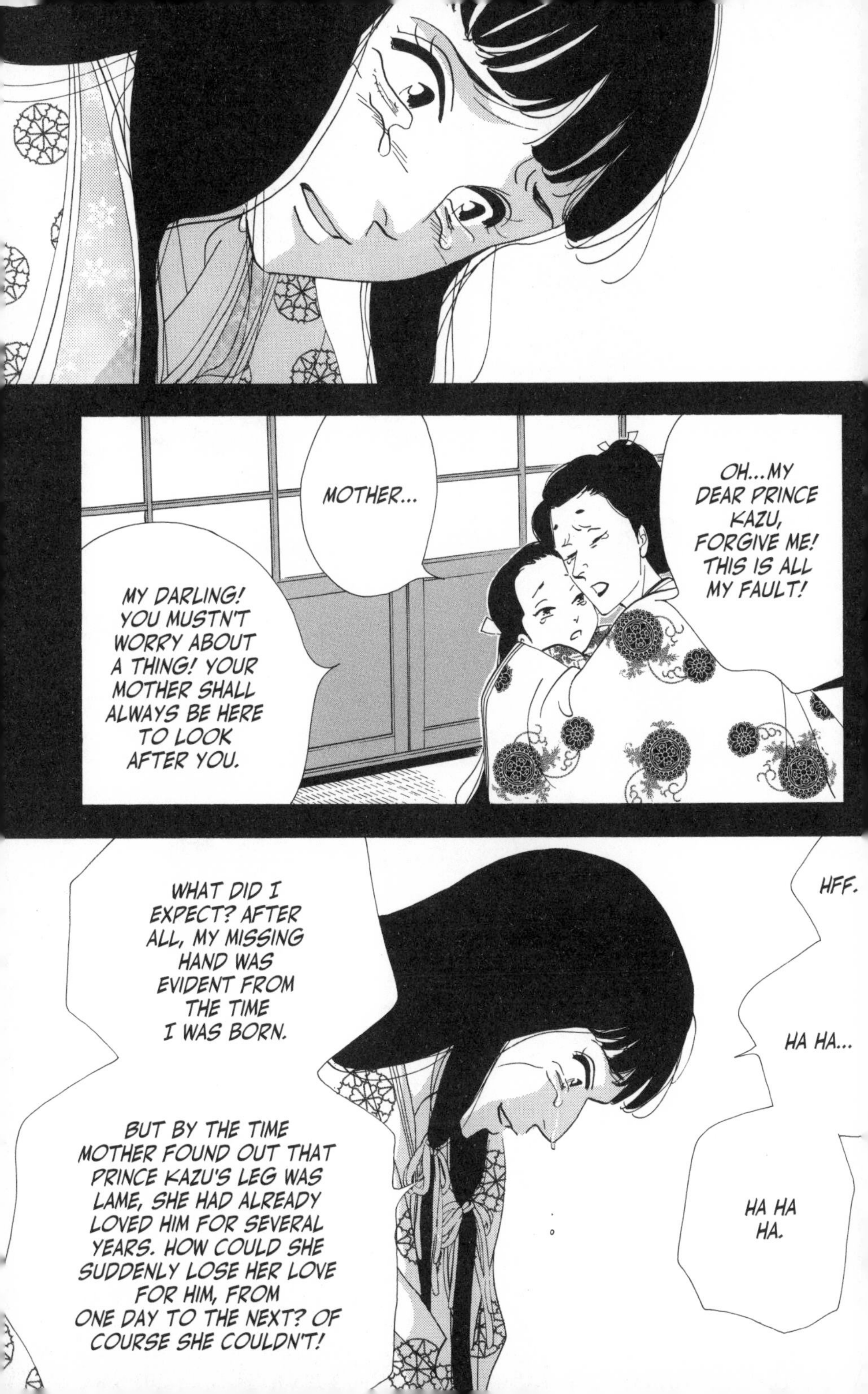
OH...MY DEAR PRINCE KAZU, FORGIVE ME! THIS IS ALL MY FAULT!
MOTHER...
MY DARLING! YOU MUSTN'T WORRY ABOUT A THING! YOUR MOTHER SHALL ALWAYS BE HERE TO LOOK AFTER YOU.
HFF.
HA HA...
HA HA HA.
WHAT DID I EXPECT? AFTER ALL, MY MISSING HAND WAS EVIDENT FROM THE TIME I WAS BORN.
BUT BY THE TIME MOTHER FOUND OUT THAT PRINCE KAZU'S LEG WAS LAME, SHE HAD ALREADY LOVED HIM FOR SEVERAL YEARS. HOW COULD SHE SUDDENLY LOSE HER LOVE FOR HIM, FROM ONE DAY TO THE NEXT? OF COURSE SHE COULDN'T!

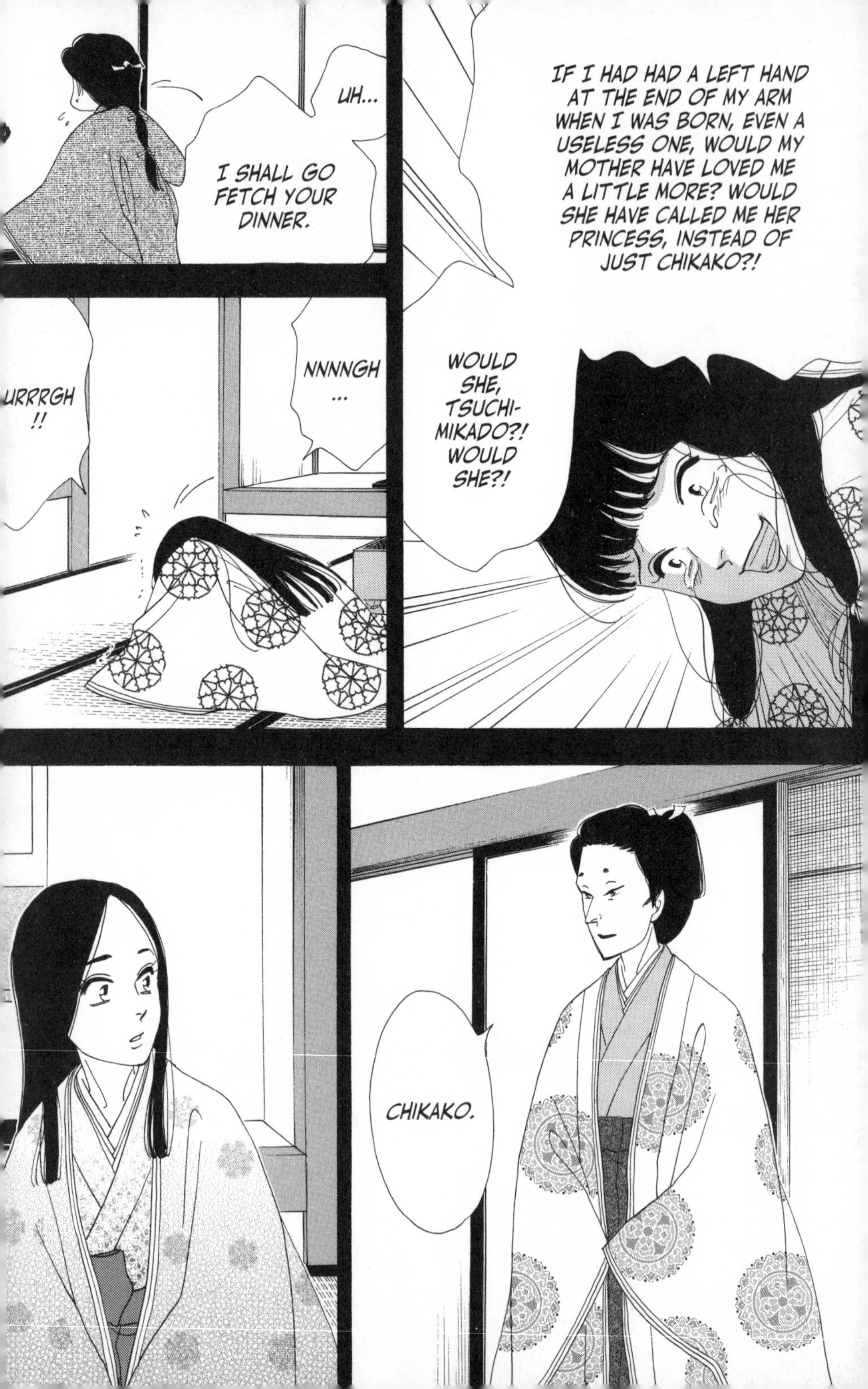
IF I HAD HAD A LEFT HAND AT THE END OF MY ARM WHEN I WAS BORN, EVEN A USELESS ONE, WOULD MY MOTHER HAVE LOVED ME A LITTLE MORE? WOULD SHE HAVE CALLED ME HER PRINCESS, INSTEAD OF JUST CHIKAKO?!
UH...
I SHALL GO FETCH YOUR DINNER.
WOULD SHE, TSUCHI-MIKADO?! WOULD SHE?!
NNNNGH...
URRRGH!!
CHIKAKO.

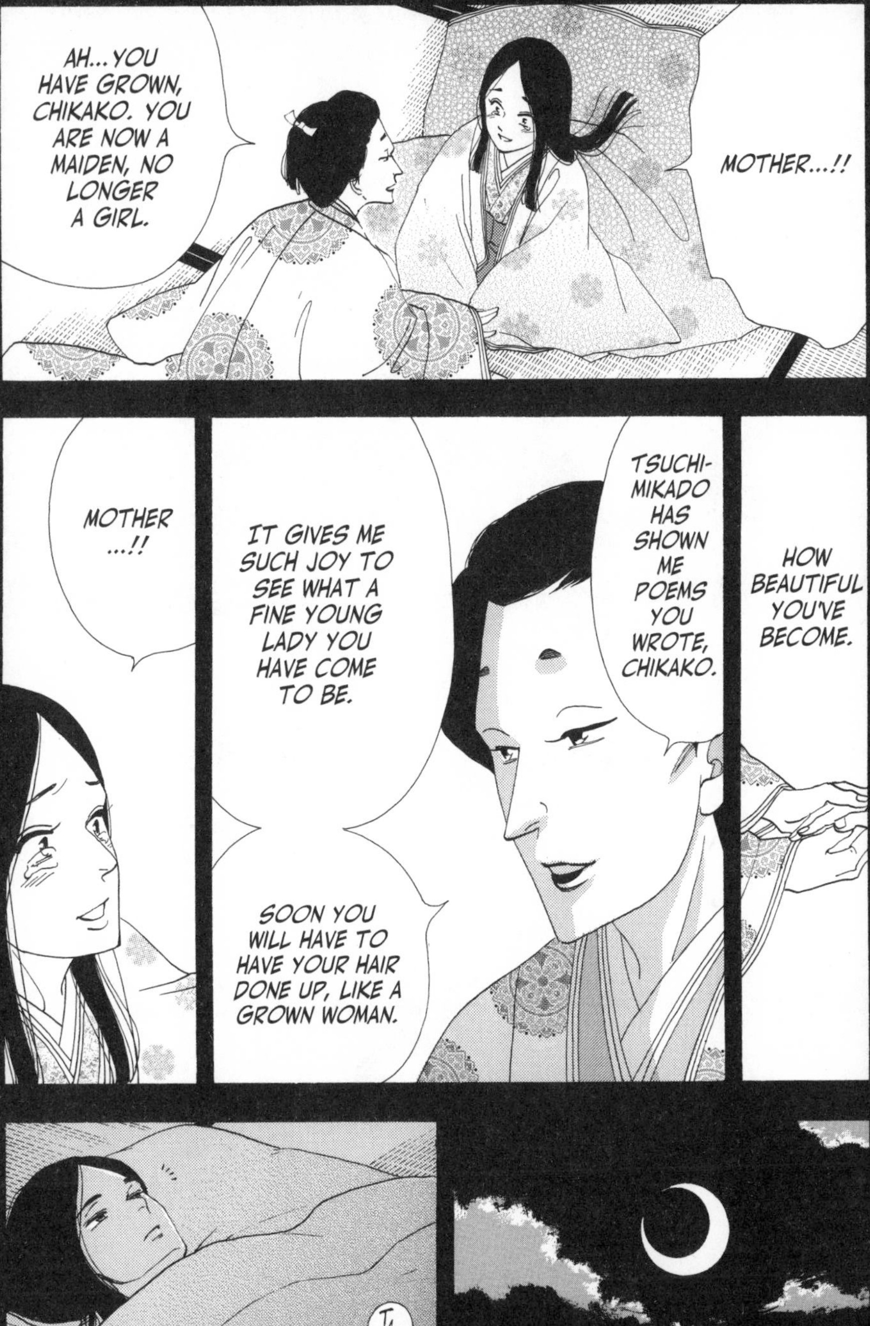
MOTHER...!!
AH...YOU HAVE GROWN, CHIKAKO. YOU ARE NOW A MAIDEN, NO LONGER A GIRL.
HOW BEAUTIFUL YOU'VE BECOME.
TSUCHI-MIKADO HAS SHOWN ME POEMS YOU WROTE, CHIKAKO.
IT GIVES ME SUCH JOY TO SEE WHAT A FINE YOUNG LADY YOU HAVE COME TO BE.
SOON YOU WILL HAVE TO HAVE YOUR HAIR DONE UP, LIKE A GROWN WOMAN.
MOTHER ...!!
TAK

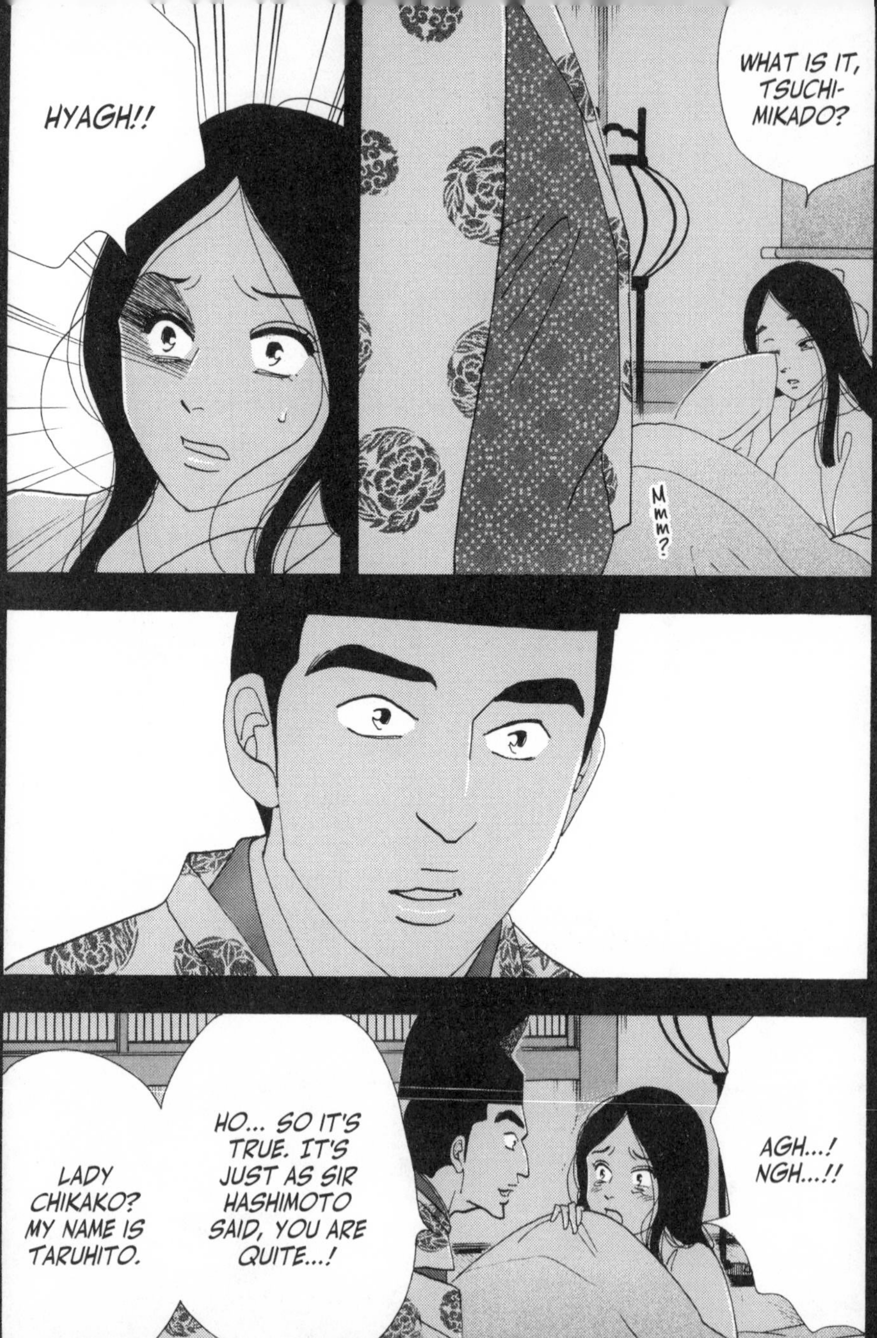
WHAT IS IT, TSUCHI-MIKADO?
Mmm?
HYAGH!!
AGH...! NGH...!!
HO... SO IT'S TRUE. IT'S JUST AS SIR HASHIMOTO SAID, YOU ARE QUITE...!
LADY CHIKAKO? MY NAME IS TARUHITO.

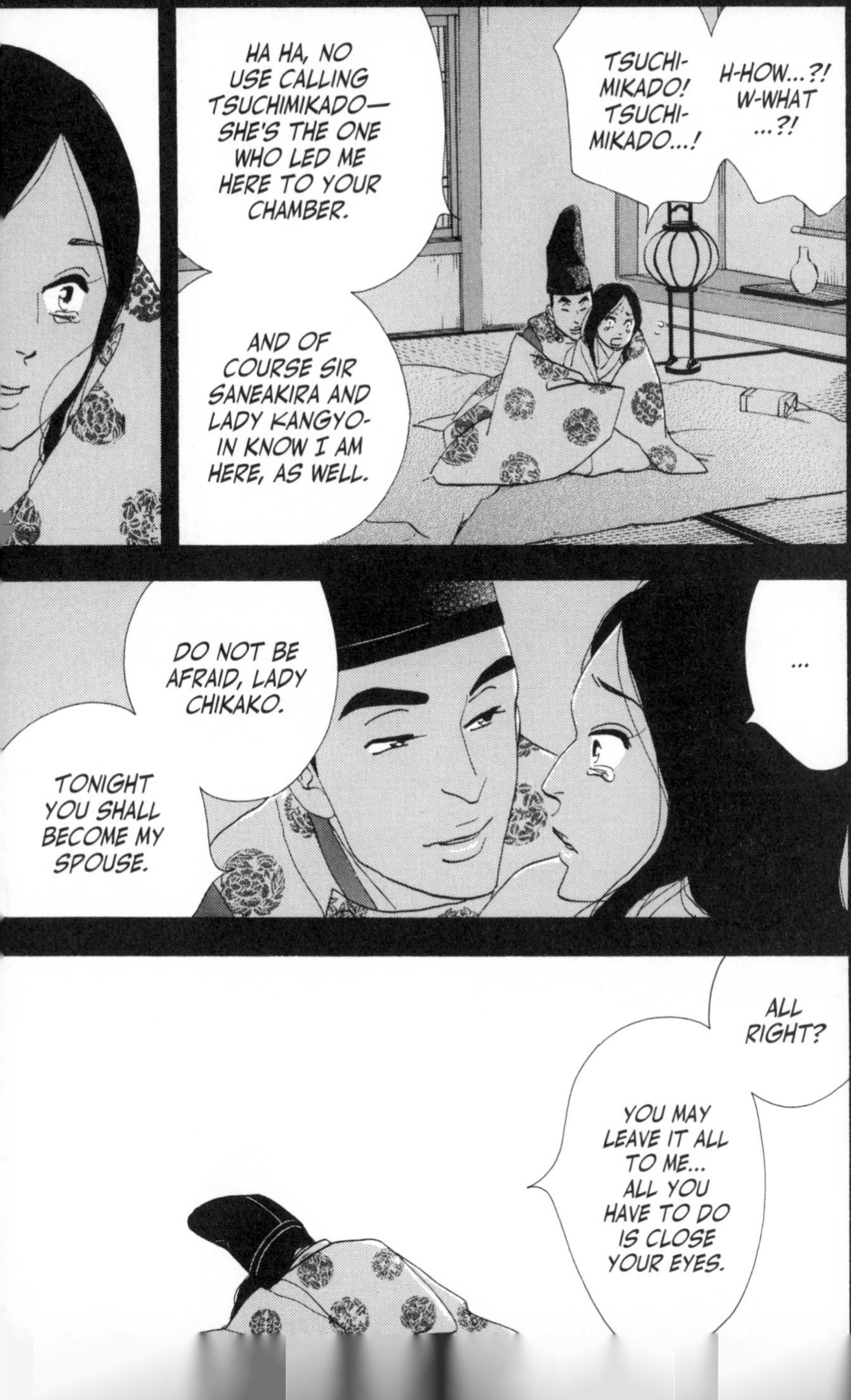
H-HOW...?! W-WHAT ...?!
TSUCHI-MIKADO! TSUCHI-MIKADO...!
HA HA, NO USE CALLING TSUCHIMIKADO—SHE'S THE ONE WHO LED ME HERE TO YOUR CHAMBER.
AND OF COURSE SIR SANEAKIRA AND LADY KANGYO-IN KNOW I AM HERE, AS WELL.
...
DO NOT BE AFRAID, LADY CHIKAKO.
TONIGHT YOU SHALL BECOME MY SPOUSE.
ALL RIGHT?
YOU MAY LEAVE IT ALL TO ME... ALL YOU HAVE TO DO IS CLOSE YOUR EYES.

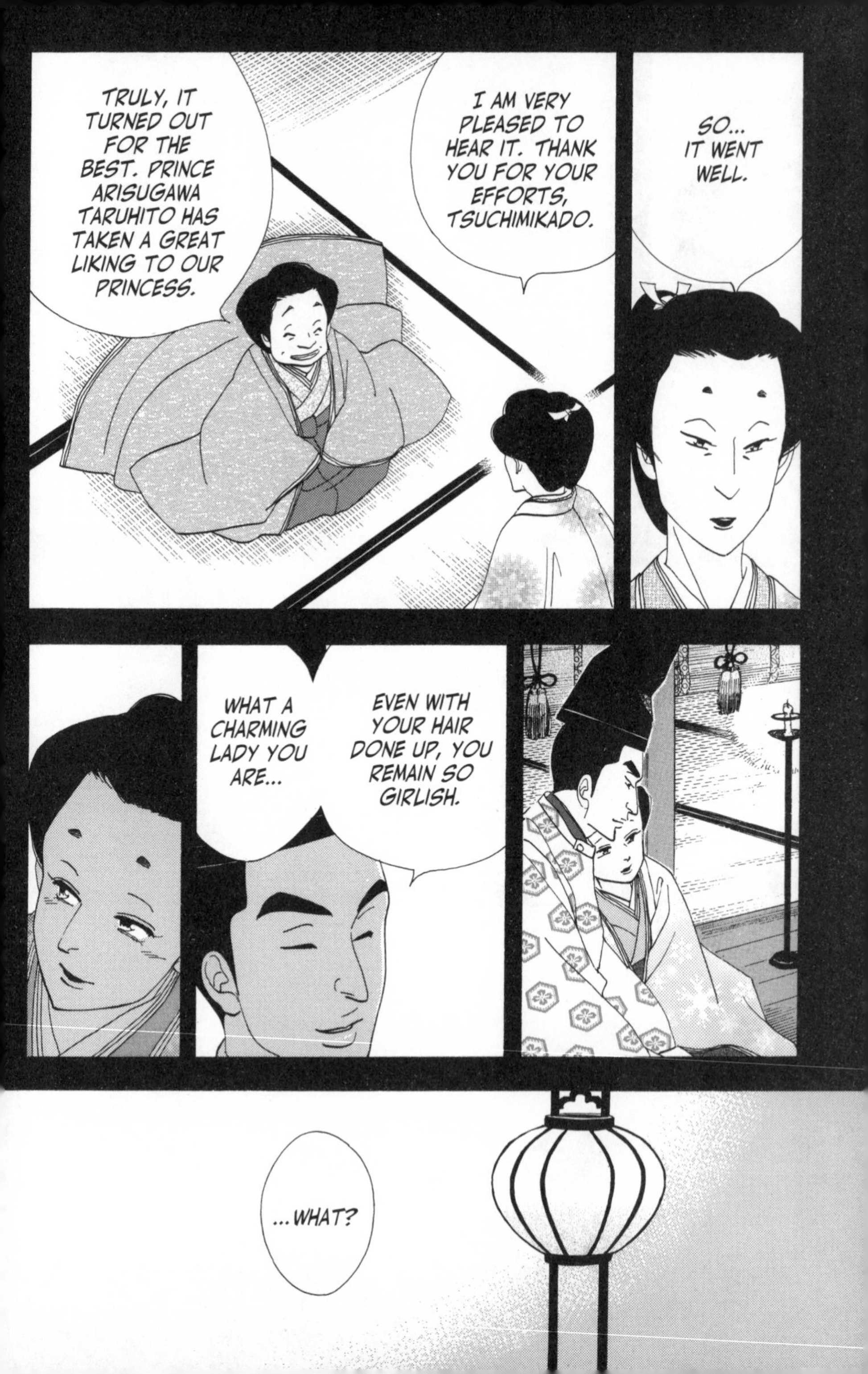
TRULY, IT TURNED OUT FOR THE BEST. PRINCE ARISUGAWA TARUHITO HAS TAKEN A GREAT LIKING TO OUR PRINCESS.
I AM VERY PLEASED TO HEAR IT. THANK YOU FOR YOUR EFFORTS, TSUCHIMIKADO.
SO... IT WENT WELL.
WHAT A CHARMING LADY YOU ARE... EVEN WITH YOUR HAIR DONE UP, YOU REMAIN SO GIRLISH.
...WHAT?

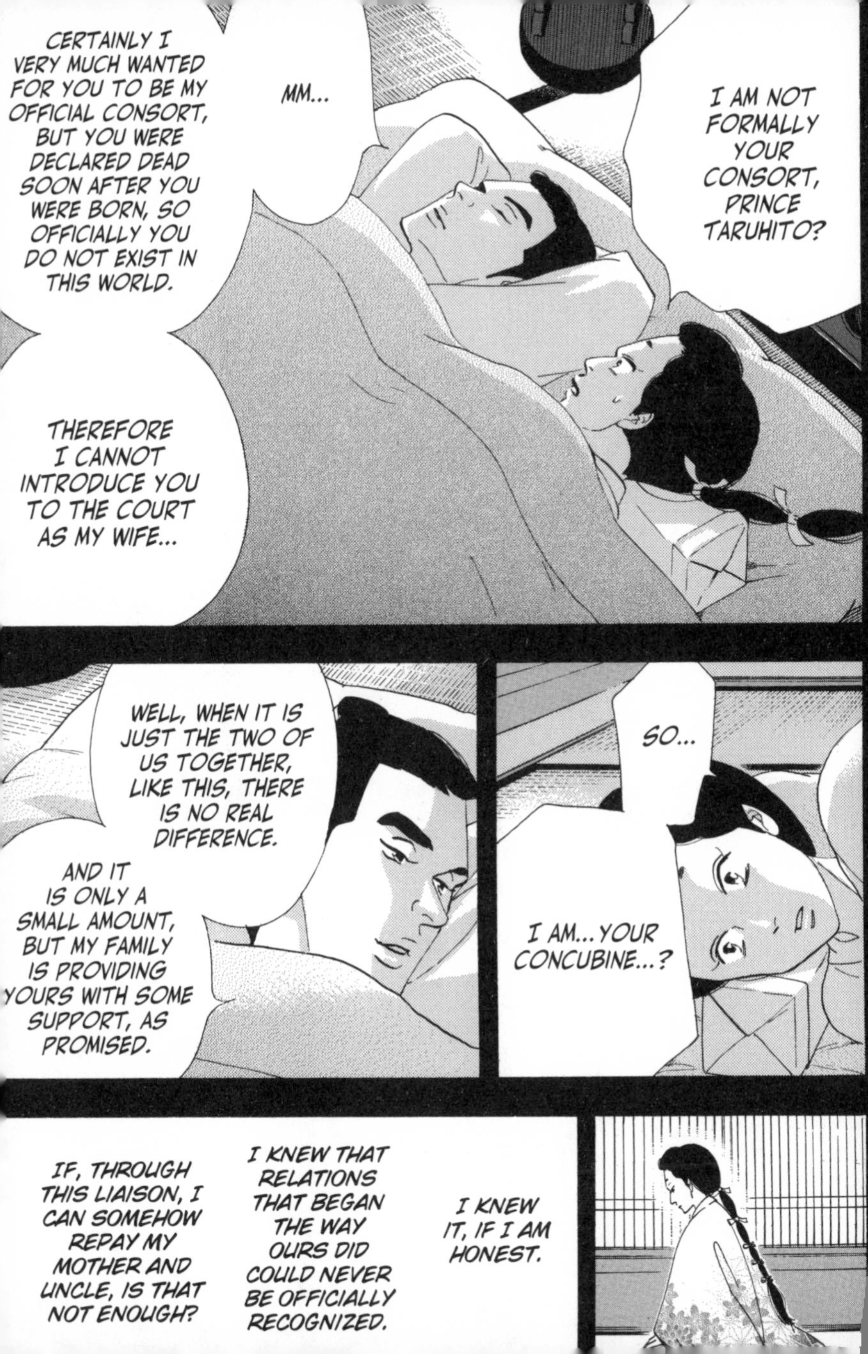
I AM NOT FORMALLY YOUR CONSORT, PRINCE TARUHITO?
MM...
CERTAINLY I VERY MUCH WANTED FOR YOU TO BE MY OFFICIAL CONSORT, BUT YOU WERE DECLARED DEAD SOON AFTER YOU WERE BORN, SO OFFICIALLY YOU DO NOT EXIST IN THIS WORLD.
THEREFORE I CANNOT INTRODUCE YOU TO THE COURT AS MY WIFE...
SO...
I AM...YOUR CONCUBINE...?
WELL, WHEN IT IS JUST THE TWO OF US TOGETHER, LIKE THIS, THERE IS NO REAL DIFFERENCE.
AND IT IS ONLY A SMALL AMOUNT, BUT MY FAMILY IS PROVIDING YOURS WITH SOME SUPPORT, AS PROMISED.
I KNEW IT, IF I AM HONEST.
I KNEW THAT RELATIONS THAT BEGAN THE WAY OURS DID COULD NEVER BE OFFICIALLY RECOGNIZED.
IF, THROUGH THIS LIAISON, I CAN SOMEHOW REPAY MY MOTHER AND UNCLE, IS THAT NOT ENOUGH?

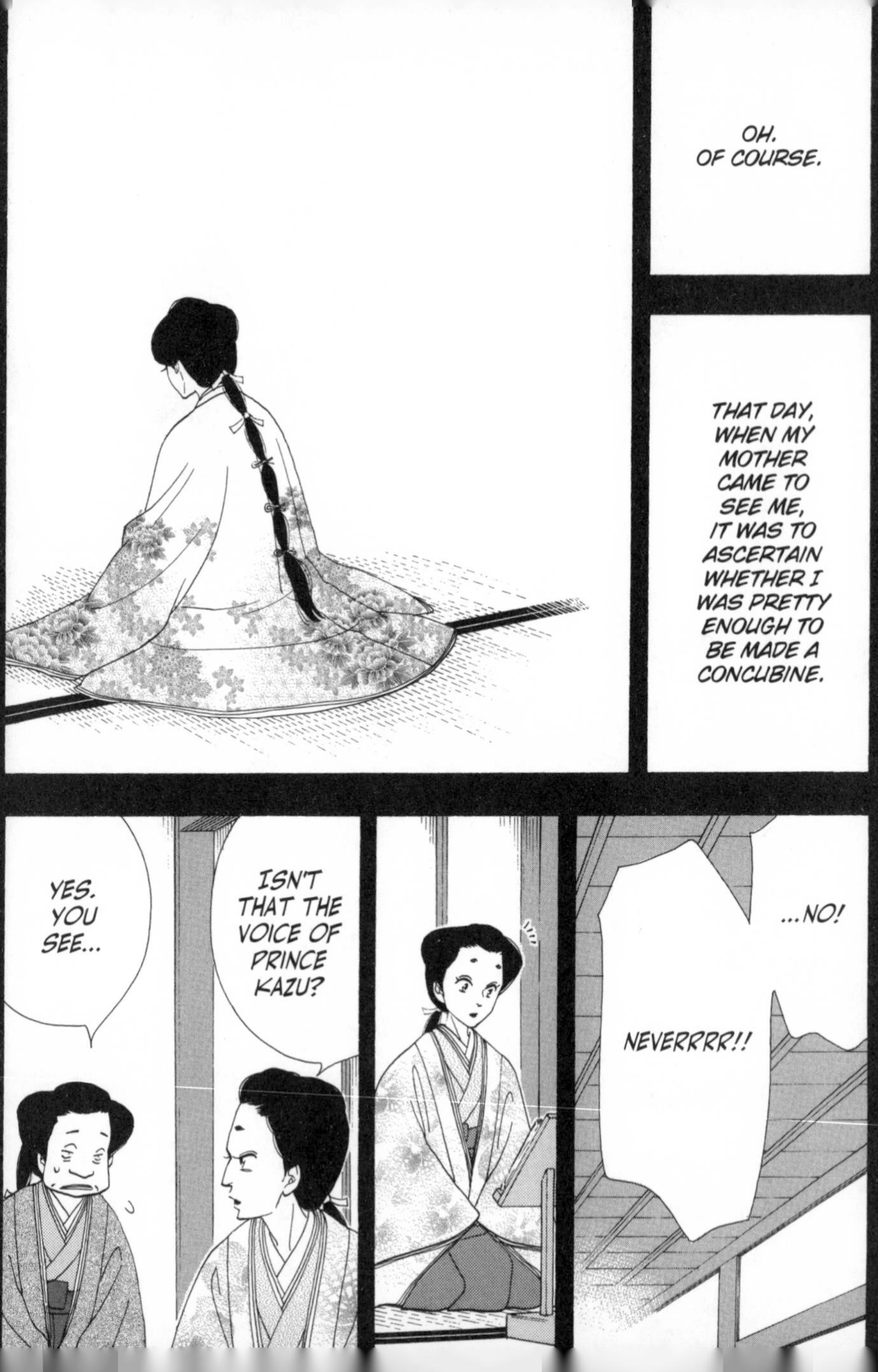
OH.
OF COURSE.
THAT DAY, WHEN MY MOTHER CAME TO SEE ME, IT WAS TO ASCERTAIN WHETHER I WAS PRETTY ENOUGH TO BE MADE A CONCUBINE.
...NO!
NEVERRRR!!
ISN'T THAT THE VOICE OF PRINCE KAZU?
YES. YOU SEE...

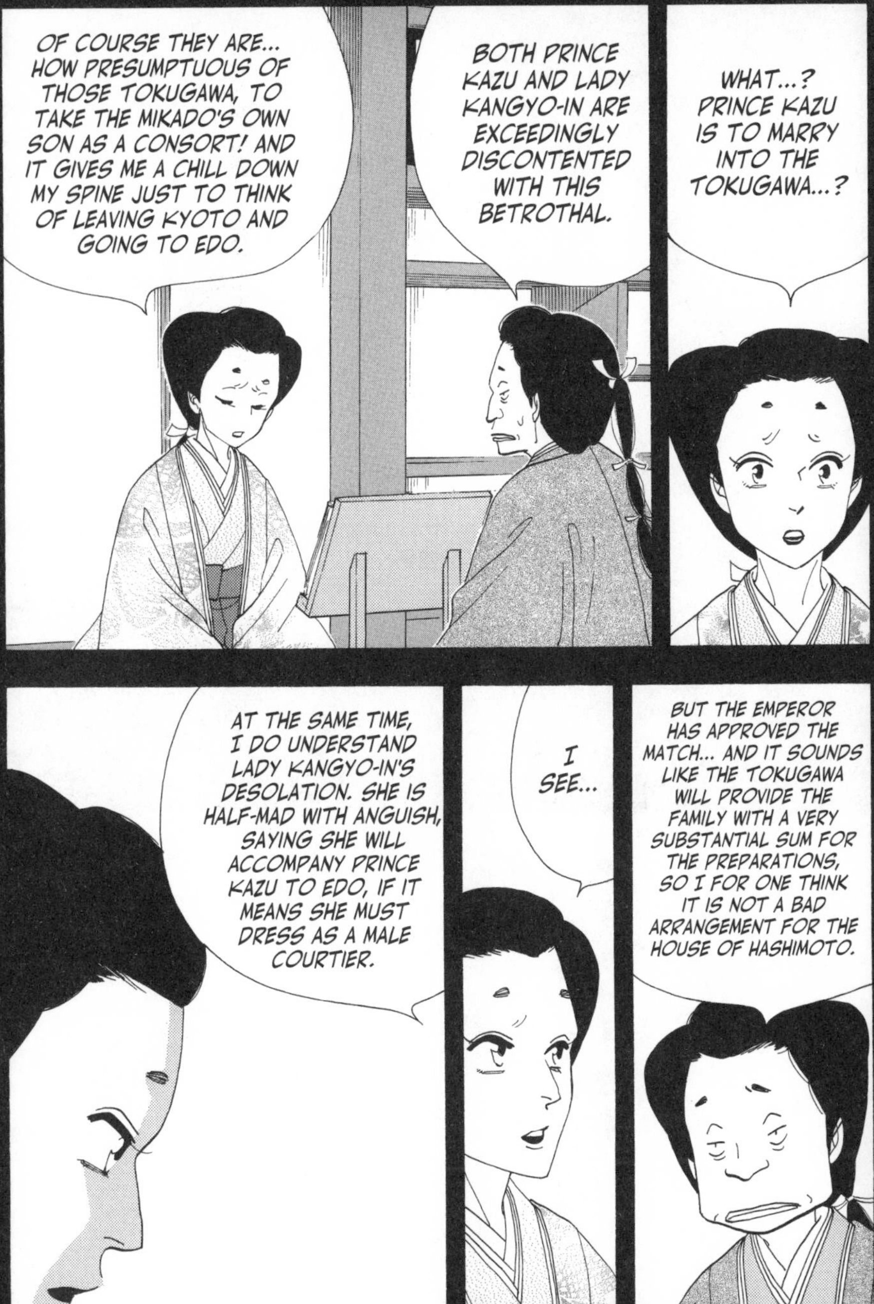
WHAT...? PRINCE KAZU IS TO MARRY INTO THE TOKUGAWA...?
BOTH PRINCE KAZU AND LADY KANGYO-IN ARE EXCEEDINGLY DISCONTENTED WITH THIS BETROTHAL.
OF COURSE THEY ARE... HOW PRESUMPTUOUS OF THOSE TOKUGAWA, TO TAKE THE MIKADO'S OWN SON AS A CONSORT! AND IT GIVES ME A CHILL DOWN MY SPINE JUST TO THINK OF LEAVING KYOTO AND GOING TO EDO.
BUT THE EMPEROR HAS APPROVED THE MATCH... AND IT SOUNDS LIKE THE TOKUGAWA WILL PROVIDE THE FAMILY WITH A VERY SUBSTANTIAL SUM FOR THE PREPARATIONS, SO I FOR ONE THINK IT IS NOT A BAD ARRANGEMENT FOR THE HOUSE OF HASHIMOTO.
I SEE...
AT THE SAME TIME, I DO UNDERSTAND LADY KANGYO-IN'S DESOLATION. SHE IS HALF-MAD WITH ANGUISH, SAYING SHE WILL ACCOMPANY PRINCE KAZU TO EDO, IF IT MEANS SHE MUST DRESS AS A MALE COURTIER.

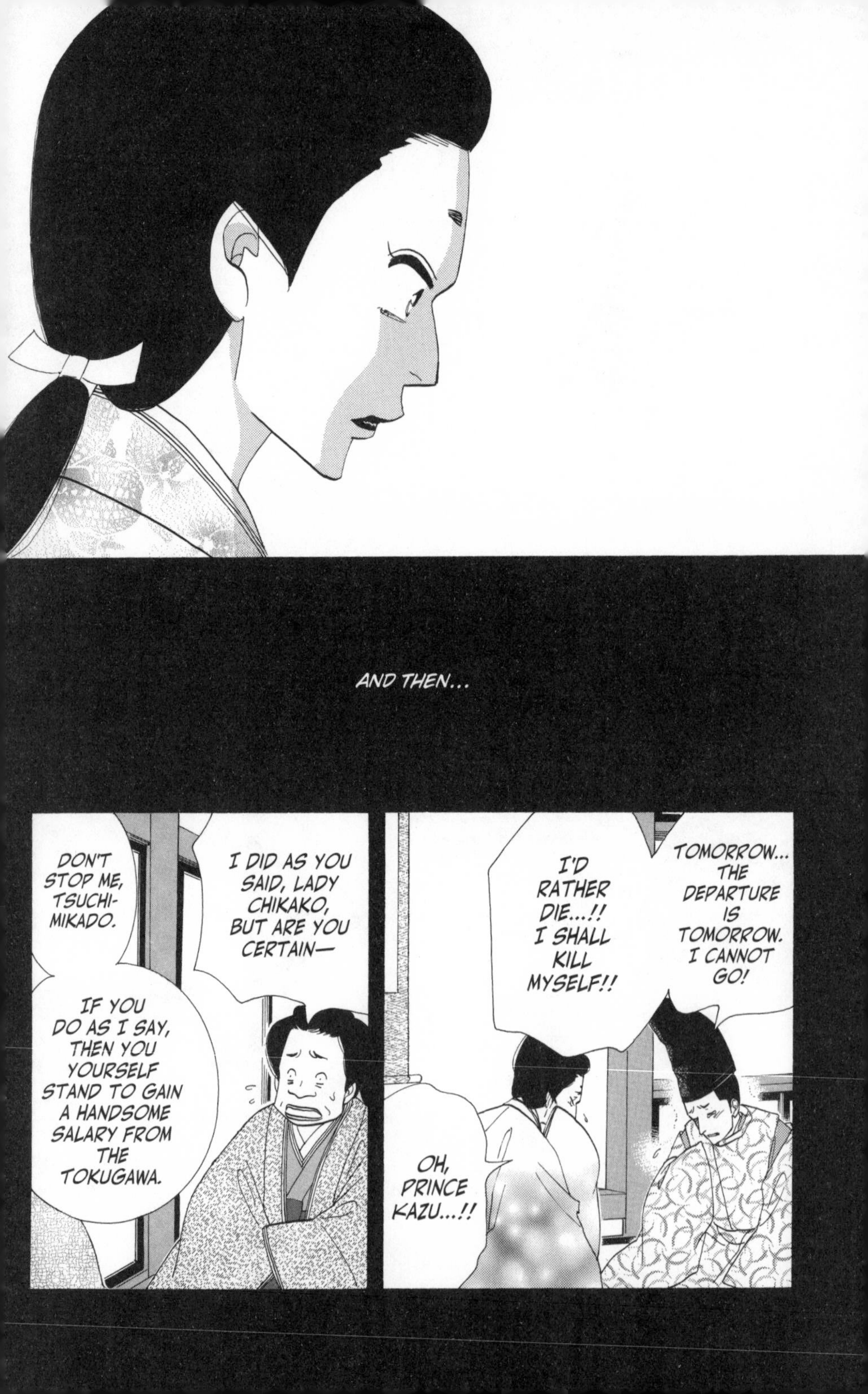
AND THEN...
TOMORROW... THE DEPARTURE IS TOMORROW. I CANNOT GO!
I'D RATHER DIE...!! I SHALL KILL MYSELF!!
OH, PRINCE KAZU...!!
I DID AS YOU SAID, LADY CHIKAKO, BUT ARE YOU CERTAIN—
DON'T STOP ME, TSUCHI-MIKADO.
IF YOU DO AS I SAY, THEN YOU YOURSELF STAND TO GAIN A HANDSOME SALARY FROM THE TOKUGAWA.

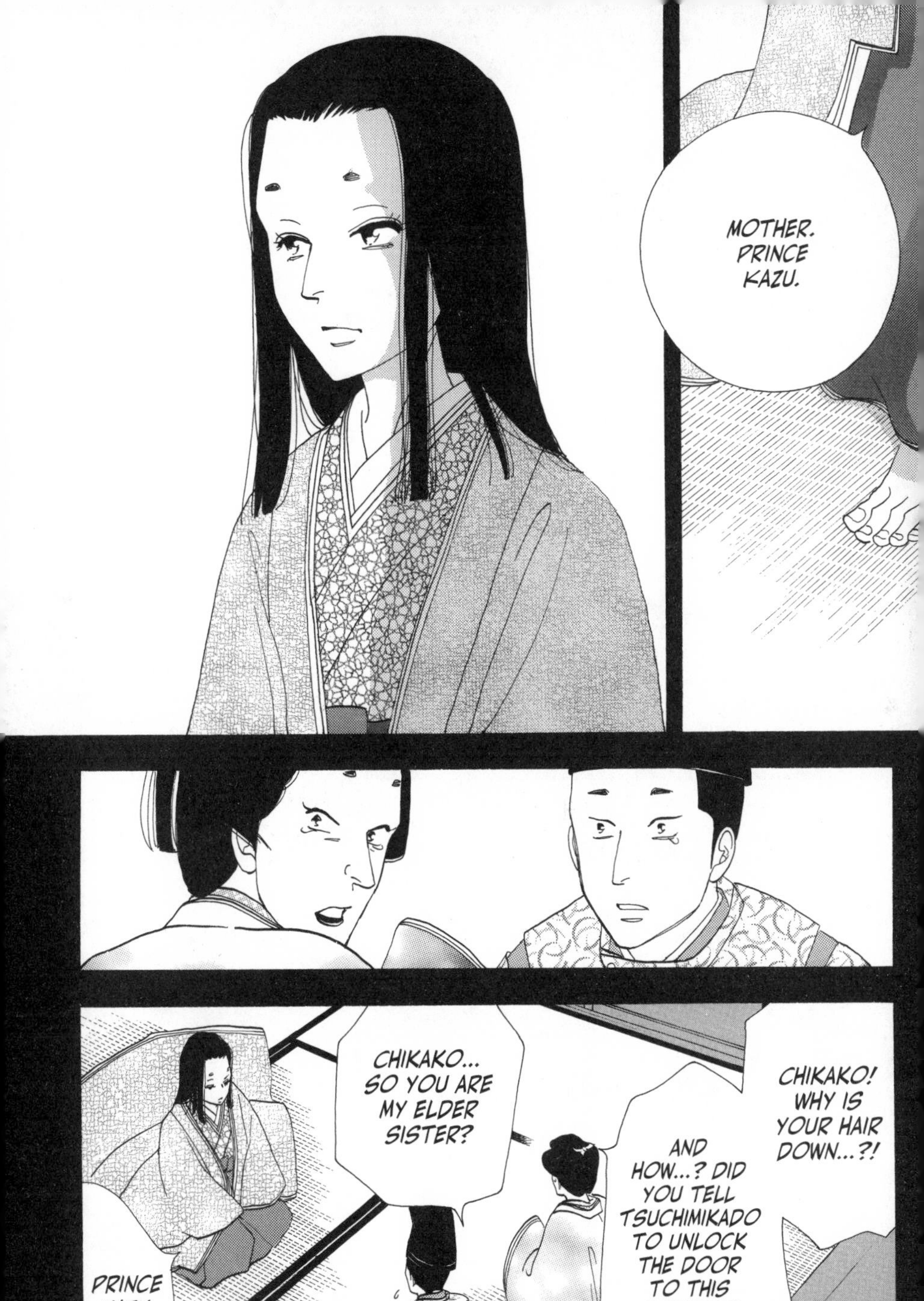
MOTHER. PRINCE KAZU.
CHIKAKO! WHY IS YOUR HAIR DOWN...?!
AND HOW...? DID YOU TELL TSUCHIMIKADO TO UNLOCK THE DOOR TO THIS CHAMBER?
CHIKAKO... SO YOU ARE MY ELDER SISTER?
PRINCE KAZU.

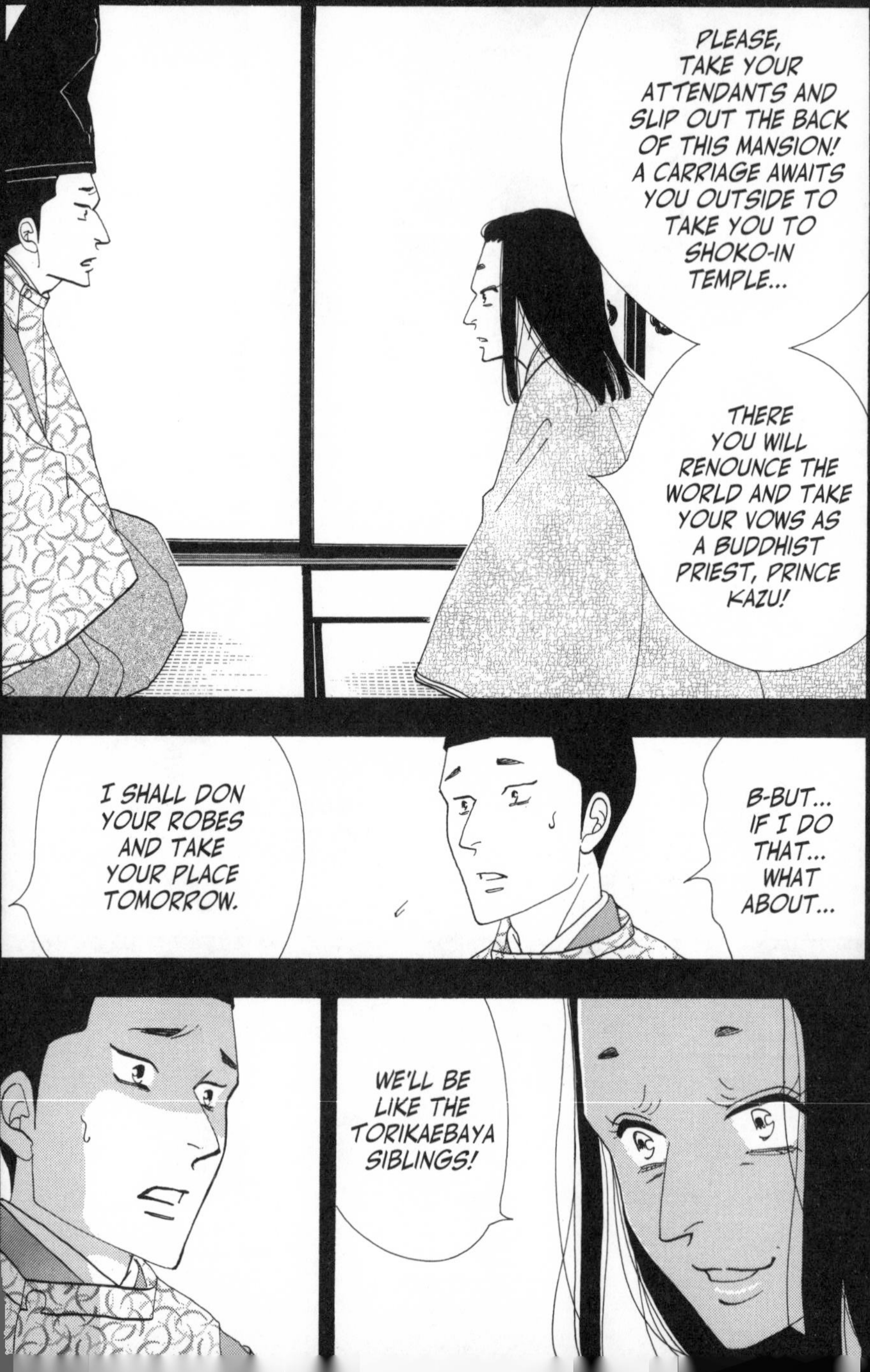
PLEASE, TAKE YOUR ATTENDANTS AND SLIP OUT THE BACK OF THIS MANSION! A CARRIAGE AWAITS YOU OUTSIDE TO TAKE YOU TO SHOKO-IN TEMPLE...
THERE YOU WILL RENOUNCE THE WORLD AND TAKE YOUR VOWS AS A BUDDHIST PRIEST, PRINCE KAZU!
B-BUT... IF I DO THAT... WHAT ABOUT...
I SHALL DON YOUR ROBES AND TAKE YOUR PLACE TOMORROW.
WE'LL BE LIKE THE TORIKAEBAYA SIBLINGS!

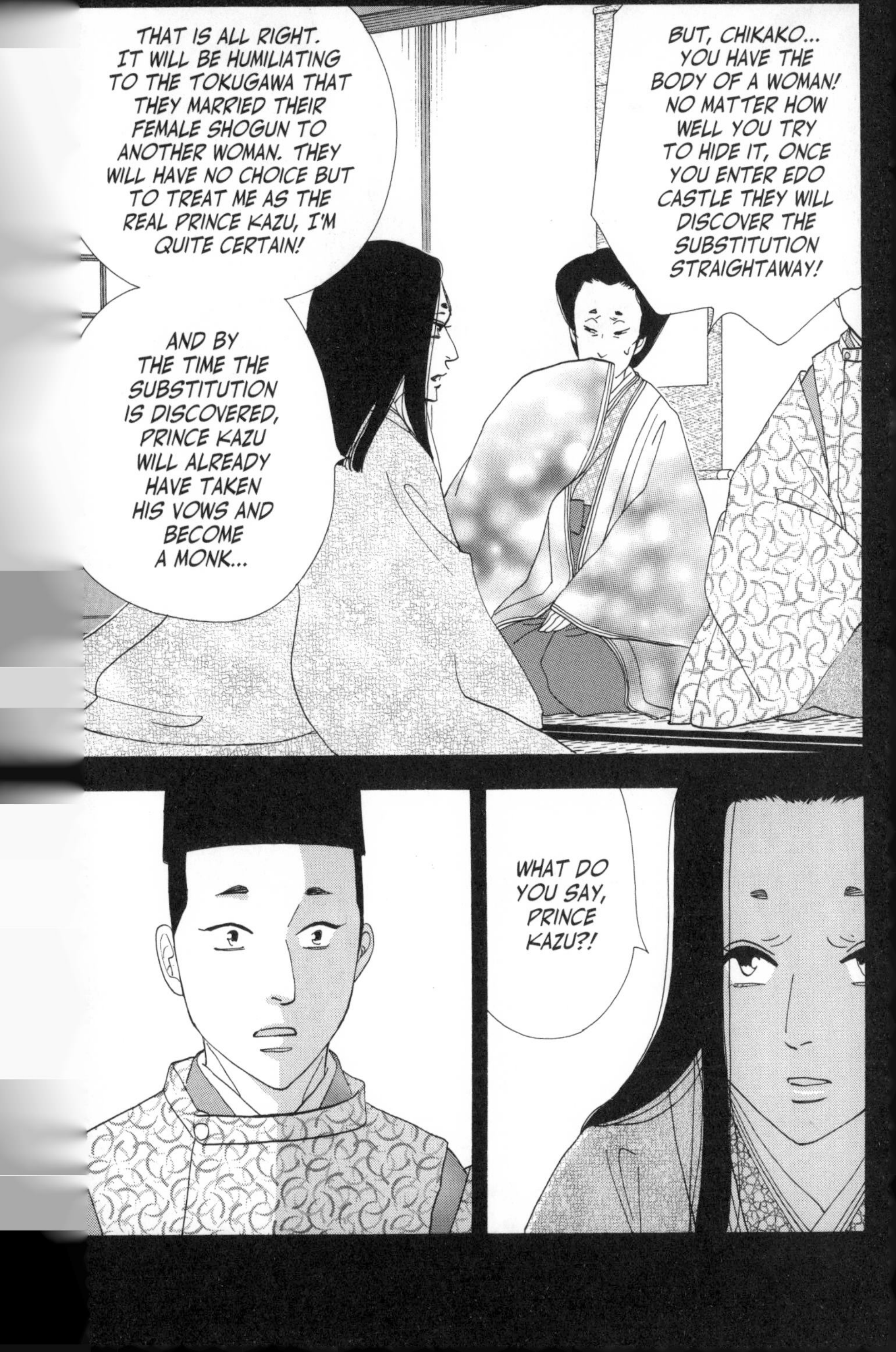
BUT, CHIKAKO... YOU HAVE THE BODY OF A WOMAN! NO MATTER HOW WELL YOU TRY TO HIDE IT, ONCE YOU ENTER EDO CASTLE THEY WILL DISCOVER THE SUBSTITUTION STRAIGHTAWAY!
THAT IS ALL RIGHT. IT WILL BE HUMILIATING TO THE TOKUGAWA THAT THEY MARRIED THEIR FEMALE SHOGUN TO ANOTHER WOMAN. THEY WILL HAVE NO CHOICE BUT TO TREAT ME AS THE REAL PRINCE KAZU, I'M QUITE CERTAIN!
AND BY THE TIME THE SUBSTITUTION IS DISCOVERED, PRINCE KAZU WILL ALREADY HAVE TAKEN HIS VOWS AND BECOME A MONK...
WHAT DO YOU SAY, PRINCE KAZU?!

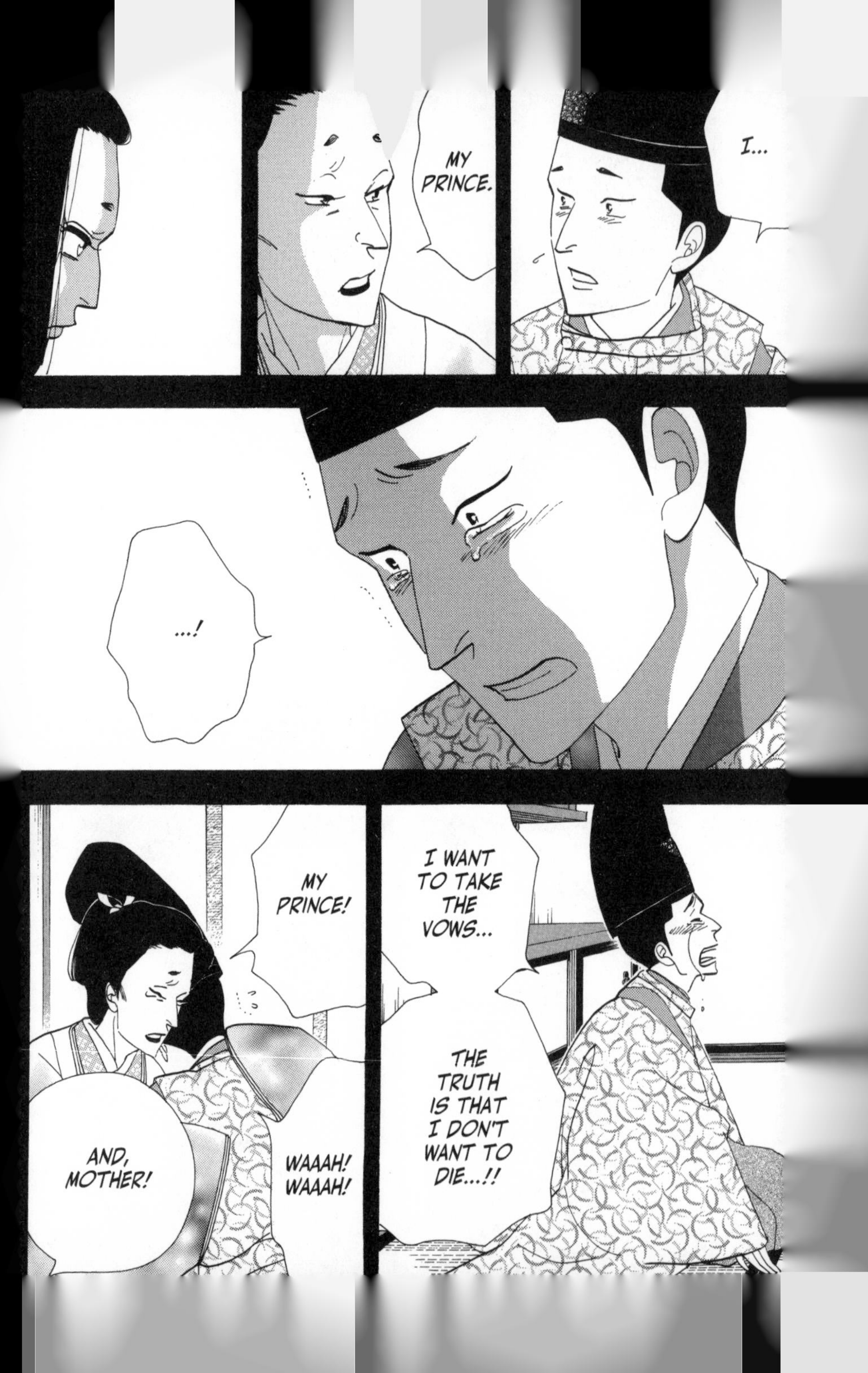
I...
MY PRINCE.
...!
I WANT TO TAKE THE VOWS...
THE TRUTH IS THAT I DON'T WANT TO DIE...!!
MY PRINCE!
WAAAH! WAAAH!
AND, MOTHER!

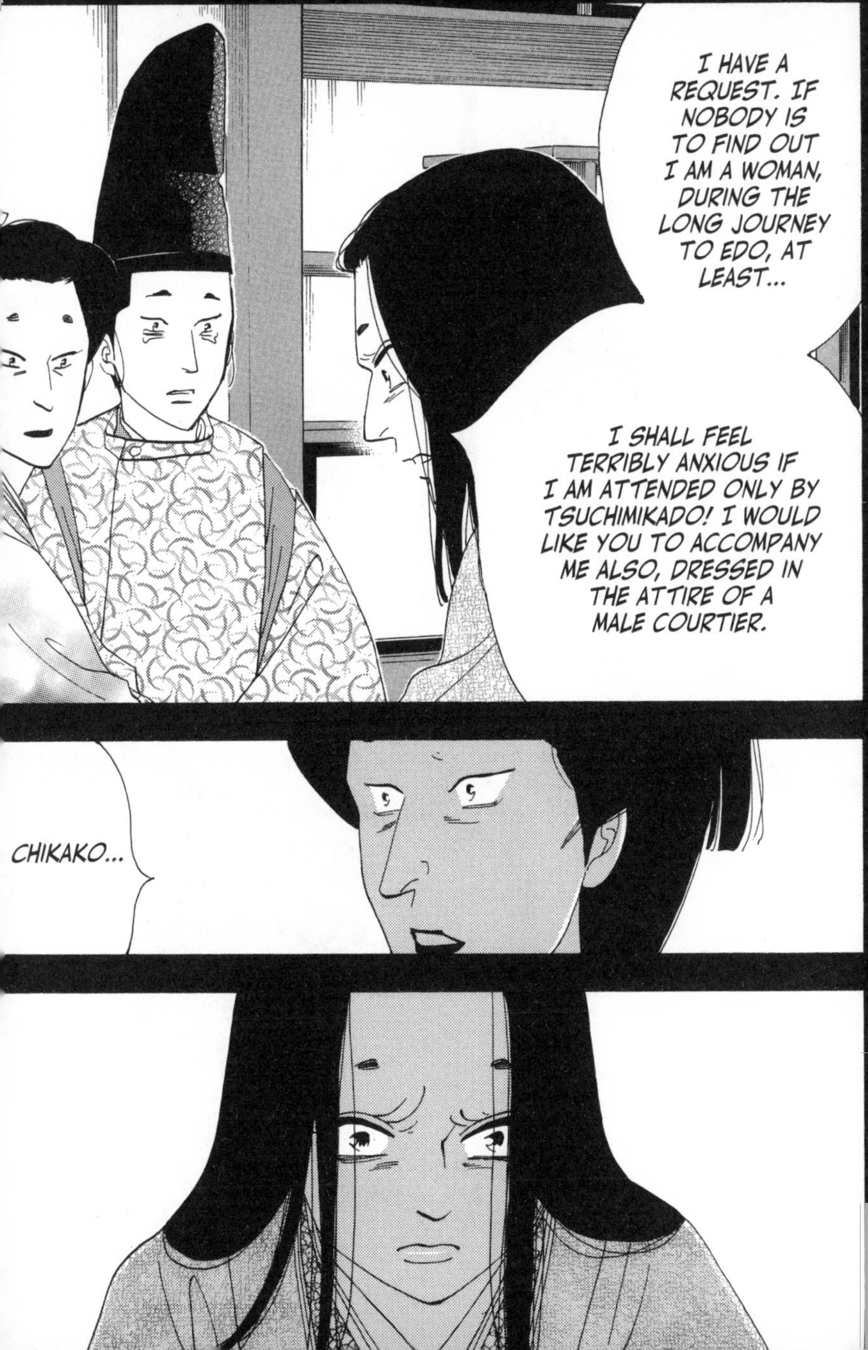
I HAVE A REQUEST. IF NOBODY IS TO FIND OUT I AM A WOMAN, DURING THE LONG JOURNEY TO EDO, AT LEAST...
I SHALL FEEL TERRIBLY ANXIOUS IF I AM ATTENDED ONLY BY TSUCHIMIKADO! I WOULD LIKE YOU TO ACCOMPANY ME ALSO, DRESSED IN THE ATTIRE OF A MALE COURTIER.
CHIKAKO...

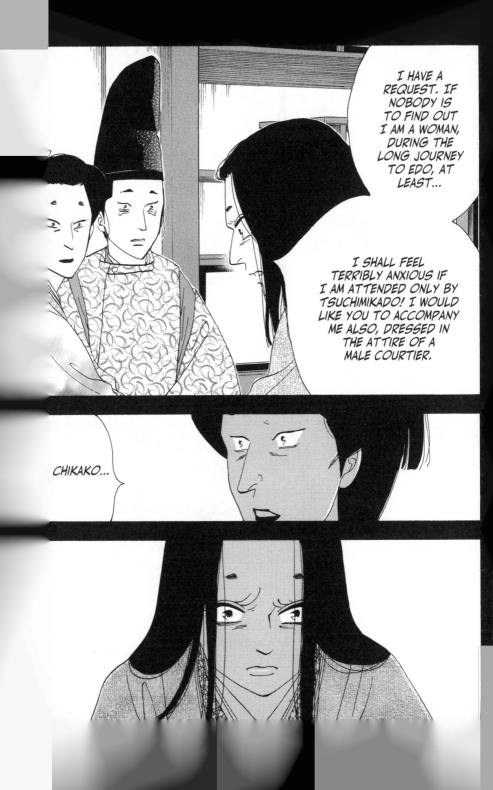

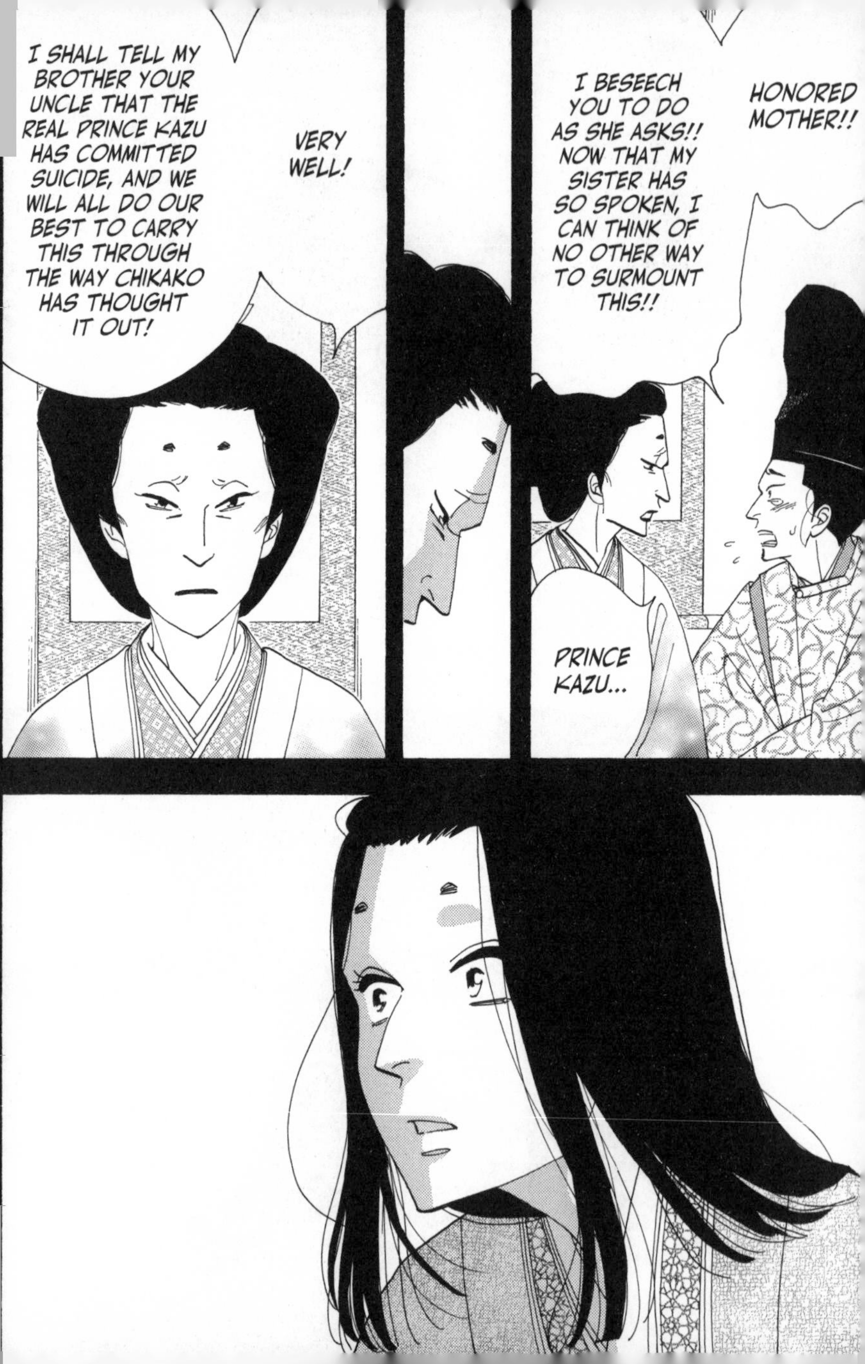
HONORED MOTHER!!
I BESEECH YOU TO DO AS SHE ASKS!! NOW THAT MY SISTER HAS SO SPOKEN, I CAN THINK OF NO OTHER WAY TO SURMOUNT THIS!!
PRINCE KAZU...
VERY WELL!
I SHALL TELL MY BROTHER YOUR UNCLE THAT THE REAL PRINCE KAZU HAS COMMITTED SUICIDE, AND WE WILL ALL DO OUR BEST TO CARRY THIS THROUGH THE WAY CHIKAKO HAS THOUGHT IT OUT!

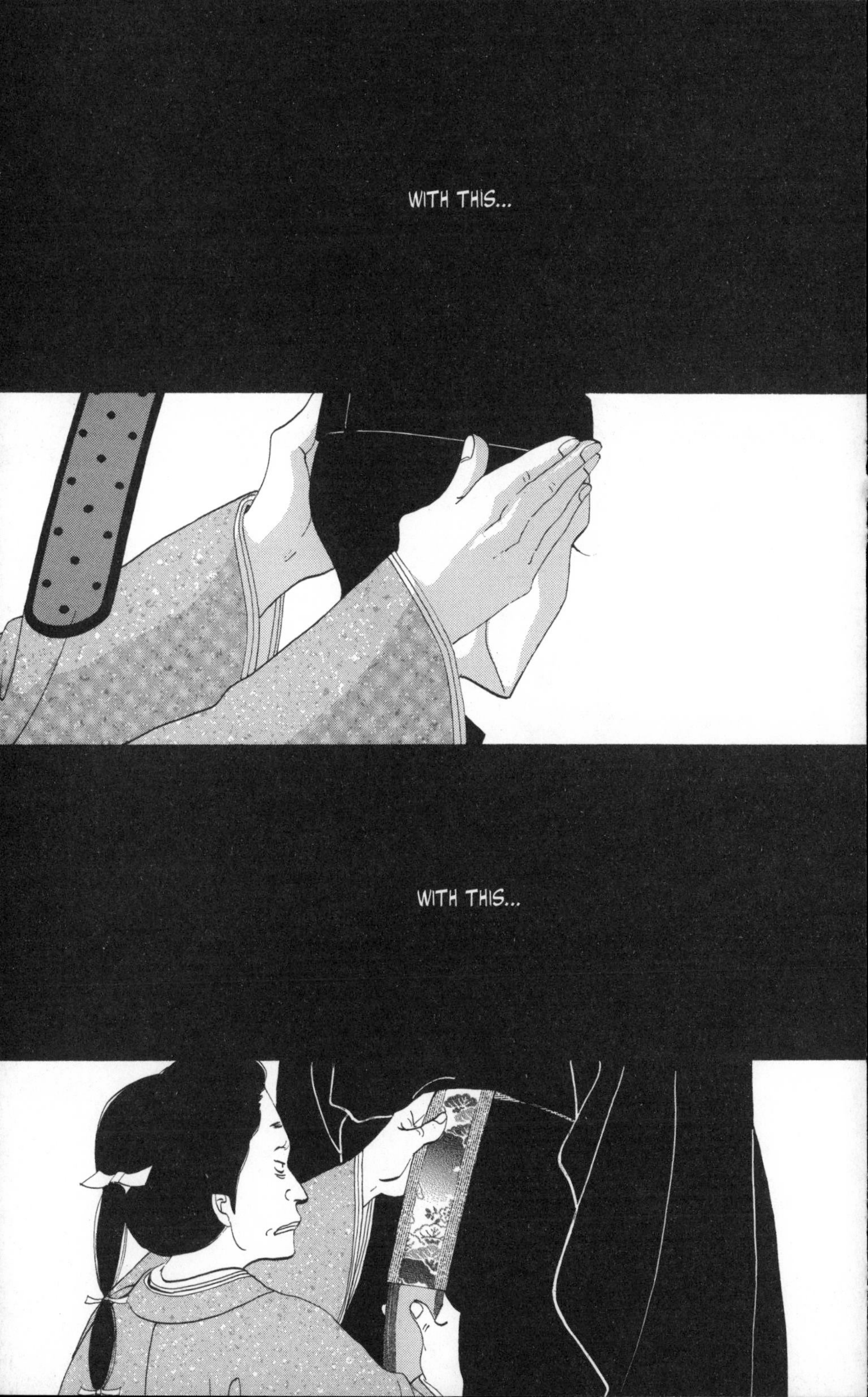
WITH THIS...
WITH THIS...

NGH!

NGH!
NGH!

I AM TRULY...
TRULY
SORRY, LADY
CHIKAKO...!!

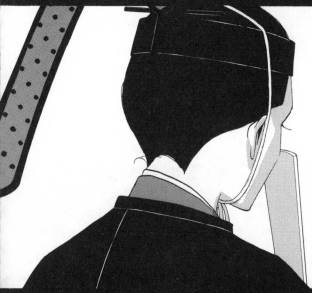

WITH THIS, MOTHER
SHALL BE MINE
ALONE.

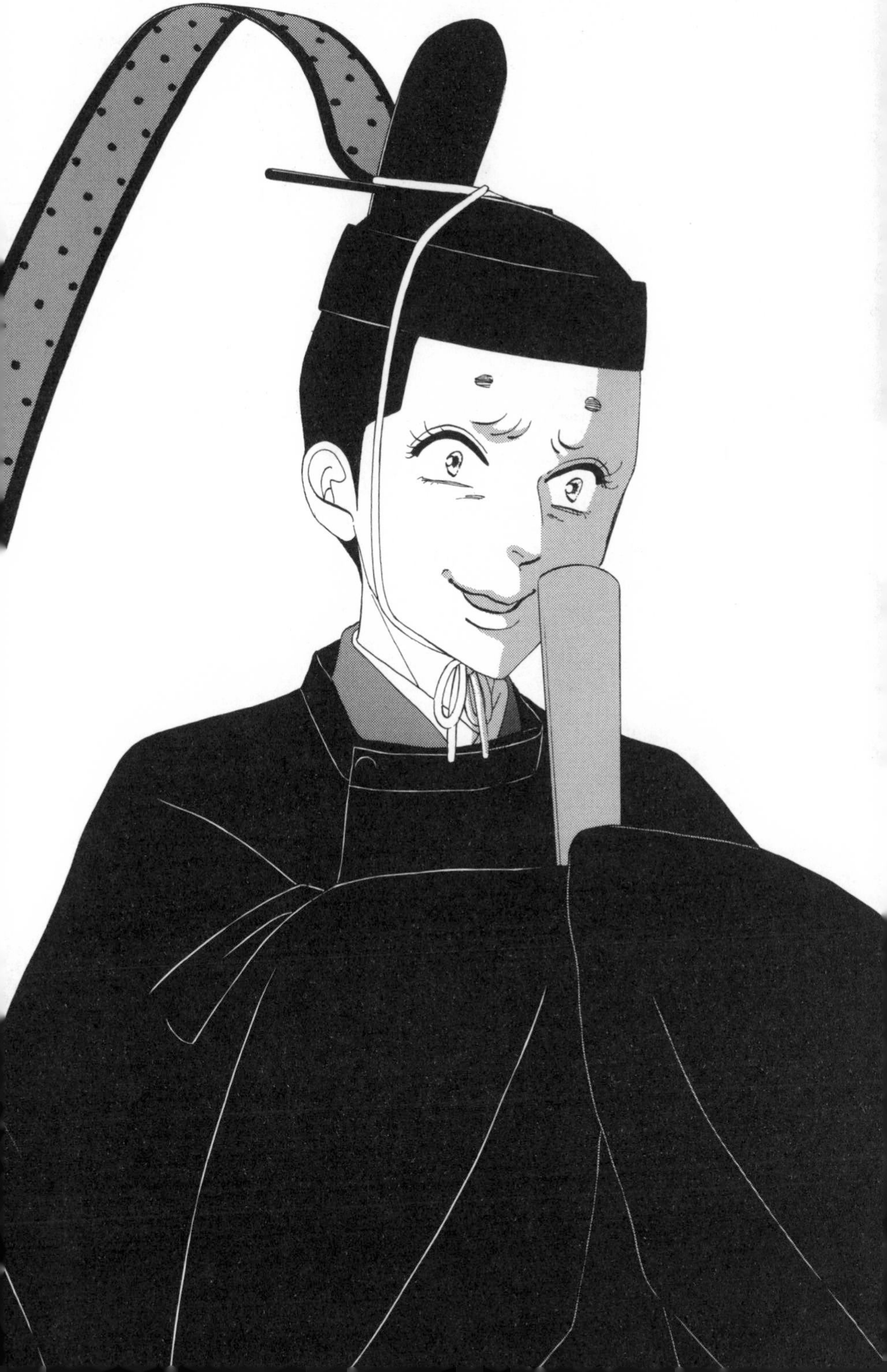

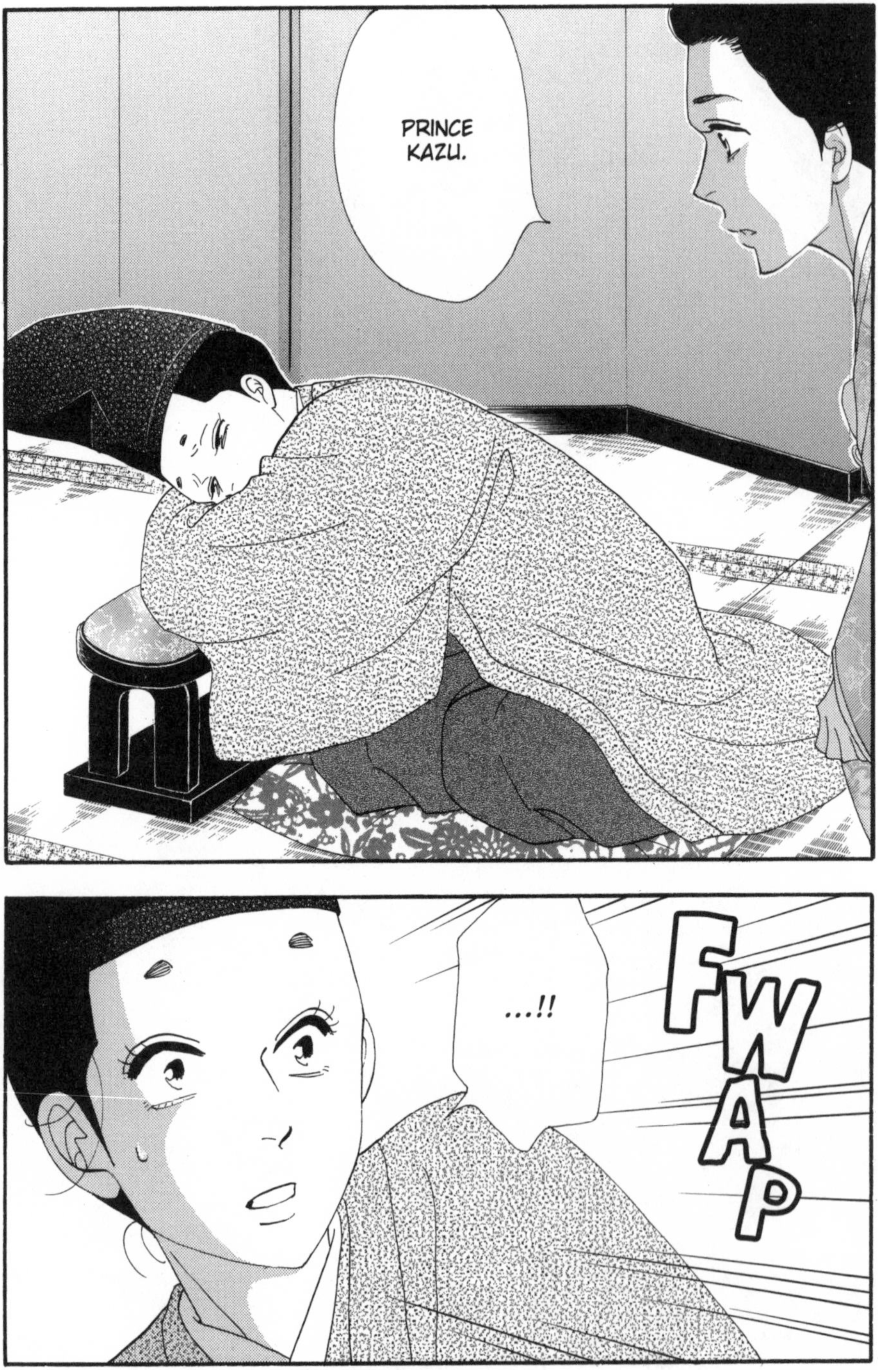
PRINCE KAZU.
FWAP
...!!

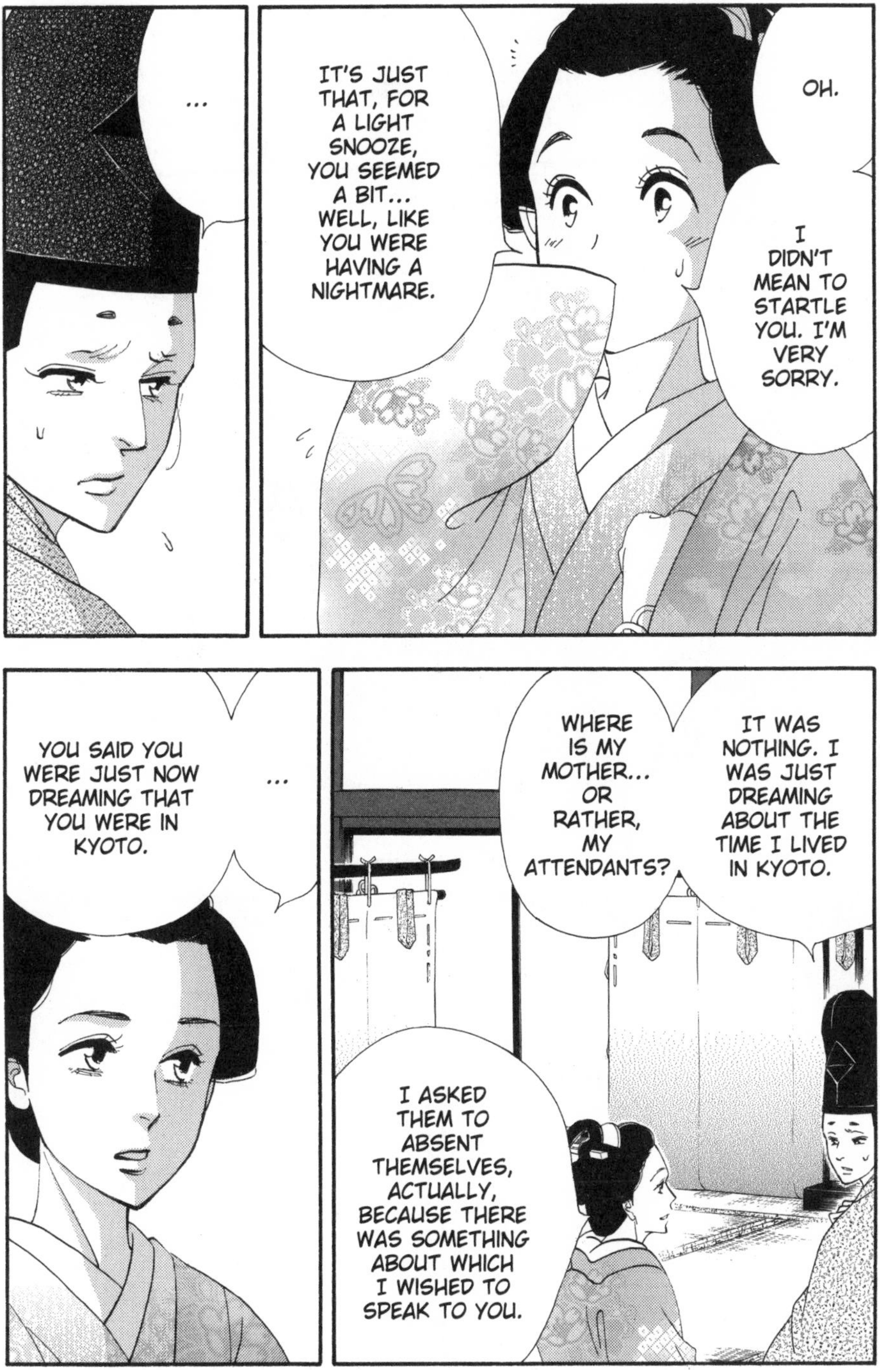
OH.
I DIDN'T MEAN TO STARTLE YOU. I'M VERY SORRY.
IT'S JUST THAT, FOR A LIGHT SNOOZE, YOU SEEMED A BIT... WELL, LIKE YOU WERE HAVING A NIGHTMARE.
...
IT WAS NOTHING. I WAS JUST DREAMING ABOUT THE TIME I LIVED IN KYOTO.
WHERE IS MY MOTHER... OR RATHER, MY ATTENDANTS?
I ASKED THEM TO ABSENT THEMSELVES, ACTUALLY, BECAUSE THERE WAS SOMETHING ABOUT WHICH I WISHED TO SPEAK TO YOU.
...
YOU SAID YOU WERE JUST NOW DREAMING THAT YOU WERE IN KYOTO.

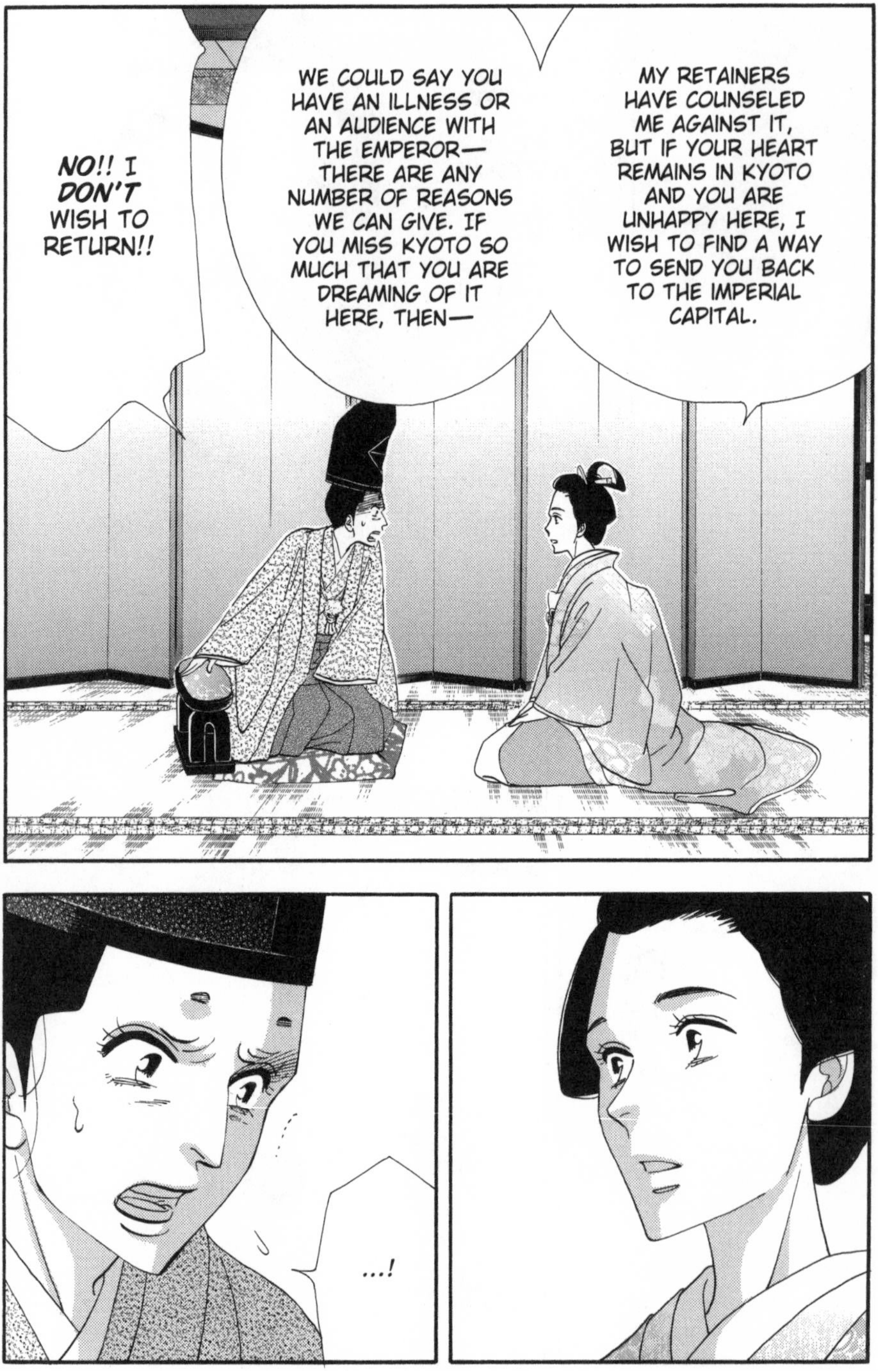
MY RETAINERS HAVE COUNSELED ME AGAINST IT, BUT IF YOUR HEART REMAINS IN KYOTO AND YOU ARE UNHAPPY HERE, I WISH TO FIND A WAY TO SEND YOU BACK TO THE IMPERIAL CAPITAL.
WE COULD SAY YOU HAVE AN ILLNESS OR AN AUDIENCE WITH THE EMPEROR—THERE ARE ANY NUMBER OF REASONS WE CAN GIVE. IF YOU MISS KYOTO SO MUCH THAT YOU ARE DREAMING OF IT HERE, THEN—
NO!! I DON'T WISH TO RETURN!!
...!

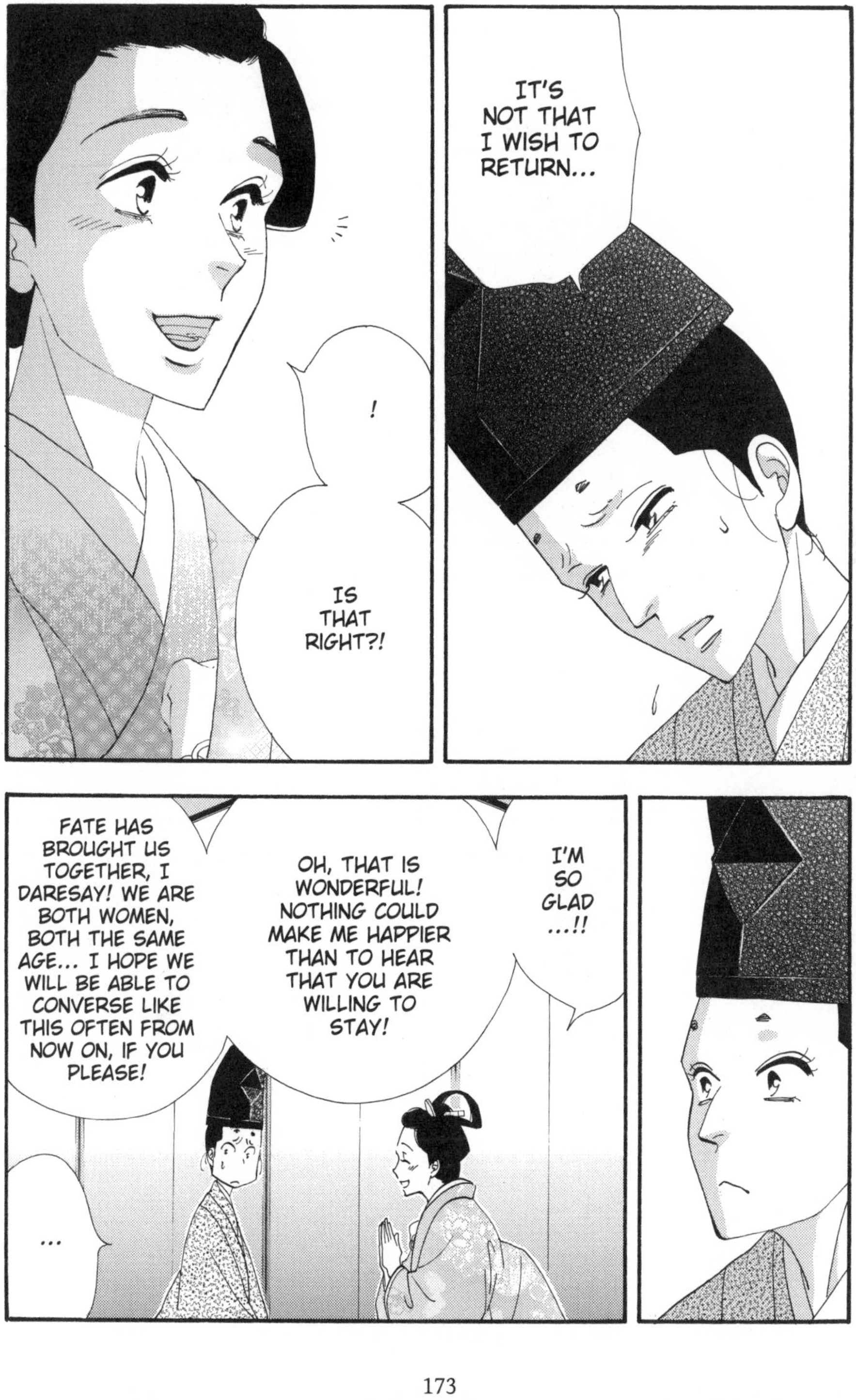
IT'S NOT THAT I WISH TO RETURN...
!
IS THAT RIGHT?!
I'M SO GLAD ...!!
OH, THAT IS WONDERFUL! NOTHING COULD MAKE ME HAPPIER THAN TO HEAR THAT YOU ARE WILLING TO STAY!
FATE HAS BROUGHT US TOGETHER, I DARESAY! WE ARE BOTH WOMEN, BOTH THE SAME AGE... I HOPE WE WILL BE ABLE TO CONVERSE LIKE THIS OFTEN FROM NOW ON, IF YOU PLEASE!
...

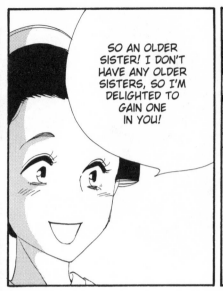

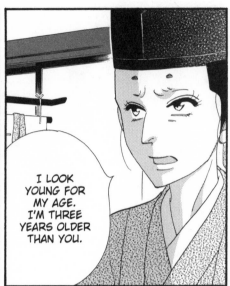

I LOOK YOUNG FOR MY AGE. I'M THREE YEARS OLDER THAN YOU.
SO AN OLDER SISTER! I DON'T HAVE ANY OLDER SISTERS, SO I'M DELIGHTED TO GAIN ONE IN YOU!
WHAT A STRANGE WOMAN!

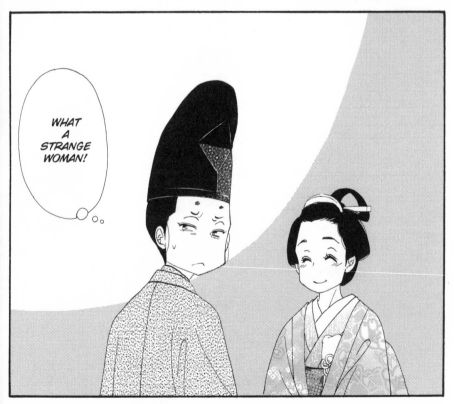

Ōoku

THE INNER CHAMBERS

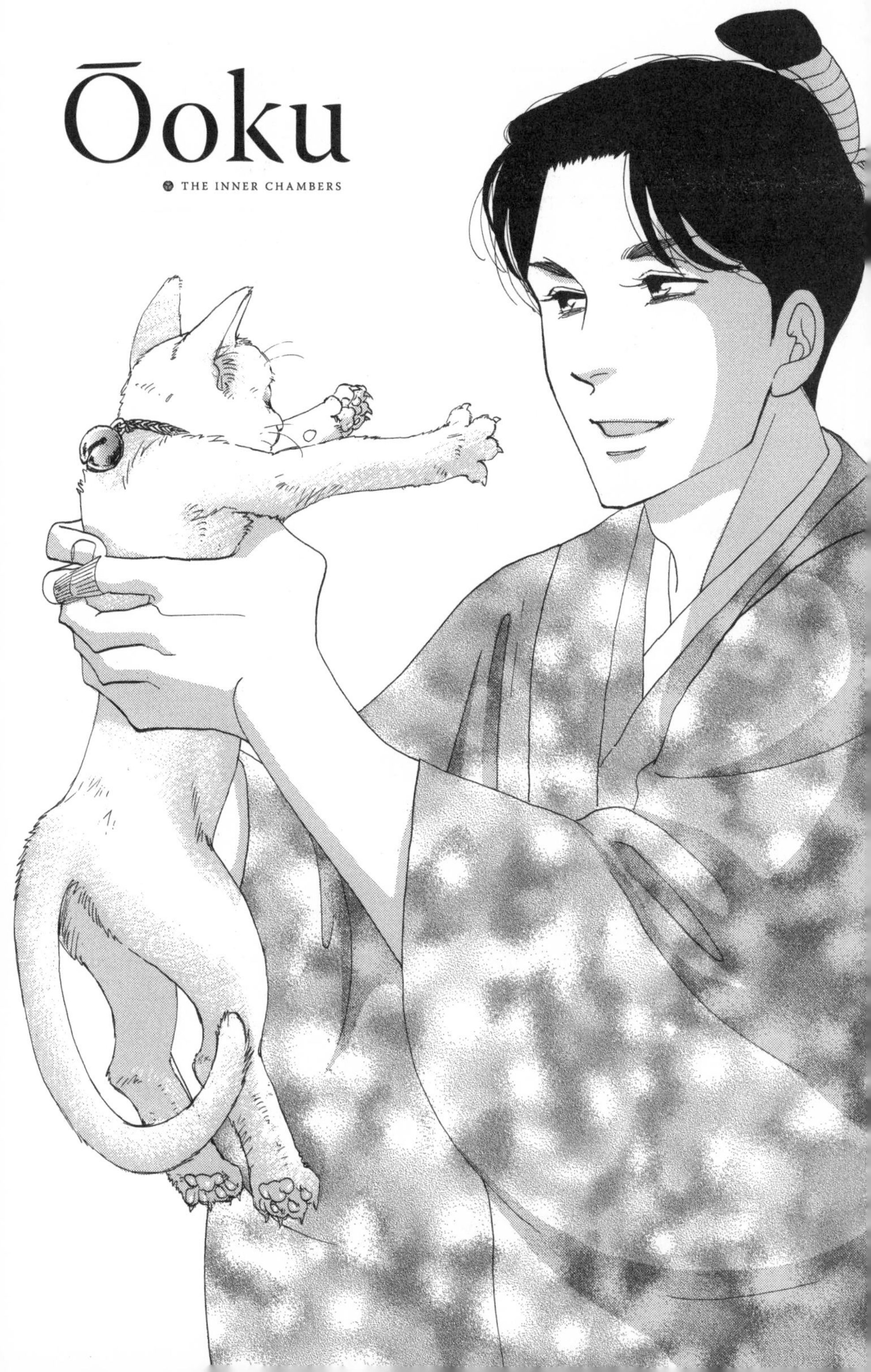

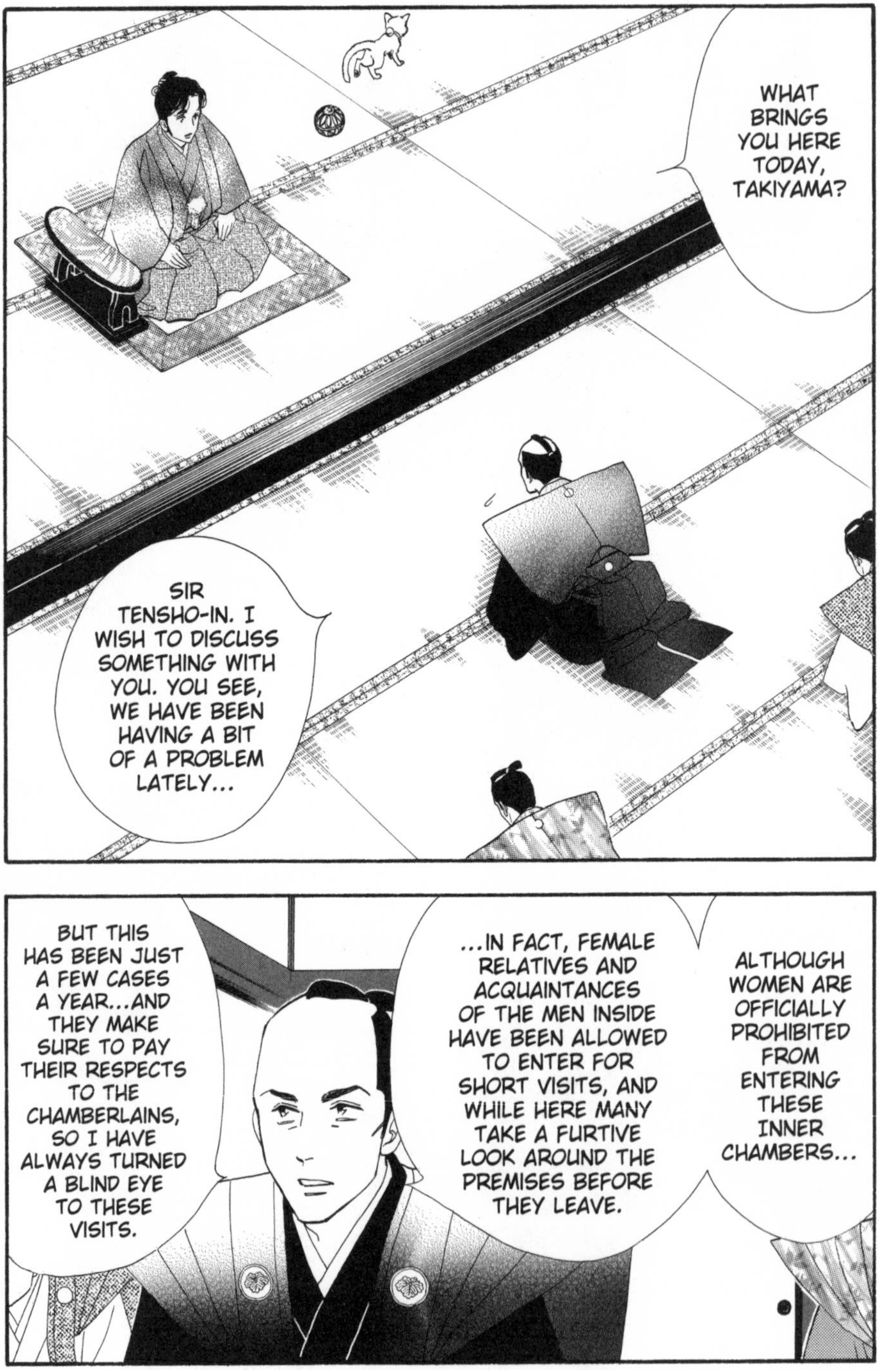
WHAT BRINGS YOU HERE TODAY, TAKIYAMA?
SIR TENSHO-IN. I WISH TO DISCUSS SOMETHING WITH YOU. YOU SEE, WE HAVE BEEN HAVING A BIT OF A PROBLEM LATELY...
ALTHOUGH WOMEN ARE OFFICIALLY PROHIBITED FROM ENTERING THESE INNER CHAMBERS...
...IN FACT, FEMALE RELATIVES AND ACQUAINTANCES OF THE MEN INSIDE HAVE BEEN ALLOWED TO ENTER FOR SHORT VISITS, AND WHILE HERE MANY TAKE A FURTIVE LOOK AROUND THE PREMISES BEFORE THEY LEAVE.
BUT THIS HAS BEEN JUST A FEW CASES A YEAR...AND THEY MAKE SURE TO PAY THEIR RESPECTS TO THE CHAMBERLAINS, SO I HAVE ALWAYS TURNED A BLIND EYE TO THESE VISITS.

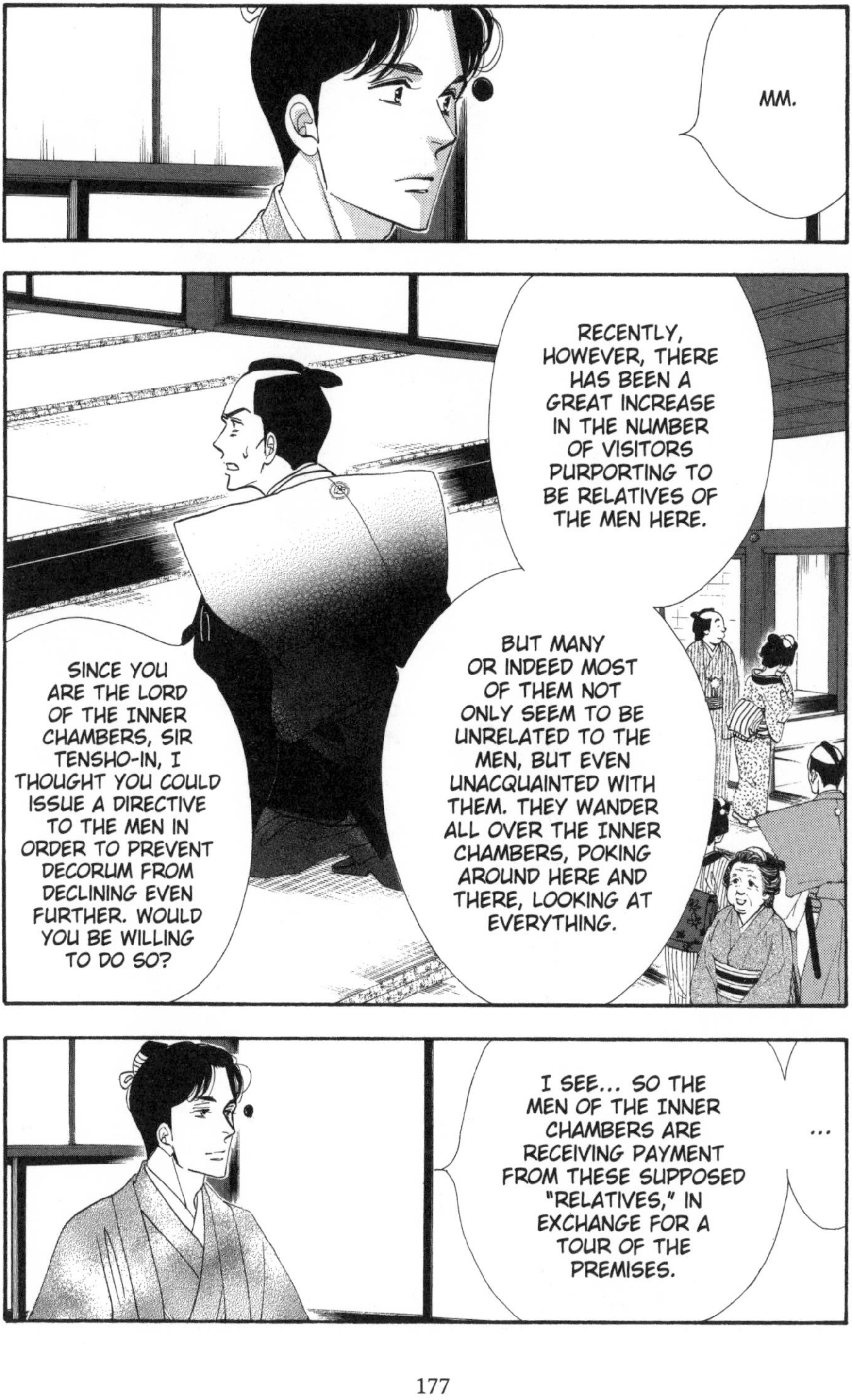
MM.
RECENTLY, HOWEVER, THERE HAS BEEN A GREAT INCREASE IN THE NUMBER OF VISITORS PURPORTING TO BE RELATIVES OF THE MEN HERE.
BUT MANY OR INDEED MOST OF THEM NOT ONLY SEEM TO BE UNRELATED TO THE MEN, BUT EVEN UNACQUAINTED WITH THEM. THEY WANDER ALL OVER THE INNER CHAMBERS, POKING AROUND HERE AND THERE, LOOKING AT EVERYTHING.
SINCE YOU ARE THE LORD OF THE INNER CHAMBERS, SIR TENSHO-IN, I THOUGHT YOU COULD ISSUE A DIRECTIVE TO THE MEN IN ORDER TO PREVENT DECORUM FROM DECLINING EVEN FURTHER. WOULD YOU BE WILLING TO DO SO?
...
I SEE... SO THE MEN OF THE INNER CHAMBERS ARE RECEIVING PAYMENT FROM THESE SUPPOSED "RELATIVES," IN EXCHANGE FOR A TOUR OF THE PREMISES.

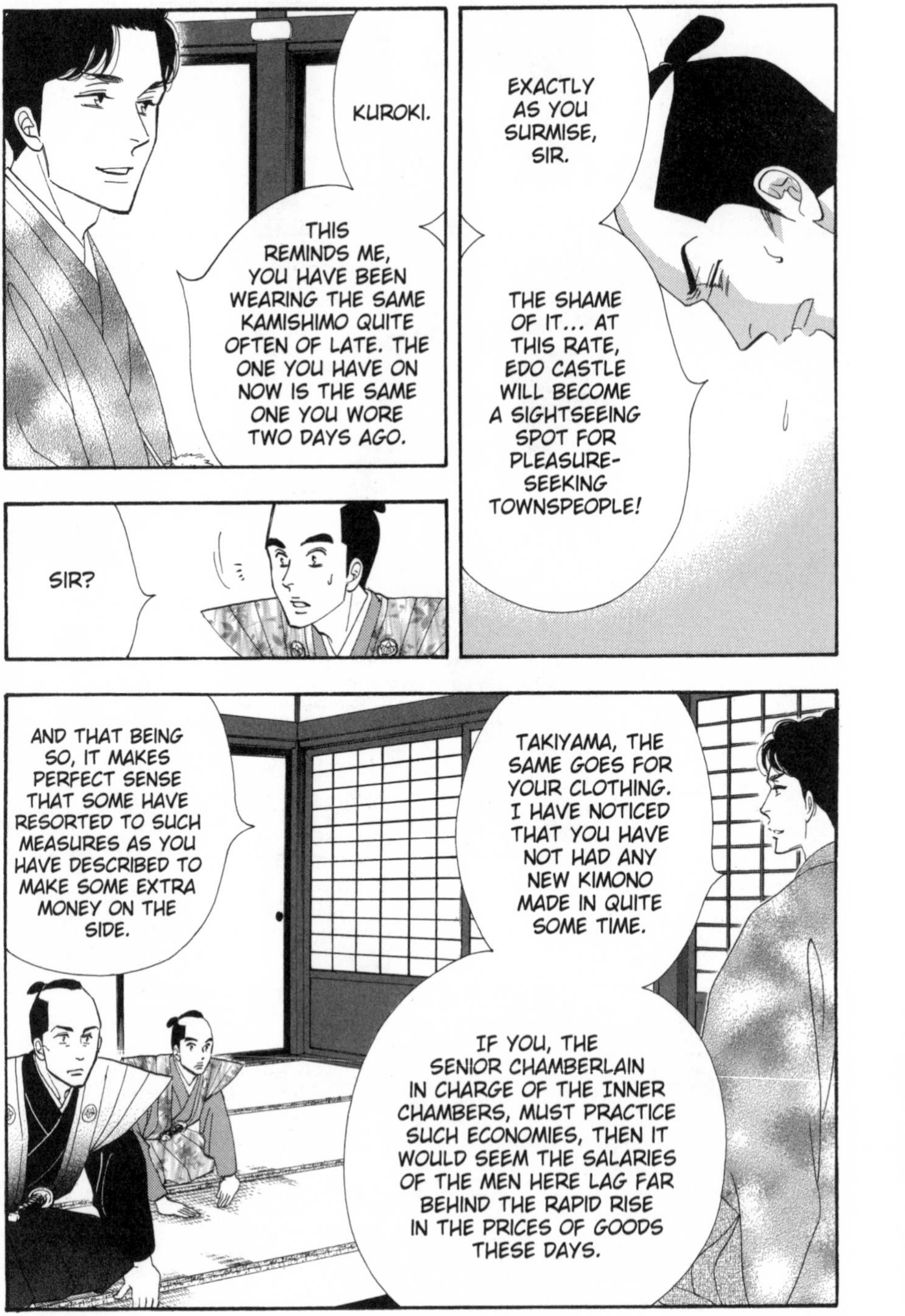
EXACTLY AS YOU SURMISE, SIR.
THE SHAME OF IT... AT THIS RATE, EDO CASTLE WILL BECOME A SIGHTSEEING SPOT FOR PLEASURE-SEEKING TOWNSPEOPLE!
KUROKI.
THIS REMINDS ME, YOU HAVE BEEN WEARING THE SAME KAMISHIMO QUITE OFTEN OF LATE. THE ONE YOU HAVE ON NOW IS THE SAME ONE YOU WORE TWO DAYS AGO.
SIR?
TAKIYAMA, THE SAME GOES FOR YOUR CLOTHING. I HAVE NOTICED THAT YOU HAVE NOT HAD ANY NEW KIMONO MADE IN QUITE SOME TIME.
IF YOU, THE SENIOR CHAMBERLAIN IN CHARGE OF THE INNER CHAMBERS, MUST PRACTICE SUCH ECONOMIES, THEN IT WOULD SEEM THE SALARIES OF THE MEN HERE LAG FAR BEHIND THE RAPID RISE IN THE PRICES OF GOODS THESE DAYS.
AND THAT BEING SO, IT MAKES PERFECT SENSE THAT SOME HAVE RESORTED TO SUCH MEASURES AS YOU HAVE DESCRIBED TO MAKE SOME EXTRA MONEY ON THE SIDE.

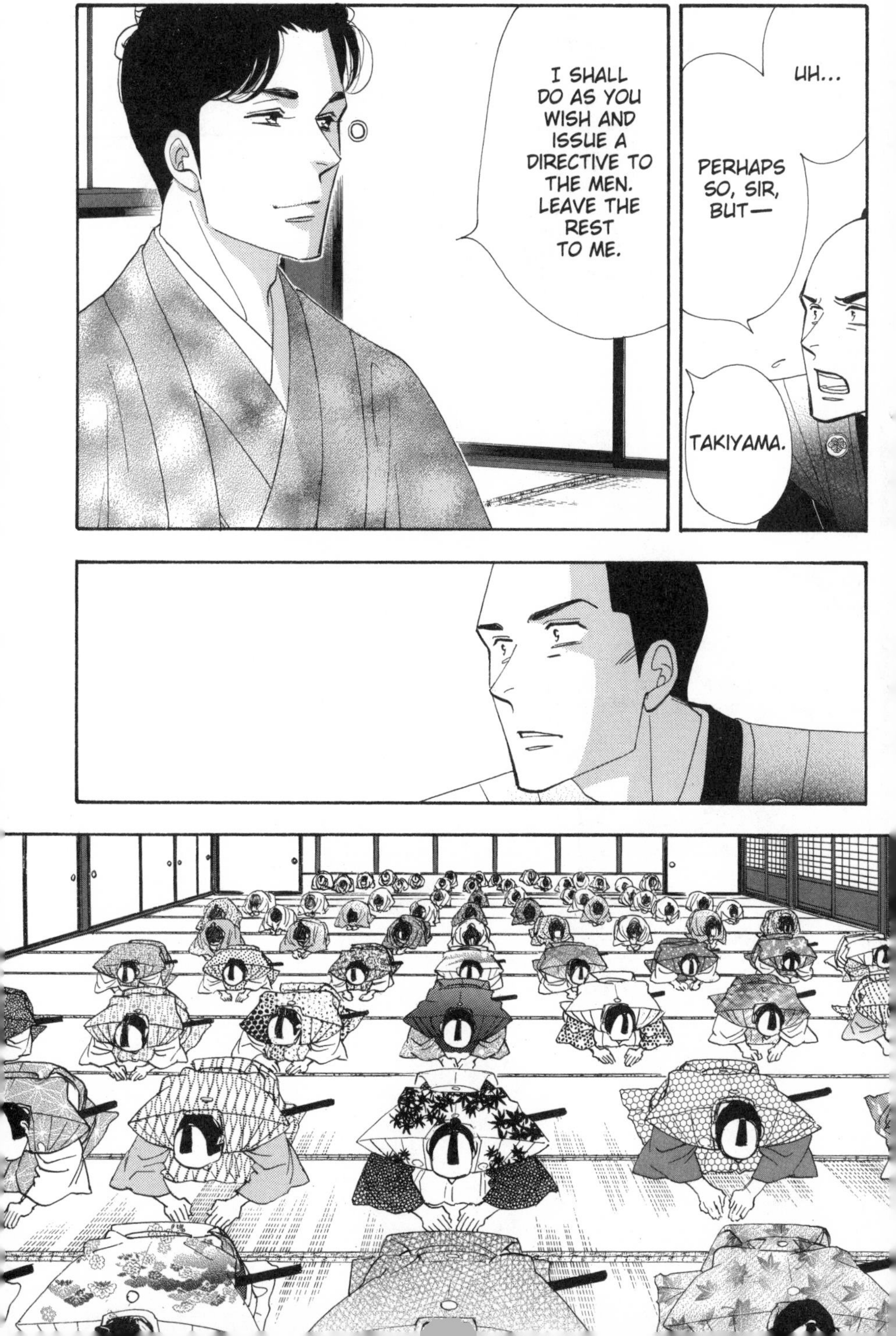
UH...
PERHAPS SO, SIR, BUT—
TAKIYAMA.
I SHALL DO AS YOU WISH AND ISSUE A DIRECTIVE TO THE MEN. LEAVE THE REST TO ME.

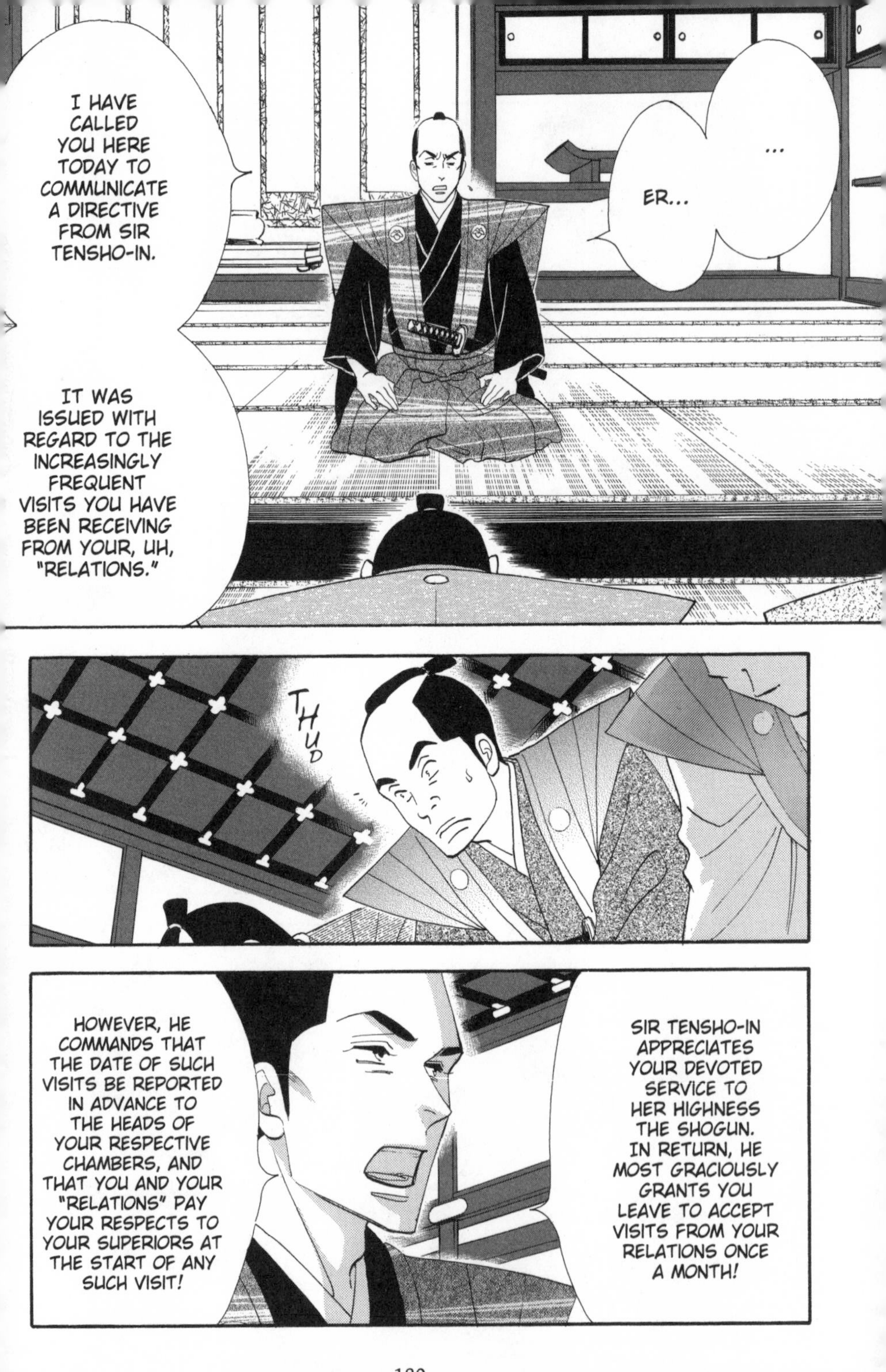
...
ER...
I HAVE CALLED YOU HERE TODAY TO COMMUNICATE A DIRECTIVE FROM SIR TENSHO-IN.
IT WAS ISSUED WITH REGARD TO THE INCREASINGLY FREQUENT VISITS YOU HAVE BEEN RECEIVING FROM YOUR, UH, "RELATIONS."
THUD
SIR TENSHO-IN APPRECIATES YOUR DEVOTED SERVICE TO HER HIGHNESS THE SHOGUN. IN RETURN, HE MOST GRACIOUSLY GRANTS YOU LEAVE TO ACCEPT VISITS FROM YOUR RELATIONS ONCE A MONTH!
HOWEVER, HE COMMANDS THAT THE DATE OF SUCH VISITS BE REPORTED IN ADVANCE TO THE HEADS OF YOUR RESPECTIVE CHAMBERS, AND THAT YOU AND YOUR "RELATIONS" PAY YOUR RESPECTS TO YOUR SUPERIORS AT THE START OF ANY SUCH VISIT!

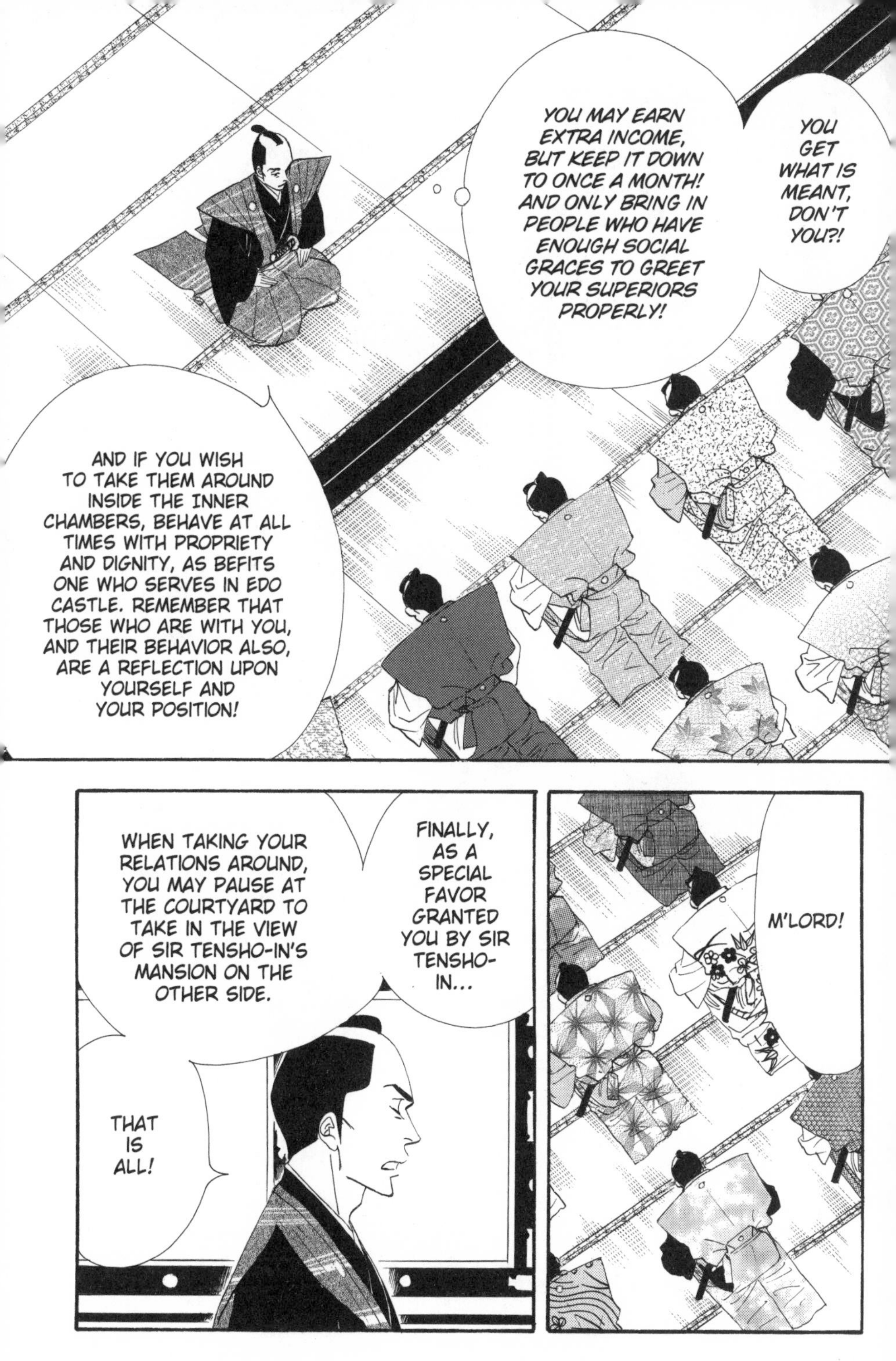
YOU GET WHAT IS MEANT, DON'T YOU?!
YOU MAY EARN EXTRA INCOME, BUT KEEP IT DOWN TO ONCE A MONTH! AND ONLY BRING IN PEOPLE WHO HAVE ENOUGH SOCIAL GRACES TO GREET YOUR SUPERIORS PROPERLY!
AND IF YOU WISH TO TAKE THEM AROUND INSIDE THE INNER CHAMBERS, BEHAVE AT ALL TIMES WITH PROPRIETY AND DIGNITY, AS BEFITS ONE WHO SERVES IN EDO CASTLE. REMEMBER THAT THOSE WHO ARE WITH YOU, AND THEIR BEHAVIOR ALSO, ARE A REFLECTION UPON YOURSELF AND YOUR POSITION!
M'LORD!
FINALLY, AS A SPECIAL FAVOR GRANTED YOU BY SIR TENSHO-IN...
WHEN TAKING YOUR RELATIONS AROUND, YOU MAY PAUSE AT THE COURTYARD TO TAKE IN THE VIEW OF SIR TENSHO-IN'S MANSION ON THE OTHER SIDE.
THAT IS ALL!

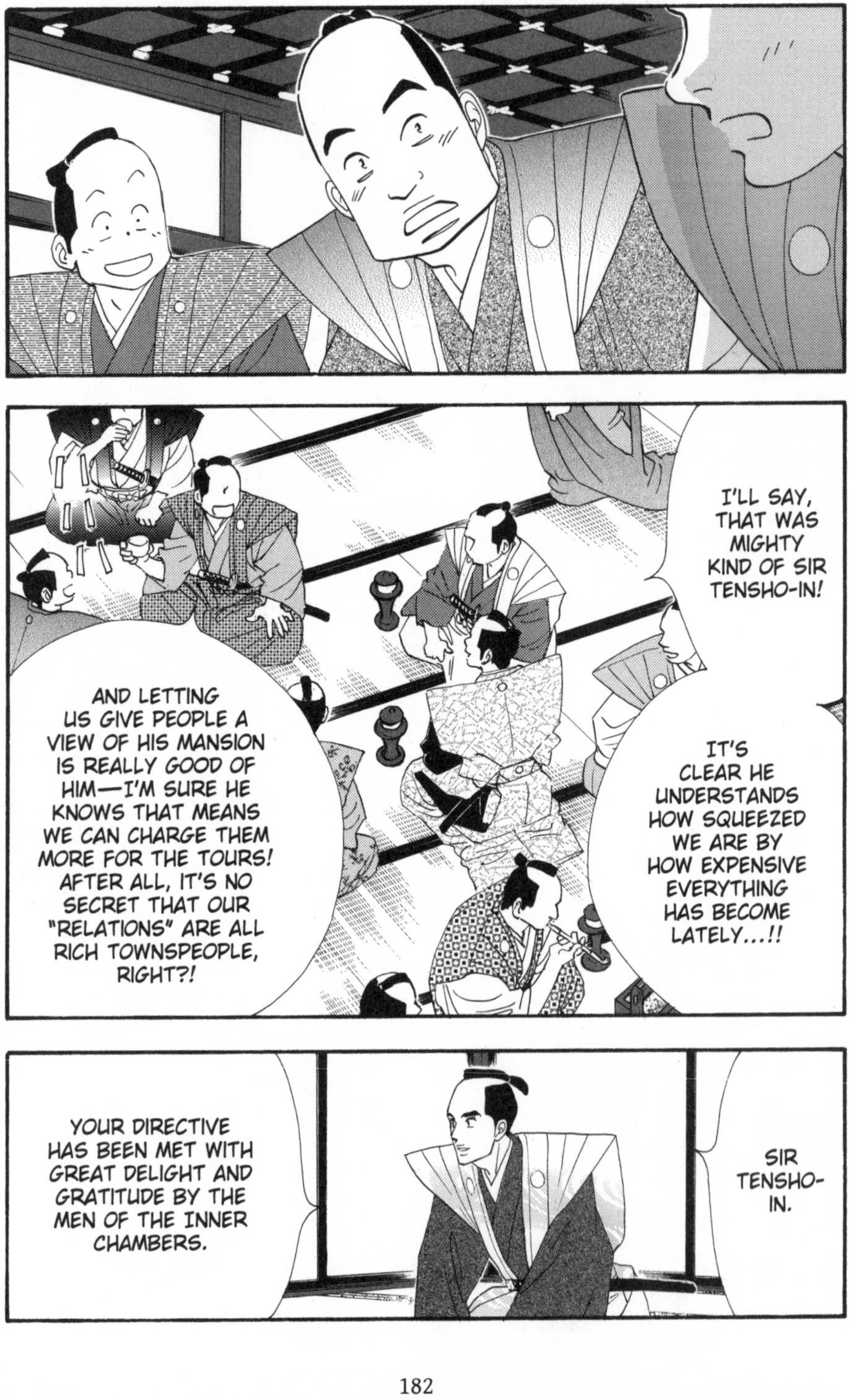
I'LL SAY, THAT WAS MIGHTY KIND OF SIR TENSHO-IN!
IT'S CLEAR HE UNDERSTANDS HOW SQUEEZED WE ARE BY HOW EXPENSIVE EVERYTHING HAS BECOME LATELY...!!
AND LETTING US GIVE PEOPLE A VIEW OF HIS MANSION IS REALLY GOOD OF HIM—I'M SURE HE KNOWS THAT MEANS WE CAN CHARGE THEM MORE FOR THE TOURS! AFTER ALL, IT'S NO SECRET THAT OUR "RELATIONS" ARE ALL RICH TOWNSPEOPLE, RIGHT?!
SIR TENSHO-IN.
YOUR DIRECTIVE HAS BEEN MET WITH GREAT DELIGHT AND GRATITUDE BY THE MEN OF THE INNER CHAMBERS.

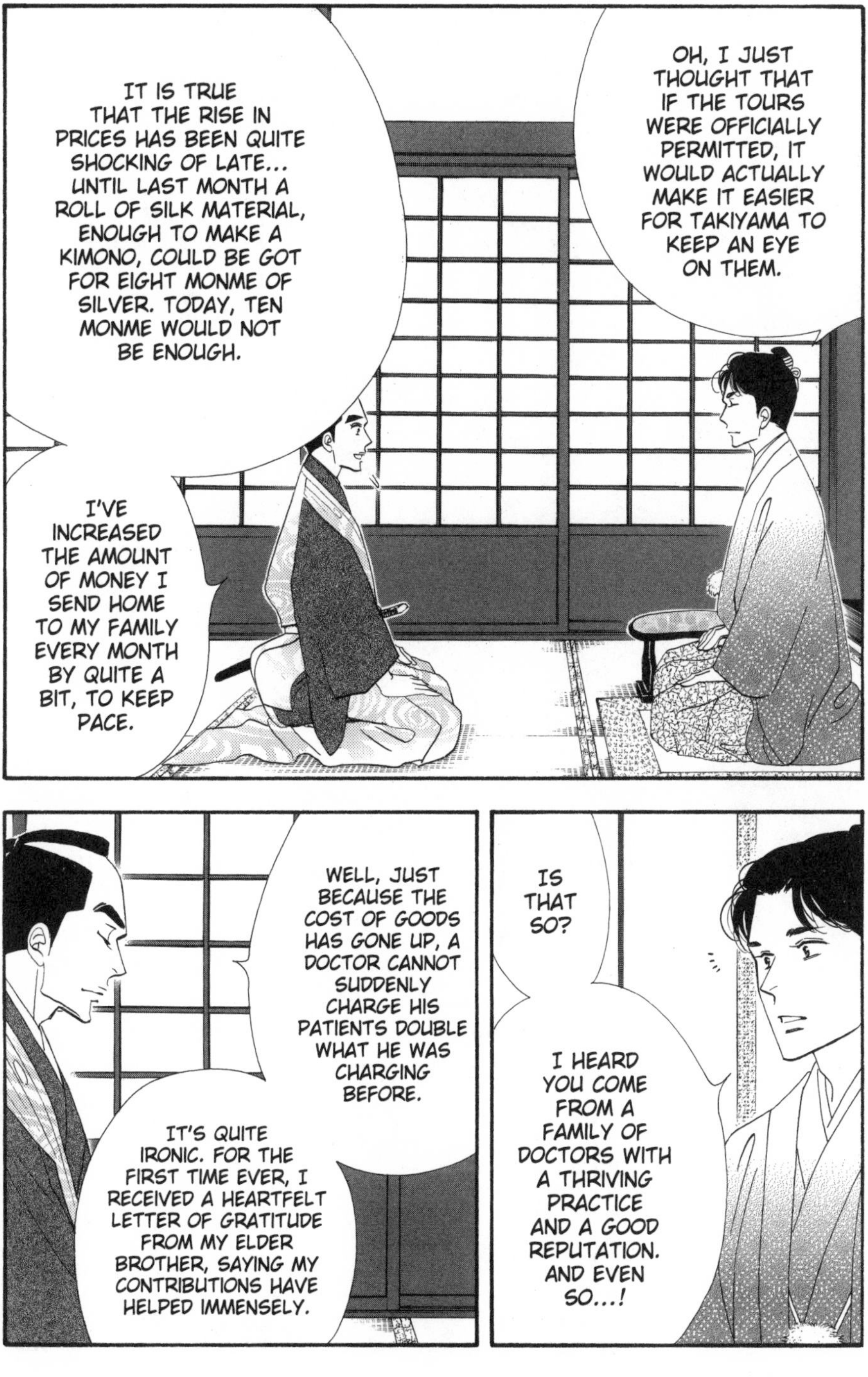
OH, I JUST THOUGHT THAT IF THE TOURS WERE OFFICIALLY PERMITTED, IT WOULD ACTUALLY MAKE IT EASIER FOR TAKIYAMA TO KEEP AN EYE ON THEM.
IT IS TRUE THAT THE RISE IN PRICES HAS BEEN QUITE SHOCKING OF LATE... UNTIL LAST MONTH A ROLL OF SILK MATERIAL, ENOUGH TO MAKE A KIMONO, COULD BE GOT FOR EIGHT MONME OF SILVER. TODAY, TEN MONME WOULD NOT BE ENOUGH.
I'VE INCREASED THE AMOUNT OF MONEY I SEND HOME TO MY FAMILY EVERY MONTH BY QUITE A BIT, TO KEEP PACE.
IS THAT SO?
I HEARD YOU COME FROM A FAMILY OF DOCTORS WITH A THRIVING PRACTICE AND A GOOD REPUTATION. AND EVEN SO...!
WELL, JUST BECAUSE THE COST OF GOODS HAS GONE UP, A DOCTOR CANNOT SUDDENLY CHARGE HIS PATIENTS DOUBLE WHAT HE WAS CHARGING BEFORE.
IT'S QUITE IRONIC. FOR THE FIRST TIME EVER, I RECEIVED A HEARTFELT LETTER OF GRATITUDE FROM MY ELDER BROTHER, SAYING MY CONTRIBUTIONS HAVE HELPED IMMENSELY.

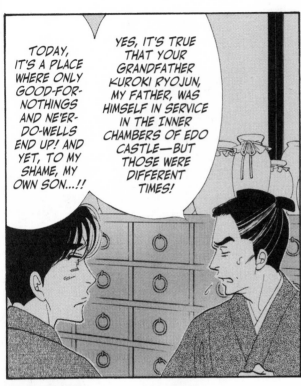

"OUR FATHER FEELS VERY BAD FOR CASTIGATING YOU WHEN YOU FIRST EXPRESSED YOUR WISH TO ENTER INTO SERVICE IN THE INNER CHAMBERS."
YES, IT'S TRUE THAT YOUR GRANDFATHER KUROKI RYOJUN, MY FATHER, WAS HIMSELF IN SERVICE IN THE INNER CHAMBERS OF EDO CASTLE—BUT THOSE WERE DIFFERENT TIMES!
TODAY, IT'S A PLACE WHERE ONLY GOOD-FOR-NOTHINGS AND NE'ER-DO-WELLS END UP! AND YET, TO MY SHAME, MY OWN SON...!!
I EXPECT THAT IN FACT MY FATHER STILL FEELS THE SAME, BUT...
THAT'S ALL RIGHT. FOR THE FIRST TIME, THE HIGH SALARY I RECEIVE AS A GROOM OF THE BEDCHAMBER HAS BEEN A BOON TO MY FAMILY...
I WAS ALWAYS A DISAPPOINTMENT TO MY FATHER, SO IT MAKES ME VERY HAPPY TO REDEEM MYSELF THIS WAY. IT FEELS GOOD TO HAVE MY FAMILY RELY ON ME.

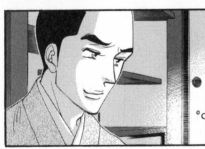

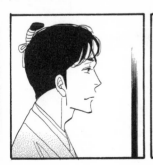

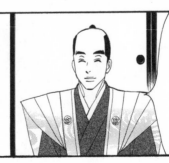

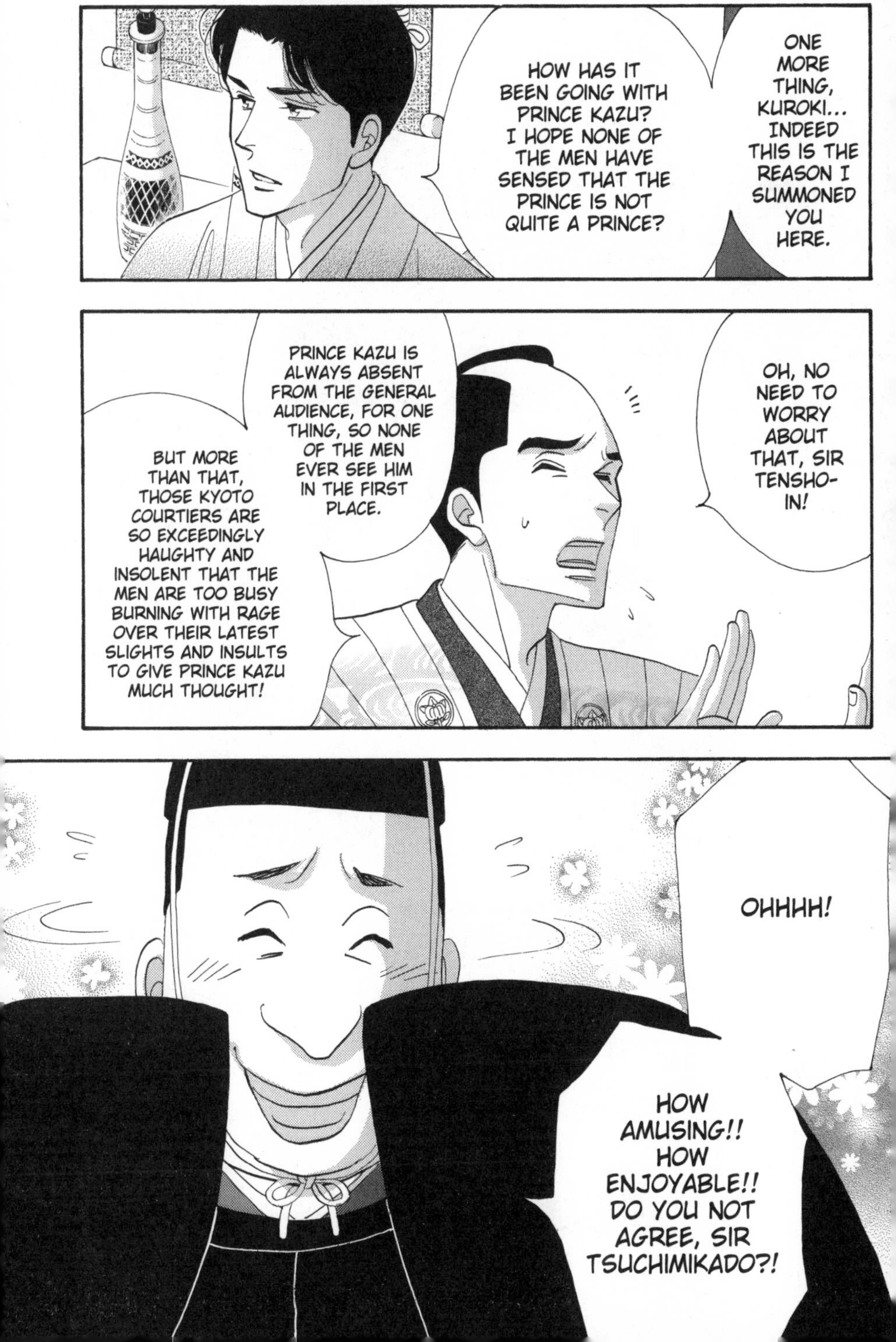
ONE MORE THING, KUROKI... INDEED THIS IS THE REASON I SUMMONED YOU HERE.
HOW HAS IT BEEN GOING WITH PRINCE KAZU? I HOPE NONE OF THE MEN HAVE SENSED THAT THE PRINCE IS NOT QUITE A PRINCE?
OH, NO NEED TO WORRY ABOUT THAT, SIR TENSHO-IN!
PRINCE KAZU IS ALWAYS ABSENT FROM THE GENERAL AUDIENCE, FOR ONE THING, SO NONE OF THE MEN EVER SEE HIM IN THE FIRST PLACE.
BUT MORE THAN THAT, THOSE KYOTO COURTIERS ARE SO EXCEEDINGLY HAUGHTY AND INSOLENT THAT THE MEN ARE TOO BUSY BURNING WITH RAGE OVER THEIR LATEST SLIGHTS AND INSULTS TO GIVE PRINCE KAZU MUCH THOUGHT!
OHHHH!
HOW AMUSING!! HOW ENJOYABLE!! DO YOU NOT AGREE, SIR TSUCHIMIKADO?!

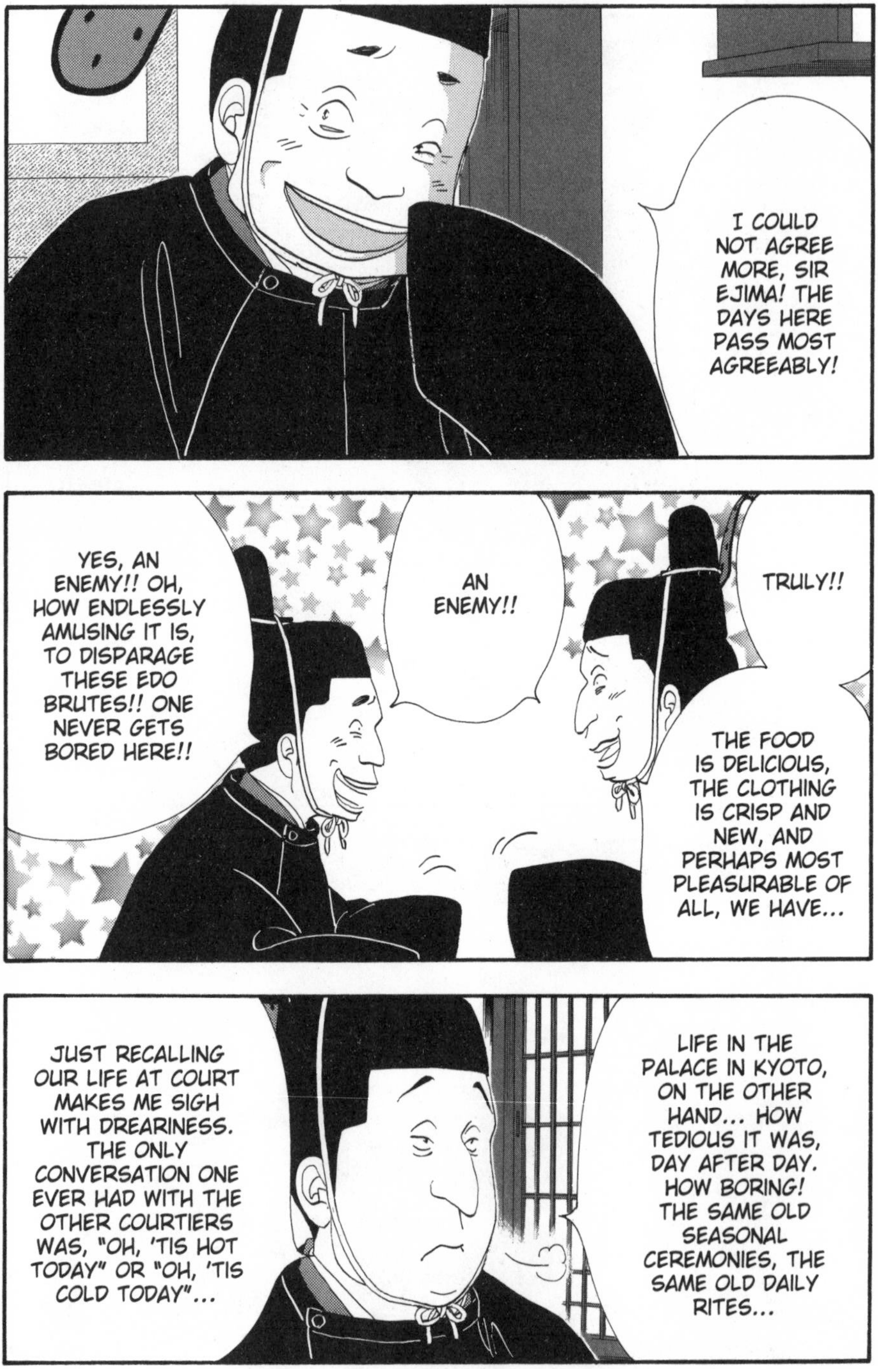
I COULD NOT AGREE MORE, SIR EJIMA! THE DAYS HERE PASS MOST AGREEABLY!
TRULY!!
THE FOOD IS DELICIOUS, THE CLOTHING IS CRISP AND NEW, AND PERHAPS MOST PLEASURABLE OF ALL, WE HAVE...
AN ENEMY!!
YES, AN ENEMY!! OH, HOW ENDLESSLY AMUSING IT IS, TO DISPARAGE THESE EDO BRUTES!! ONE NEVER GETS BORED HERE!!
LIFE IN THE PALACE IN KYOTO, ON THE OTHER HAND... HOW TEDIOUS IT WAS, DAY AFTER DAY. HOW BORING! THE SAME OLD SEASONAL CEREMONIES, THE SAME OLD DAILY RITES...
JUST RECALLING OUR LIFE AT COURT MAKES ME SIGH WITH DREARINESS. THE ONLY CONVERSATION ONE EVER HAD WITH THE OTHER COURTIERS WAS, "OH, 'TIS HOT TODAY" OR "OH, 'TIS COLD TODAY"...

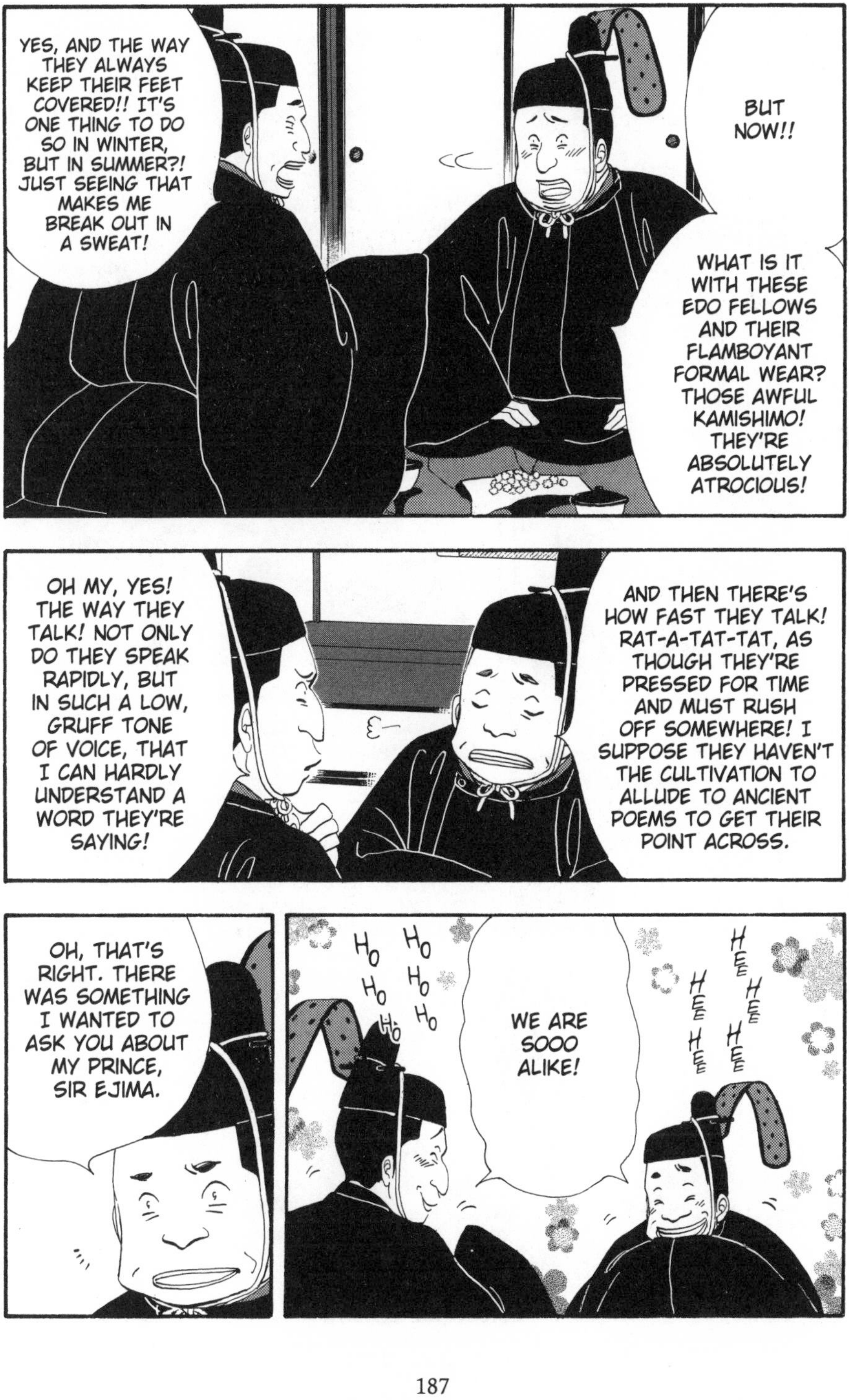
BUT NOW!!
WHAT IS IT WITH THESE EDO FELLOWS AND THEIR FLAMBOYANT FORMAL WEAR? THOSE AWFUL KAMISHIMO! THEY'RE ABSOLUTELY ATROCIOUS!
YES, AND THE WAY THEY ALWAYS KEEP THEIR FEET COVERED!! IT'S ONE THING TO DO SO IN WINTER, BUT IN SUMMER?! JUST SEEING THAT MAKES ME BREAK OUT IN A SWEAT!
AND THEN THERE'S HOW FAST THEY TALK! RAT-A-TAT-TAT, AS THOUGH THEY'RE PRESSED FOR TIME AND MUST RUSH OFF SOMEWHERE! I SUPPOSE THEY HAVEN'T THE CULTIVATION TO ALLUDE TO ANCIENT POEMS TO GET THEIR POINT ACROSS.
OH MY, YES! THE WAY THEY TALK! NOT ONLY DO THEY SPEAK RAPIDLY, BUT IN SUCH A LOW, GRUFF TONE OF VOICE, THAT I CAN HARDLY UNDERSTAND A WORD THEY'RE SAYING!
HEE HEE HEE HEE HEE HEE
WE ARE SOOO ALIKE!
HO HO HO HO HO HO HO
OH, THAT'S RIGHT. THERE WAS SOMETHING I WANTED TO ASK YOU ABOUT MY PRINCE, SIR EJIMA.

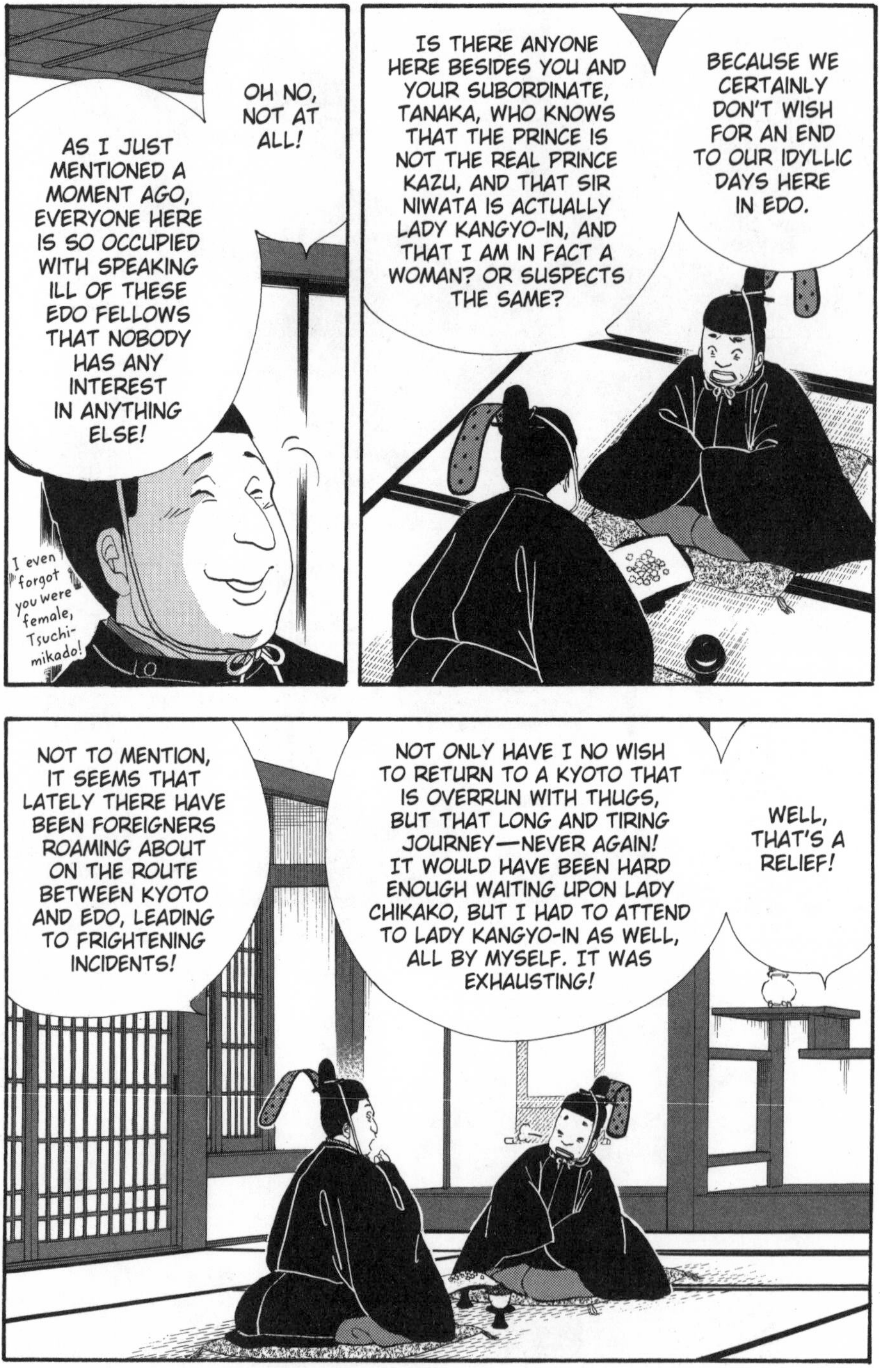
IS THERE ANYONE HERE BESIDES YOU AND YOUR SUBORDINATE, TANAKA, WHO KNOWS THAT THE PRINCE IS NOT THE REAL PRINCE KAZU, AND THAT SIR NIWATA IS ACTUALLY LADY KANGYO-IN, AND THAT I AM IN FACT A WOMAN? OR SUSPECTS THE SAME?
BECAUSE WE CERTAINLY DON'T WISH FOR AN END TO OUR IDYLLIC DAYS HERE IN EDO.
OH NO, NOT AT ALL!
AS I JUST MENTIONED A MOMENT AGO, EVERYONE HERE IS SO OCCUPIED WITH SPEAKING ILL OF THESE EDO FELLOWS THAT NOBODY HAS ANY INTEREST IN ANYTHING ELSE!
I even forgot you were female, Tsuchi-mikado!
WELL, THAT'S A RELIEF!
NOT ONLY HAVE I NO WISH TO RETURN TO A KYOTO THAT IS OVERRUN WITH THUGS, BUT THAT LONG AND TIRING JOURNEY—NEVER AGAIN! IT WOULD HAVE BEEN HARD ENOUGH WAITING UPON LADY CHIKAKO, BUT I HAD TO ATTEND TO LADY KANGYO-IN AS WELL, ALL BY MYSELF. IT WAS EXHAUSTING!
NOT TO MENTION, IT SEEMS THAT LATELY THERE HAVE BEEN FOREIGNERS ROAMING ABOUT ON THE ROUTE BETWEEN KYOTO AND EDO, LEADING TO FRIGHTENING INCIDENTS!

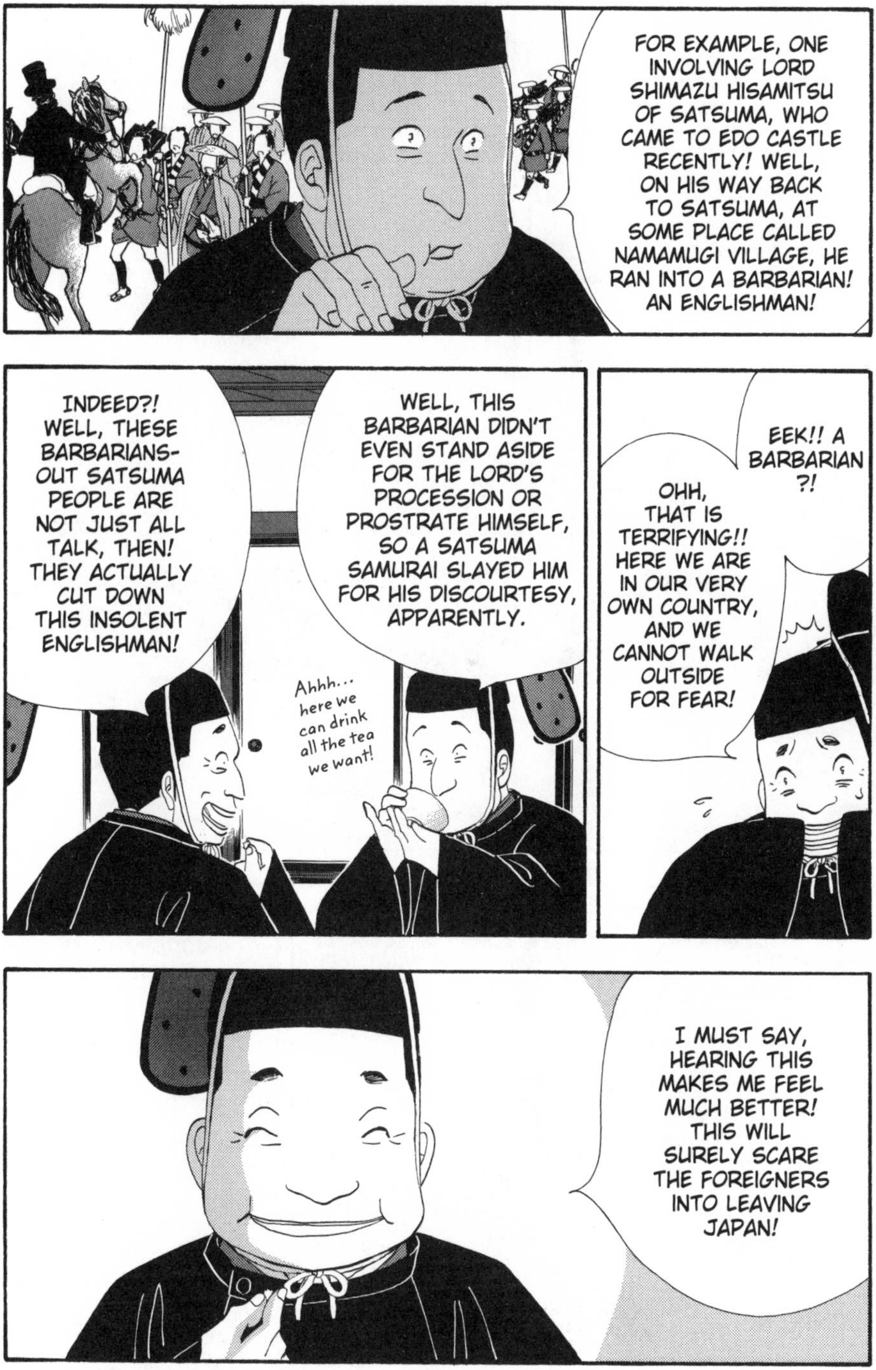
FOR EXAMPLE, ONE INVOLVING LORD SHIMAZU HISAMITSU OF SATSUMA, WHO CAME TO EDO CASTLE RECENTLY! WELL, ON HIS WAY BACK TO SATSUMA, AT SOME PLACE CALLED NAMAMUGI VILLAGE, HE RAN INTO A BARBARIAN! AN ENGLISHMAN!
EEK!! A BARBARIAN ?!
OHH, THAT IS TERRIFYING!! HERE WE ARE IN OUR VERY OWN COUNTRY, AND WE CANNOT WALK OUTSIDE FOR FEAR!
WELL, THIS BARBARIAN DIDN'T EVEN STAND ASIDE FOR THE LORD'S PROCESSION OR PROSTRATE HIMSELF, SO A SATSUMA SAMURAI SLAYED HIM FOR HIS DISCOURTESY, APPARENTLY.
Ahhh... here we can drink all the tea we want!
INDEED?! WELL, THESE BARBARIANS-OUT SATSUMA PEOPLE ARE NOT JUST ALL TALK, THEN! THEY ACTUALLY CUT DOWN THIS INSOLENT ENGLISHMAN!
I MUST SAY, HEARING THIS MAKES ME FEEL MUCH BETTER! THIS WILL SURELY SCARE THE FOREIGNERS INTO LEAVING JAPAN!

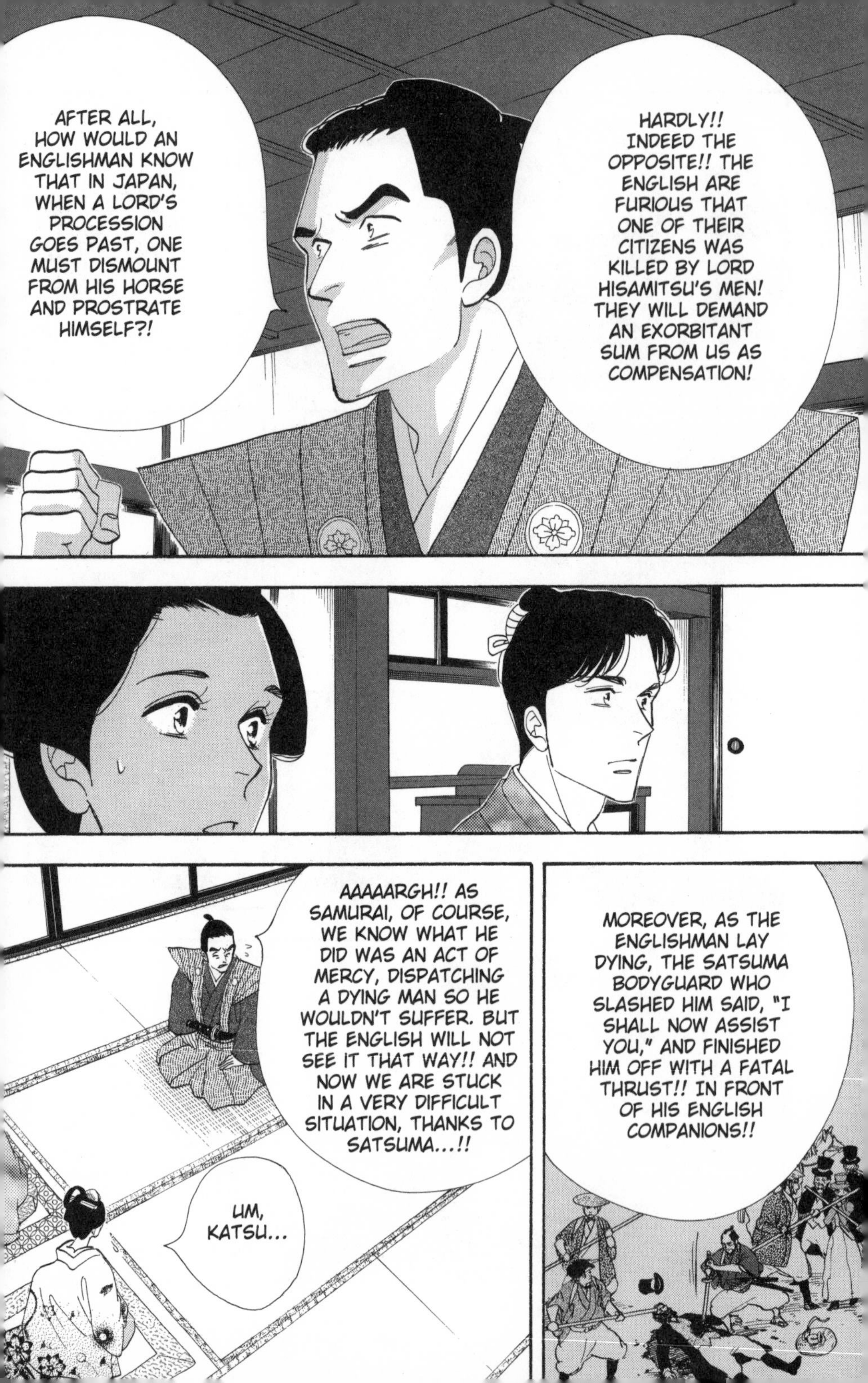
HARDLY!! INDEED THE OPPOSITE!! THE ENGLISH ARE FURIOUS THAT ONE OF THEIR CITIZENS WAS KILLED BY LORD HISAMITSU'S MEN! THEY WILL DEMAND AN EXORBITANT SUM FROM US AS COMPENSATION!
AFTER ALL, HOW WOULD AN ENGLISHMAN KNOW THAT IN JAPAN, WHEN A LORD'S PROCESSION GOES PAST, ONE MUST DISMOUNT FROM HIS HORSE AND PROSTRATE HIMSELF?!
MOREOVER, AS THE ENGLISHMAN LAY DYING, THE SATSUMA BODYGUARD WHO SLASHED HIM SAID, "I SHALL NOW ASSIST YOU," AND FINISHED HIM OFF WITH A FATAL THRUST!! IN FRONT OF HIS ENGLISH COMPANIONS!!
AAAAARGH!! AS SAMURAI, OF COURSE, WE KNOW WHAT HE DID WAS AN ACT OF MERCY, DISPATCHING A DYING MAN SO HE WOULDN'T SUFFER. BUT THE ENGLISH WILL NOT SEE IT THAT WAY!! AND NOW WE ARE STUCK IN A VERY DIFFICULT SITUATION, THANKS TO SATSUMA...!!
UM, KATSU...

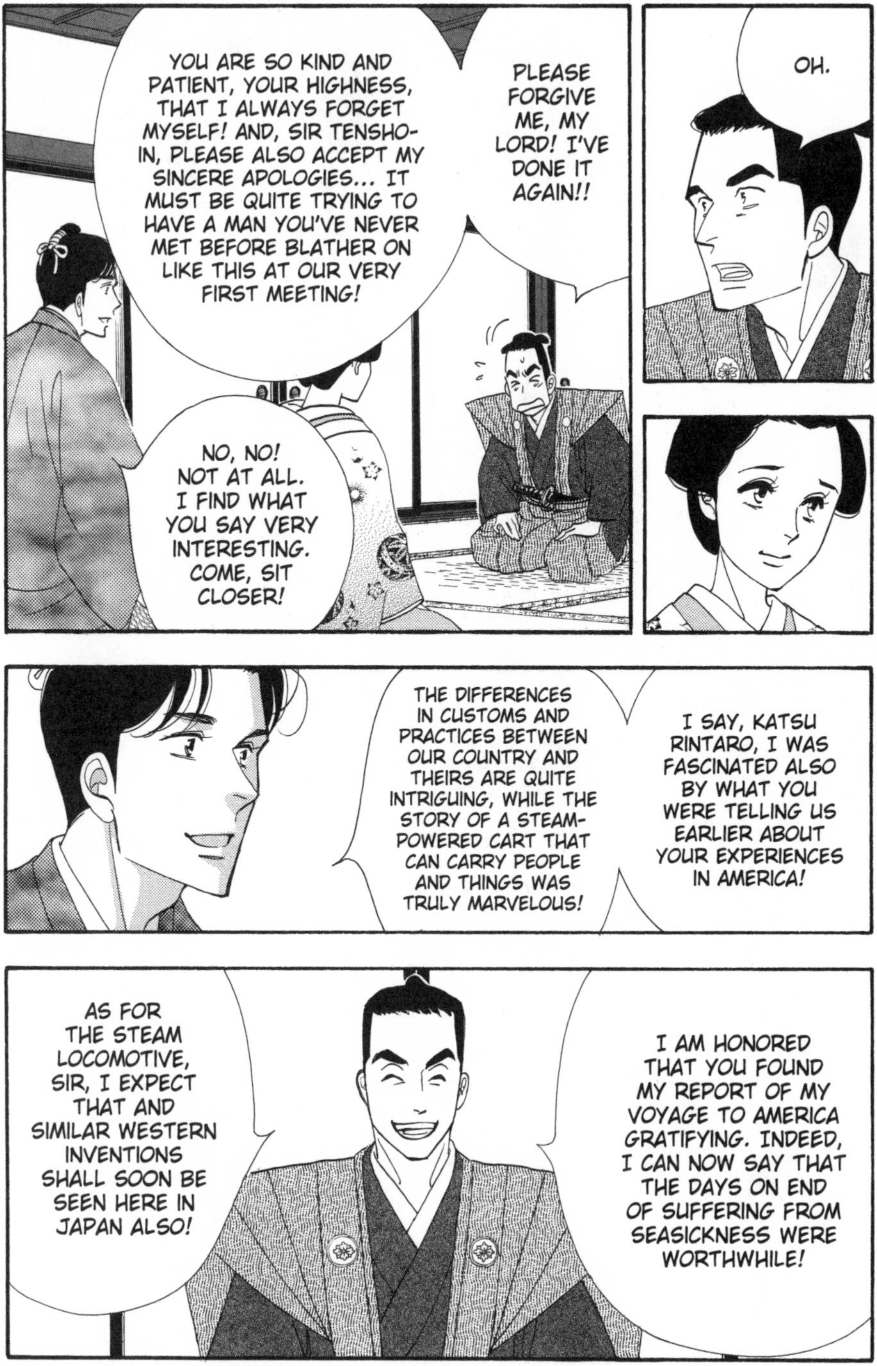
OH.
PLEASE FORGIVE ME, MY LORD! I'VE DONE IT AGAIN!!
YOU ARE SO KIND AND PATIENT, YOUR HIGHNESS, THAT I ALWAYS FORGET MYSELF! AND, SIR TENSHO-IN, PLEASE ALSO ACCEPT MY SINCERE APOLOGIES... IT MUST BE QUITE TRYING TO HAVE A MAN YOU'VE NEVER MET BEFORE BLATHER ON LIKE THIS AT OUR VERY FIRST MEETING!
NO, NO! NOT AT ALL. I FIND WHAT YOU SAY VERY INTERESTING. COME, SIT CLOSER!
I SAY, KATSU RINTARO, I WAS FASCINATED ALSO BY WHAT YOU WERE TELLING US EARLIER ABOUT YOUR EXPERIENCES IN AMERICA!
THE DIFFERENCES IN CUSTOMS AND PRACTICES BETWEEN OUR COUNTRY AND THEIRS ARE QUITE INTRIGUING, WHILE THE STORY OF A STEAM-POWERED CART THAT CAN CARRY PEOPLE AND THINGS WAS TRULY MARVELOUS!
I AM HONORED THAT YOU FOUND MY REPORT OF MY VOYAGE TO AMERICA GRATIFYING. INDEED, I CAN NOW SAY THAT THE DAYS ON END OF SUFFERING FROM SEASICKNESS WERE WORTHWHILE!
AS FOR THE STEAM LOCOMOTIVE, SIR, I EXPECT THAT AND SIMILAR WESTERN INVENTIONS SHALL SOON BE SEEN HERE IN JAPAN ALSO!

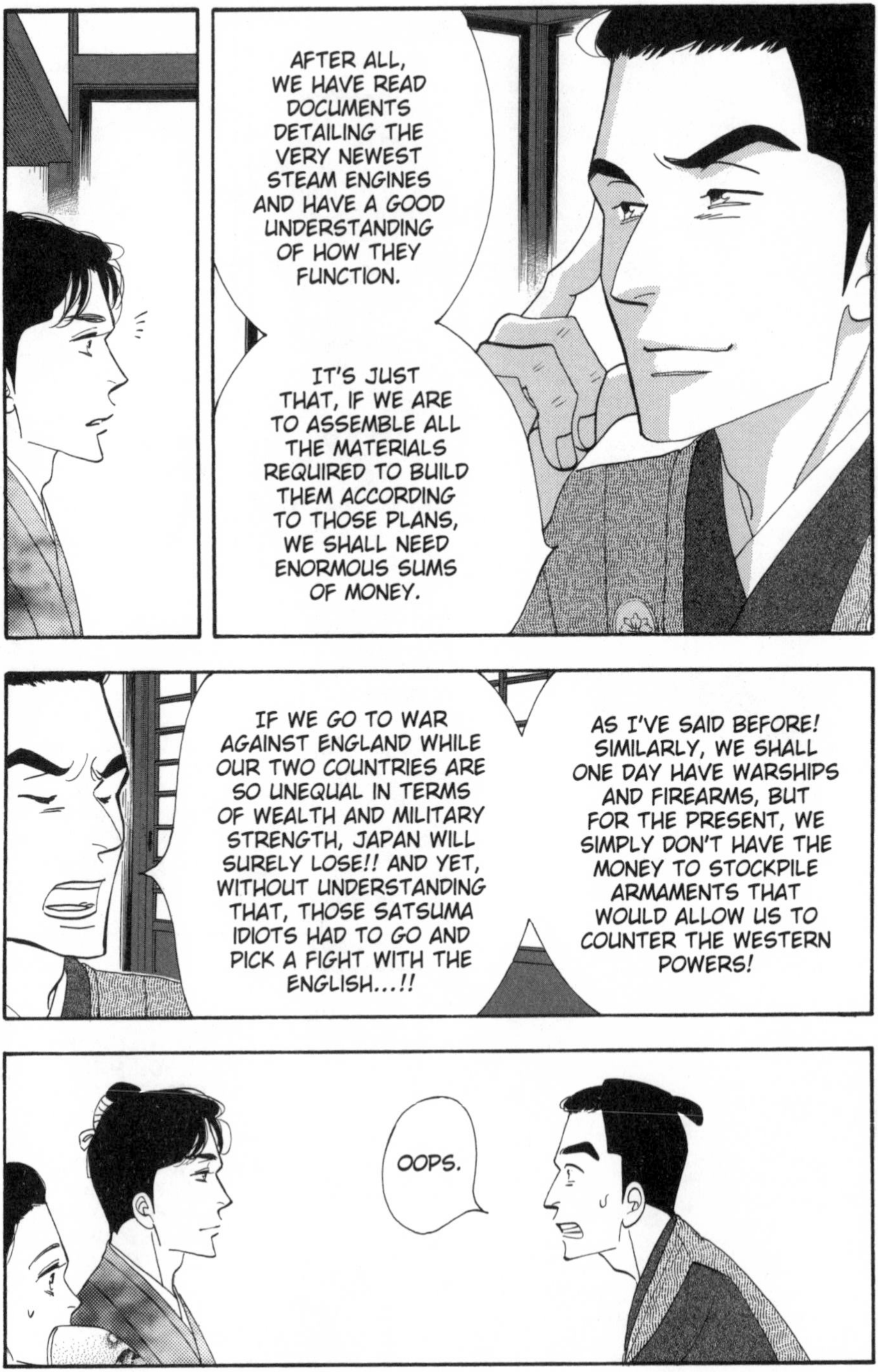
AFTER ALL, WE HAVE READ DOCUMENTS DETAILING THE VERY NEWEST STEAM ENGINES AND HAVE A GOOD UNDERSTANDING OF HOW THEY FUNCTION.
IT'S JUST THAT, IF WE ARE TO ASSEMBLE ALL THE MATERIALS REQUIRED TO BUILD THEM ACCORDING TO THOSE PLANS, WE SHALL NEED ENORMOUS SUMS OF MONEY.
AS I'VE SAID BEFORE! SIMILARLY, WE SHALL ONE DAY HAVE WARSHIPS AND FIREARMS, BUT FOR THE PRESENT, WE SIMPLY DON'T HAVE THE MONEY TO STOCKPILE ARMAMENTS THAT WOULD ALLOW US TO COUNTER THE WESTERN POWERS!
IF WE GO TO WAR AGAINST ENGLAND WHILE OUR TWO COUNTRIES ARE SO UNEQUAL IN TERMS OF WEALTH AND MILITARY STRENGTH, JAPAN WILL SURELY LOSE!! AND YET, WITHOUT UNDERSTANDING THAT, THOSE SATSUMA IDIOTS HAD TO GO AND PICK A FIGHT WITH THE ENGLISH...!!
OOPS.

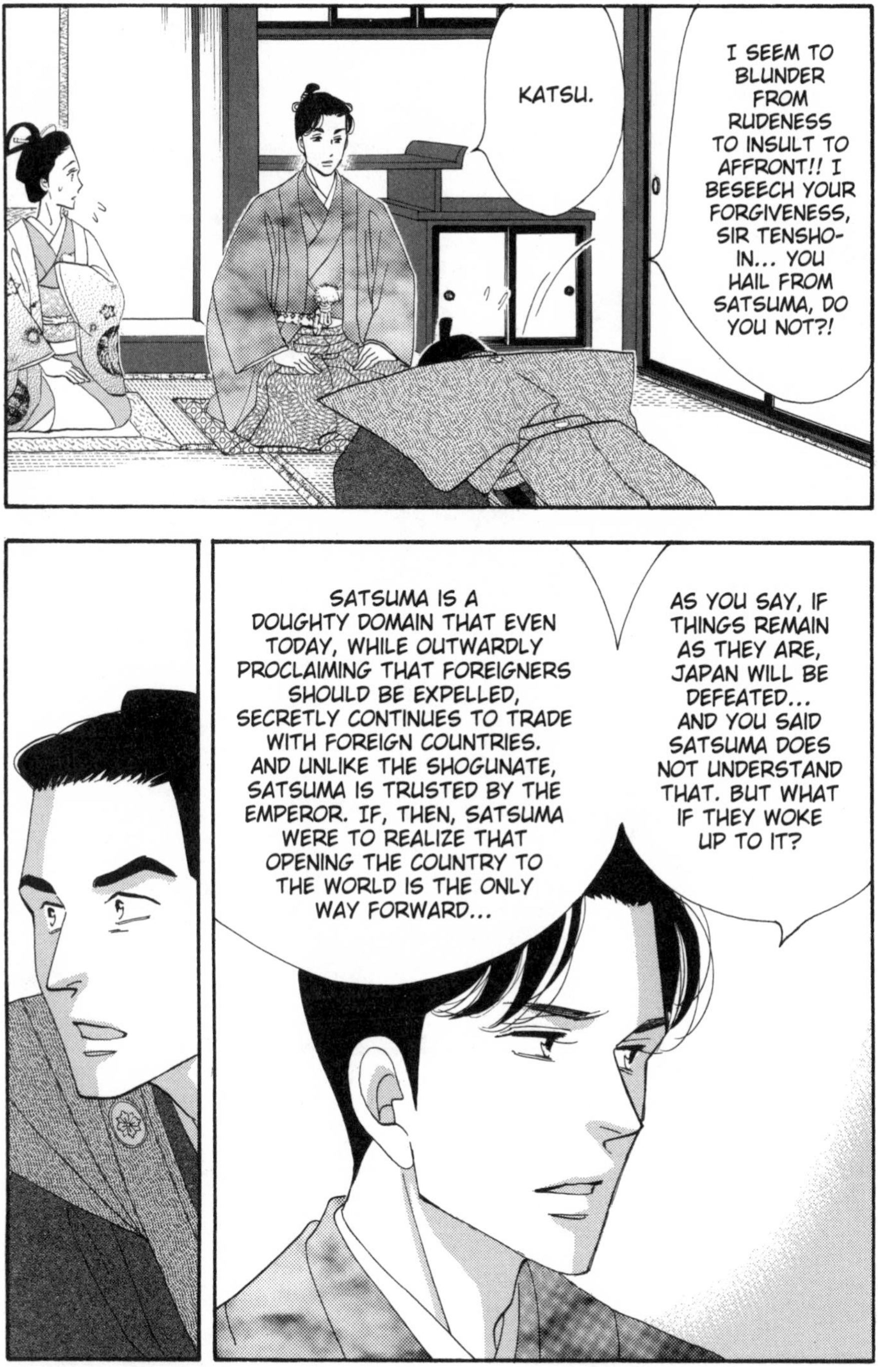
I SEEM TO BLUNDER FROM RUDENESS TO INSULT TO AFFRONT!! I BESEECH YOUR FORGIVENESS, SIR TENSHO-IN... YOU HAIL FROM SATSUMA, DO YOU NOT?!
KATSU.
AS YOU SAY, IF THINGS REMAIN AS THEY ARE, JAPAN WILL BE DEFEATED... AND YOU SAID SATSUMA DOES NOT UNDERSTAND THAT. BUT WHAT IF THEY WOKE UP TO IT?
SATSUMA IS A DOUGHTY DOMAIN THAT EVEN TODAY, WHILE OUTWARDLY PROCLAIMING THAT FOREIGNERS SHOULD BE EXPELLED, SECRETLY CONTINUES TO TRADE WITH FOREIGN COUNTRIES. AND UNLIKE THE SHOGUNATE, SATSUMA IS TRUSTED BY THE EMPEROR. IF, THEN, SATSUMA WERE TO REALIZE THAT OPENING THE COUNTRY TO THE WORLD IS THE ONLY WAY FORWARD...

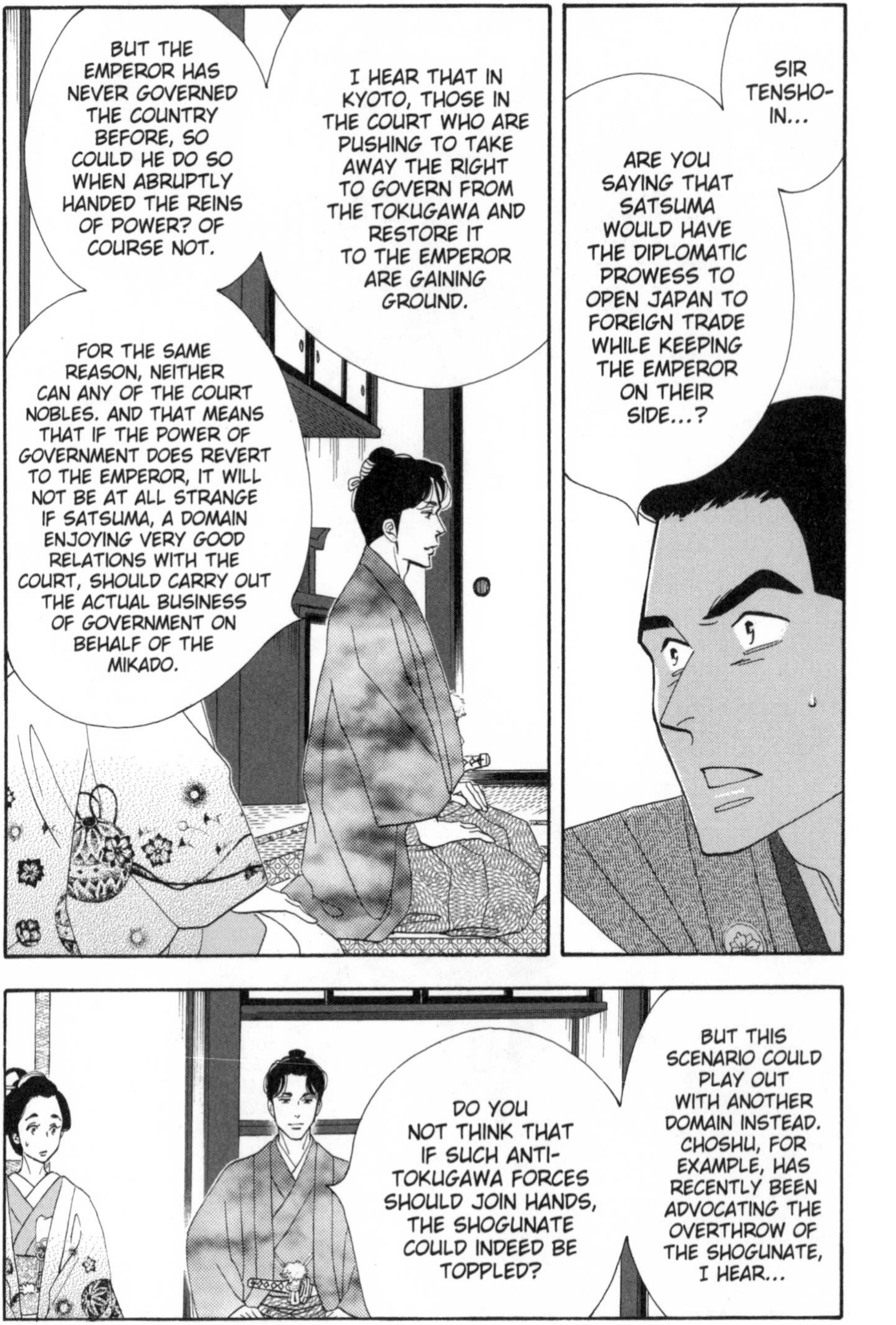
SIR TENSHO-IN...
ARE YOU SAYING THAT SATSUMA WOULD HAVE THE DIPLOMATIC PROWESS TO OPEN JAPAN TO FOREIGN TRADE WHILE KEEPING THE EMPEROR ON THEIR SIDE...?
I HEAR THAT IN KYOTO, THOSE IN THE COURT WHO ARE PUSHING TO TAKE AWAY THE RIGHT TO GOVERN FROM THE TOKUGAWA AND RESTORE IT TO THE EMPEROR ARE GAINING GROUND.
BUT THE EMPEROR HAS NEVER GOVERNED THE COUNTRY BEFORE, SO COULD HE DO SO WHEN ABRUPTLY HANDED THE REINS OF POWER? OF COURSE NOT.
FOR THE SAME REASON, NEITHER CAN ANY OF THE COURT NOBLES. AND THAT MEANS THAT IF THE POWER OF GOVERNMENT DOES REVERT TO THE EMPEROR, IT WILL NOT BE AT ALL STRANGE IF SATSUMA, A DOMAIN ENJOYING VERY GOOD RELATIONS WITH THE COURT, SHOULD CARRY OUT THE ACTUAL BUSINESS OF GOVERNMENT ON BEHALF OF THE MIKADO.
BUT THIS SCENARIO COULD PLAY OUT WITH ANOTHER DOMAIN INSTEAD. CHOSHU, FOR EXAMPLE, HAS RECENTLY BEEN ADVOCATING THE OVERTHROW OF THE SHOGUNATE, I HEAR...
DO YOU NOT THINK THAT IF SUCH ANTI-TOKUGAWA FORCES SHOULD JOIN HANDS, THE SHOGUNATE COULD INDEED BE TOPPLED?

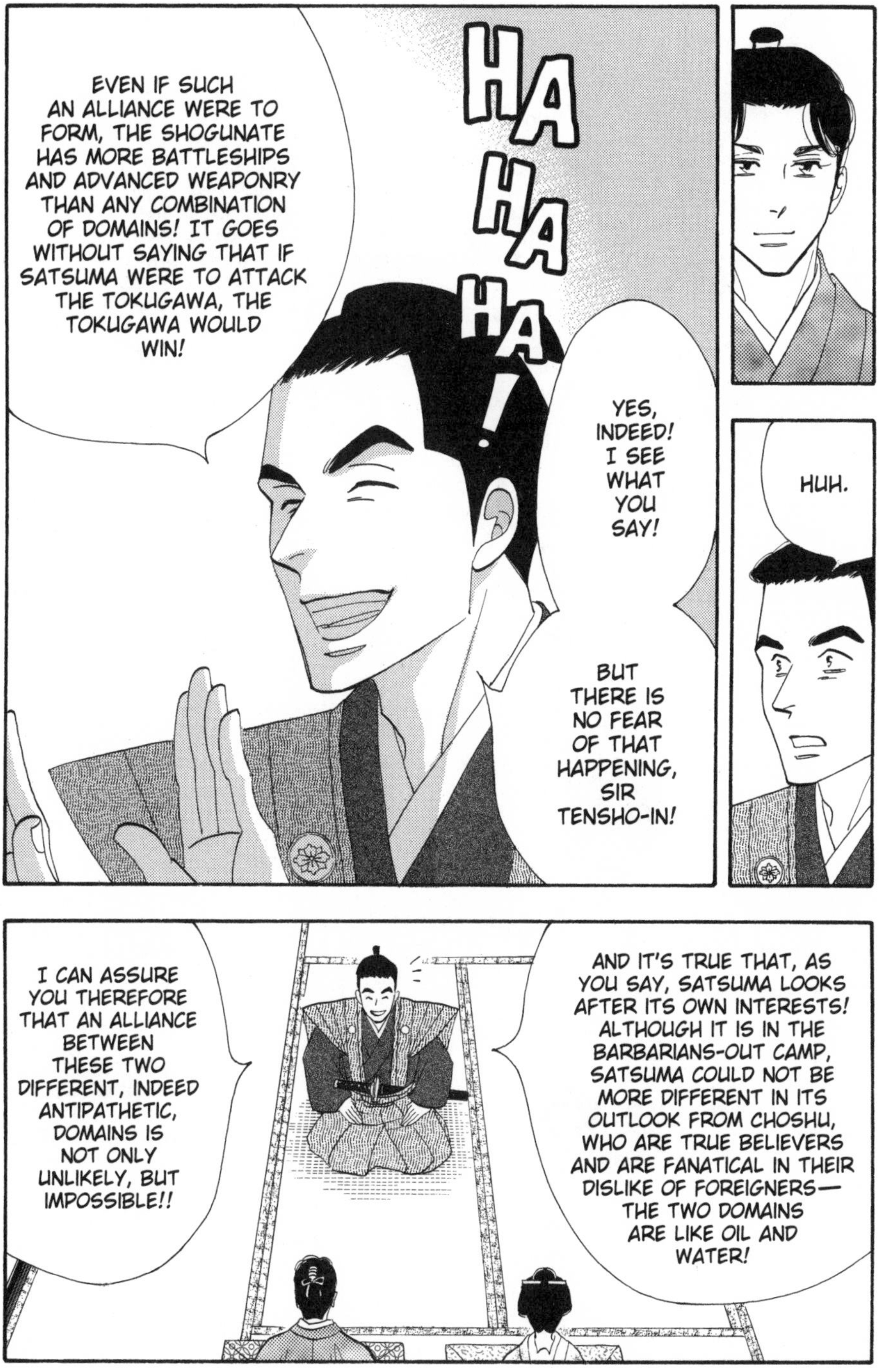
HUH.
HA HA HA!
YES, INDEED! I SEE WHAT YOU SAY!
BUT THERE IS NO FEAR OF THAT HAPPENING, SIR TENSHO-IN!
EVEN IF SUCH AN ALLIANCE WERE TO FORM, THE SHOGUNATE HAS MORE BATTLESHIPS AND ADVANCED WEAPONRY THAN ANY COMBINATION OF DOMAINS! IT GOES WITHOUT SAYING THAT IF SATSUMA WERE TO ATTACK THE TOKUGAWA, THE TOKUGAWA WOULD WIN!
AND IT'S TRUE THAT, AS YOU SAY, SATSUMA LOOKS AFTER ITS OWN INTERESTS! ALTHOUGH IT IS IN THE BARBARIANS-OUT CAMP, SATSUMA COULD NOT BE MORE DIFFERENT IN ITS OUTLOOK FROM CHOSHU, WHO ARE TRUE BELIEVERS AND ARE FANATICAL IN THEIR DISLIKE OF FOREIGNERS—THE TWO DOMAINS ARE LIKE OIL AND WATER!
I CAN ASSURE YOU THEREFORE THAT AN ALLIANCE BETWEEN THESE TWO DIFFERENT, INDEED ANTIPATHETIC, DOMAINS IS NOT ONLY UNLIKELY, BUT IMPOSSIBLE!!

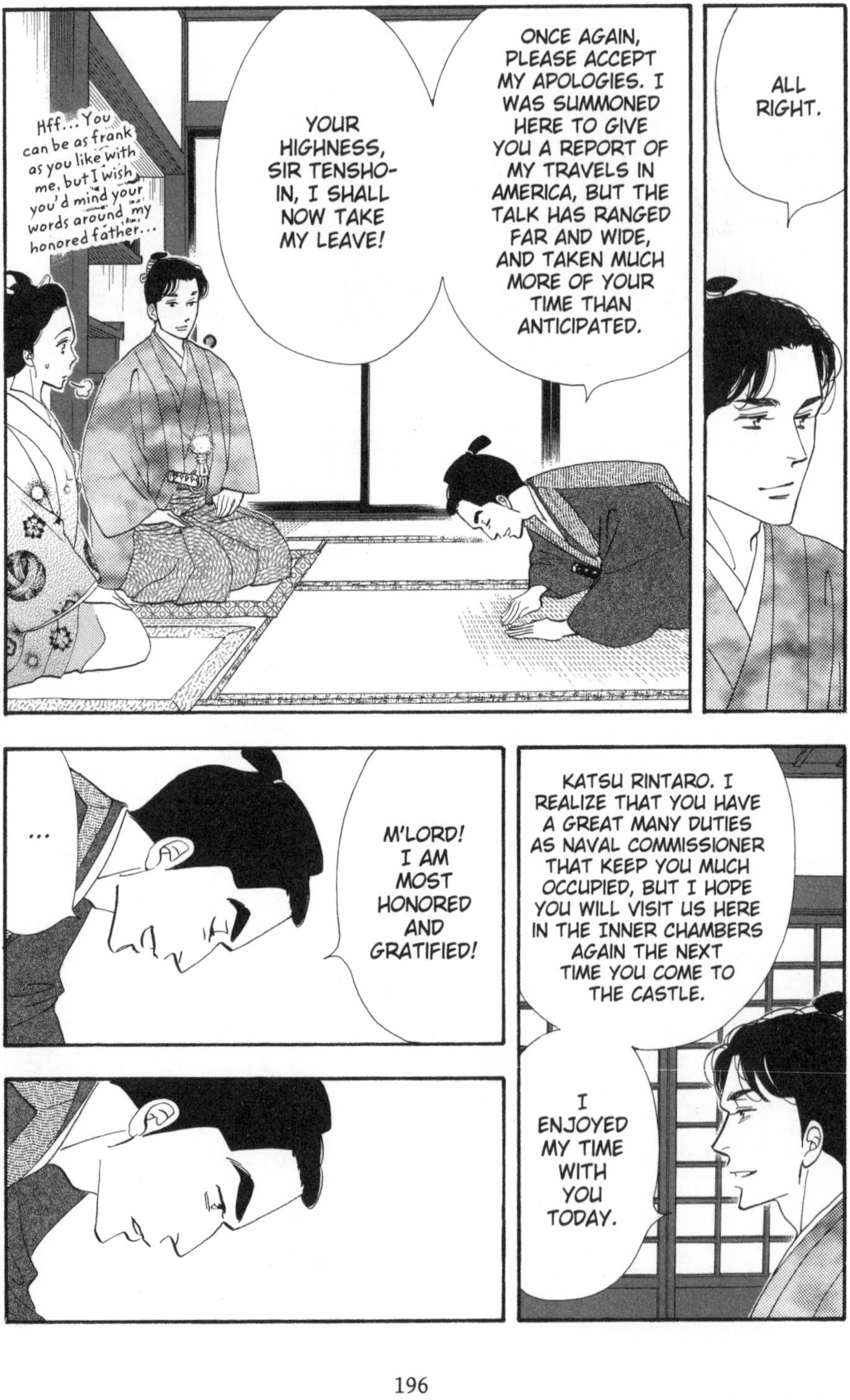
ALL RIGHT.
ONCE AGAIN, PLEASE ACCEPT MY APOLOGIES. I WAS SUMMONED HERE TO GIVE YOU A REPORT OF MY TRAVELS IN AMERICA, BUT THE TALK HAS RANGED FAR AND WIDE, AND TAKEN MUCH MORE OF YOUR TIME THAN ANTICIPATED.
YOUR HIGHNESS, SIR TENSHO-IN, I SHALL NOW TAKE MY LEAVE!
Hff... You can be as frank as you like with me, but I wish you'd mind your words around my honored father...
KATSU RINTARO. I REALIZE THAT YOU HAVE A GREAT MANY DUTIES AS NAVAL COMMISSIONER THAT KEEP YOU MUCH OCCUPIED, BUT I HOPE YOU WILL VISIT US HERE IN THE INNER CHAMBERS AGAIN THE NEXT TIME YOU COME TO THE CASTLE.
I ENJOYED MY TIME WITH YOU TODAY.
M'LORD! I AM MOST HONORED AND GRATIFIED!
...

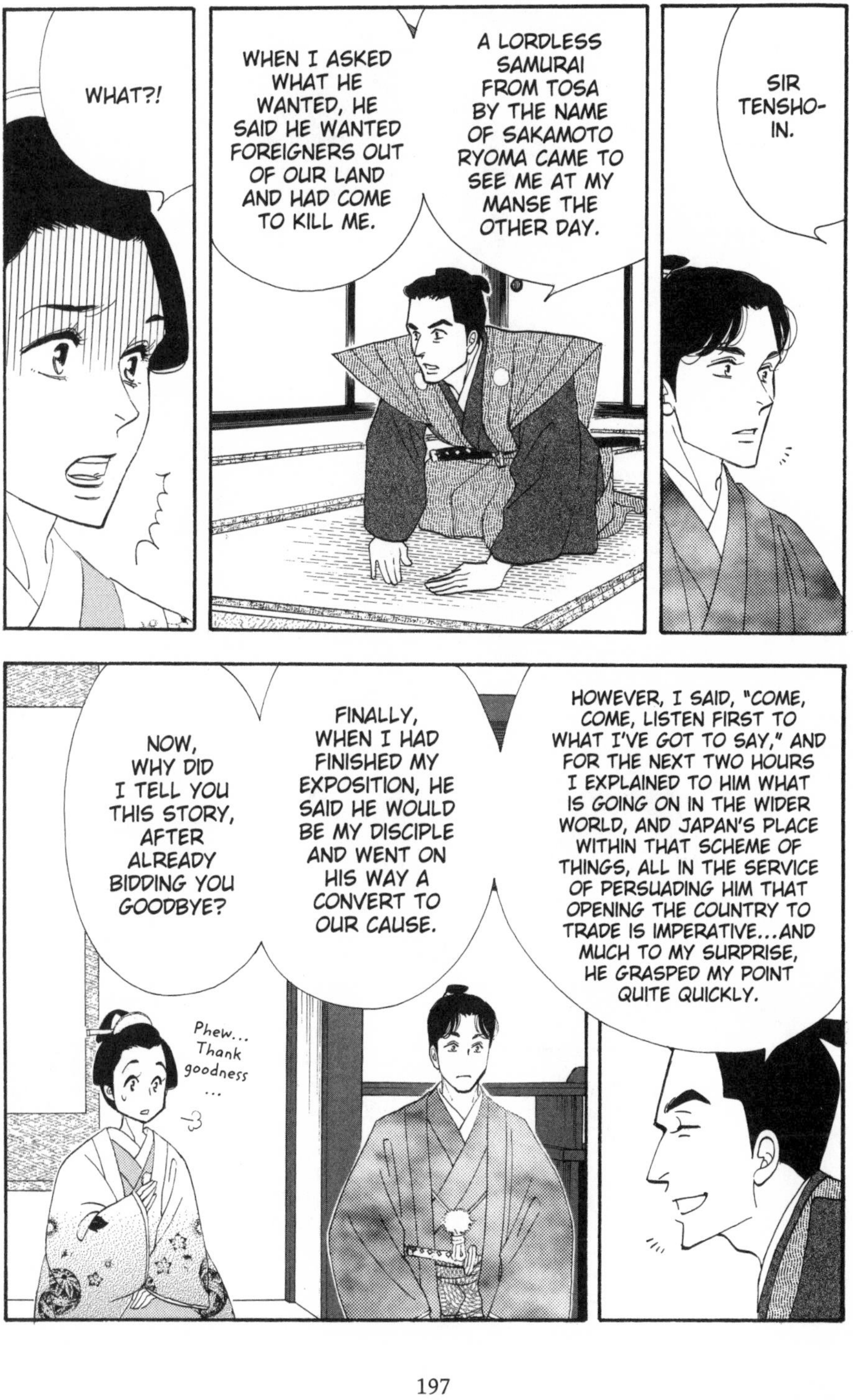
SIR TENSHO-IN.
A LORDLESS SAMURAI FROM TOSA BY THE NAME OF SAKAMOTO RYOMA CAME TO SEE ME AT MY MANSE THE OTHER DAY.
WHEN I ASKED WHAT HE WANTED, HE SAID HE WANTED FOREIGNERS OUT OF OUR LAND AND HAD COME TO KILL ME.
WHAT?!
HOWEVER, I SAID, "COME, COME, LISTEN FIRST TO WHAT I'VE GOT TO SAY," AND FOR THE NEXT TWO HOURS I EXPLAINED TO HIM WHAT IS GOING ON IN THE WIDER WORLD, AND JAPAN'S PLACE WITHIN THAT SCHEME OF THINGS, ALL IN THE SERVICE OF PERSUADING HIM THAT OPENING THE COUNTRY TO TRADE IS IMPERATIVE...AND MUCH TO MY SURPRISE, HE GRASPED MY POINT QUITE QUICKLY.
FINALLY, WHEN I HAD FINISHED MY EXPOSITION, HE SAID HE WOULD BE MY DISCIPLE AND WENT ON HIS WAY A CONVERT TO OUR CAUSE.
NOW, WHY DID I TELL YOU THIS STORY, AFTER ALREADY BIDDING YOU GOODBYE?
Phew... Thank goodness...

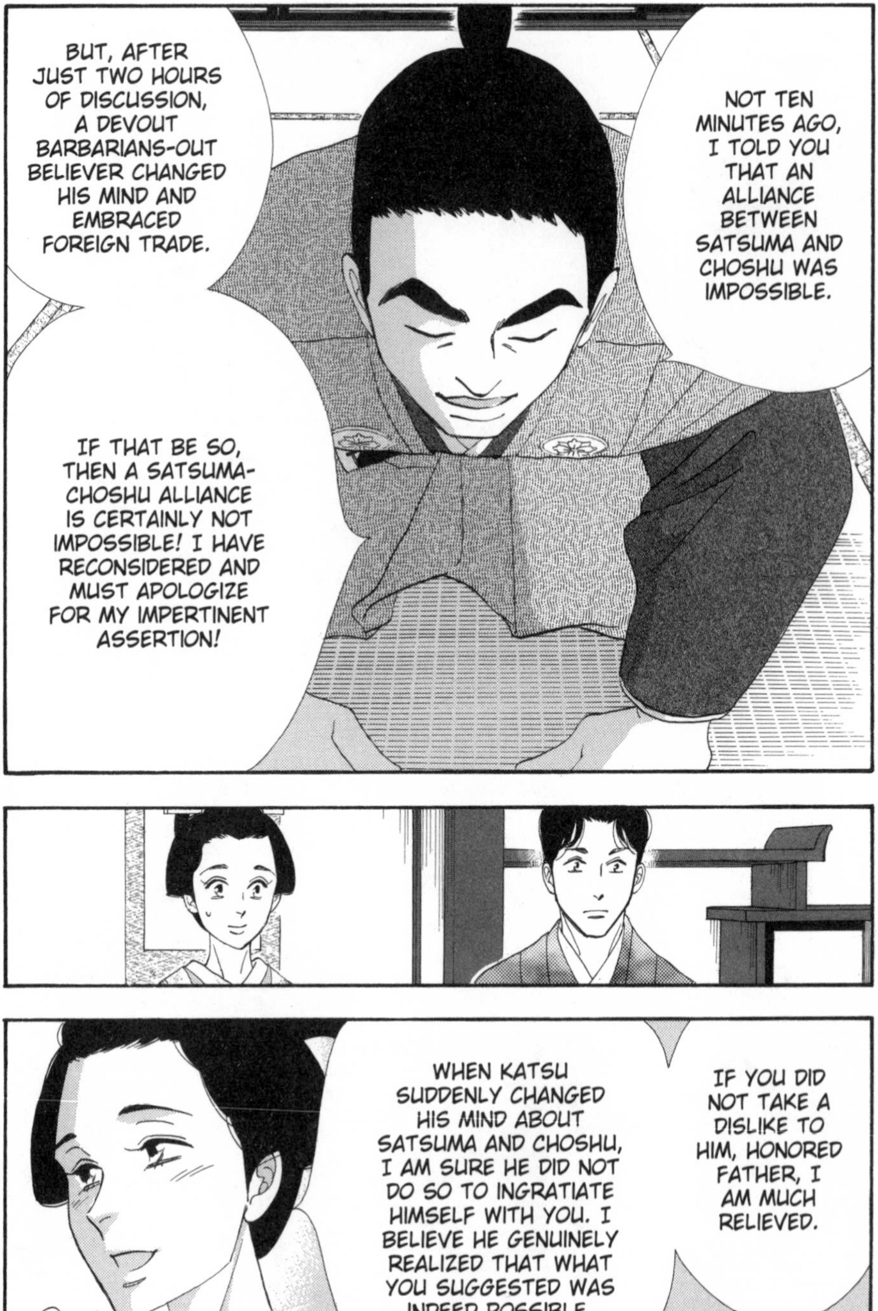
NOT TEN MINUTES AGO, I TOLD YOU THAT AN ALLIANCE BETWEEN SATSUMA AND CHOSHU WAS IMPOSSIBLE.
BUT, AFTER JUST TWO HOURS OF DISCUSSION, A DEVOUT BARBARIANS-OUT BELIEVER CHANGED HIS MIND AND EMBRACED FOREIGN TRADE.
IF THAT BE SO, THEN A SATSUMA-CHOSHU ALLIANCE IS CERTAINLY NOT IMPOSSIBLE! I HAVE RECONSIDERED AND MUST APOLOGIZE FOR MY IMPERTINENT ASSERTION!
IF YOU DID NOT TAKE A DISLIKE TO HIM, HONORED FATHER, I AM MUCH RELIEVED.
WHEN KATSU SUDDENLY CHANGED HIS MIND ABOUT SATSUMA AND CHOSHU, I AM SURE HE DID NOT DO SO TO INGRATIATE HIMSELF WITH YOU. I BELIEVE HE GENUINELY REALIZED THAT WHAT YOU SUGGESTED WAS INDEED POSSIBLE.

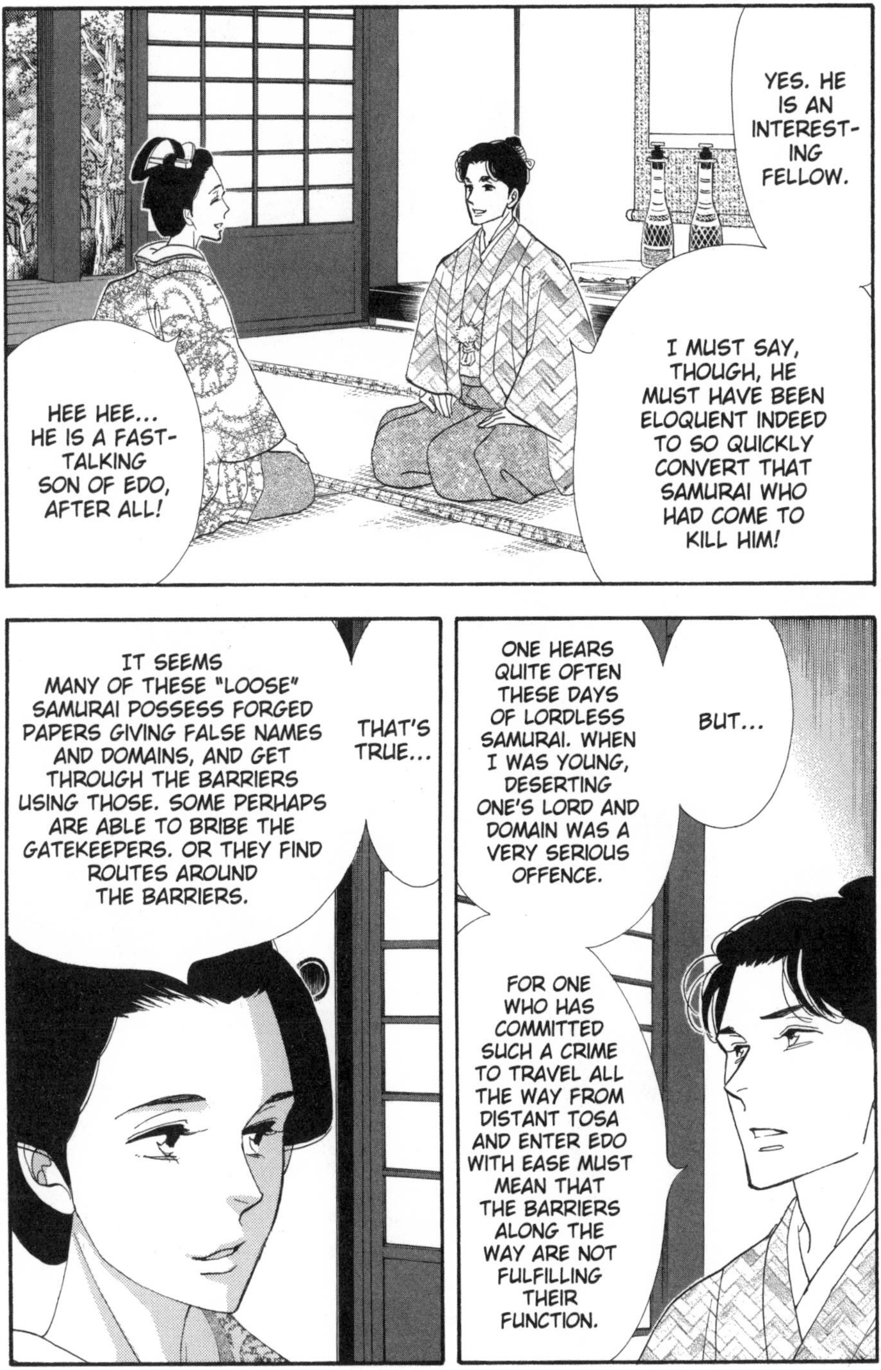
YES. HE IS AN INTERESTING FELLOW.
I MUST SAY, THOUGH, HE MUST HAVE BEEN ELOQUENT INDEED TO SO QUICKLY CONVERT THAT SAMURAI WHO HAD COME TO KILL HIM!
HEE HEE... HE IS A FAST-TALKING SON OF EDO, AFTER ALL!
ONE HEARS QUITE OFTEN THESE DAYS OF LORDLESS SAMURAI. WHEN I WAS YOUNG, DESERTING ONE'S LORD AND DOMAIN WAS A VERY SERIOUS OFFENCE.
BUT...
FOR ONE WHO HAS COMMITTED SUCH A CRIME TO TRAVEL ALL THE WAY FROM DISTANT TOSA AND ENTER EDO WITH EASE MUST MEAN THAT THE BARRIERS ALONG THE WAY ARE NOT FULFILLING THEIR FUNCTION.
THAT'S TRUE...
IT SEEMS MANY OF THESE "LOOSE" SAMURAI POSSESS FORGED PAPERS GIVING FALSE NAMES AND DOMAINS, AND GET THROUGH THE BARRIERS USING THOSE. SOME PERHAPS ARE ABLE TO BRIBE THE GATEKEEPERS. OR THEY FIND ROUTES AROUND THE BARRIERS.

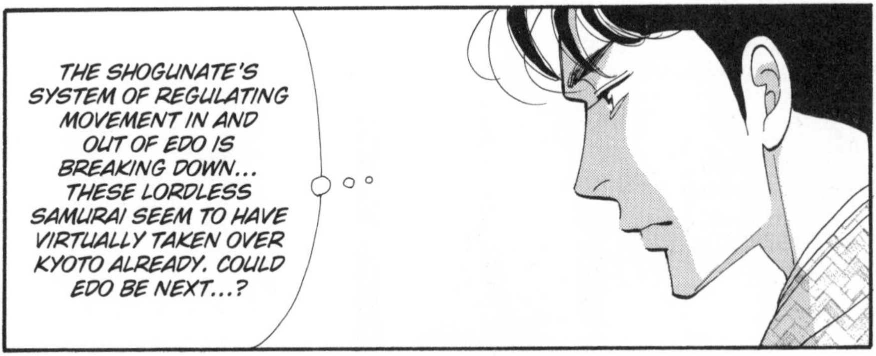
THE SHOGUNATE'S SYSTEM OF REGULATING MOVEMENT IN AND OUT OF EDO IS BREAKING DOWN... THESE LORDLESS SAMURAI SEEM TO HAVE VIRTUALLY TAKEN OVER KYOTO ALREADY. COULD EDO BE NEXT...?

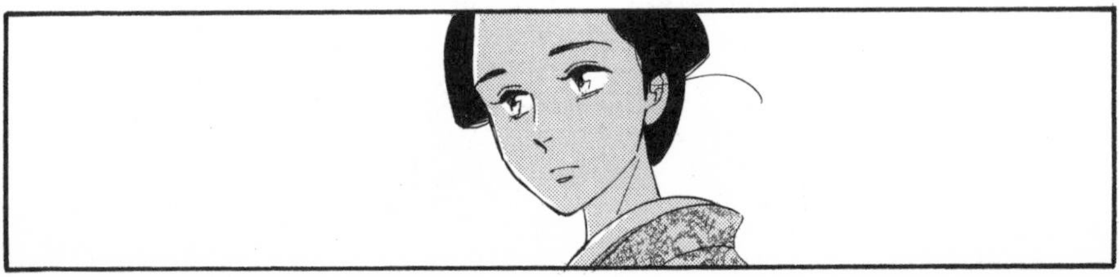

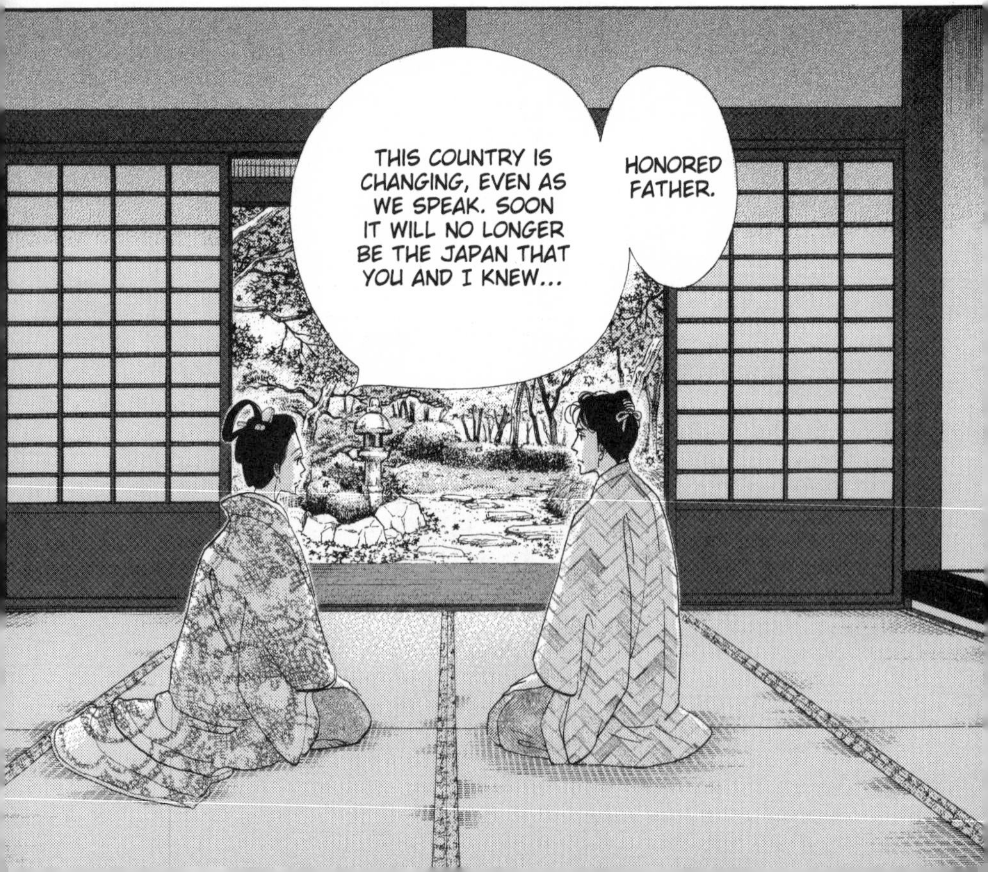
HONORED FATHER.
THIS COUNTRY IS CHANGING, EVEN AS WE SPEAK. SOON IT WILL NO LONGER BE THE JAPAN THAT YOU AND I KNEW...

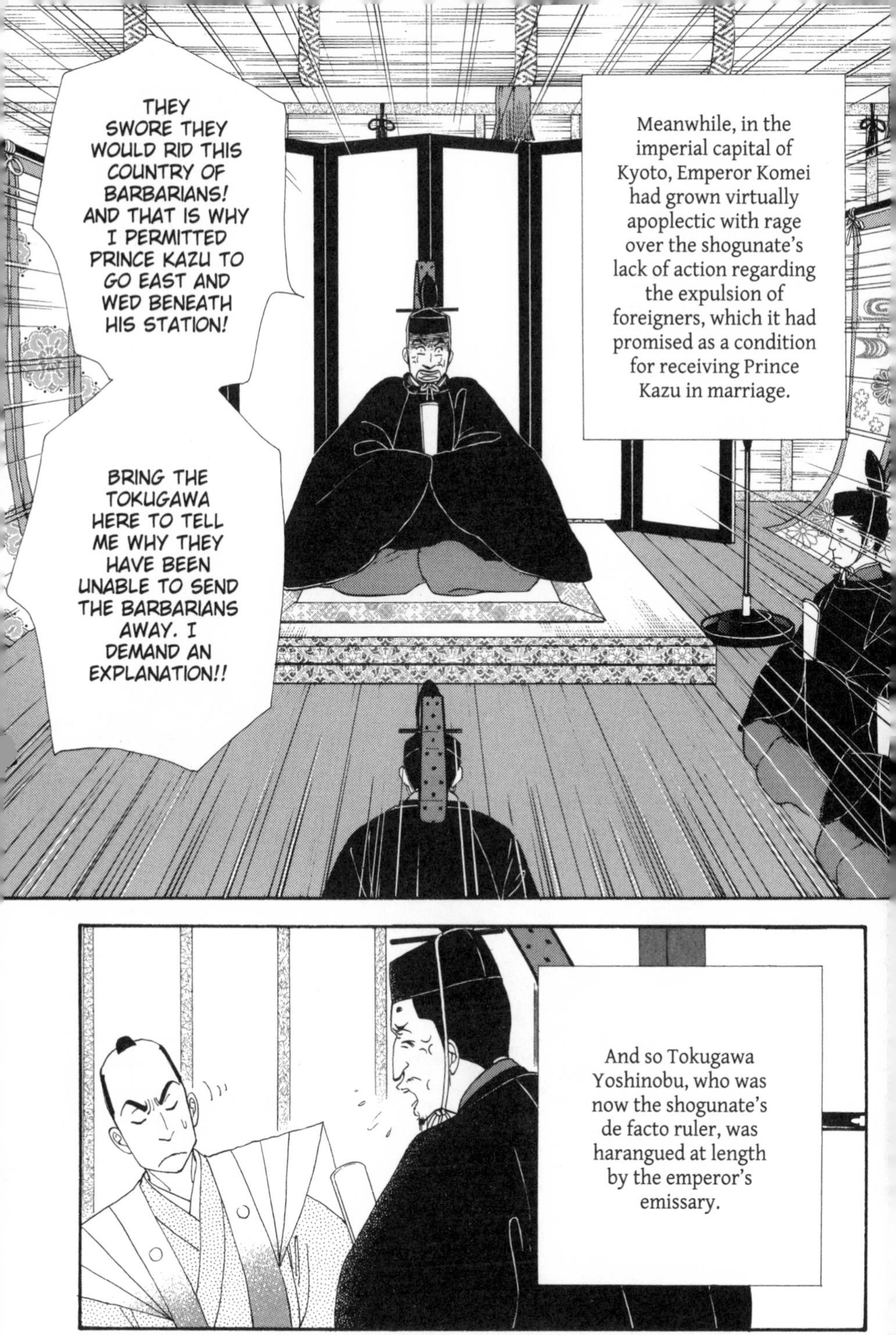

Meanwhile, in the imperial capital of Kyoto, Emperor Komei had grown virtually apoplectic with rage over the shogunate's lack of action regarding the expulsion of foreigners, which it had promised as a condition for receiving Prince Kazu in marriage.
THEY SWORE THEY WOULD RID THIS COUNTRY OF BARBARIANS! AND THAT IS WHY I PERMITTED PRINCE KAZU TO GO EAST AND WED BENEATH HIS STATION!
BRING THE TOKUGAWA HERE TO TELL ME WHY THEY HAVE BEEN UNABLE TO SEND THE BARBARIANS AWAY. I DEMAND AN EXPLANATION!!
And so Tokugawa Yoshinobu, who was now the shogunate's de facto ruler, was harangued at length by the emperor's emissary.

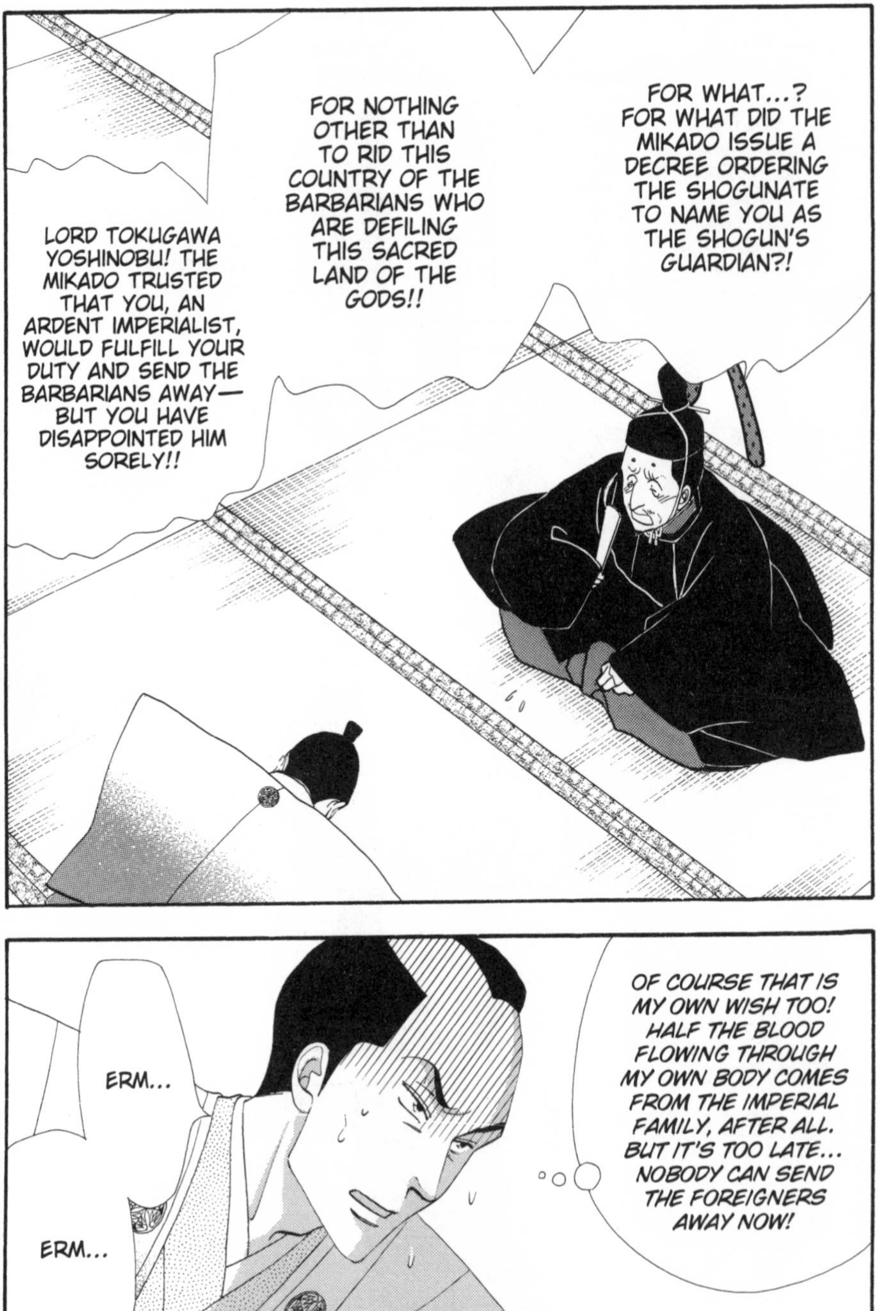
FOR WHAT...? FOR WHAT DID THE MIKADO ISSUE A DECREE ORDERING THE SHOGUNATE TO NAME YOU AS THE SHOGUN'S GUARDIAN?!
FOR NOTHING OTHER THAN TO RID THIS COUNTRY OF THE BARBARIANS WHO ARE DEFILING THIS SACRED LAND OF THE GODS!!
LORD TOKUGAWA YOSHINOBU! THE MIKADO TRUSTED THAT YOU, AN ARDENT IMPERIALIST, WOULD FULFILL YOUR DUTY AND SEND THE BARBARIANS AWAY—BUT YOU HAVE DISAPPOINTED HIM SORELY!!
OF COURSE THAT IS MY OWN WISH TOO! HALF THE BLOOD FLOWING THROUGH MY OWN BODY COMES FROM THE IMPERIAL FAMILY, AFTER ALL. BUT IT'S TOO LATE... NOBODY CAN SEND THE FOREIGNERS AWAY NOW!
ERM...
ERM...

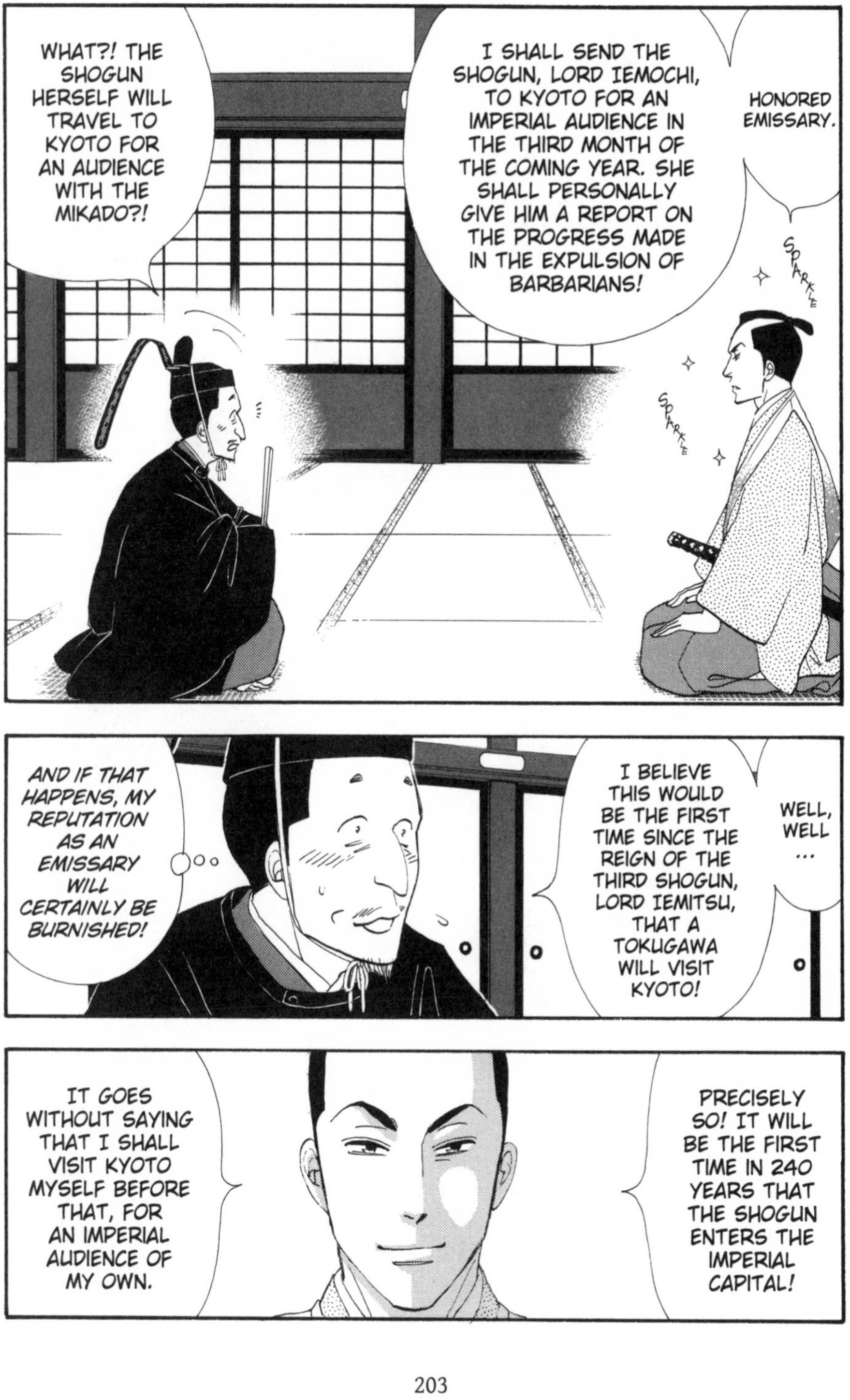
HONORED EMISSARY.
I SHALL SEND THE SHOGUN, LORD IEMOCHI, TO KYOTO FOR AN IMPERIAL AUDIENCE IN THE THIRD MONTH OF THE COMING YEAR. SHE SHALL PERSONALLY GIVE HIM A REPORT ON THE PROGRESS MADE IN THE EXPULSION OF BARBARIANS!
SPARKLE
SPARKLE
WHAT?! THE SHOGUN HERSELF WILL TRAVEL TO KYOTO FOR AN AUDIENCE WITH THE MIKADO?!
WELL, WELL ...
I BELIEVE THIS WOULD BE THE FIRST TIME SINCE THE REIGN OF THE THIRD SHOGUN, LORD IEMITSU, THAT A TOKUGAWA WILL VISIT KYOTO!
AND IF THAT HAPPENS, MY REPUTATION AS AN EMISSARY WILL CERTAINLY BE BURNISHED!
PRECISELY SO! IT WILL BE THE FIRST TIME IN 240 YEARS THAT THE SHOGUN ENTERS THE IMPERIAL CAPITAL!
IT GOES WITHOUT SAYING THAT I SHALL VISIT KYOTO MYSELF BEFORE THAT, FOR AN IMPERIAL AUDIENCE OF MY OWN.

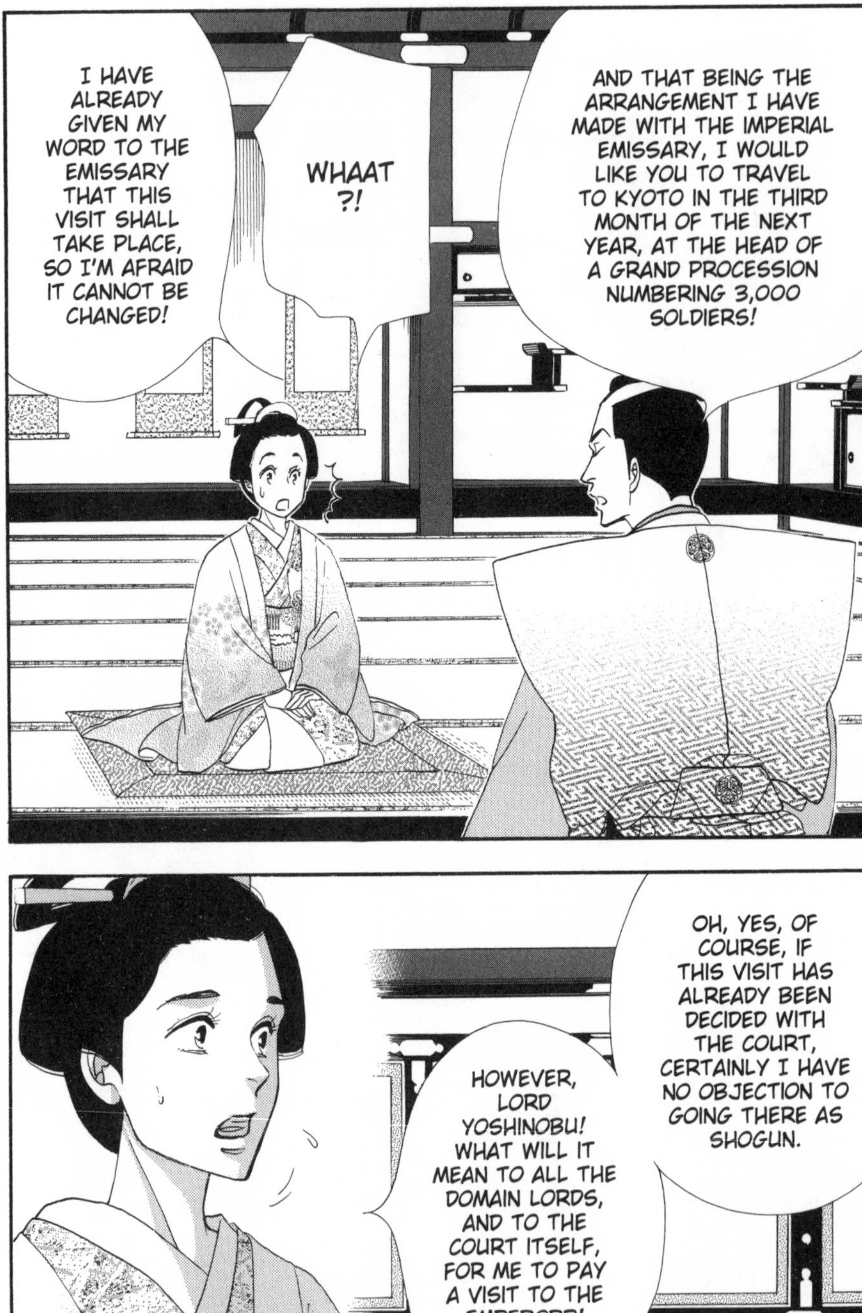
AND THAT BEING THE ARRANGEMENT I HAVE MADE WITH THE IMPERIAL EMISSARY, I WOULD LIKE YOU TO TRAVEL TO KYOTO IN THE THIRD MONTH OF THE NEXT YEAR, AT THE HEAD OF A GRAND PROCESSION NUMBERING 3,000 SOLDIERS!
WHAAT?!
I HAVE ALREADY GIVEN MY WORD TO THE EMISSARY THAT THIS VISIT SHALL TAKE PLACE, SO I'M AFRAID IT CANNOT BE CHANGED!
OH, YES, OF COURSE, IF THIS VISIT HAS ALREADY BEEN DECIDED WITH THE COURT, CERTAINLY I HAVE NO OBJECTION TO GOING THERE AS SHOGUN.
HOWEVER, LORD YOSHINOBU! WHAT WILL IT MEAN TO ALL THE DOMAIN LORDS, AND TO THE COURT ITSELF, FOR ME TO PAY A VISIT TO THE EMPEROR?!

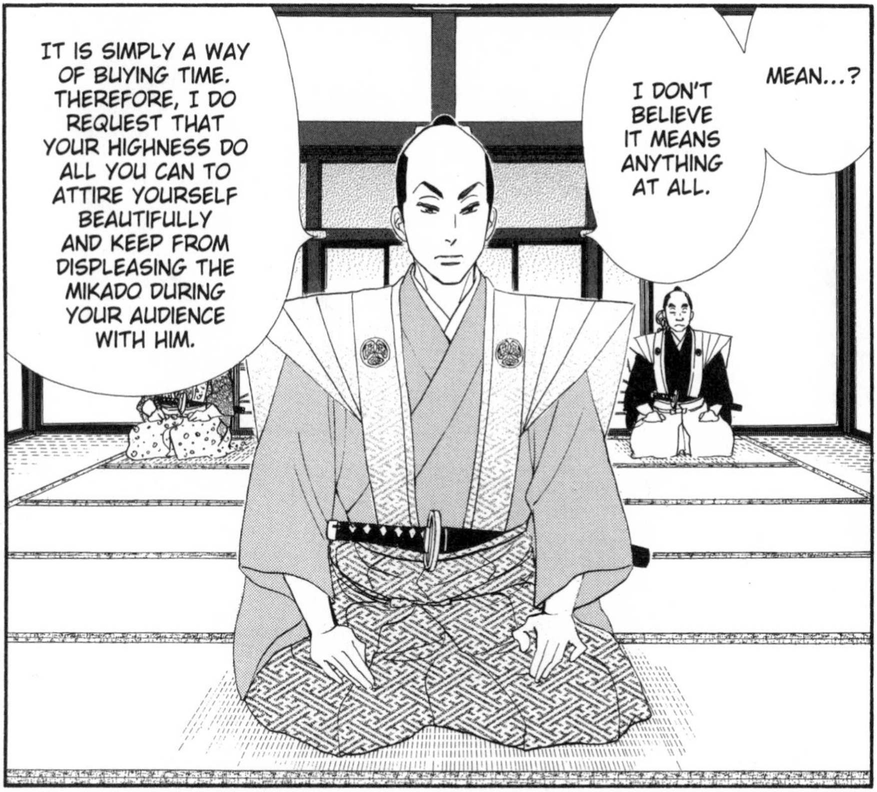
MEAN...?
I DON'T BELIEVE IT MEANS ANYTHING AT ALL.
IT IS SIMPLY A WAY OF BUYING TIME. THEREFORE, I DO REQUEST THAT YOUR HIGHNESS DO ALL YOU CAN TO ATTIRE YOURSELF BEAUTIFULLY AND KEEP FROM DISPLEASING THE MIKADO DURING YOUR AUDIENCE WITH HIM.

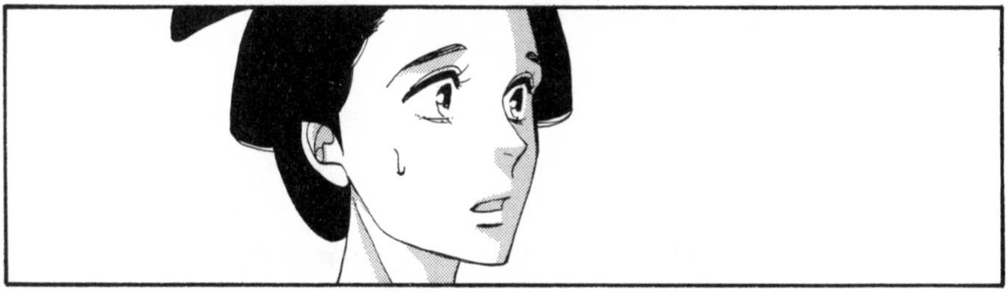

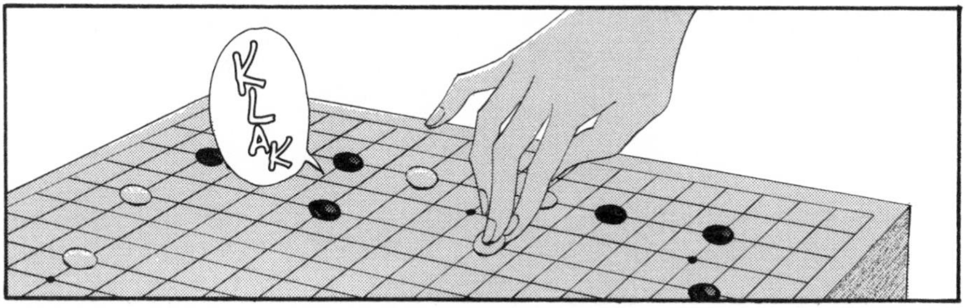
KLAK

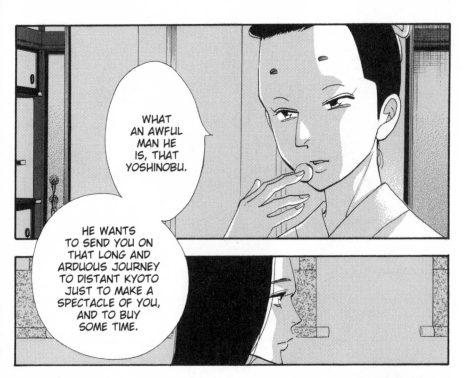

WHAT AN AWFUL MAN HE IS, THAT YOSHINOBU.
HE WANTS TO SEND YOU ON THAT LONG AND ARDUOUS JOURNEY TO DISTANT KYOTO JUST TO MAKE A SPECTACLE OF YOU, AND TO BUY SOME TIME.
PRINCE KAZU.
IF I MUST GO TO KYOTO, THEN I INTEND TO FIND MEANING IN THAT FOR MYSELF, FOR IT IS A RARE OPPORTUNITY.
FOR EXAMPLE, I COULD USE MY AUDIENCE WITH THE MIKADO TO EXPLAIN TO HIM WHY IT IS NECESSARY TO OPEN OUR COUNTRY TO FOREIGN TRADE, AFTER APOLOGIZING FOR MAKING THE IMPOSSIBLE PROMISE OF DRIVING OUT THE BARBARIANS, OF COURSE.
KLAK

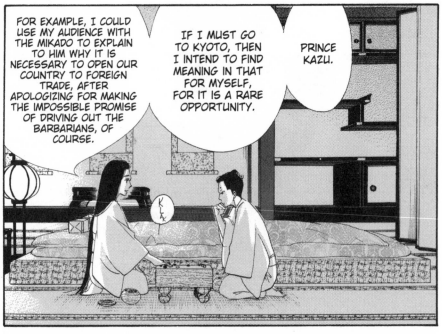

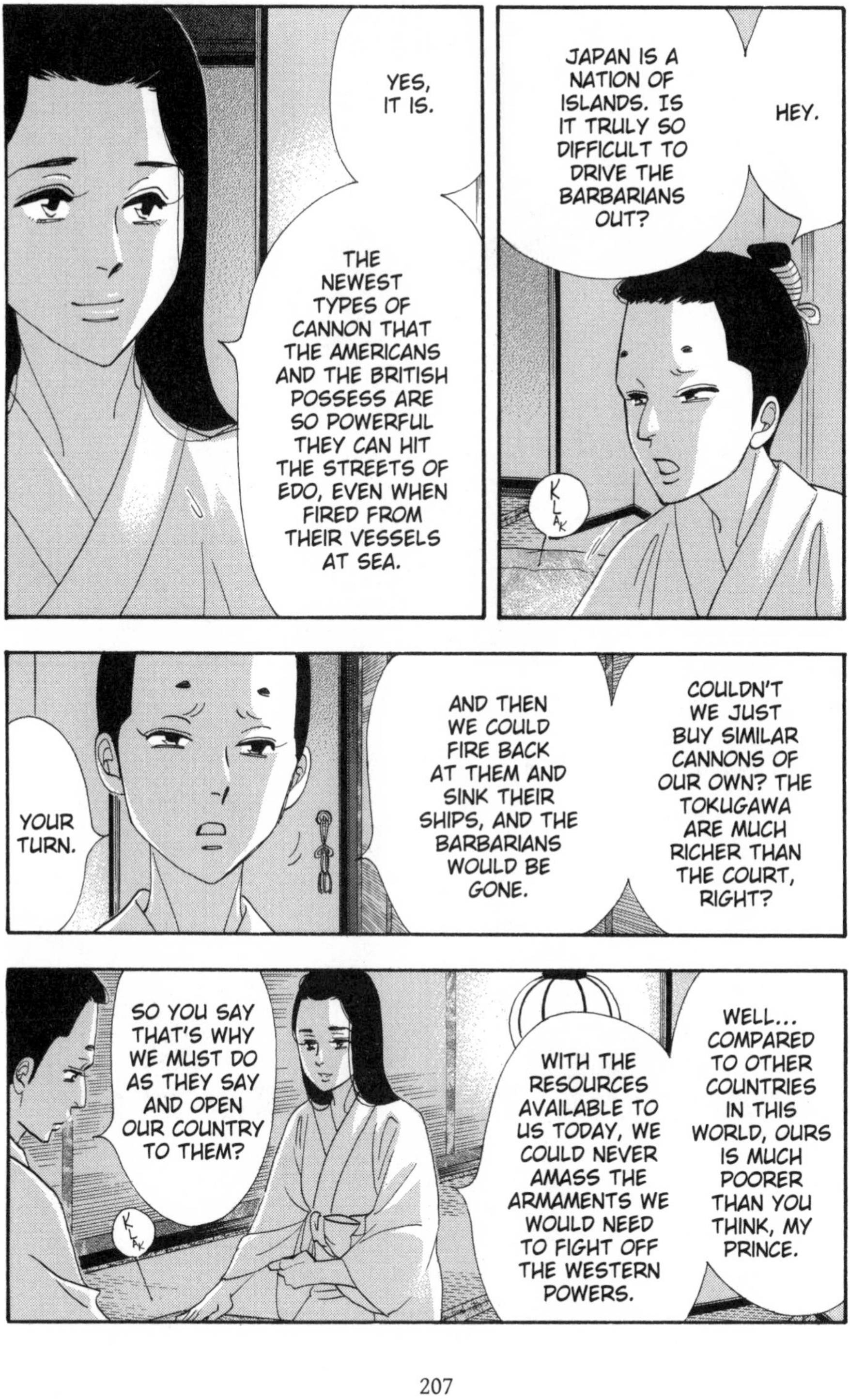
HEY.
JAPAN IS A NATION OF ISLANDS. IS IT TRULY SO DIFFICULT TO DRIVE THE BARBARIANS OUT?
KLAK
YES, IT IS.
THE NEWEST TYPES OF CANNON THAT THE AMERICANS AND THE BRITISH POSSESS ARE SO POWERFUL THEY CAN HIT THE STREETS OF EDO, EVEN WHEN FIRED FROM THEIR VESSELS AT SEA.
COULDN'T WE JUST BUY SIMILAR CANNONS OF OUR OWN? THE TOKUGAWA ARE MUCH RICHER THAN THE COURT, RIGHT?
AND THEN WE COULD FIRE BACK AT THEM AND SINK THEIR SHIPS, AND THE BARBARIANS WOULD BE GONE.
YOUR TURN.
WELL... COMPARED TO OTHER COUNTRIES IN THIS WORLD, OURS IS MUCH POORER THAN YOU THINK, MY PRINCE.
WITH THE RESOURCES AVAILABLE TO US TODAY, WE COULD NEVER AMASS THE ARMAMENTS WE WOULD NEED TO FIGHT OFF THE WESTERN POWERS.
SO YOU SAY THAT'S WHY WE MUST DO AS THEY SAY AND OPEN OUR COUNTRY TO THEM?
KLAK

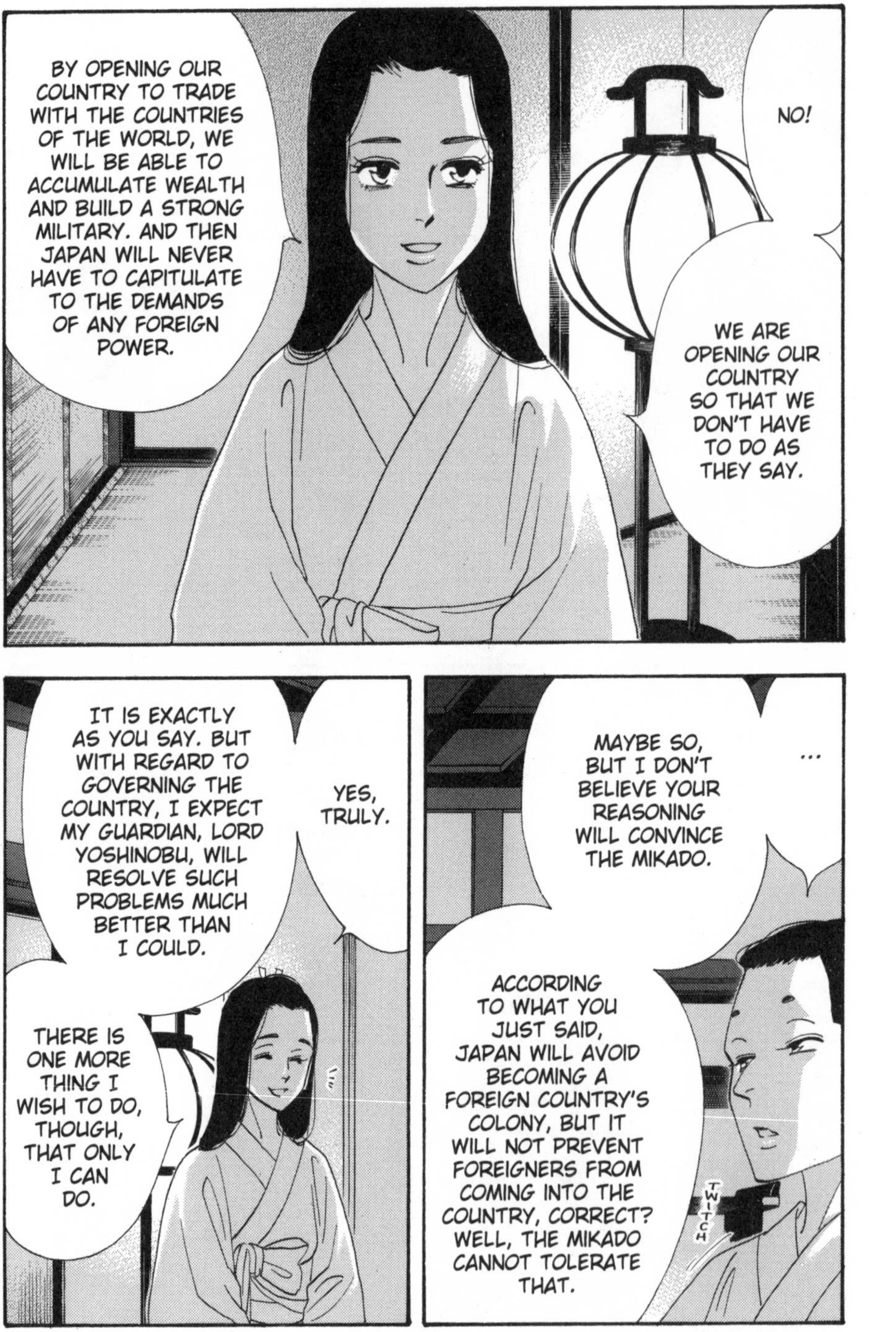
NO!
BY OPENING OUR COUNTRY TO TRADE WITH THE COUNTRIES OF THE WORLD, WE WILL BE ABLE TO ACCUMULATE WEALTH AND BUILD A STRONG MILITARY. AND THEN JAPAN WILL NEVER HAVE TO CAPITULATE TO THE DEMANDS OF ANY FOREIGN POWER.
WE ARE OPENING OUR COUNTRY SO THAT WE DON'T HAVE TO DO AS THEY SAY.
...
MAYBE SO, BUT I DON'T BELIEVE YOUR REASONING WILL CONVINCE THE MIKADO.
ACCORDING TO WHAT YOU JUST SAID, JAPAN WILL AVOID BECOMING A FOREIGN COUNTRY'S COLONY, BUT IT WILL NOT PREVENT FOREIGNERS FROM COMING INTO THE COUNTRY, CORRECT? WELL, THE MIKADO CANNOT TOLERATE THAT.
TWITCH
YES, TRULY.
IT IS EXACTLY AS YOU SAY. BUT WITH REGARD TO GOVERNING THE COUNTRY, I EXPECT MY GUARDIAN, LORD YOSHINOBU, WILL RESOLVE SUCH PROBLEMS MUCH BETTER THAN I COULD.
THERE IS ONE MORE THING I WISH TO DO, THOUGH, THAT ONLY I CAN DO.

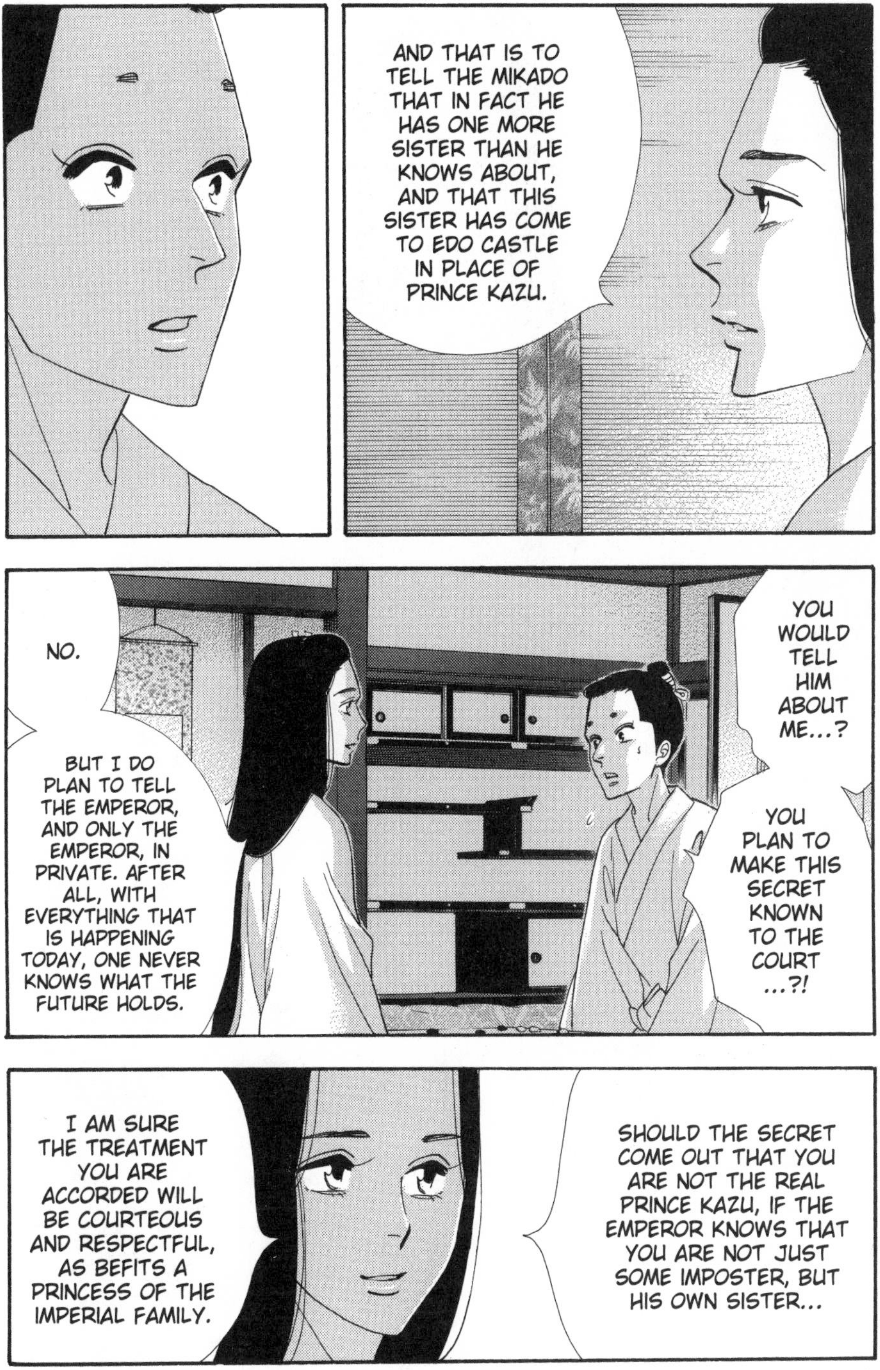
AND THAT IS TO TELL THE MIKADO THAT IN FACT HE HAS ONE MORE SISTER THAN HE KNOWS ABOUT, AND THAT THIS SISTER HAS COME TO EDO CASTLE IN PLACE OF PRINCE KAZU.
YOU WOULD TELL HIM ABOUT ME...?
YOU PLAN TO MAKE THIS SECRET KNOWN TO THE COURT ...?!
NO.
BUT I DO PLAN TO TELL THE EMPEROR, AND ONLY THE EMPEROR, IN PRIVATE. AFTER ALL, WITH EVERYTHING THAT IS HAPPENING TODAY, ONE NEVER KNOWS WHAT THE FUTURE HOLDS.
SHOULD THE SECRET COME OUT THAT YOU ARE NOT THE REAL PRINCE KAZU, IF THE EMPEROR KNOWS THAT YOU ARE NOT JUST SOME IMPOSTER, BUT HIS OWN SISTER...
I AM SURE THE TREATMENT YOU ARE ACCORDED WILL BE COURTEOUS AND RESPECTFUL, AS BEFITS A PRINCESS OF THE IMPERIAL FAMILY.

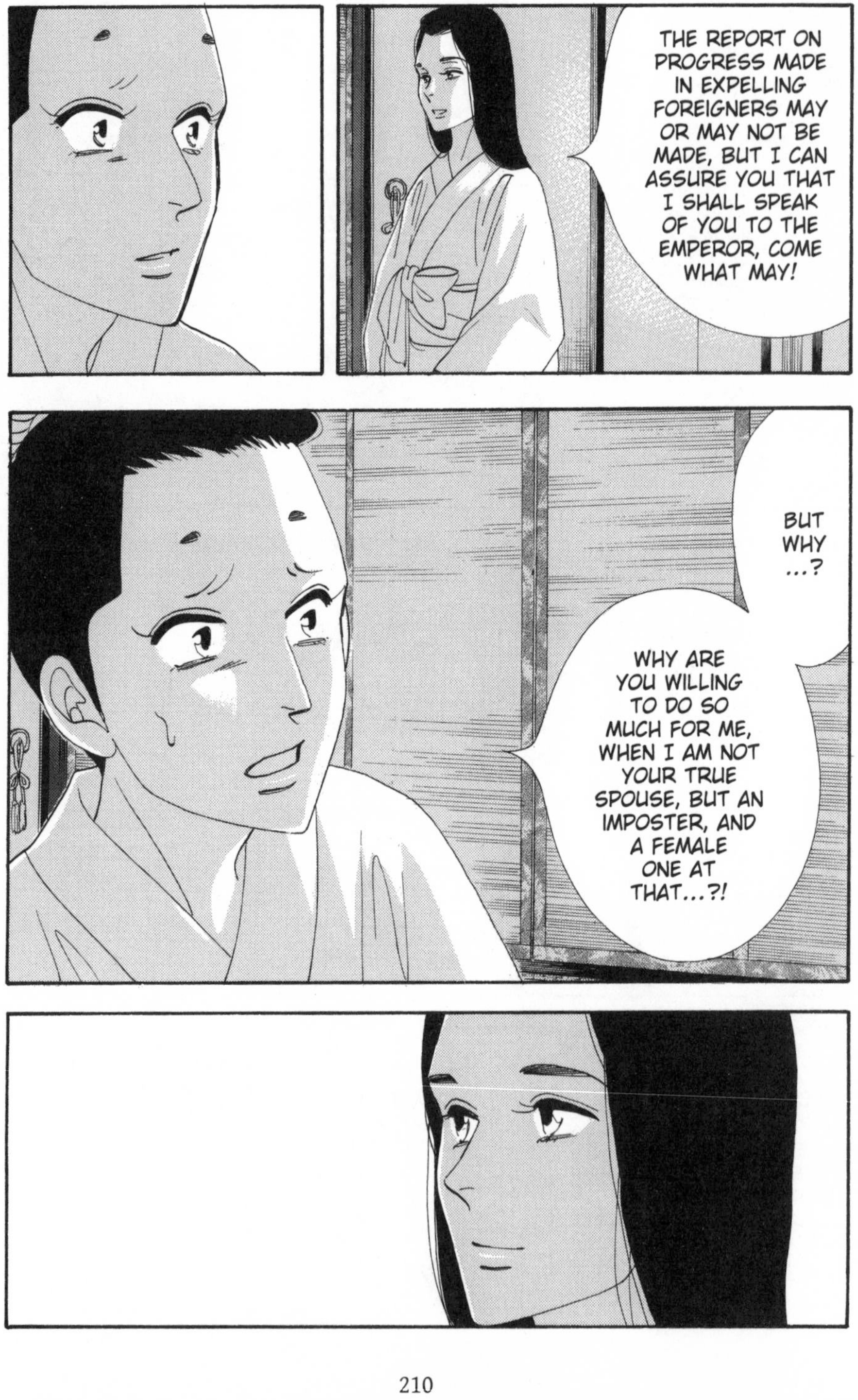
THE REPORT ON PROGRESS MADE IN EXPELLING FOREIGNERS MAY OR MAY NOT BE MADE, BUT I CAN ASSURE YOU THAT I SHALL SPEAK OF YOU TO THE EMPEROR, COME WHAT MAY!
BUT WHY ...?
WHY ARE YOU WILLING TO DO SO MUCH FOR ME, WHEN I AM NOT YOUR TRUE SPOUSE, BUT AN IMPOSTER, AND A FEMALE ONE AT THAT...?!

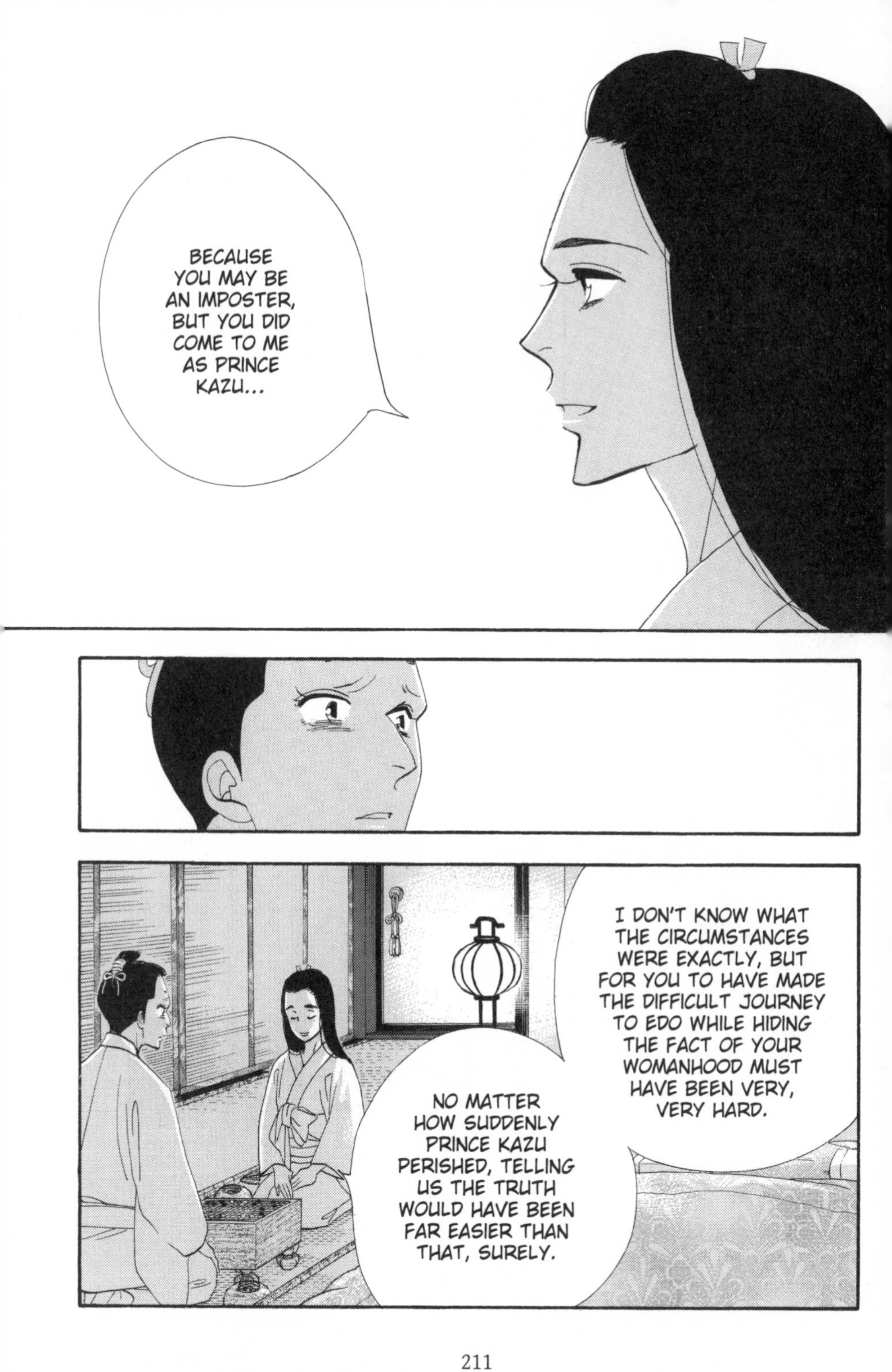
BECAUSE YOU MAY BE AN IMPOSTER, BUT YOU DID COME TO ME AS PRINCE KAZU...
I DON'T KNOW WHAT THE CIRCUMSTANCES WERE EXACTLY, BUT FOR YOU TO HAVE MADE THE DIFFICULT JOURNEY TO EDO WHILE HIDING THE FACT OF YOUR WOMANHOOD MUST HAVE BEEN VERY, VERY HARD.
NO MATTER HOW SUDDENLY PRINCE KAZU PERISHED, TELLING US THE TRUTH WOULD HAVE BEEN FAR EASIER THAN THAT, SURELY.

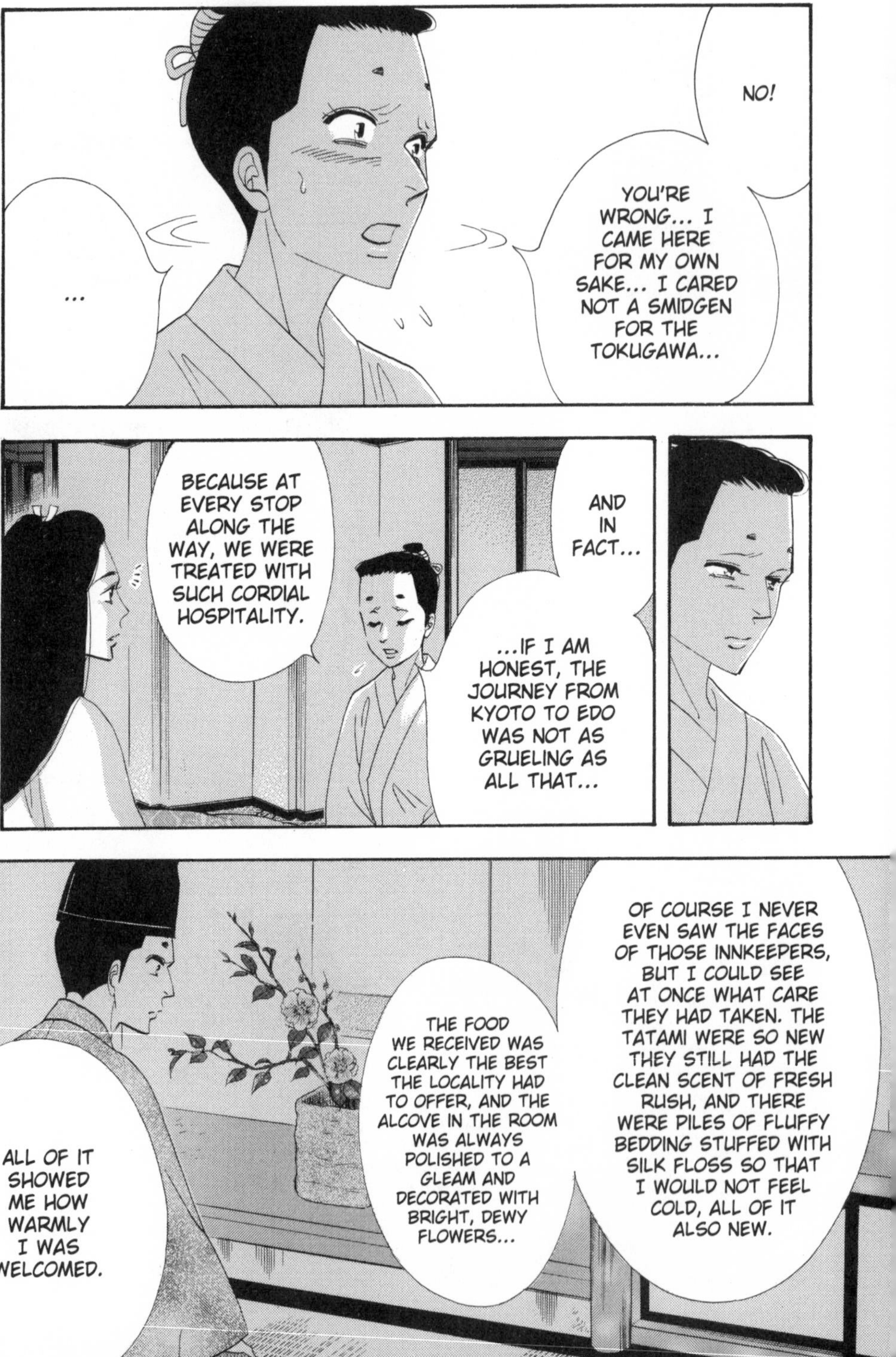
NO!
YOU'RE WRONG... I CAME HERE FOR MY OWN SAKE... I CARED NOT A SMIDGEN FOR THE TOKUGAWA...
...
AND IN FACT...
...IF I AM HONEST, THE JOURNEY FROM KYOTO TO EDO WAS NOT AS GRUELING AS ALL THAT...
BECAUSE AT EVERY STOP ALONG THE WAY, WE WERE TREATED WITH SUCH CORDIAL HOSPITALITY.
OF COURSE I NEVER EVEN SAW THE FACES OF THOSE INNKEEPERS, BUT I COULD SEE AT ONCE WHAT CARE THEY HAD TAKEN. THE TATAMI WERE SO NEW THEY STILL HAD THE CLEAN SCENT OF FRESH RUSH, AND THERE WERE PILES OF FLUFFY BEDDING STUFFED WITH SILK FLOSS SO THAT I WOULD NOT FEEL COLD, ALL OF IT ALSO NEW.
THE FOOD WE RECEIVED WAS CLEARLY THE BEST THE LOCALITY HAD TO OFFER, AND THE ALCOVE IN THE ROOM WAS ALWAYS POLISHED TO A GLEAM AND DECORATED WITH BRIGHT, DEWY FLOWERS...
ALL OF IT SHOWED ME HOW WARMLY I WAS WELCOMED.

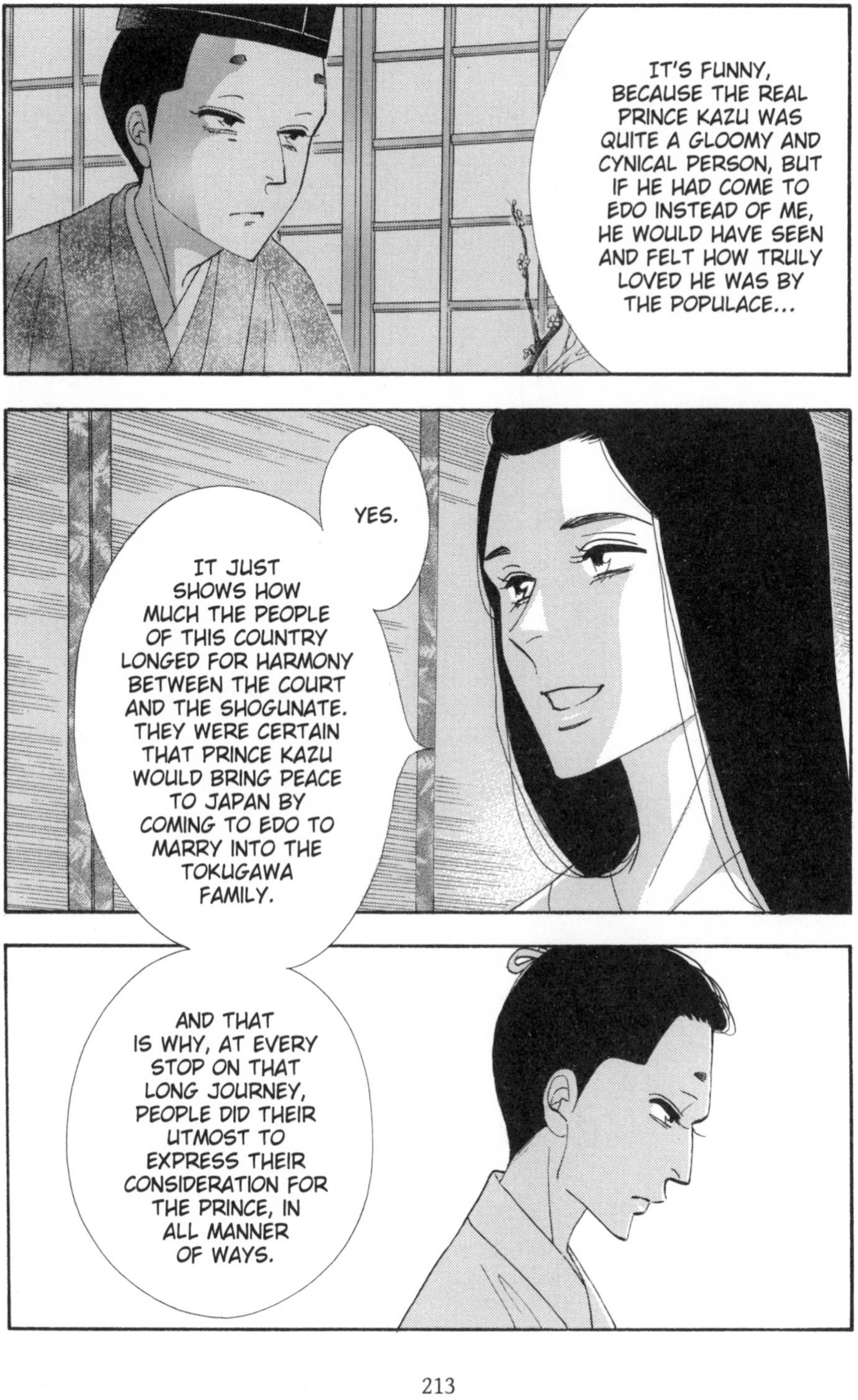
IT'S FUNNY, BECAUSE THE REAL PRINCE KAZU WAS QUITE A GLOOMY AND CYNICAL PERSON, BUT IF HE HAD COME TO EDO INSTEAD OF ME, HE WOULD HAVE SEEN AND FELT HOW TRULY LOVED HE WAS BY THE POPULACE...
YES.
IT JUST SHOWS HOW MUCH THE PEOPLE OF THIS COUNTRY LONGED FOR HARMONY BETWEEN THE COURT AND THE SHOGUNATE. THEY WERE CERTAIN THAT PRINCE KAZU WOULD BRING PEACE TO JAPAN BY COMING TO EDO TO MARRY INTO THE TOKUGAWA FAMILY.
AND THAT IS WHY, AT EVERY STOP ON THAT LONG JOURNEY, PEOPLE DID THEIR UTMOST TO EXPRESS THEIR CONSIDERATION FOR THE PRINCE, IN ALL MANNER OF WAYS.

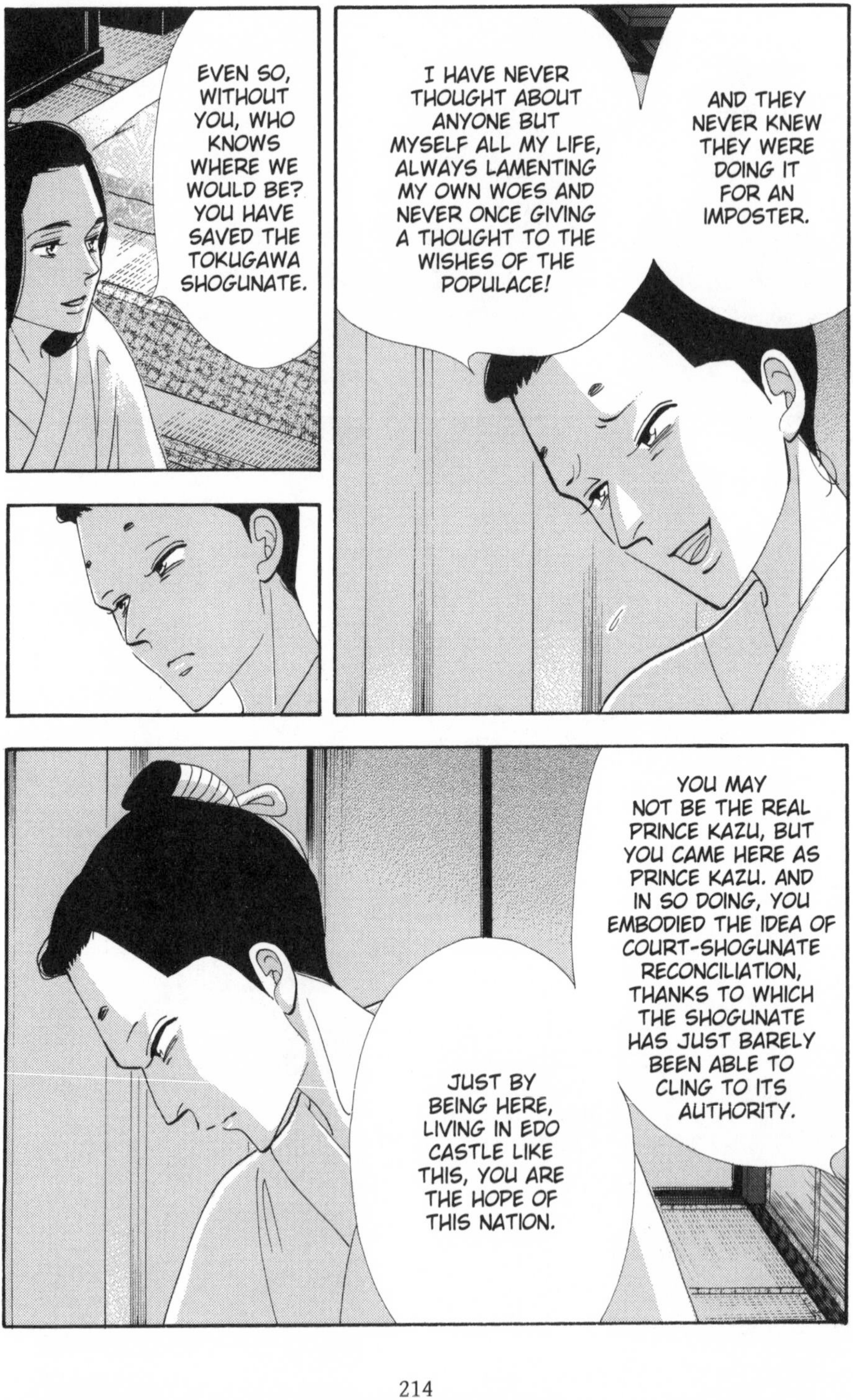
I HAVE NEVER THOUGHT ABOUT ANYONE BUT MYSELF ALL MY LIFE, ALWAYS LAMENTING MY OWN WOES AND NEVER ONCE GIVING A THOUGHT TO THE WISHES OF THE POPULACE!
AND THEY NEVER KNEW THEY WERE DOING IT FOR AN IMPOSTER.
EVEN SO, WITHOUT YOU, WHO KNOWS WHERE WE WOULD BE? YOU HAVE SAVED THE TOKUGAWA SHOGUNATE.
YOU MAY NOT BE THE REAL PRINCE KAZU, BUT YOU CAME HERE AS PRINCE KAZU. AND IN SO DOING, YOU EMBODIED THE IDEA OF COURT-SHOGUNATE RECONCILIATION, THANKS TO WHICH THE SHOGUNATE HAS JUST BARELY BEEN ABLE TO CLING TO ITS AUTHORITY.
JUST BY BEING HERE, LIVING IN EDO CASTLE LIKE THIS, YOU ARE THE HOPE OF THIS NATION.

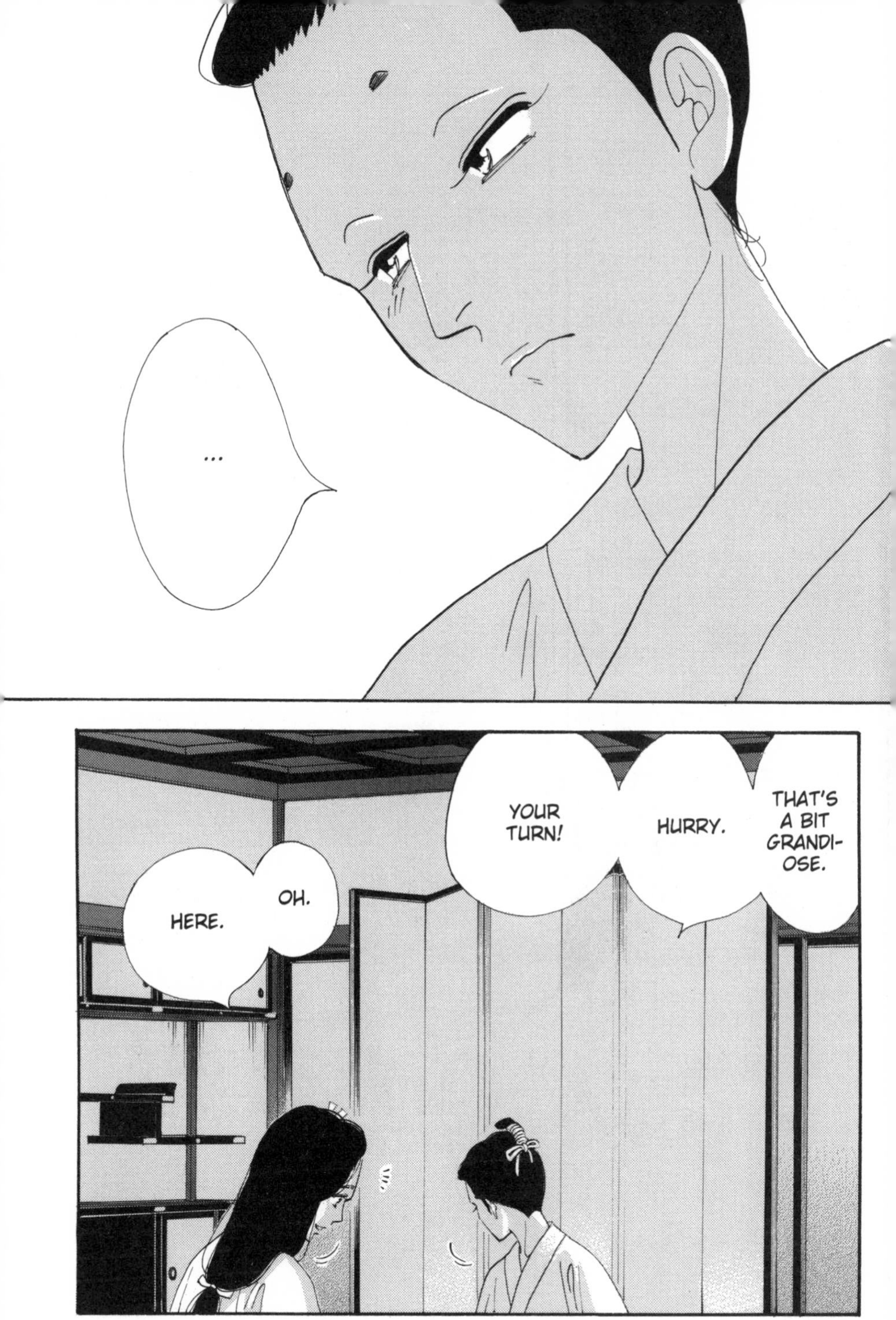
...
THAT'S A BIT GRANDIOSE.
HURRY.
YOUR TURN!
OH.
HERE.

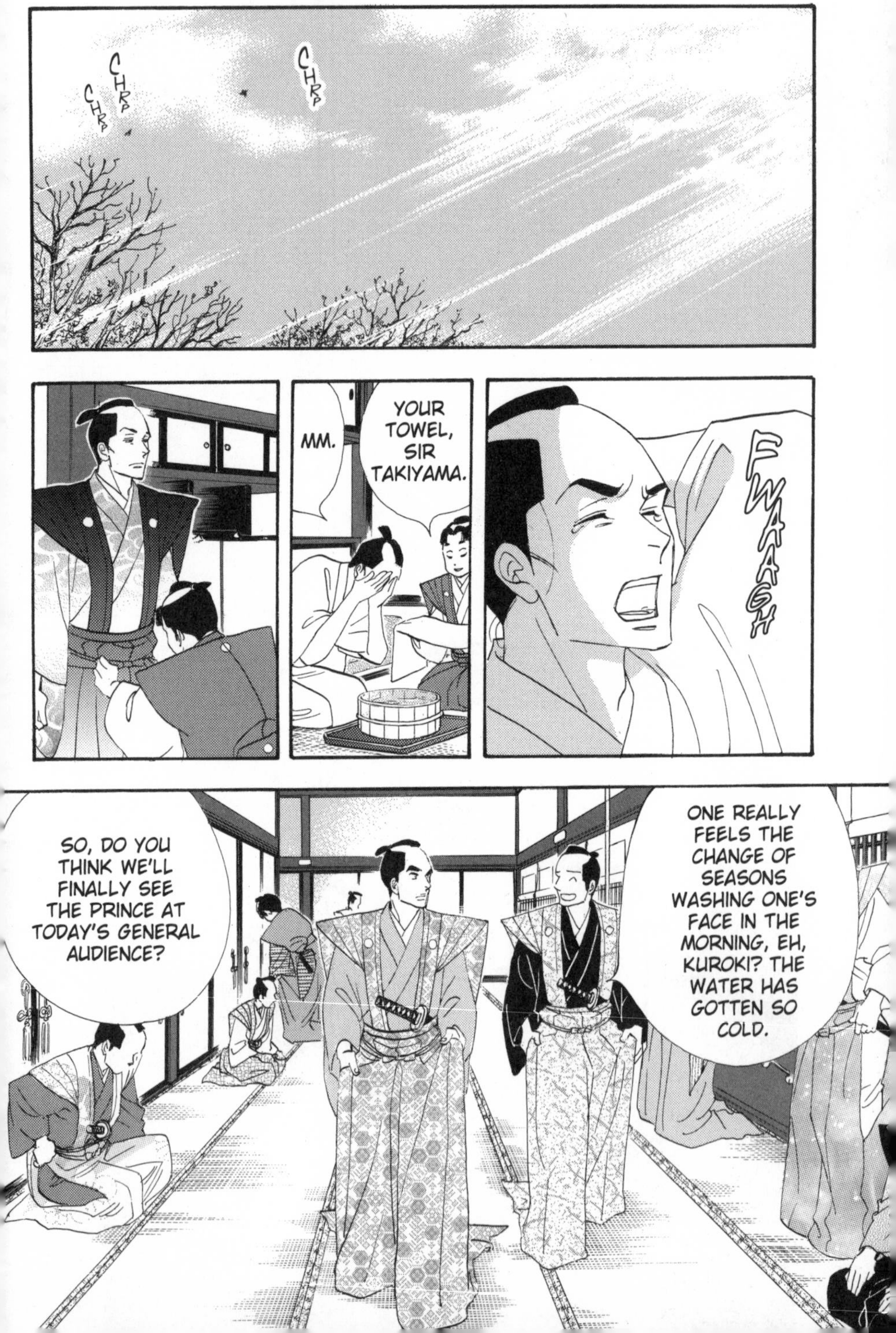
CHRP
CHRP
CHRP
FWAAGH
YOUR TOWEL, SIR TAKIYAMA.
MM.
ONE REALLY FEELS THE CHANGE OF SEASONS WASHING ONE'S FACE IN THE MORNING, EH, KUROKI? THE WATER HAS GOTTEN SO COLD.
SO, DO YOU THINK WE'LL FINALLY SEE THE PRINCE AT TODAY'S GENERAL AUDIENCE?

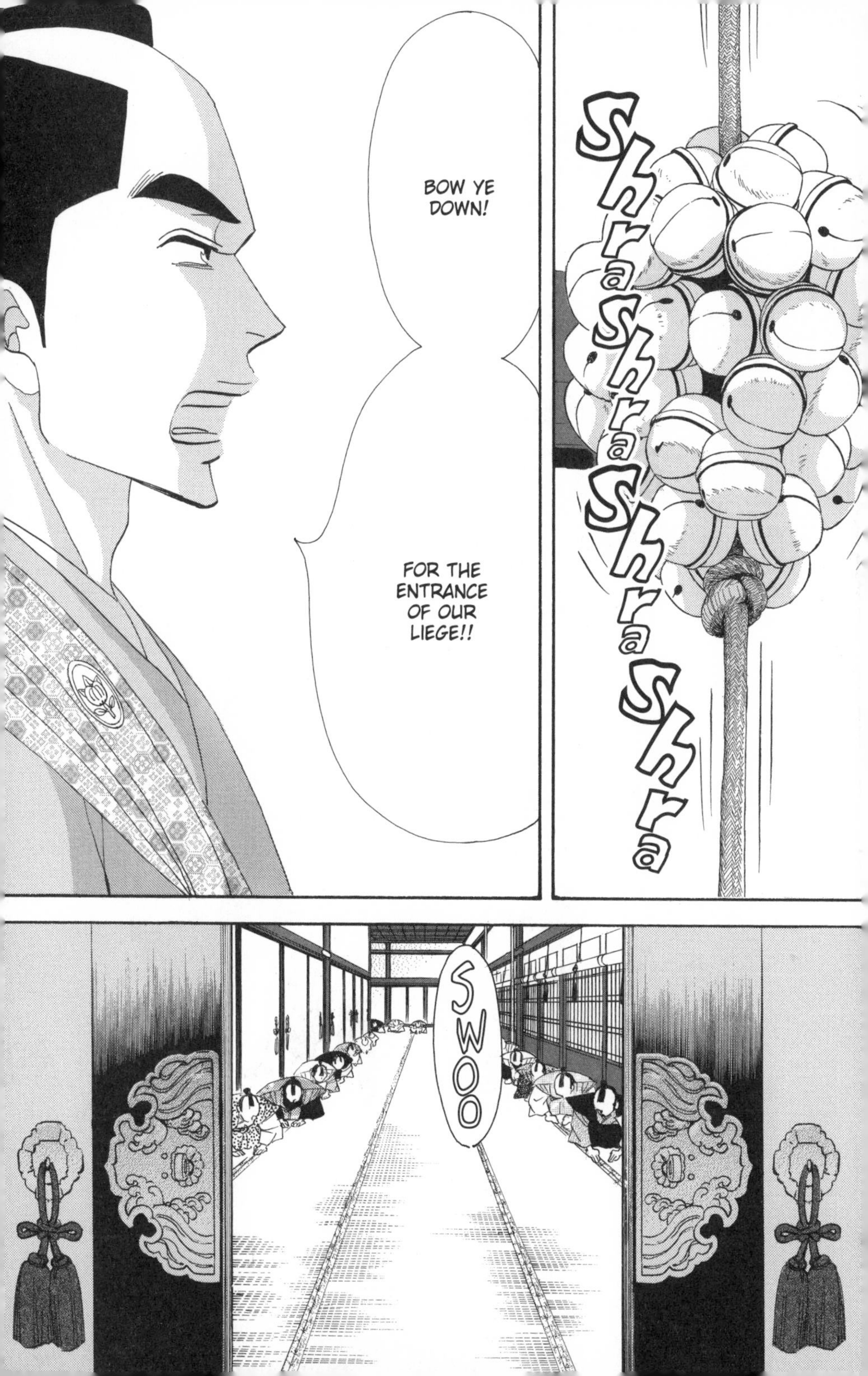
ShraShraShraShra
BOW YE DOWN!
FOR THE ENTRANCE OF OUR LIEGE!!
SWOO

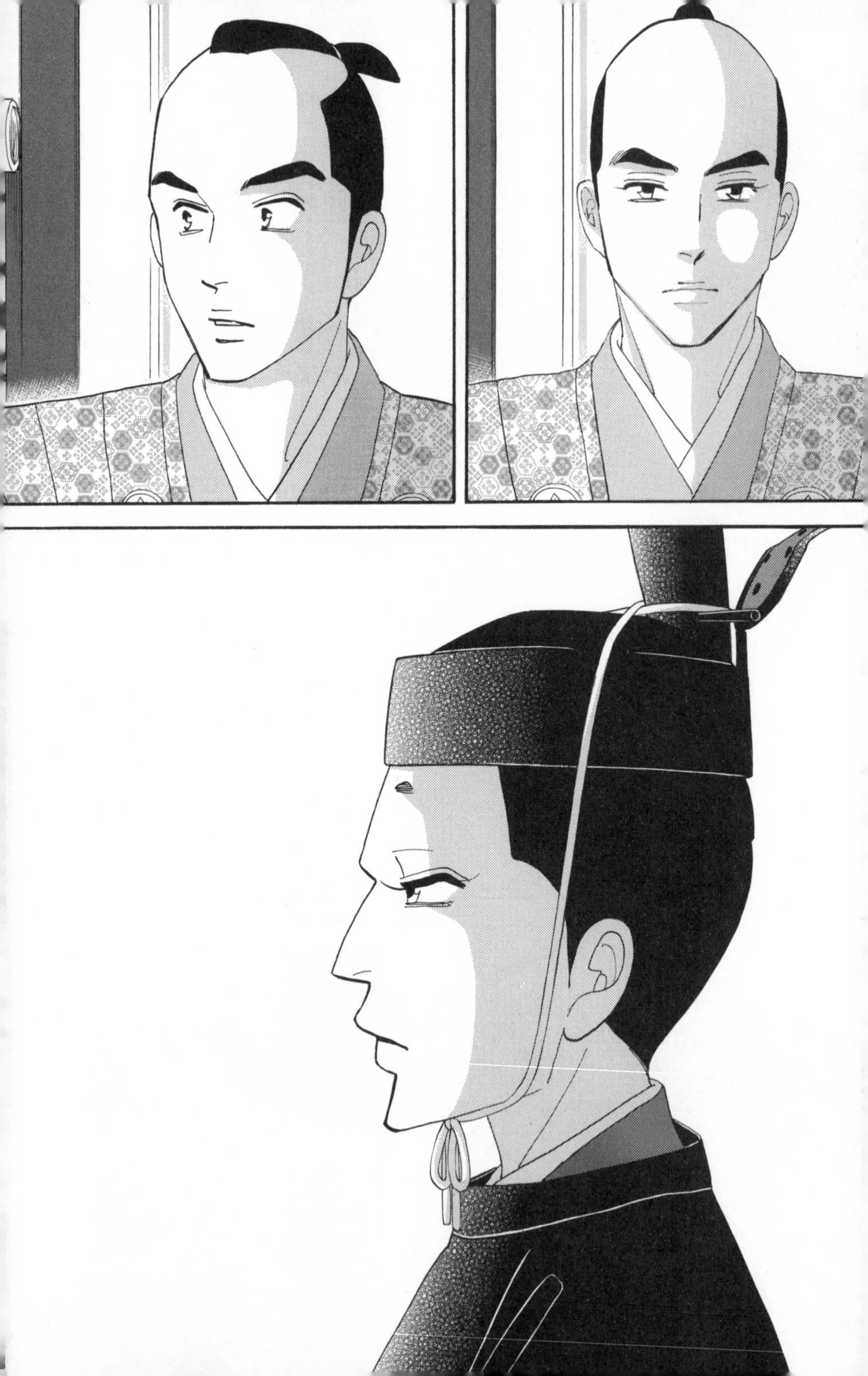

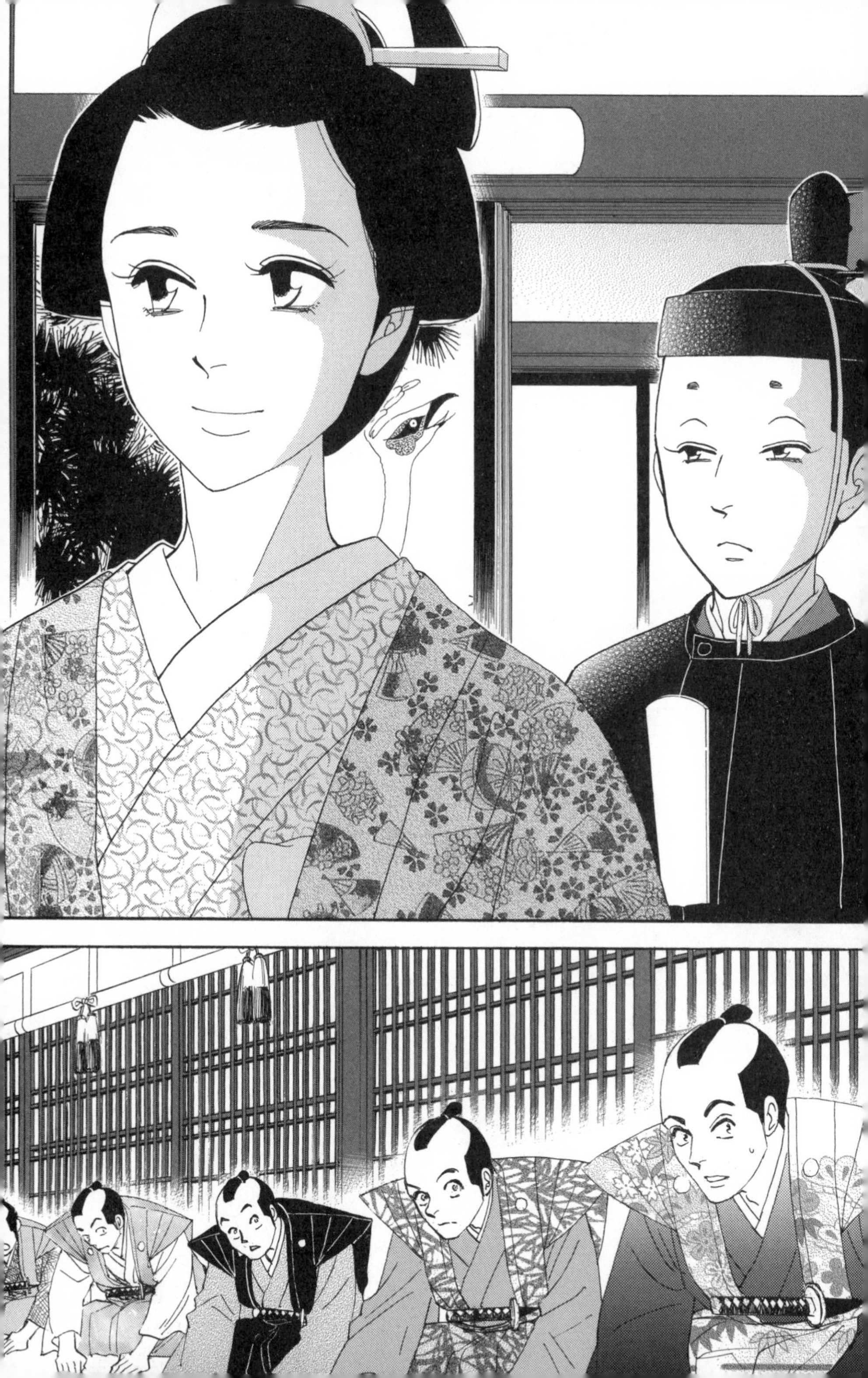

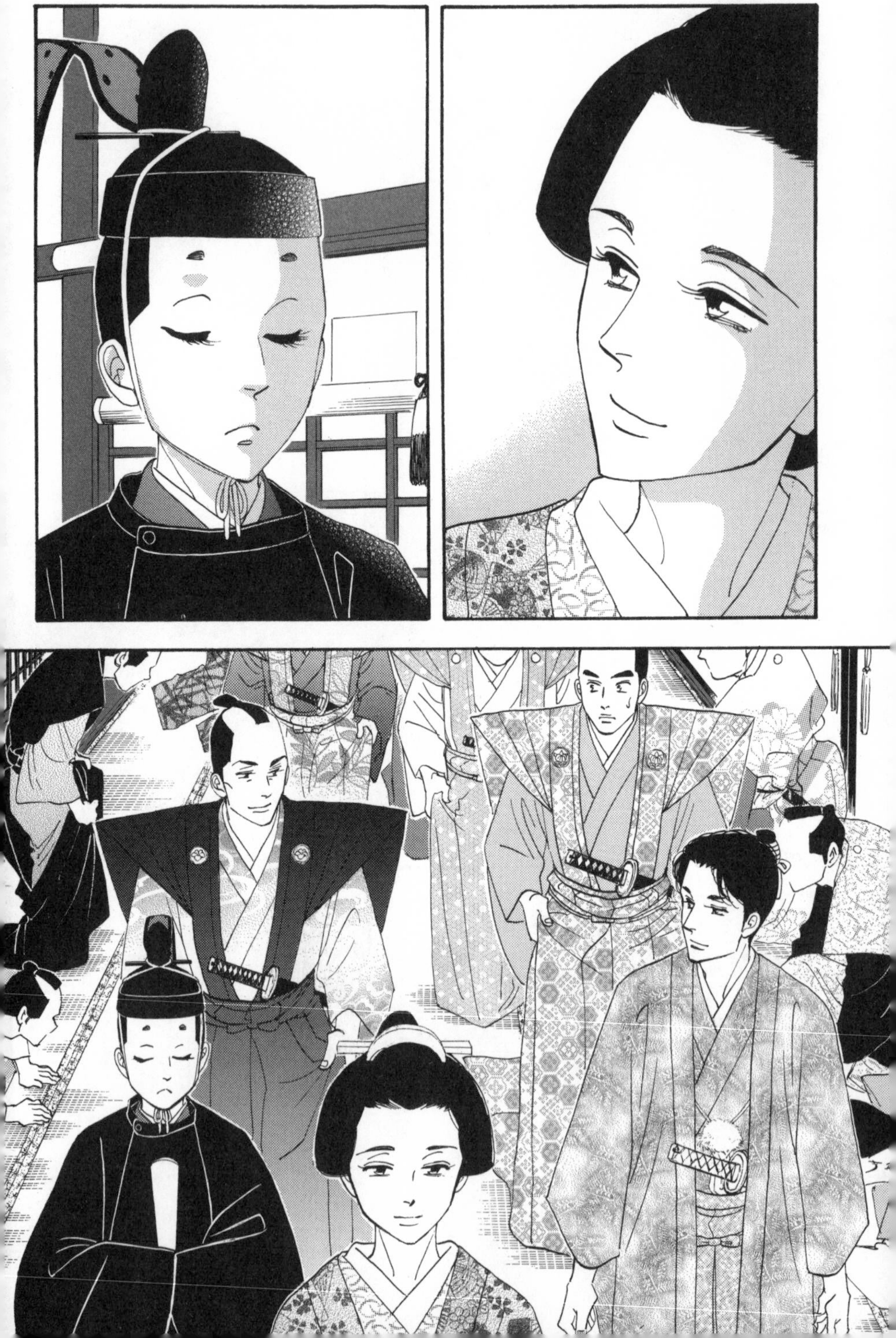

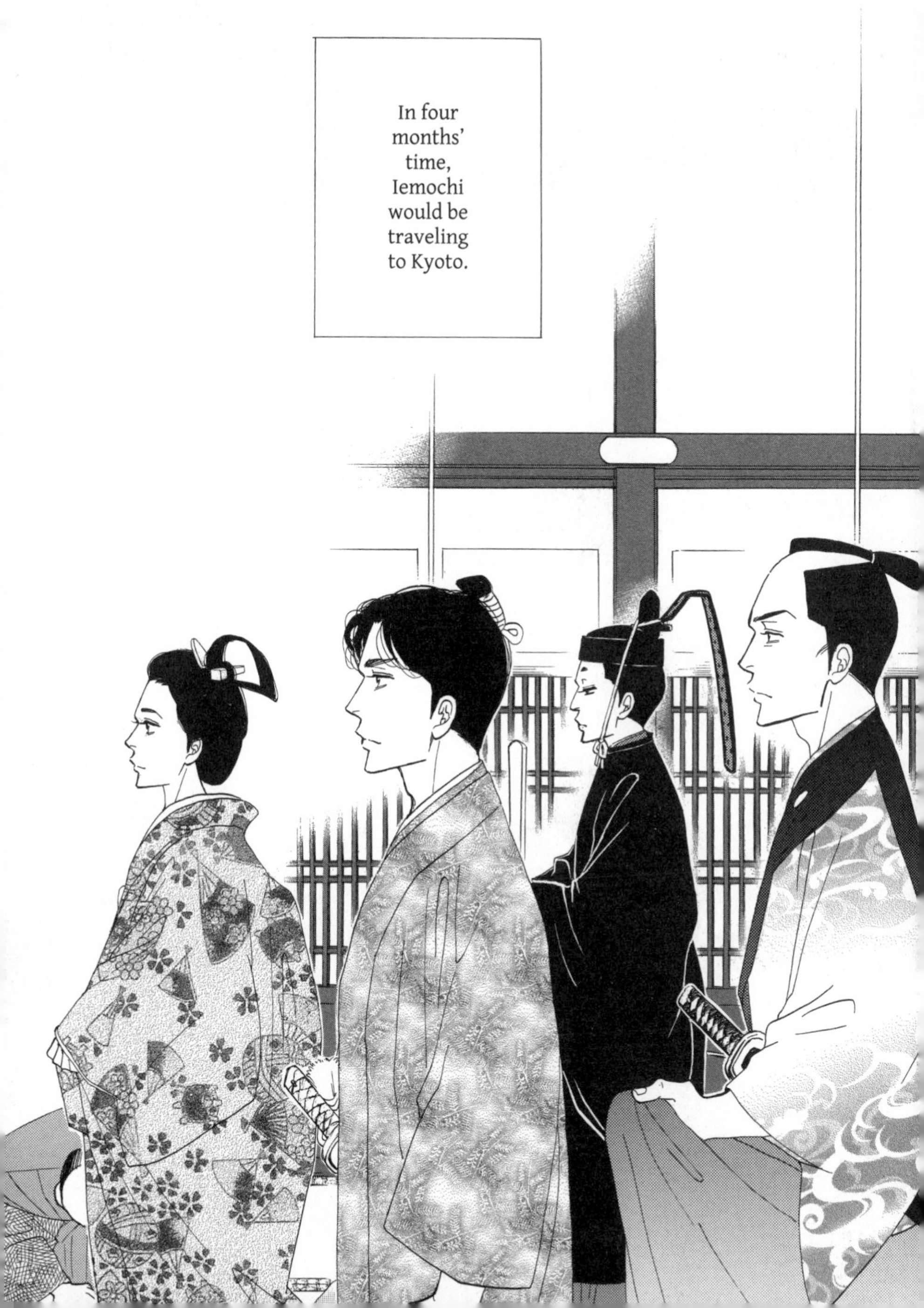
In four months' time, Iemochi would be traveling to Kyoto.

Ōoku

❀ THE INNER CHAMBERS

Ōoku: The Inner Chambers

VOLUME 16 · END NOTES

by Akemi Wegmüller

Page 21, panel 2 · HAORI
Hip- or thigh-length jackets. Unlike kimono, haori are worn open or secured by string ties at the lapels.

Page 99, panel 4 · GYUHI
A glutinous rice flour made into a soft dough and steamed, to which sugar or syrup is added. It is then heated and kneaded until it has the consistency of pliable marzipan.

Page 124, panel 3 · INCIDENT AT THE TERADA-YA INN
Around 70 pro-imperialists met at the Terada-ya Inn to plot rebellion, with as many as 50 of them hailing from Satsuma.

PAGE 125, panel 2 · GREAT ANSEI PURGE
See volume 15.

PAGE 154, panel 4 · HASHIMOTO
Chikako's family name is Hashimoto.

PAGE 162, panel 3 · TORIKAEBAYA SIBLINGS
A Heian-era story, wherein a pair of siblings swap genders and places at the imperial court.

PAGE 178, panel 2 · KAMISHIMO
Formal attire. It literally means "upper and lower" and is an ensemble that goes over the kimono for formal occasions. The upper section is a sleeveless robe with wide starched shoulders, and the lower section is an undivided hakama.

PAGE 183, panel 1 · MONME
A Japanese unit of weight equal to 3.75 grams.

PAGE 189, panel 1 · NAMAMUGI
The attack on British subjects by Lord Shimazu Hisamitsu is known as the Namamugi Incident, Kanagawa Incident or Richardson Affair. It eventually led to the outbreak of the Anglo-Satsuma war in 1863.

CREATOR BIOGRAPHY

FUMI YOSHINAGA

Fumi Yoshinaga is a Tokyo-born manga creator who debuted in 1994 with *Tsuki to Sandaru* (*The Moon and the Sandals*). Yoshinaga has won numerous awards, including the 2009 Osamu Tezuka Cultural Prize for *Ôoku*, the 2002 Kodansha Manga Award for her series *Antique Bakery* and the 2006 Japan Media Arts Festival Excellence Award for *Ôoku*. She was also nominated for the 2008 Eisner Award for Best Writer/Artist.

Ōoku

⊙ THE INNER CHAMBERS

Ōoku: The Inner Chambers
Vol. 16

VIZ Signature Edition

Story and Art by Fumi Yoshinaga

Translation & Adaptation/Akemi Wegmüller
Touch-up Art & Lettering/Monaliza De Asis
Design/Yukiko Whitley
Editor/Pancha Diaz

Printed in Canada

Published by VIZ Media, LLC
P.O. Box 77010
San Francisco, CA 94107

PARENTAL ADVISORY
ŌOKU: THE INNER CHAMBERS is rated M for
Mature and is recommended for ages 18 and up.
Contains violence and sexual situations.

10 9 8 7 6 5 4 3 2 1
First printing, December 2019

VIZ MEDIA
viz.com

VIZ SIGNATURE
vizsignature.com

THIS IS THE LAST PAGE.

Ōoku: The Inner Chambers has been printed in
the original Japanese format in order to preserve
the orientation of the original artwork.